T0305364

Global Environmental Economics

Global Environmental Economics
Equity and the Limits to Markets

Edited by

Mohammed H. I. Dore and Timothy D. Mount

Copyright © Blackwell Publishers Ltd, 1999

First published 1999

Blackwell Publishers Inc.
350 Main Street
Malden, Massachusetts 02148
USA

Blackwell Publishers Ltd
108 Cowley Road
Oxford OX4 1JF
UK

Library of Congress Cataloging-in-Publication Data

Global environmental economics: equity and the limits of markets
edited by Mohammed H. I. Dore and Timothy D. Mount.
p.   cm.
Includes bibliographical references and index.
ISBN 978-1-55786-551-3

1. Environmental economics.   2. Economics–Moral and ethical
aspects.   3. Environmental justice.   I. Dore, M. H. I.   II. Mount,
Tim.

British Library Cataloguing in Publication Data

A CIP catalogue record for this book is available from the
British Library

Contents

Figures

Tables

Contributors

Jean Agras
Ph.D. candidate, Environmental Economics
Department of Agricultural, Resource, & Managerial Economics
Cornell University
Ithaca, NY 14853

Jean Agras is a Ph.D. Candidate and Research Assistant for the Economic Research Laboratory for Energy and Environment at Cornell University. In 1995/96, she was the Project Coordinator for the Institute of Economic Studies (IES), a joint graduate level program between Cornell University and the University of Agriculture, Nitra, Slovakia. She has conducted research on solar energy in Zimbabwe, and is currently completing her dissertation on trade, environment, and development.

Marcello Basili
Assistant Professor, Economics
Departimento di Economia Politica
Università di Siena
Piazza S. Francesco 17
53100 Siena
Italy

Marcello Basili received his post-graduate degree (MA) in Banking and his Ph.D. in Economics from the University of Siena. His research interests include option value theory, environmental and ecological economics, decision theory and capacity theory.

Duane Chapman
Professor, Environmental Economics
Cornell University
Ithaca, NY 14853

Duane Chapman headed the USAID group on Energy, Industry, and the Urban Environment. He has worked at the University of Natal in South Africa, and the University of Zimbabwe. His work on trade and environmental pollution has been presented at hearings before the US Federal Trade commission and the New York Legislature. His text *Environmental Economics: Theory, Application, Policy* is to be published in 1999.

Paul Demeny
Economist and Demographer
One Dag Hammarskjold Plaza
Population Council
New York, NY

Paul Demeny received his Ph.D. in economics at Princeton University in 1961. Currently, he is Distinguished Scholar at the Population Council, New York. Previously, he served on the economics faculties of Princeton University, the University of Michigan, and the University of Hawaii, and was director of the East-West Center's Population Institute. A past president of the Population Association of America, his scientific work and publications center on the study of the relationships between population dynamics and economic and social development. Most recently, he coedited (with Bernardo Columbo and Max F. Perutz) the book *Resources and Population: Natural, Institutional, and Demographic Dimensions of Development* (Oxford, Clarendon Press). He is founding editor of the quarterly journal *Population and Development Review*.

Mohammed Dore
Professor, Economics
Brock University
St Catherines, Ontario
Canada

Mohammed H. I. Dore, a co-editor of this volume, did his doctoral studies at Oxford University. He is Professor of Economics at Brock University and has published three other books, including *The Macrodynamics of Business Cycles* (Blackwell 1993). A Japanese language edition of this book appeared in 1996. He has published a number of articles which have appeared in: *Theory and Decision*; *Journal of Environmental Economics and Management*; *Nonlinear Dynamics, Psychology and the Life Sciences*; *Environmental Ethics*; *Journal of Post-Keynesian Economics*; *Science and Society*; *Ambio: the Journal of the Human Environment*; *Economics Letters*; *International Review of Applied Economics*; *Canadian Journal of Development Studies*; *History of Political Economy*; *Canadian Journal of Economics*; and the *Journal of Comparative Economics*. His current research interests are global environmental change and its distributional consequences on the rich and the poor. He leads an inter-American team of researchers from South, Central and North America on the role of forests in mitigating global warming. His research has been funded by the Social Sciences and Humanities Research Council of Canada, the National Science Foundation of the USA, the Inter-American Institute of Global Change Research (which is now based in Brazil) and also the National Science Foundation of Brazil. He is also a member of an international consortium of research, called NEPAMA, based at the University of Brasilia.

Johan Eyckmans
Senior Research Assistant, Energy, Transport & the Environment
Centre for Economic Studies
Catholic University Leuven, Naamsestraat 69
B-3000 Leuven, Belgium

Johan Eyckmans is a Senior Research Assistant for the research group of Energy, Transport and the Environment. In 1990, he obtained his MA in Economics degree at the Katholieke Universiteit Leuven in Belgium, specializing in public economics and mathematical economics. In 1997, he completed his Ph.D. thesis: "On the incentives of nations to join international environmental agreements." His main research interests are normative and axiomatic economics, and game theory. He has published in *Kyklos*, and *Journal of Environmental Economics and Management*.

Raúl García-Barrios
Professor, Resource Economics
Centro Regional de Investigaciones Multidisciplinarias
Cuernavaca, Mexico

Raúl García-Barrios' research interests are in the areas of rural institutional economics and resource management, as well as morality and rationality of contracts.

Daniel V. Gordon
Professor, Economics
The University of Calgary
Calgary T2N 1N4
Canada

Daniel V. Gordon is Professor of Economics at the University of Calgary. He holds a visiting position of Professor at the Institute of Fisheries Economics, Norwegian School of Economics and Business Administration. He specializes in natural resource economics and econometrics, and has published extensively in the field.

Ronald Herring
Director, Mario Einaudi Center for International Studies
Cornell University
Ithaca, NY 14853

Ronald Herring is the John S. Knight Professor of International Relations and Professor of Government. Herring has been Editor of Comparative Political Studies. His earliest academic interests were with land relations (*Land to the Tiller: The Political Economy of Agrarian Reform in South Asia*, Yale University Press, 1983), which fed into concern for environmental degradation. His current work is concerned with authority in nature and international environmental treaties – leading to work on the Montreal Protocol under the auspices of a project initiated by the Social Science Research Council, and funded by the MacArthur and Ford Foundations and the National Science Foundation.

K. K. Klein
Professor, Department of Economics
The University of Lethbridge
Lethbridge, Alberta T1K 3M4
Canada

K. K. Klein is an agricultural economist who has spent most of his career as a member of teams conducting multi-disciplinary research. He has studied and written extensively in the areas of economics of new technologies in agriculture, efficiency of water use in agriculture, economic impacts of climate warming on agriculture, and other agricultural policy and trade areas.

Timothy D. Mount
Professor, Resource and Environmental Economics
Agricultural, Resource & Managerial Economics and Director of CISER
(Cornell Institute for Social and Economic Research)
Cornell University
Ithaca, NY 14853

Tim Mount received his Ph.D. from the University of California, Berkeley in 1970. His research and teaching interests are econometric modeling and policy analysis relating to the demand for fuels and electricity, and to environmental policies. Currently, he is involved with research being conducted on the implications for long-run planning of incorporating the costs of environmental damage from emissions of sulfur dioxide, nitrogen oxides and carbon dioxide, and the selection of economically efficient strategies for meeting ozone standards and stabilizing emissions of greenhouse gases.

P. S. Ramakrishnan
Professor, Ecology
School of Environmental Sciences
Jawaharlal Nehru University
New Delhi-110067, India

P. S. Ramakrishnan was the founding Director of the G.B. Pant Institute of Himalayan Environment and Development of the Ministry of Environment and Forests, in India. He has written on plant population ecology and forest ecosystem dynamics, linking ecosystem processes with the multi-faceted socio-economics and socio-cultural interface of traditional mountain societies, centered around shifting agriculture (*jhum*), forestry and other land use related activities, including sustainable development of traditional societies.

Erik Schokkaert
Professor, Centre for Economic Studies and Director of the Centre for Economics and Ethics
Catholic University of Leuven, Naamsestraat 69
B-3000 Leuven, Belgium

Professor Schokkaert teaches public economics. His research focuses on ethical questions concerning economic policy and on the role of government intervention, specifically with respect to taxation and social security. He has published in the academic journals: *Journal of Public Economics, European Economic Review, Social Choice and Welfare, Kyklos, European Journal of Political Economy, Public Finance, Economics Letters,* and *Journal of Economic Psychology.*

Henry Shue
Professor, Ethics & Public Life
Cornell University
Ithaca, NY 14853

Henry Shue is the Wyn and William Y. Hutchinson Professor of Ethics & Public Life at Cornell University and the first Director of Cornell's Program on Ethics & Public Life. After studying at Merton College, Oxford, as a Rhodes Scholar, he received his Ph.D. from Princeton in the Interdepartmental Program on Political Philosophy. In 1976, he became a founding member of the Institute for Philosophy and Public Policy, a research center in the Washington area devoted to the examination of the ethical aspects of public affairs. He is the author of *Basic Rights* (1996, 2nd edn, Princeton). Professor Shue has concentrated on ethical issues in transnational relations, including the appropriate response to human rights' violations in nations other than one's own, moral issues concerning specific weapons systems and war in general, and the fairness of the terms of international agreements to deal with global environmental challenges like climate change.

Vivek Suri
Consultant
World Bank
Washington, DC

Vivek Suri is a Research Associate with the Tata Energy Research Institute, India, and a consultant to the World Bank, Washington DC. He received his Ph.D. in Environmental and Resource Economics from Cornell University, and an MA in Economics from the Delhi School of Economics. His research interests include: trade, environment, development, and their interactions; the economics of global climate change; and energy-economy modeling.

Peter Taylor
Ecologist; Science, Technology and Society (STS)
Swarthmore College
Swarthmore, PA 19081

Peter Taylor's work links scientific research on environmental change with interpretation of such research in its changing social and historical context. He pays particular attention to how researchers deal with the complexity generated by the intersection of social and natural processes involving differentiated agents and occurring at different scales, from the local to the transnational – and how STS deals with the equivalent complexity of influences on the sciences investigating such processes. He is co-editor of *Changing Life: Genomes, Ecologies, Bodies, Commodities* (1997, Minneapolis: University of Minnesota Press), and is currently Eugene Lang Professor of Social Change at Swarthmore College.

Alessandro Vercelli
Dipartimento di Economia Politica
Università di Siena
Piazza S. Francesco 17
53100 Siena
Italy

Alessandro Vercelli is Professor of Economics at the University of Siena. He did his doctoral studies at Oxford University and has published widely on macroeconomics, methodology, public policy, and environmental economics.

Tony Ward
Associate Professor, Economics
Brock University
St Catherines, Ontario
Canada

Tony Ward received his Ph.D. in economics from the University of British Columbia in 1990. His research interests include the historical process of climate change and its impact on economic activity, and other aspects of environmental policy. He has also published in the fields of Canadian and European economic history, on the impacts of technological change and climate change on both agriculture and forestry.

Marc Willinger
Professor of Economics
Université Louis Pasteur
bd d'Anvers
67000 France

Marc Willinger is Professor of Economics at University Louis Pasteur in Strasbourg (France), and member of Institut Universitaire de France. He teaches economics of the environment, information economics and experimental economics. His research areas cover decision making under uncertainty and irreversibility, and preference assessment. More recently, his research has focused on the design of experiments covering various research areas: information asymmetries, voluntary contribution to public goods, and informational externalities.

Preface

Following the successful negotiation of the Montreal Protocol in 1987, a major international conference in 1992 recognized that the world now faced serious global environmental problems calling for broad and concerted action at the global level. Because there was and still is no authority at the global level that might carry this out, action had to be implemented at the state level by individual nations who signed the protocols and the conventions. At a time when government funds for environmental control and regulation were shrinking, it was obvious that any action would have to be demonstrated to be an effective use of public money. For this reason, an economic approach to environmental problems was bound to play a major role. However, public action required a *social* perspective as opposed to the individualist and consumptionist bias of received economic theory. The only part of received theory that could be applied to the analysis of the environment was "welfare economics," which was at best agnostic on the key theoretical issue of who gains and who loses. The agnosticism follows from the assumption that economics has no business in making such judgments, which require interpersonal comparisons of well-being. Welfare economics has been developed mainly within an individualist and utilitarian framework. It tolerates only the "weakest" Paretian value judgments, although Pareto himself was deeply concerned with justice and equity. Being wedded to these weak value judgments, surprisingly little has changed in welfare economics since J. de V. Graaf wrote his masterful book in 1957 (*Theoretical Welfare Economics*, Cambridge: Cambridge University Press). Graaf expressed his despair at the fact that welfare economics was not much of a guide to policy, and had nothing to say on the difficult ethical choices that have to be made before policy is formulated.

It is therefore not surprising to see that welfare economic analysis of environmental degradation has not integrated concern for the interests of future generations. Neither does it incorporate any regard for the distributional impacts of any adjustments required to adapt to the new reality of serious environmental damage to the air, land and oceans. For example, it is clear that curbs on the use of fossil fuels would affect income growth and economic development in the third world, although most agree that raising the income levels of these people must indeed be an international priority. Since the industrialized world has contributed most to the current global environmental problems, any curbs on the development of the poor must be examined in an ethically responsible framework. Hence, the required adjustments raise intergenerational, intra-national and international equity issues. Traditional welfare economics is not equipped to handle these issues.

For these reasons, it is the aim of this book to contribute to a reform of the economic analysis of environmental problems, and to develop a framework that is both practical and intellectually sound by acknowledging the importance of the ethical dimension, a point made emphatically by Graaf in his book. Fortunately, the publication of John Rawls' *A Theory of Justice* in 1971 provided a return to an earlier deontological tradition that had been largely forgotten in the English speaking world. His work gave a new impetus to the analysis of ethical issues, not only in political theory but in economics as well, within the broader fields of social choice theory and modern public economics. Rawls' cogent critique of utilitarianism in his book also enabled others to see the limitations of "welfarism" in welfare economics and led to the further development of new deontological perspectives. Pareto wrote a great deal about justice, but the economics profession has chosen largely to ignore most of his work and has focused entirely on "Pareto efficiency." However, with the development of the new perspectives, social choice theory has once again rehabilitated concepts of *rights* and *justice*. In this book, we have sought to draw lessons from the social choice literature and applied it to environmental concerns.

Thus we are able to argue that issues of equity for future generations, and for people in developing nations, should play a central role in the analysis of environmental economics, since economics as a guide to policy is first and foremost a moral science. Consequently, we claim that distribution matters; and it matters most when adjustments will have to be made that will affect the entire industrial culture and future economic development of that vast majority of humanity that is still waiting to enjoy the benefits of industrial development. Of course, this will require close attention to the impacts of these adjustments. Fortunately, the need for adjustments is already being reflected in international agreements.

Two recent international agreements clearly recognized the need for adjustments which will have intergenerational, intra-national and international equity dimensions. The Montreal Protocol on the phasing out of chlorofluorocarbons (CFCs) is one of these agreements. This agreement even made explicit financial provisions for the developing nations, called "Article 5 countries", to meet the costs of these adjustments. The second agreement is the Kyoto Protocol, signed in December 1997, on cutting greenhouse gas emissions. While this agreement does not have the financial provisions for adjustment costs, it recognizes that the time needed for the adjustment must be equitable and, therefore, contains a differential schedule for CO_2 reductions for industrialized countries. However, China and India are not party to it, and it does not go as far as the Montreal Protocol in its resolve to respond to the challenges of global climate change. Nevertheless, it is a good beginning.

It remains to be seen whether the US Congress will ratify the Kyoto Protocol.

The current position of Congress is that reductions of GHGs in the USA should only be made if reductions are made in developing economies like China, effectively ignoring the complexity of the equity issue. The ratification issue in the USA is also likely to focus on an equity principle, but it is bound to be framed in a self-serving manner: why should the USA cut its CO_2 emissions and suffer a "decline" in the standard of living, if India and China do not do their "fair" share for the global environment? But, who was responsible for the current level of CO_2 concentrations in the atmosphere, in the first place? Should the industrialized countries compensate the developing countries for re-equipping their industrial capital stock in the light of the environmental damage? Should their development be slowed down to accommodate the industrialized North? Should Brazil be required to preserve its forests when Europe has all but eliminated hers in the name of development? Should India have to forego putting a refrigerator in every Indian household for fear of the damage that the CFCs cause to the global stratosphere? As the largest producer of CO_2 emissions, should the USA be required to be the "polluter that pays"? Should environmentally-friendly new technology be transferred to the developing countries at favorable prices, even when this technology belongs to private entrepreneurs in the North? This book throws light on some of these questions, and clarifies some of the complexities of the equity issue. As this book appears at a particularly critical time in the evolution of thinking about the global environment, we hope the reader will be exposed to some new ideas which will show that what is fair and what is just requires a much richer informational basis, and certainly one that goes beyond "utility" information.

Of course, ethics is a difficult subject and no single discipline has a monopoly on applied ethics. Here, we attempt an interdisciplinary focus on the equity dimension. Authors of papers in this book include economists, ethicists, political scientists, demographers, and ecologists. The papers were first discussed at a conference held at Cornell University, and were later revised in the light of discussions and referee reports. Participants were also asked to make their papers self-contained, with a minimum of technical apparatus. We wanted the book to be useful to as wide a readership as possible. For that reason, some papers were completely rewritten as broad survey papers to reflect the "state of the art" that would be useful in considering equity for a wider readership. With this in mind, the Introduction offers a much needed critique of Paretian welfare economics, and draws attention of the reader to the importance of distributive justice, a topic that is usually neglected in the standard economics curriculum. This part of the Introduction is an important background which the reader would be advised to read through. The full force of the critique requires some elementary calculus; however, it is self-contained and does not require the reader to have had a course in welfare economics. The Introduction also sketches some elements of the new theory of justice in a non-technical manner.

The need to produce a self-contained reader led to the present structure of the book, beginning with rights, preferences and well-being. Thus the first paper (by Dore) reviews Amartya Sen's approach to interpersonal comparisons of well-being in a practical and applied manner, which could make use of a number of widely available indexes of well-being. The second essay, written by a well-known ethicist, Henry Shue, is a compelling argument for the rights of future generations, a theme which is continued in part II. The second essay in part II (a survey of option values) integrates much diverse and technical material.

The first three parts are essentially theoretical. Part IV is about international equity actions taken just before, and after, the 1992 Rio Conference. It is a close scrutiny of global actions and the need to include the interests of developing countries. The two international agreements – the Montreal Protocol and the Kyoto Protocol – show that equity issues are already of practical importance.

The inclusion of some specialized topics such as population growth and its impact on the environment, sectoral studies of industrial location, energy, and fisheries round off the major aspects of environmental degradation and its distributional impacts on the people of developing countries as well as on future generations.

In short, we hope that the essays in this book present a coherent focus on the equity issue as it might be applied to global environmental problems. At the same time, each essay is self-contained, requiring a minimum of technical preparation on the part of the reader. The book will therefore be suitable for both advanced undergraduate and graduate students in a number of environmental economics courses, as well as in environmental studies programs now being taught at universities in North America and Europe.

The editors wish to thank the following organizations for providing the financial support that made the initial conference on equity and the environment possible: The Cornell Center for the Environment, The Cornell International Institute for Food, Agriculture and Development, The Mario Einaudi Center for International Studies, The Cornell Institute for Social and Economic Research and the Department of Agricultural, Resource and Managerial Economics. In addition, thanks are due to Jean Agras, Will Reidhead and Vivek Suri for their help with editing, to Joyce Knuutila for secretarial support, and to Cindy Chase and Cherie Hulse for making arrangements for the conference. We thank the authors of the papers for their valuable contributions and their willingness to make major revisions to the original papers.

We also owe a great deal to four referees, chosen by Blackwell, for their helpful comments which led to further re-writing and re-organization of the book: Jane V. Hall, California State University – Fullerton; Richard B. Howarth, University of California – Santa Cruz; Richard G. Newell, Resources for the Future; and Richard B. Norgaard, University of California – Berkeley. Finally, we would like to thank Al Bruckner, the Executive Editor at Blackwell Publishers, and his staff, for their patient guidance and meticulous help. The book would not have been possible without this cooperation and the support of many individuals and organizations.

M. D.
T. M.

Introduction

Both the environmental activist and the average citizen know that the world faces a host of global environmental problems: the depletion of the ozone layer, global warming, depletion of the fish and contamination of the oceans, loss of forests and soil erosion, loss of biodiversity, desertification, industrial pollution, and deteriorating quality of water, to name the most important problems. The UN Conference on the Environment and Development of 1992 (UNCED) marks an important watershed in the official recognition of these global environmental problems, and the need to re-think our way of life along the lines of "sustainable development." Indeed, UNCED produced the most highly quoted definition of sustainable development that would preserve the quality of life for future generations; the definition emphasized the necessity of meeting "the needs of the present without compromising the ability of future generations to meet their own needs." Sustainable development thus established a link to equity, both across the globe and across future generations. In the very definition of sustainable development promulgated at UNCED, it was recognized that the global environmental problems cannot be tackled unless the equity dimension is given some priority.

For this reason, the 1992 conference recognized that improving environmental quality cannot be accomplished at the expense of the development and increase in per capita incomes in developing countries and, as this book shows, attempting to do so will not succeed. The major international agreements on the global environment, both before and after UNCED, have recognized the special position of the developing countries. In many ways, practice is already far ahead of theory, as often happens. However, in much of research on environmental policy, the important questions of equity are avoided, perhaps in the futile search for a "value-free" guide to policy. Yet, almost all the environmental problems, including those listed above, are predominantly equity problems – they affect the well-being of our neighbors, either in spatial location, or a "neighbor" in time, such as the next generation. The neighbor in location is the resident across the street or in nearby states in developing countries. My comfortable car journey into the city is the city resident's smog; my capital gains from shares in a chemical company that is maintaining its high profitability partly by dumping chemical pollutants into a nearby river is a concern to the farmer next door who relies on that river for water. Profligate use of fossil fuels, which make life in the Northern Hemisphere comfortable, will also cause increasing greenhouse gases in the atmosphere, which will raise global temperatures and raise sea levels for some developing island nation in the Pacific ocean.

While sometimes the neighbor across the street can speak up and claim damages, often the complainant – like the resident of the Pacific island – is powerless and has no world authority to which the damage claim can be taken. Class action suits, such as the one brought by the Natural Resources Defence Council against the US Environmental protection Agency have proved to be effective *within* the USA but the wanton disregard by the Japanese ships of international conservation measures for oceans resources leaves all citizens, even citizens of Japan, powerless to act.

Future generations were called our neighbors in time, but these neighbors are particularly powerless with respect to what state of the biosphere they wish to inherit. My summertime comfort requires the use of the air conditioner but, if this appliance uses CFCs, then my air conditioner means more skin cancer for a future resident of this earth. The cattle rancher in Brazil, who wants a bigger ranch, clears virgin forests; but this act contributes to an increase in future climate variability, with more extreme weather events, such as floods, hurricanes and ice storms. Thus *all* acts of environmental degradation or abuse impinge on the rights of some other persons, whether alive now or to be alive in the future. Consequently, environmental degradation is largely – and almost completely – a matter of equity, between citizens across the globe or equity between people alive now and citizens of some future date. Time and again, such equity issues are treated as "efficiency problems," either as a matter of bilateral negotiation (à la Coase) or marginal amelioration, through least-cost implementation, by equating the marginal benefit with the marginal cost of abatement. Such an approach is not an adequate response to the challenge.

This book is a plea for the recognition of the equity dimension in the environment. The recognition of the importance of equity means that economics must go beyond the treatment of environmental problems as "externalites" that required either Coasean-type bargaining solutions, or simple lump sum corrective taxes, to induce mitigation behavior. We believe that it is no longer necessary to show the inadequacies of this conventional approach. Indeed, if these conventional policy tools had been adequate, the major environmental problems that we now face would not have occurred. Therefore, this book is mainly concerned with the analysis of environmental degradation and the implications of distributive justice, both across the present and future generations in a fairly concrete and applied manner. The objective of this Introduction is not only to draw attention to the main strands of thought and findings of these papers, but also to reflect on some key issues in the treatment of distribution in economics which the papers in this book treat as background information. This is best done by contrasting the treatment of distribution in the received theory, and in the new and emerging theory of distributive justice. First, we cover the treatment of distribution in the received theory, in so far as the latter can be said to do so. We repeat: this is a necessary theoretical background to elements of distribution that have been neglected in the traditional teaching curriculum, and the reader is advised to absorb the main lessons of a technical argument that show the biases and limitations of Paretian welfare economics as it is applied to environmental issues which includes standard social cost-benefit analysis (CBA) and its foundations.

Then (on page 10) we reflect on some elements of the new theory of distributive justice. This new literature is vast and growing. Of course, the approach in this Introduction is merely suggestive; it is designed to stimulate the intellectual appetite of the reader to explore this new theory, and to consider the topics and essays in this book in the light of this new theory. The crucial issue separating the two distinct approaches is that the received theory assumes that efficiency and equity are separable, whereas the newer theory makes no such assumption. Finally (on page 14) we offer an integrated review of the main findings of the papers in this book in relation to equity.

The treatment of distribution: The received theory

In economics, the received theory of perfect markets both glorifies markets and puts a huge burden on them. For economists, the benchmark is general competitive equilibrium, as portrayed by the Walrasian "general equilibrium" model. *All* policy prescriptions – whether they be in the field of anti-trust policy, international trade, taxation, labor management, environmental control or CBA – use the competitive equilibrium as the benchmark. It is implicitly assumed that the "closer" the real economy is to this perfect state of perfect competition, the greater the happiness of the population. In the general equilibrium model, the system of interrelated markets economizes on information flows, as the only relevant information for "efficient exchange" is beautifully summarized in *one* signal, namely price; that is the huge burden. The glorification occurs by showing that when markets are perfect, orderly, and with zero transactions costs, then the markets are the socially preferred mechanism for the "efficient" allocation of resources, as such markets promote the general good with a minimum of resource costs. The "general good" in Walrasian general equilibrium theory is assumed to coincide with "efficiency" in production, associated with a competitive equilibrium. The properties of a competitive equilibrium are well known; they may be summarized as the two fundamental theorems of welfare economics:

Theorem 1: *every competitive equilibrium is a Pareto optimum*

and, with slightly stronger assumptions,

Theorem 2: *any particular Pareto optimum can be reached in a decentralized manner with a suitable redistribution of the initial endowments of the agents.*

Theorem 1 states that at the competitive equilibrium, no consumer's utility can be increased without decreasing the utility of some other consumer. Since

CBA is a major theoretical tool of environmental regulation, it might be instructive to re-state Theorem 1 in terms of consumer's surplus (CS), a concept well known to second-year economics students. One may state Theorem 1 as Theorem 1′:

> at a competitive equilibrium the sum of consumers' surpluses is maximized, and no individual consumer's surplus can be increased without decreasing that of another consumer.

As is well known, CBA justifies any "project" that increases CS. If a project were justified on the basis of an increase in CS, the project has also increased at least on person's utility without decreasing the utility of another. In other words, the project was "Pareto improving." Equivalently, a Pareto-improving project is accepted on the basis of the Pareto criterion. (We can assume that the Pareto-improving project must have been a "public good," since in a Walrasian general equilibrium, public goods are excluded at the outset by assumption.)

Theorem 2 identifies "efficiency" with a Pareto optimum, and assures the separability of "efficiency" and "equity." This theorem in effect says: guarantee efficiency first, and policy makers can reach any particular Pareto optimum by lump-sum redistribution and compensation. In its earlier (partial equilibrium) guise, Theorem 2 was known as the "Hicks-Kaldor Compensation Principle" (HK, for short), which went beyond the well-known Pareto criterion stated above. According to the Pareto criterion, any project or "move" that enhances the utility of one consumer without lowering the utility of another is not objectionable, since envy is treated as a base emotion. Thus, such a move is socially desirable as it promotes the general good. However, if there are more than one moves, or projects, that satisfy the Pareto criterion, then the criterion itself cannot rank them (see below).

In HK, Hicks and Kaldor strengthened the Pareto criterion by claiming that any move that enables the gainers to compensate the losers (at least potentially), and would leave the gainers still better off, promotes the general good. As argued below, when HK is taken to be the net benefit criterion, which values CS in monetary terms, then any number of projects can be ranked if "efficiency" and equity are separable.

Note that the compensation should be only potentially feasible, for if the compensation is actually paid, then of course HK is equivalent to the Pareto criterion. The microeconomic application of Theorem 2 is nothing but HK, according to which compensation does not actually have to be paid; that is left to the policy makers that actually chose a particular Pareto optimum. From Walrasian general equilibrium theory, it is Theorem 2 that guarantees the separability of "efficiency" and "equity;" the Hicks-Kaldor compensation principle is merely its partial equilibrium analogue.

One can now define (Pareto) efficiency strictly: given two objectives, efficiency requires that it should not be possible to enhance one objective without foregoing a bit of the other objective. In other words, a situation in which *both* objectives can be simultaneously enhanced is a position where "efficiency gains" (whatever

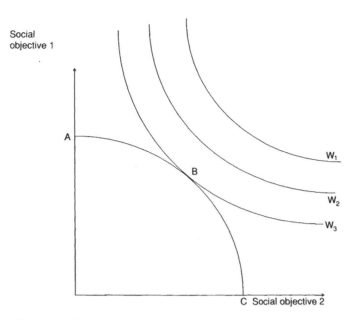

Figure I.1 The trade-off between two social objectives

they may be) have not been exhausted. Hence, given a production possibility curve between the production of two goods, productive efficiency requires that it should not be possible to increase the output of one without decreasing the output of the other. Thus, efficiency is required in production, a process which is the "transformation" of goods into other goods. In production, the efficiency is nothing but non-wastefulness, as Amartya Sen has convincingly shown. In consumption, Pareto efficiency requires that in the space of utilities, no person's utility can be increased without decreasing the utility of any other.

Therefore, if the economy operated on the "Pareto frontier," any particular Pareto optimum can be chosen and the gains can be costlessly redistributed among those who lose, as a result of the choice of this particular Pareto optimum, by those who gain. The separability of efficiency and equity suggests that there is a trade-off between the two. But, is the trade-off between Pareto optima the same thing as a trade-off between efficiency and equity?

Consider figure I.1, in which there are two social objectives, objective 1 and objective 2. Suppose that resources available to fulfil these objectives are limited, and that the "transformation curve" ABC between them is concave to the origin. The curve ABC is then the "objectives possibility frontier," where all points on the curve are Pareto efficient, as defined above. It is the defining characteristic of efficiency that establishes the trade-off between the two social objectives. Therefore, efficiency itself cannot be a social objective (Le Grand, 1991). This idea is important and worth restating: if efficiency establishes a trade-off, the social objectives remain *the* social objectives; and these objectives are not themselves supplanted by making efficiency the only objective.

Now suppose the social objective is to raise the "utilities" of individuals 1 and 2, u^1 and u^2, where utility is defined over money incomes y^1 and y^2. Suppose there is a fixed amount of total income so that

$$y^1 + y^2 = y$$

Then the utility possibility curve can be obtained as

$$y = f(u^1, u^2) \tag{I.1}$$

Differentiate the above equation totally and set $dy = 0$. Then the slope of the frontier is

$$-\frac{du^1}{du^2} = \frac{\dfrac{\partial f}{\partial u^2}}{\dfrac{\partial f}{\partial u^1}} \tag{I.2}$$

From the inverse function rule

$$\frac{\partial u^1}{\partial y^1} = \frac{1}{\dfrac{\partial f}{\partial u^1}} \tag{I.3}$$

and

$$\frac{\partial u^2}{\partial y^2} = \frac{1}{\dfrac{\partial f}{\partial u^2}}$$

Therefore

$$-\frac{du^1}{du^2} = \frac{\dfrac{\partial u^1}{\partial y^1}}{\dfrac{\partial u^2}{\partial y^2}} \tag{I.4}$$

Thus, the slope of the utility possibility frontier is equal to the ratio of the marginal utilities of income of the two individuals. Now, it is well known that one cannot "choose" a point on the utility possibility frontier without some exogenous choice mechanism. In the older welfare economics, such a choice mechanism is a "social welfare function" (Sen, 1970). After the publication of Arrow's impossibility theorem, the social welfare functions went out of fashion; but to those who appreciated the narrowness of Arrow's four conditions required to prove the impossibility (Sen, 1970, p. 37–8), a social welfare function continued to be a useful heuristic devise and, for some welfare economists, such as Paul Samuelson, it never lost its charm.

Consider a Paretian social welfare ordering, which belongs to the general class of Bergson-Samuelson social welfare orderings,

$$W = w(u^1, u^2)$$

This ordering has four properties.

1 **Welfarism**   The welfare function depends only on the utilities of the two individuals.
2 **Pareto-inclusiveness**   The function increases for each increase in u^1, given a level of u^2; and it increases for each increase in u^2, given a level of u^1.
3 **Maximal property**   Because of Pareto-inclusiveness, it follows that increasing the utility of one can only be obtained by decreasing the utility of the other. This means that the contours of this function are downward-sloping, i.e. convex to the origin (see figure I.1).
4 **Continuity**   When the social welfare ordering of all *possible* states is continuous, it becomes a social welfare function.

A social welfare function satisfying properties 1–4 is called a Bergson–Samuelson social welfare function.

Differentiate this function totally:

$$dW = \frac{\partial w}{\partial u^1} \cdot du^1 + \frac{\partial w}{\partial u^2} \cdot du^2 \tag{I.5}$$

Along each welfare contour, $dW = 0$. Therefore, the slope of the contour which is given by

$$-du^1 / du^2$$

and is equal to

$$\frac{\dfrac{\partial W}{\partial u^2}}{\dfrac{\partial W}{\partial u^1}} = \frac{\dfrac{\partial u^1}{\partial y^1}}{\dfrac{\partial u^2}{\partial y^2}} \tag{I.6}$$

For all Pareto improvements to constitute improvements in welfare, the utility possibility frontier must lie along a welfare contour. Therefore at the social optimum, the slopes of the two must be the same, i.e.

$$-\frac{du^1}{du^2} = \frac{\dfrac{\partial W}{\partial u^2}}{\dfrac{\partial W}{\partial u^1}} = \frac{\dfrac{\partial u^1}{\partial y^1}}{\dfrac{\partial u^2}{\partial y^2}} \tag{I.7}$$

It follows that the welfare weight attached in the Paretian social welfare function to a change in a given individual's utility varies inversely with that individual's marginal utility of income. If there is diminishing marginal utility of income, then it is clear from the above equation that the *higher* the individual's income, the *higher* the welfare weight of that individual. Quite apart from the optimum, consider the social welfare function alone and apply the inverse function rule to (I.5), and re-arrange the result:

$$\frac{\partial W}{\partial u^2} = \frac{1}{\dfrac{\partial u^2}{\partial y^2}} \quad \text{and} \quad \frac{\partial W}{\partial u^1} = \frac{1}{\dfrac{\partial u^1}{\partial y^1}} \tag{I.8}$$

The interpretation of (I.8) is: the lower the denominator, the higher the social welfare weight for that particular individual. Note that the implication of the inverse function rule in (I.8) is true "everywhere" along the Paretian social welfare function, and not just at the point of tangency of the Paretian welfare function and the utility possibility curve. It is (I.7) that represents the point of tangency, but the bias towards "those with a lower marginal utility of income" is a property of the Paretian social welfare function, as shown in (I.8). In fact, the bias carries over to the entire class of Bergson–Samuelson social welfare functions that have the Pareto-inclusiveness property. (This result was first demonstrated by Le Grand but its full implications have not been appreciated.) Thus a Bergson–Samuelson and the Paretian social welfare functions favor the better-off in judging social improvements. This is indeed a particular notion of equity built into the Paretian approach; it is not value neutral, as has been customarily supposed in welfare economics.

It is true that, since Arrow's famous impossibility theorem, Bergson–Samuelson and Paretian welfare functions are not *explicitly* used. When a social welfare function does not exist, environmental economists use the Hicks-Kaldor compensation principle (or Theorem 2), as the foundation of *all* social CBA, and the Pareto criterion is subsumed as a special case of HK. Does the equity bias of the Pareto social welfare function carry over to HK, which is also Paretian? We consider this question next. It needs some elaboration.

Note first that the Pareto criterion *by itself* is not objectionable, but it is useless as Sen (1970, pp. 21–4) has shown. By itself, the Pareto criterion generates a "collective choice rule" but it is incomplete and cannot rank Pareto optimal points. Thus it is pair-wise incomplete and, hence, indecisive. To overcome this indecisiveness, environmental economists use social CBA to judge new projects as "moves," relying either on Theorem 2 or on HK. In CBA, it is typically assumed that the *rest* of the economy is at some optimum identified by (I.7), and that a

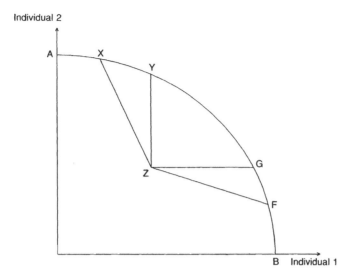

Figure I.2 The non-separability of equity and efficiency

further move from there in the "north-east direction" is justifiable if the move is a Pareto improvement. If the full social welfare function were available, there would be no difficulty in determining the actual distribution of utilities between the two parties, and the new social optimum would be unique. But, when a social welfare function is not available, environmental economists implicitly rely on Theorem 2 or its partial equilibrium analogue, HK, which overcomes the limitations of the Pareto criterion by enlarging the domain of the validity of HK to the *entire* Pareto frontier. It is this principle which forms the basis of the net benefit criterion in social CBA. HK is decisive over the entire Pareto frontier, with hypothetical compensation for those who lose from the "winnings" of those who gain by the move to any point on the new Pareto frontier. If there is more than one project, then the projects can all be ranked on the basis of net benefit criterion or net present value, which ranks projects according to the money estimate of CS. Thus, when HK is taken to be the net benefit criterion, all projects can be ranked in terms of the consumer surplus or the sum of consumer surpluses. In this way, HK enables society to "improve" on the initial general equilibrium.

The above point can be illustrated by an example, using HK. For simplicity, suppose that the utility possibility curve (for individuals 1 and 2) is concave to the origin, as shown in figure I.2. In the space of utilities, the point Z is inferior, since a move to the frontier can increase the utility of either individual, or indeed that of both. According to HK, the move from Z to the point X is a social improvement even though u^1 (the utility for individual 1) declines, because individual 2 can potentially compensate individual 1. The move from Z to X is an "efficient" move, which is separable from the compensating, or "equity", move from X to Y. In fact any move from Z to the segment AXY would be a social improvement.

Similarly, any move from Z to the segment GFB would be a social improvement. Thus HK covers *all* points on the frontier *not* covered by the Pareto criterion, and points covered by the latter become a special case of HK. Thus, HK in effect replaces the Pareto criterion. According to HK, only those who gain more can possibly compensate the losers. Then, without actually requiring that compensation be paid, the project is pronounced to be a social improvement. Thus HK shares the same equity bias (towards the better off) that was shown to be the case with the Pareto social welfare function. We therefore conclude that the Paretian approach to welfare *as a whole* shares the same bias towards the better off. Thus, even without an explicit social welfare function, HK does what the Paretian social welfare function would have done. We conclude that, as far as equity is concerned, Paretian welfare economics has the same equity bias.

To summarize so far: it is assumed that the rest of the economy is in general equilibrium. At the optimum, if a Paretian social welfare function is assumed to characterize it then, the utility of the rich is weighted more highly than the utility of the poor, assuming a declining marginal utility of money. Without the function, a new project is worthy of consideration if the project increases CS in net terms, i.e. the gainers can, in principle, compensate the losers. That project is pronounced to be a Pareto improvement. In this formulation, the separability of efficiency and equity is assured by relying on Theorem 2, or on HK which is simply the partial equilibrium analogue of Theorem 2. The indecisive nature of the Pareto criterion is overcome by making it a special case of HK. Even when the calculus is in terms of *social* gain, the criterion of value is CS, the CS of the gainers. By the definition of the Pareto-inclusiveness property, marginal social gain is the gain of the gainers.

Next, we concentrate only on points along the segment YG (i.e. points over which the Pareto Criterion is indecisive) in figure I.2 and consider some principles of the new theory of justice. However, only a bare sketch is provided.

The new theory of distributive justice

Let us now return to points along the segment YG in figure I.2. Again, in principle, there is nothing to stop one from applying HK to a move from Z to this segment, where any unequal gains can be compensated, but HK requires the assumption that efficiency and equity be separated, which is an unwarranted assumption. Furthermore, it throws no light on questions of sharing the gains through some concept of distributional equity. We will therefore now turn to some elements of the theory of distributive justice to consider how the move from Z to the Pareto frontier YG can be analyzed. This theory of distributive justice has been developed by Rawls, Nozick, Kolm, Sen, Arrow, Atkinson, Williams, Roemer, Varian, Le Grand, Binmore, Van Parijs, Barry, Dorkin, Fleurbaey, and others. Indeed, the literature is vast, but here only one or two central principles will be touched upon, concentrating on the work of John Rawls (1971) and Ken Binmore (1994).

A simple first step is to view the segment ZYG to be a cake of known and fixed size, which is to be divided between the two people by some agreeable principle when:

- separability is not assumed
- there is no known and agreed upon exogenous criterion, such as a social welfare function, and
- there is no dictator.

In this case, equal division emerges as both a feasible and just solution. For a decentralized solution, the individuals agree to an independent criterion: the person cutting the cake takes the last slice. Then a 45° line from Z to the frontier will determine a just solution to the distributional problem. What happens if there is no agreed upon independent criterion for distribution, or the size of the "cake" is not known? We can turn to Rawls for a possible answer.

The most important single idea in Rawls' *Theory of Justice* is the concept of pure procedural justice. The latter must be distinguished from allocative justice, for which

- a perfect procedure for allocation exists, and
- there exists an independent and exogenous criterion for judging the outcome of the procedure.

For example, for the above problem of the just division of a cake of fixed size, the independent criterion is equal shares. The perfect procedure for fulfilling the objective of the independent criterion is to dictate that the person cutting the cake (assuming he or she is self-interested) takes the *last* slice. Then, the self-interested cutter will cut *all* slices to be equal. Hence, for the problem of the allocation of a fixed resources, a perfect (allocation) procedure exists.

Perfect procedural justice is to be distinguished from imperfect procedural justice, which holds when we have an independent and exogenous criterion for a just outcome, but we lack a procedure that would always guarantee the just outcome. A criminal trial is an example of imperfect procedural justice. We have an exogenous criterion for a just outcome – the innocent should be acquitted and the guilty should be convicted – but the trial procedure is always imperfect and the just outcome cannot be guaranteed.

When there is no exogenous and independent criterion for judging the outcome, Rawls calls it "pure procedural justice." When there is no exogenous criterion, then the procedure must be fair or right; if we can guarantee a fair procedure then, by extension, the outcome, no matter what it is, will also be fair. Thus, the outcome of a series of fair bets is fair, no matter what the distribution of the outcomes. However, this example simply illustrates what might be fair; it does not say that a just distribution should be determined by a system of fair bets.

According to Rawls, social distributive justice is a matter of pure procedural justice; we do not have an independent and exogenous criterion for judging the outcomes of a political and social process, and so there is no ideal distribution.

Without an independent exogenous criterion, there is no way of knowing whether any resulting distribution is right or just. For example, the distribution resulting from a Walrasian competitive general equilibrium model requires that one accepts the exogenous criterion of the maximization of utility, as a "God's Law." The resulting distribution is a function of the initial distribution of endowments. All it guarantees is *some* Pareto allocation, if the number of agents is infinite; and as has been said before, in Walrasian theory to get to a particular Pareto point, we have to rely on Theorem 2.

Suppose there is no agreed exogenous criterion of allocation. How are two individuals in figure I.2 to agree on some allocation on the YG frontier? This problem has all the essential elements of a social contract. It is surprising how the existence of an exogenous criterion simplifies things and how, without it, the matter becomes complex. The solution to the social contract raises all the Arrow difficulties in finding a non-dictatorial social welfare function (SWF). However, some Bergson–Samuelson type of a SWF would be an exogenous criterion, which "true" liberals like Rawls would reject, since the essence of liberty is that individuals pursue their own good, whatever it happens to be. It is for this reason, too, that Rawls and other deontologists reject utilitarianism, since the latter involves imposing an exogenous unidimensional criterion, a "God's law," which is the maximization of the sum or average utility. Thus, those who reject utilitarianism, also reject Harsanyi's utilitarian solution to the Arrow problem. This means that either one treats the issue of the social contract as being unsolved, or one tries to improve on the "solution" offered by Rawls himself, as Binmore (1994) has done.

There are two possible answers here, depending on whether the segment ZYG is known in advance or not. If the "pie" or "cake" ZYG is known then the just division of the pie is a matter of allocative justice, as argued above. Approaching it from the perspective of game theory, the pie is the Nash bargaining set. It is clear that the two "players" in the game need to co-operate and agree on some move to get them to a point on YG.

If the two players had equal bargaining strength, then the solution would be the so-called "regular Nash bargaining" solution. That is, the gains from the move from Z to the frontier would be shared equally by the two players, a solution we have met before when there is a perfect procedure of allocative justice. If, however, they had unequal bargaining strengths, then a generalized Nash bargaining solution can be found which preserves some inequalities embodied in Z. However, both types of solutions would be "technocratic," and would lack an ethical dimension. Both types of solution, therefore, do not interest theorists like Rawls and Binmore. A brief comment on their respective solutions would be of some interest.

Rawls presents us with a thought experiment. If each individual were equally likely to be in the shoes of the other, what sort of social contract would they all finding appealing? Then, in the *original* position, when each individual is stripped of his or her particular identity, Rawls argues that they would accept two principles of justice:

1 guarantee equal liberty to all, and
2 agree to a redistributional policy that attempts to make the worst off, as
   better of as possible; this is his "difference principle," or *maximin*.

For Rawls (1971, p. 88), as said before, justice is the search for "pure
procedural justice." This follows because, in Rawls, there is no independent
criterion for judging what is a right outcome, and no assumptions imposed on the
nature of preferences of the agents, except that one may infer that, in the original
position, the agents must be risk averse to accept the difference principle. (Risk
aversion is then an implicit statement about the nature of the underlying preferences. Apart from this implicit assumption, individuals pursue and define their
own goals.) Hence, for Rawls, the social contract is a matter of pure procedural
justice. If the procedure is fair, then the resulting distribution must be judged to
be fair by extension.

Rawls' two principles could serve as the theoretical justification of the so-
called "welfare state," for the kind of redistributional policies that Western
Europe, Japan and Canada have adopted towards their own citizens. As a
distributional principle, maximin has attracted a great deal of attention, and
Schokhaert and Eyckmans (in this book) apply it to the North-South negotiations
on global warming. In their paper, the authors formulate maximin as the priority
of the poorest in the developing countries.

In Rawls' proposed society, the market mechanism would be fully utilized; but
the allocative achievements of the market mechanism are improved upon by
judicious social intervention. In other words, while the market assures production
efficiency, it is incapable of achieving equity. In Rawls, there is a presumption in
favor of equality as the basic guiding principle but, when some inequality can also
benefit the worst off through maximin, the worst off cannot object to it. (However, the standard argument against redistribution and the "welfare state" is that
redistribution blunts incentives and that there would be some loss not of efficiency but of *growth of income*. For reasons of space, this line of thought will not
be pursued here.)

The Rawlsian maximin was a positive solution to Arrow's negative result (i.e.
the impossibility theorem) but, while stimulating, and indeed brilliant, it required
reformulation along rigorous mathematical lines. In a liberal society, is it possible
to choose among Pareto efficient outcomes that enhance equity without sacrificing efficiency? That is the question Binmore (1994) tackles. He shows that while
the Harsanyi utilitarian solution is possible, a non-utilitarian Rawlsian solution
can also be rigorously determined. Furthermore, the Rawlsian solution is more
equitable than the Harsanyi solution. Binmore offers a game theoretic solution,
but it is formulated in terms of evolutionary games. He shows that if the two
individuals in figure I.2 had empathetic preferences, in addition to their normal
preferences, then they will have ethical values on who deserves what, i.e. values
about "deservingness." These values will eventually converge to a common set of
values (through evolution) and determine the slope of the line from Z to some
point between Y and G. Binmore's solution to the distributional problem (which

is what a social contract is) belongs to the same family as Rawls' maximin criterion. Binmore's approach has at least four advantages (see Dore, 1997).

First, Binmore's treatise on game theory and the social contract is a positive response to Arrow's negative result. Binmore shows that there are ways of thinking about social justice, without the Arrovian straightjacket. It is true that the solution needs empathetic preferences and evolutionary games, but this is really no worse than Arrow's requirement of the independence of irrelevant alternatives to obtain his impossibility result. Second, if there is no externally given criterion (or God's law) such as to maximize the sum or "average" utility, it is still possible to think rigorously about social justice along Rawlsian (maximin) lines. Third, in seeking social justice, judgements about who deserves what (interpersonal comparisons) can be done in a non-dictatorial way that preserves liberal values. Fourth, as a logical consequence of the third, social philosophers and even economists need not be silent about the social choice *among* Pareto optima. This is where the so-called old welfare economics reached an impasse. Developing a "post" welfarist intersection of ethics and economics is both possible and essential; see chapter 1 by Dore, who discusses Sen's post welfarist approach to interpersonal comparisons of well-being. Finally, Binmore also shows that any given Pareto efficient allocation is not necessarily a "social optimum"; it is indeed disingenuous and "unscrupulous" (Binmore, 1994, p. 71n) to claim that. The search for a social optimum cannot rely on Walrasian general equilibrium theory and its first and second theorems of welfare economics. The real challenge lies in theorizing and formulating a choice *among* Pareto optima, without evading and avoiding serious ethical choices. Indeed, that is precisely what social choice theorists such as Sen and Binmore are engaged in and, in our opinion, social choice theory has much more to offer to the development of social policy than conventional welfare economics.

Rawls (or Binmore's) commitment to the worst off is, in logic, certainly no better or worse that the Paretian commitment to giving a higher weight to the better off, but outside the realm of logic, it would be difficult to justify the Paretian commitment as a persuasive guide to policy. As soon as it is admitted that human societies are always guided by some minimal principles of ethics, then the Rawlsian commitment to the worst off acquires a clearly superior status to the Paretian commitment which, in the light of minimal ethics, would become morally repugnant.

Equity: An integrated review

It is this same minimal commitment to ethics that serves as the guiding principle to thinking about environmental problems and their possible solution throughout the papers in this book. Part I is about rights, preferences, and well-being. In chapter 1, Mohammed Dore reviews a new approach to interpersonal comparisons of well-being. The measurement of benefits is, of course, central to the determination of what constitutes well-being, a calculus that cannot be completed if information is restricted to utility information alone. Reviewing the work of

Amartya Sen, Dore argues that an economics of well-being can be reconstructed using social choice theory that goes beyond utility by taking into account a person's functioning and capability. Dore shows that the result is both an "economics of well-being," as well as a usable theory of justice, in a way that welfare economics never was. He contrasts the welfarist analysis of the consequences of global warming, with that which might be based on the functionings–capability approach. The latter approach shows how the well-being of the developing countries will be reduced by global warming. Viewing the functionings–capability approach as a theory of justice, it is possible to say that the differential impacts will be unjust; but this could not be said from within the framework of welfare economics.

In chapter 2, Henry Shue presents a stimulating thought experiment about burying small land mines now with covers that will last for a very long time, so that the harm will only befall future generations. He argues that the right to the integrity of the body is an unalienable right: it cannot be "sold" or traded off for anything else. He also makes a careful distinction between compensation for an injury (say through some accident) and the purchase of a right to injure. He questions the assumed primacy of the preferences of the present generation and the use of discounting to reduce the "weights" attached to the inalienable rights of future generations.

Marc Willinger, in chapter 3, examines preferences further. He argues that standard CBA is based on the assumption of a well-defined and stable system of preferences. For most environmental valuation, such preferences do not exist. As a counterfactual, Willinger constructs three desirable properties of an invariant and stable preference structure. He then reviews the literature that shows how each of these three properties is repeatedly violated in practice. His results show the limitations of standard CBA which has a shaky foundation in valuation and cannot come to grips with the questions of whose benefits should be measured.

Part II of the book is about environmental options, equity and uncertainty. Vercelli contributes two papers here. In chapter 4, he argues that an important dimension of sustainable development requires taking into account the opportunities of future generations. The set of options open to them should be at least as large as the set of options open to the current generation. Vercelli also raises an important methodological point: the Benthamite view that the problem of conflicting and inconsistent rights of generations can be resolved by reducing all ethical evaluations to one homogeneous measure, called utility, is false. This view has been rejected in the philosophy of law, and persists only in the neoclassical economic models. Even Harsanyi and Hare combine their "neo-utilitarianism" with Kantian deontological principles. In chapter 5, Vercelli (with co-author Basili) surveys "environmental option values." The main conclusion of these two papers, taken together, is that the presence of uncertainty does not diminish the rights of future generations – quite the reverse. The survey of the rigorous literature on option values shows that an increase in uncertainty necessitates increasing the intertemporal flexibility of decision strategies, and irreversibilities increase the value of future options.

In the last paper in part II, in chapter 6, Tony Ward considers the treatment of risk and uncertainty in CBA of environmental issues. He argues that CBA was developed with economic growth as the social objective, whereas sustainable development involves incorporating the social objective of distribution, including distribution across generations. This requires fundamental changes to the methodology of project evaluation. The priority he gives to negative rights, i.e. the right not to be harmed, ties in well with the essay by Henry Shue.

Part III has two papers under the rubric of "population and the environment," in which the two papers present opposing points of view. In chapter 7, Peter Taylor and Raúl García-Barrios analyse the connection between population growth and environmental degradation. They ask: is the so-called "population problem" to blame for the rampant evidence of deforestation, soil erosion, and deteriorating water quality in the developing countries? Does India have too many people? Is controlling population growth a sensible way to address environmental problems? The authors argue that the "think-globally-act-locally" cliché is not adequate to answer the challenges that need to be faced. They argue that it is the nature of income and wealth distribution (specifically land holdings) that determines the extent of the population pressure. Brazil and Mexico are good examples. The authors argue that the focus on population growth as the source of environmental degradation is not correct; this is what they call "neo-Malthusian" environmentalism. In Mexico, rather than population growth being the cause, it is the breakdown of traditional authority and the "moral economy" brought about by the proletarianization of the rural population that has led to severe soil erosion. Similarly, the out-migration of the most able-bodied young people has left the land short of resource management.

On the other hand, in chapter 8, Paul Demeny, who is at the Population Council in New York, views population pressures in a longer term perspective. He argues that the problem can be seen largely as the case of the fertility rate being incompatable with the equilibrium levels of population. He sees no direct environmental stresses arising from population pressure, and is critical of the notion of carrying capacity. He is sceptical, on the whole, of the role of the state in population policy and reviews the history of Europe where the consequences of state policy have had no effect on either encouraging or discouraging population growth.

Part IV is devoted to global action on the environment with equity constraints, after the Rio conference. In chapter 9, the first paper, by Schokkaert and Eyckmans, focuses on negotiations for reductions of greenhouse gases (GHGs) which began with the UNCTAD recommendations, but the authors anticipate what must indeed follow in this arena, in the wake of the Montreal negotiations on the depletion of the ozone layer. This paper very ably reviews the evidence of the effects of GHGs and the differential impacts on the richer North and the poorer South. The available evidence suggests that the South will be affected more heavily than the North, and the authors argue persuasively that the abatement of GHGs cannot be separated from the issue of the overall development and the basic needs of the poor. According to the authors, the top ethical priority in these negotiations should be the need to raise the living standard of millions of people in the third world to some minimum level; and if GHG emissions abatement leads to a new and higher production possibility curve, then most of the gains should be redistributed to the poorest nations. Thus, issues of international justice should be central in the negotiations, as was well recognized by the negotiating parties in the "Montreal process," to which Ronald Herring turns in chapter 10.

Herring shows how issues of international justice dominated the negotiations over reducing CFC emissions, under the Montreal Protocol. Montreal is a clear example of two contradictory policies that the North is promoting: on the one hand, it is demanding that the South implement deregulation and "free" markets and reduce the role of the state but, on the other hand, it is asking the states of the South to enforce compliance with the Montreal Protocol. The South, led by India, won a partial victory in establishing the "polluter-pays" principle by requiring compensation from the North to the South for the period of adjustment necessary to phase out the use of CFCs. Herring's paper neatly complements the Schokkaert–Eyckmans paper; while the latter is theoretical, Herring deals with the hard realities of relative political bargaining power. It is also clear from Herring's paper that in the realm of the global commons, the South was able to assert itself through the leadership given by India to the demands of the Group of 7, and Montreal would prove to become an important precursor for negotiations on global warming, which began in earnest in Berlin, that led to the Kyoto Protocol signed in December 1997. The Montreal Protocol has been improved and strengthened several times, but it remains to be seen whether the further meetings will strengthen and reinforce the Kyoto Protocol which, as it stands (in January 1998), only makes sense as a first legally binding attempt to come to grips with the problem of GHGs.

The third paper in part IV, by P. S. Ramakrishnan is also concerned with international justice in the area of the protection of the biodiversity in the developing countries, which will require strengthening the Biodiversity Convention. He argues that biodiversity depletion is threatened by population pressure in the developing countries, and over consumption in the developed countries. These two factors interact and create market pressures that result in deforestation and the consequent loss of biodiversity. At the policy level, what is required is the need for a new economic order through institutional change at the global level that will harmonize the interests of the North and the South. Such an order will only emerge if the equity issues are taken seriously.

Part V of the book is a more detailed look at three sectoral studies of policy and the environment in: changes in industrial location, the management of a fishery which is a common property resource, and energy policies in the USA.

In chapter 12, Duane Chapman and his co-authors look at the dramatic growth of manufacturing in East Asia and the distribution of the benefits from the migration of environmentally polluting industry from "industrial" countries to new locations. They argue that such "trade" benefits the consumers of the North, as they obtain products, made with imported pollution-intensive raw materials, at a lower price. They also benefit from a cleaner environment in the North. What has happened is that the decline in the energy intensity per dollar of real GNP of the OECD has been exactly offset by an increase in energy intensity elsewhere. As a result, world energy intensity has remained almost constant, while world energy use is accelerating. The distribution of the gains from this

industrial growth remains skewed; not only has the distribution of income between nations become more unequal but the inequality within nations has also
increased.

In chapter 13, Daniel Gordon and Kurt Klein consider the failure of the
management of the North Atlantic cod fishery, a classic tragedy of the international commons. They show evidence from Iceland that when overfishing exceeds
some critical threshold, the fish stock may *never* recover. The North Atlantic cod
stocks have already been depleted seriously but perhaps not as badly as around
Iceland. Nevertheless, the total allowable catch quotas have been too generous in
the past, with no regard to equity between nations and equity for future generations. This is an example where the scientific knowledge needed for good management did exist; the problem came from the inability of political institutions to
take the rules of good management seriously.

The final paper by Timothy Mount, in chapter 14, discusses the environmental
problem of global warming and the need for changes in energy policy in the USA.
It complements the paper by Schokkaert and Eyckmans on equity relating to
negotiations for reducing GHGs. Mount shows that the USA is a major contributor to global emissions of GHGs due largely to having a policy of inexpensive
energy in a country with a high income. Mount also shows that most of the future
growth in energy use will be in low income countries, such as China and India.
Since current forecasts imply that global emissions of GHGs will continue to
grow in all regions, Mount argues that any credible global policy to stabilize
emissions of GHGs will require leadership and action from the USA. He offers
a Marshallian interpretation of energy, that contrasts with the conventional
Hotelling theory of extraction, to explain why economists and environmentalists
differ so widely on energy policy. In the end, Mount is pessimistic about the
ability of the USA to adopt a new energy policy. He proposes using a surrogate
policy with more immediate environmental benefits as a way to move forward.
The surrogate policy proposed by Mount is to reduce urban smog. This would
lead to more energy efficiency in transportation, reducing GHG emissions. Developing new technologies would be valuable to low income as well as high income
countries because urban smog is a global problem. Forming a partnership between the USA and China, for example, to address global warming may be an
effective way to proceed. The paper illustrates the main theme of this book which
is that the issue of equity is central to the public economics of the environment.

References

Binmore, K. (1994) *Game Theory and the Social Contract. Volume 1: Playing Fair.*
   Cambridge, Mass: MIT Press.
Dore, M. H. I. (1997) On Playing Fair: Professor Binmore on game theory and the social
   contract, *Theory and Decision*, 43, 3, 219–39.
Le Grand, J. (1991) *Equity and Choice.* London, UK: Harper Collins Academic.
Rawls, J. (1971) *A Theory of Justice.* Cambridge, Mass: Harvard University Press.
Sen, A. K. (1970) *Collective Choice and Social Welfare.* London: Oliver and Boyd.

I
Rights, Preferences, and Well-being

1

The Economics of Well-being: A Review of Post Welfarist Economics[1]

Mohammed H. I. Dore

How can one compare the well-being of individuals or groups? It would be natural to begin by saying that one needs a consistent theory on the basis of which comparisons of well-being can be made. Indeed, it could be argued that it is conventional welfare economics that provides a consistent theoretical foundation on such comparisons for all public policy issues in general. In economics, this welfare-theoretic approach provides the theoretical foundations for most state activity in the economic domain: taxation, public finance, competition policy, regulation of public utilities, cost-benefit analysis (CBA), environmental policy, and indeed even the microeconomic basis of law, in civil disputes. In an attempt to be as close as possible to positivism, conventional welfare economics is based on an ethical theory that attempts to minimize disagreement. Consequently welfare economics is based only on four tenets: welfarism; ordinalism; Paretianism; and an *ex-ante* assumption of the non-comparable nature of utilities and utility "scales" between persons. The first tenet confines the analysis to utility information only, and yet the last tenet rules out any possibility of interpersonal comparability of utility information. From this, it follows that in making any judgements about well-being or any improvement (or deterioration in well-being), the only acceptable and noncontroversial criterion is the Pareto criterion (i.e. the third tenet), which avoids disagreements on ethics.[2] However, this criterion is so restrictive that any non-utility information, such as a pollution index or information on income distribution, is irrelevant in making judgements about well-being; there is simply no way of incorporating such an index in the Pareto criterion. Within welfare economics, the only alternative to the Pareto criterion is the Hicks-Kaldor compensation criterion (HK), which is of dubious validity (Boadway, 1974; Sen, 1979, 1987; Chipman 1987; Broome 1991). We shall return to HK below.

The objective of this paper is to review an alternative theory, one that does not rely on the four tenets of welfare economics mentioned above. It can be shown that the standard welfare-theoretic approach is a special case of this more general theory, and that in this theory, systematic (although not necessarily complete) interpersonal comparisons of well-being are possible. Much of this new theory relies on the work of Amartya Sen. Indeed, after a significant output of research into the limitations of the utilitarian approach to economics and to public policy, Amartya Sen has made the development of an alternative theory a high priority. While this work has reached a certain degree of maturity, it is yet to be reflected fully in textbooks dealing with "public economics," or "public sector" economics, although it has stimulated much scholarly work.[3] Until the development of modern social choice theory, conventional welfare economics was the only theoretical foundation of public policy in general; social choice theory, which began with Arrow (1951) as a new corner of the subject of welfare economics, now serves as the larger framework for a critique of welfare economics and also as a rigorous foundation of an alternative theory that goes beyond utility information. It is this larger social choice theory framework that shows that received welfare economics is a special case.

The restriction in welfare economics to utility information has also been a straightjacket that has excluded debate in economics, and in welfare economics in particular, on important issues of inequality in income distribution, well-being, hunger, malnutrition, gender inequality, and indeed all aspects of liberty, freedom, and the fulfilment of human potentials.

In contrast, the new theory, which is now known as "post welfarist theory," developed by Amartya Sen – see especially Sen (1985) – is both an "economics of well-being," as well as a usable theory of justice, in a way that welfare economics never was. The post welfarist theory has at its very core, concepts of freedom and capabilities. Following Sen's lead, post welfarist theory has also influenced a number of economists and philosophers to go beyond utilitarianism. However, for reasons of space it will not be possible to do justice to this growing body of work. Therefore, this paper will be confined almost exclusively to a review of some of the work of Amartya Sen, in building an economic theory of well-being.

First the motivating framework for post welfarist theory will be presented as a critique of welfare economics. Then, the major elements of the theory are presented. Finally, it is shown how this new theory can be used to make interpersonal comparisons of well-being. The conclusion suggests that this theory, which encompasses welfare economics as a special case, may one day become a stepping stone to building a new foundation for public policy.

The framework for post welfarist theory

In standard welfare economics, any pollution index, such as an index of air quality or UV index, has no "standing;" it is of no theoretical relevance and cannot logically be incorporated in welfare comparisons, except insofar as it indirectly lowers a consumer's utility. Even if global warming melts the polar ice caps and the thirty-one island nations are submerged, and Manhattan is protected by high dykes, these changes have no direct bearing on individual utility functions, which are a function of commodities only. Only insofar as such flooding affects the *relative* prices of commodities will it affect the levels of utilities reached but, apart from that, nothing can be said about changes in well-being, as explained next.

Consider the following thought experiment. Suppose the ice caps melt. How can the catastrophic effects of global warming be incorporated directly into a utilitarian welfare analysis? As a result of the effects of global warming, some commodity prices will rise and others may fall, so that some relative prices will change as a result of the exogenous effects of climate change on production possibilities. Consumers will adapt to the new relative prices, and the commodity composition of the goods consumed at the optimum may change. Thus, one scenario is to treat the momentous changes as any other exogenous (marginal) change, equivalent to a redistribution of initial endowments, or a change in production possibilities. It all depends on how the world production possibility frontier shifts as a result of global warming; a full "rightward" shift could even be a Pareto improvement. If this turns out to be the case, then at least someone is made even better off, as some consumers reach a higher indifference curve. Equivalently, the utility possibility frontier expands. However, this is a very optimistic scenario, which is not plausible; it will occur only if technological change more than offsets any declines in outputs due strictly to global climate change, so that, in fact, technological change associated with global warming is a Pareto improvement.

Next, consider a less optimistic scenario. Suppose that global warming is an externality. Since an externality is a violation of the assumptions of Walrasian general equilibrium, there is no simple way of incorporating it. When an externality is *entirely* private, the solution given by the Coase Theorem is that it is best left as a bargaining problem between the parties. For there may be potential gains from trade (through bargaining) which must be exhausted in order to be on the "efficiency frontier." When externalities affect a large number of people, or perhaps *all* humanity, as in the destruction of the ozone layer, or indeed global warming, then such an externality is dubbed an external social cost. Such a social cost arises only because of ambiguous and unclear property rights, i.e. rights to land, water or space (including air). As a result of climate change, the utility possibility frontier shifts unequally so the utility of some consumer declines (that of the thirty-one island nations), while that of some other consumers (consumers in Northern latitudes) increases. There are two possible responses in this situation.

One possibility is to suppose that the actions of the consumers in Northern latitudes (who burn most of the fossil fuels) lead to "injuries," or reduces the utility of the consumers of the thirty-one island nations. If the injury is entirely private, then the two parties must bargain, as in the Coase Theorem. Clearly, the property rights to the atmosphere are unclear. In law, there may even be a presumption that those who "appropriate" the atmosphere first may be deemed to "own" it, just as those who declared sovereignty on land (new or old, by means of enclosures, or by declaring new limits deep into the oceans) are deemed to be legitimate. The legitimation becomes entrenched by virtue of recognition of this new sovereignty by not challenging it within a reasonable time. Thus the northern latitude consumers may have acquired proprietary rights in the atmosphere, as they were the "first" to use (or abuse) the atmosphere, i.e. they were the first to establish property rights in the atmosphere. The Coase Theorem then dictates that an "efficient" solution will emerge through bargaining, assuming the transaction costs of bargaining are nil. At the efficient solution, the consumers of the Northern latitudes will be persuaded to limit their use of fossil fuels, and a new equilibrium with no *further* increases in carbon and other emissions will occur. The new equilibrium will again reflect the standard marginal conditions. In return, the thirty-one island nations will give up some x million coconuts for the consumers of the Northern latitudes.

A second possibility is that consumers of Northern latitudes explicitly recognize that the thirty-one nations also have property rights in the atmosphere, but the North also has rights to use the atmosphere. The North can afford to take any required defensive action (build dykes for Manhattan and for The Netherlands) and still continue with their present way of life; they can grow more food in the Northern latitudes as the grain belt shifts further North, and, as they have the technology, they can supply more food and more air conditioners to the thirty-one nations. This means that, in principle, if the thirty-one nations have equal property rights in the atmosphere, then the HK compensation test can be applied to compensate the thirty-one nations *hypothetically*, and the North will still be better off with their present way of life, even after the compensation. However, according to the HK principle, no compensation has to be paid, because redistribution of income is not the responsibility of the consumers of the North. All they must do is to show that, in principle, global warming is a "good" thing for them because *their* gains outweigh the losses of the thirty-one island nations.[4] In other words, the claim is that the *net* benefits are positive. As for the actual payment of compensation, the HK principle is silent. Perhaps this matter should be taken up by the thirty-one nations at the UN. The HK principle requires only that gains exceed costs, and the questions of whether compensation is actually paid is not within the purview of the HK principle. The fact that the UV index has also shot up and the poorer people of the thirty-one nations are further disadvantaged cuts no ice, as the marginal net benefits (measured with utility as numeraire) are positive. In fact, says the north, if "global warming" was to be regarded as a project then, on the basis of CBA, the project should be implemented because, in principle, the marginal gains outweigh the marginal losses. This would be the case even if the externalities (such as the increase in the UV index) were taken into account, using shadow pricing or some other non-market valuation technique, in a standard social CBA!

The above is a logically plausible welfare-theoretic analysis of global warming. Clearly, it is a cogent and logical theory, based on the Pareto criterion and its illegitimate offshoot, the HK compensation test. However, it fails to take into account the effects of rising sea levels on the well-being of the citizens for the thirty-one island nations; they may even face extinction due to rising sea levels. Next, the alternative post welfarist theory is outlined. Later, the implications of that theory for global warming will also be considered.

An alternative post-welfarist theory

In the standard neoclassical theory, it is assumed that utility is derived from consuming commodities, which are limited only by the consumer's budget constraint. In contrast, Sen (1985), building on the work of Gorman (1956) and Lancaster (1966), argues that commodities are desired because of their characteristics, whether it is to satisfy hunger, meet a nutritional need, or to nourish the soul. The extent to which a person succeeds in utilizing the commodities at his or her command may be called a "functioning." A functioning is an achievement of a person: what he or she manages to do or to be. It reflects the part of a "state" of a person, which must be distinguished from commodities, which are used to achieve those functionings. The state of persons can be reflected in any number of grouped statistics collected by a statistical agency. These may cover diverse statistics such as levels of food intake and nutrition, health and literacy.

A functioning can be determined *after* having received the commodities, and their corresponding characteristics. Let

$\mathbf{x}_i$ = the vector of commodities possessed by person i

$c(\cdot)$ = the function converting a commodity vector into a vector of characteristics of those commodities

$f_i(\cdot)$ = a personal utilization function of i reflecting the pattern of use of commodities that i can actually succeed in doing

$F_i(\cdot)$ = the feasible set of utilization functions f_i, anyone of which persons i can in fact choose and achieve

If i chooses the utilization function $f_i(\cdot)$, then with his or her commodity vector $\mathbf{x}_i$, the achieved functions will be given by the vector $\mathbf{b}_i$.

$$\mathbf{b}_i = f_i(c(\mathbf{x}_i)) \tag{1.1}$$

The vector $\mathbf{b}_i$ denotes the state of the person, i.e. whether the person is well-nourished, well-clothed, literate, and so on.

The important issue is a class of evaluations of the state $\mathbf{b}$ of person i. Of course, i may also have her own "happiness evaluations" of $\mathbf{b}$, specified as

$$\mathbf{u}_i = h_i(f_i(c(\mathbf{x}_i))) \tag{1.2}$$

where $\mathbf{u}_i$ is personal happiness with the achieved functionings.[5] Later on in this paper, it is shown that personal happiness or desire fulfilment is the not the only kind of evaluation of state $\mathbf{b}$ by person i. If (1.2) were the only form of valuation, the individual would be acting like a "pleasure machine." Such a personal valuation would be devoid of any personal ethical views that might legitimately influence an individual in evaluating his or her personal state.

To contrast personal happiness from a substantive individualist valuation, what is needed is some form of evaluation of $\mathbf{b}$. The evaluation, one for each i, will reflect some ethical judgements, as will become clear.

It will be useful to begin with some constraint sets as functionings will typically be bounded, and these bounds may change over time.

For a given commodity vector $\mathbf{x}_i$, the functioning vectors feasible for person i are given by the set $P_i(\mathbf{x}_i)$.

$$P_i(\mathbf{x}_i) = \{\mathbf{b}_i | \mathbf{b}_i = f_i(c(\mathbf{x}_i)), \text{ for some } f_i(\cdot) \in F_i\} \tag{1.3}$$

$$Q_i(X_i) = \{\mathbf{b}_i | \mathbf{b}_i = f_i(c(\mathbf{x}_i))\}, \text{ for some } f_i(\cdot) \in F_i \text{ and some } \mathbf{x}_i \tag{1.4}$$

If the choice of commodity vectors is constrained and restricted to set X_i, then the person's feasible functioning vectors are given by the set $Q_i(X_i)$. Thus,

$$Q_i(X_i) \subset P_i \qquad\qquad (1.5)$$

$Q_i(X_i)$ represents the freedom that a person has in terms of the choice of functions, given his or her personal features F_i (conversion of characteristics into functionings) and his or her command over commodities X_i, which may be called his or her "entitlements." A failure of entitlements could restrict him or her to some subset $\overline{X}_i$ where

$$\overline{X}_i \subset X_i \qquad\qquad (1.6)$$

Naturally such a failure will affect $Q(\cdot)$.

In general, Q_i can be called "capabilities" of person i. It reflects the various combinations of functionings (or "beings") that he or she can achieve.

We now return to the valuation exercise. The valuation will, *inter alia*, reflect that person's ethical beliefs. Thus it will still be an individualist valuation; it is not some valuation imposed by a dictator.

Let $v_i(\cdot)$ be a valuation function for i, reflecting the well-being that can be achieved from some set V_i.

$$V_i = \{v_i | v_i = v_i(\mathbf{b}_i), \text{ for some } \mathbf{b}_i \in Q_i\} \qquad\qquad (1.7)$$

It is assumed that this individualist valuation ordering is complete. This completeness property is required to generate a partial ordering of individual well-being.

It should be noted that there is no presumption that the "highest" v_i in V_i (when it exists) will be chosen; given deontological considerations, a v_i that is not the maximal element of V_i may indeed be chosen to express the person's valuation. In other words, the individual is not presumed (or required) to be "maximizing" anything; it is merely a personal evaluation of his or her personal state. It is this valuation as a substantive individual ethical position that is missing in utilitarianism, in which it is supposed that there is no need to go beyond happiness or desire fulfilment, as happiness is assumed to be the only determinant of value. Hence utilitarianism stops at (1.2), with only utility information. Consequently, in utilitarian welfare economics, there is no valuation exercise, as value rests in utility only. In contrast here, the individual evaluates his or her own state, reflecting his or her ethical beliefs. In part, this valuation may reflect the person's evaluation of his or her happiness with his or her personal state, but the evaluation need not just reflect desire fulfilment.

On the other hand, a utilitarian analysis places value in personal utility only. However, there is no agreed metric by which the utilities can be compared between persons. The "utility" of a debt ridden African peasant surviving on the edge cannot be compared to that of a Texan rancher. Relative deprivation cannot be incorporated into the welfare calculus since, by definition, only utility information is available and, of course, utility comparisons between the African peasant and Texan rancher are not possible. Indeed, it may even be argued that it is possible that the African farmer may be "happier" than the Texan, unless of course he were able to see how his Texan counterpart is doing, i.e. what the

Texan rancher's functionings are. Then, some envy might creep in, but, in any case, this level of envy cannot be incorporated into the analysis.

In contrast, in Sen's approach, the valuation is central: starting with a functioning vector b_i, it is converted into a real valued scalar measure v_i, mapping functioning vectors into numerical representations of well-being. However, this is still an individualist valuation; it is not ipsedixist, i.e. it is not dictatorial. No one dictates what the level of well-being should be, or how that individual "should" evaluate his or her well-being; i.e. there are no "objective" or exogenously given standards for determining well-being.

Could this valuation change with information on other people's functioning vectors? Quite possibly, but here we are concerned only with a static picture of valuations obtained at a given time, based on the information available to persons at that time. It is these personal evaluations that can then be used to generate a partial ordering. This is explained below.

In an expository article on functionings and their valuations, it is necessary to go over much ground that Sen takes for granted. Not only is it necessary to distinguish these particular valuations from the standard utilitarian valuations, but it is also necessary to explain the difference between complete and partial orderings. The next three sections consider these issues in some detail: partial orderings; complete orderings, and the difference between the two; and the informational basis of a partial ordering.

Partial orderings

It was stated that the valuation v for each individual i is his or her valuation of his or her functionings vector b. To obtain these individualist valuations, some formal mechanisms will have to used to solicit the information. Sen refers to three different sources of information:

1   market purchase data
2   responses to questionnaires, and
3   non-market observation of personal states.

For the moment, it will be convenient to suppose that questionnaires would provide the necessary valuations. We return to the other sources of information on page 31.

If one solicits individual valuations, through questionnaires, one would expect that there will be a large number of valuations v_i. In that case, how is it possible to rank these measures of well-being? In some cases, the valuations will *vector dominate* others. This might occur, for example, in the ranking of the well-being of the very deprived, but even when there is no vector domination, there is no need to insist on generating *complete* orderings; a *partial* ordering will still yield important information about the rankings of well-being.

It will be instructive to consider an example of a partial ordering that has proved to be very useful, and Sen (1973) himself has made use of it. Consider figure 1.1, in which three different Lorenz curves of income distribution, x, y, and z are given. In this diagram, the Lorenz curve x lies wholly outside z, but x and y intersect. It is clear that we can say that x is "less unequal" than z. Let "less unequal" be represented by L. Then we can write the previous sentences as: xLz. Also, yLz, but it is not possible to say xLy or yLx, since they intersect. Hence the Lorenz curve ordering is a partial ordering, but nevertheless it gives useful information in ranking different income distributions.

If there are indeed a large number of valuation orderings, the scope for uncontroversial assessment of well-being will be restricted by the actual extent of variations among the orderings. Suppose that there is a n-set of orderings of functioning vectors, labelled $(P^1, P^2, \ldots, P^n)$. There will be a non-empty intersection of these orderings which will yield a partial ordering P^* such that:

$$xP^*y \text{ iff } xP^iy \,\forall\, i = 1, \ldots, n \tag{1.8}$$

This idea of the intersection is illustrated in figure 1.2.

Let I^1 to I^n represent a family of indifference curves going through X, corresponding to P^*. It is clear that all points to the right of AXD are superior to X, and all points below CXB are clearly inferior. The intersection partial ordering P^* is the minimum that can be safely said without contradicting any of the remaining orderings. This partial ordering P^* can then be used to rank well-being.

The idea of an intersection partial ordering, introduced above, can be explained further. Suppose there are k individuals, $i = 1, 2, \ldots, k$. Let each of these individuals have complete orderings C^i. Then we can define their intersection Q such that

$$yQx, \text{ iff } yC^ix \,\forall\, i = 1, 2, \ldots, k \tag{1.9}$$

Then it is clear that Q is a partial ordering,[6] which is by definition incomplete; just how incomplete it is depends on the extent to which each C^i are noncomparable and conflicting.[7]

It should be noted that the valuation of functionings is individualist, but not welfarist. The valuations can be obtained by the questionnaire method, as mentioned earlier. In principle, one may seek valuations from the entire population. In practice, a well stratified and representative sample (stratified by income, gender, education, location, etc.) would provide the necessary information.

Having collected the valuations, any one of a number of normalization techniques may be used to generate a partial ordering; the interested reader may consult Sen (1970, chapters 7 and 7*) for details on how a partial ordering may be obtained.

Granted that each v_i is an independent individualist valuation that orders the person's respective vector **b**. In what way is it different from a utilitarian valuation, in the sense of one's notion of "happiness," or desire fulfilment? The valuation v (the "i" argument is suppressed for simplicity) need not coincide with the personal valuation of happiness; indeed if it were the same, then the entire functioning approach would collapse and would be no different from other varieties of utilitarianism.

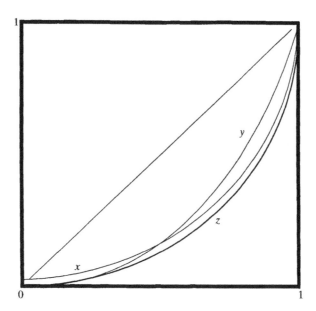

Figure 1.1 Partial orderings

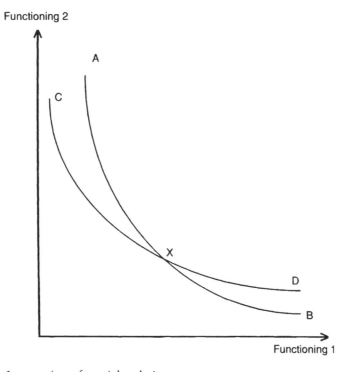

Figure 1.2 Intersection of partial orderings

The logic of valuation is demonstrated in Statement 1. The alternative is given in Statement 2.

Statement 1   I value x. Therefore I am happy with x.
Statement 2   I am happy with x. Therefore I value x.

The valuation v is consistent with the logic of Statement 1, but not with Statement 2. It should also be noted that the valuation v is not some "objective" measure of valuation; and it is not ipsedixist. If an objective valuation measure existed, it would be a *complete* ordering, by definition. Two examples will make this clear.

Complete orderings

In the classical theory of value, let **A** be the matrix of input coefficients and let **B** be the matrix of capital coefficients. The classical theory of value can be expressed by the vector **p**, which are production prices:

$$\mathbf{p}(\mathbf{A} + \lambda\mathbf{B}) = \mathbf{p} \tag{1.10}$$

The vector **p** is a *complete* valuation; it *orders* all goods produced with the input–output matrices **A** and **B**. As is well known, the vector **p** is determined up to a factor of proportionality.

The same underlying convexity theory may be used to find competitive equilibrium prices, in the sense of Arrow–Debreu. A competitive equilibrium yields a complete ranking of all goods in terms of "competitive equilibrium" prices.

Both of the above are complete valuations; they succeed in ordering all goods. The valuations are "objective" in some sense: the classical value proportions reflect the direct and indirect labor and capital content of production. The neoclassical values are "objective" in that they reflect marginal social opportunity costs. The only difference between the two is that production prices reflect current technological possibilities with the commodity composition reflected in the choice of "columns" of the matrices **A** and **B**. In the neoclassical case, demand (through utility maximization) dictates the point on the production possibility curve, but both provide relative values that completely order all goods produced in the economy. In this strict sense, the resulting valuations in both cases are objective measures.

Referring to (1.10), two price vectors **p** (associated with matrices **A** and **B**) and **p′** (associated with matrices **A′** and **B′**) will differ if and only if at least one of the elements of the matrix pair (**A**, **B**) differs from the elements of the matrix pair (**A′**, **B′**).[8] With a complete ordering, we can value each and every good in the production system. Hence, considering the elements of the price vector **p** as $(p_1, p_2, \ldots, p_n)$, either the value of one good is greater than, or less than another good, or the two goods are of equal value. With a complete ordering, there can be no indeterminateness, i.e. no gaps.

The informational bases of a partial ordering

We return to the partial ordering v. On page 27, it was assumed that the partial ordering would be obtained by a questionnaire completed by the relevant population. Here, the informational bases of the valuation are considered further.

To repeat, the valuation scheme v is not objective in the sense of the previous section; in contrast, there is no invariant rule for determining them. Neither is it utilitarian in the sense of "I am happy with x, and therefore I value x." However, being an individualist valuation scheme, it would be subject to the same difficulties encountered in the contingent valuation method (CVM).

A contingent valuation (of, say, an environmental good) is obtained by putting forth a questionnaire to the affected group of people. CVM generates a forward-looking valuation based on people's expectations; consequently, CVM is referred to in the literature as a "stated preference" method of valuation, as opposed to a "revealed preferred" method. A revealed preferred method would look at revealed behaviour and infer a valuation from such data through a pattern of actual use. Actual use reveals preferences and valuations, as opposed to asking people to anticipate their potential use of some environmental amenity, and by asking them to form expectations about their potential willingness to pay for an environmental amenity. Again, data that is based on a revealed preference valuation may in some sense be treated as "objective," as each act of using an environmental amenity is an established fact, a datum, a given. On the other hand, CVM will be a hypothetical valuation based on a hypothetical demand, and subject to a large number of biases. In the case of a public environmental good, there will be a strategic (i.e. free-rider) bias in addition to all the other possible statistical biases (Mitchell and Carson, 1989).

Could the individual valuations v possibly reflect such strategic biases? Would it be in the interest of an individual to understate the valuation of his or her beings and doings, i.e. understate the valuation of his or her vector **b**?

It very much depends to what uses the valuations would be put. Clearly, if taxes were to be based on the valuations, then individuals would have an incentive for systematic under-valuation in the reported valuations v. If the valuations were to be used for "international comparisons of well-being" the individual might have an incentive to overstate his or her respective well-being, from nationalistic motives.

It seems inevitable that the individual valuations must be compared with what Sen calls non-market data, so as to check for consistency. For example, reported literacy data must be consistent with census data on literacy; reported income data must be consistent with national income data; morbidity data must be checked with data on medical insurance claims, and so on. Of course, at least some of the aggregate data will itself be survey data such as family budget data, panel data on expenditures, and so on. If multiple sources are used, then the danger of biases (including strategic biases) can be minimized.

In this way, individualist valuations need not be purely fanciful. At the same time, individual valuations, which will always be subject to information available to the individual, need not be ipsedixist. Neither is the search for valuations a search for an "objective" measure of well-being. An objective measure, if found, would have to be a *complete* ordering; otherwise, it cannot be called objective.

The ranking of well-being will not face the same kind of Arrow-type impossibility problems for two reasons. First, the object of the present exercise is to obtain a *common* standard of well-being rather than to resolve interpersonal conflicts in the assessments of social states; it is not an exercise in interpersonal aggregation of rankings of *all* social states. The common standard is obtained by using any of the usual normalization methods, as stated earlier. Second, we are not interested in completeness (of orderings) in any case. The partial ordering v will be weakly "supervenient" (i.e. contingent) on the functionings; i.e. the valuation will depend on the individual's perception of what he or she has achieved with the commodities at his or her command.[9]

We may conclude that well-being is decidable strictly on the basis of the specification and assessment of functionings. To use some partial ordering P^* to judge the well-being of a particular individual, or a country or a population, the functionings approach can be combined with three different sources of information: market purchase data; responses to questionnaires; and non-market observation of personal states. It should be noted that the last mentioned will, in part, reflect the consequences of public policy actions. Thus the non-market observation of personal states could include data on literacy, life-expectancy, incidence of cancer, pollution indexes, and so on. The resulting ordering of well-being can then be used to assess the effectiveness of the public policies; or they could indicate the relative "distance" in the well-being of two different populations, where "distance" is of course ordinal. For example population x may be compared to population z through a comparison with y, k, and m. The idea was illustrated in figure 1.1. Hence, comparisons of well-being will be possible.

The three sources of information – and particularly non-market observation – will give information of the "states" of persons, of their living conditions, in fact on the functionings achieved. Questionnaires will give individual valuations; non-market observation will give aggregate data with which the former must be compared for consistency.

Well-being and Capability Set

Well-being reflects particular achievements, but the picture of well-being is incomplete without taking into account real opportunities open to the person. This is what Sen calls "advantage." Assessment of advantage involves the evaluation of a set of potential achievements, not just actual ones. Advantage can also be called a set of potential functionings, or a person's "capability set."

As an example of the capability set, consider the set composed of the three vectors in table 1.1. The first vector is the ratio of the distribution of income of the top 20 percent divided by the bottom 20 percent of the population of the country. The next vector is the income of the top 10 percent of the population, and the third vector is the purchasing power parity (PPP) adjusted per capita GNP

Table 1.1 Income distribution and PPP adjusted real GNP per capita index (US = 100)

Country	80/20[a]	Share of top 10% in per cent	GNP[b] 1987	1993
1 USA	8.9	25.0	100	100
2 Switzerland	8.6	29.8	101	96
3 Japan	4.3	22.4	75	84
4 Canada	7.1	24.1	88	82
5 Denmark	7.1	22.3	79	79
6 France	7.5	26.1	76	77
7 Netherlands	4.5	21.9	67	70
8 United Kingdom	9.6	27.8	71	70
9 Sweden	4.6	20.8	78	69
10 Germany	5.8	24.4	66	68
Upper middle income				
11 Chile	18.3	45.8	25	34
12 Mexico	13.6	39.5	28	28
13 Hungary	3.2	20.8	29	25
14 Brazil	32.1	51.3	25	22
15 South Africa	19.2	47.3	N/A	N/A
Lower middle income				
16 Algeria	6.7	31.7	27	22
17 Russia	11.4	31.5	36	20
18 Bulgaria	4.7	24.7	29	17
19 Indonesia	4.9	27.9	10	13
20 Sri Lanka	4.4	25.2	8	12
21 Bolivia	8.6	31.7	9	10
Low income				
22 China	6.5	24.6	6	9
23 India	4.7	27.1	5	5
24 Zambia	9.6	34.2	5	4
25 Tanzania	26.1	46.5	2	2

[a] 80/20 is the ratio of the slope of the Lorenz curve; it is the share of the top 20 percent divided by the share of the bottom 20 percent of income.
[b] GNP per capita is adjusted for PPP, as computed by the World Bank.
Source: *Word Bank Development Report*, 1994

index, with that of the USA expressed as 100. The GNP index is an indicator of the "size" of the national income "cake," whereas the other two are indices of its relative distribution. This set contains information on the functionings and advantage of persons in the various countries considered in table 1.1.

Table 1.1 contains a sample of twenty-five countries out of 132 countries for which the World Bank publishes data on income distribution and an index of per capita GNP, adjusted by PPP. It is this sort of data that would make up a capability set. Note first that the GNP data are used to rank and group the countries into four groups: high income, upper middle income, lower middle income, and low income. This capability set enables us to use the idea of a partial ordering to derive some information on the well-being of the citizens of the respective countries. It is apparent that, in the high income group, the highest inequality is observed in the UK, the USA and Switzerland. The worst record of inequality in the entire sample of 132 countries is Brazil, followed by South Africa and Chile. The poorest country in the sample, Tanzania, has a very unequal distribution of income, second only to Brazil. Of the large lower middle income countries, the Russian Federation has the most unequal distribution. However, as might be expected, not all countries can be ranked in terms of inequality, and even some pairwise comparisons cannot be made. For example, the income distribution of China and India are noncomparable. This is of course character-istic of all partial orderings. Nevertheless partial orderings can yield useful information about comparative and *relative* well-being.

The data on the nature of the distribution of income indicate the degree to which the number of people in different income strata have command over commodities, which will in turn suggest the level of functioning achieved, but as this is always a comparative matter, the above analysis also indicates how far some countries will have to go to increase the well-being of the lowest 20 percent of their population, compared to what the richest receive.

Capabilities is a freedom type notion, or a notion of realizing one's potential; it encompasses both negative freedom and positive freedom, and therefore both negative and positive rights. The underlying judgement is that humans should be free to reach their full potential in all dimensions, but it is also clear that some humans face a smaller capability set than others, who have more options through a larger or a different capability set. Sen shows that it is important to compare (and rank) capability sets too through a partial ordering.

A complete picture of the evaluation of human life thus requires the twin concepts of both well-being, and advantage or capabilities. Capabilities are also indicative of what can be achieved and what public policy might wish to strive for in the future for the citizenry.

The functionings–capability approach can be used not only for ranking of well-being but for other interpersonal comparisons too. It can also be used in the analysis of inequality (Sen, 1992). Consequently, it can form a basis for a theory of justice. All theories of justice can be distinguished on the basis of the metric used in judging a persons' advantage. In a utilitarian theory of justice, the metric is, of course, utility derived by command over goods. In Rawls's theory, it is the primary goods' index, and, in Sen's theory of justice, it is functionings and capabilities, i.e. what persons can do and achieve; it is this that serves as the metric.

Thus, the economics of well-being is one aspect of a theory of justice, a theory that has room for, and remains open to, the widest possible fulfilment of human potentialities in all dimensions chosen by humans. As has been shown, the functionings–capability approach reflects not only current well-being achieved by a group, but also the future potential well-being. In doing this, the approach goes beyond utility information; that is why it has been called *post* welfarist.

The implications for global warming

It will be recalled that the motivational question posed earlier was how to incorporate the differential impact on persons of the long-term, possibly catastrophic, effects of global warming. This is no place to catalogue a long list of possible effects of global warming. We cannot assume either that technological change will completely neutralize the effects, or that the effects of global warming will be Pareto improvements for all citizens of the world. The most likely outcome is that global warming will affect different people differently.

A differential impact will mean that the set Q will change, so that for some set of people it will

$$\overline{Q}_i \subset Q_i \tag{1.11}$$

and there will be a failure of entitlements. Increased incidence of cancer, for example, will alter the set F; and every possible index of functionings of some people will reduce their well-being. The small island nations (the group of thirty-one) will also face the possibility of extinction. Thus, the burdens of adaptations to changes induced by global warming will fall unequally on nations, with the heaviest burden falling on those least able to do much about it.

All this is nothing new; it has been said before. The point being made here is that the welfarist analysis of the consequences of global warming, sketched on pages 23–4, is not consistent with real features of life, whereas on the basis of the functionings–capability approach we can say that the well-being of many, mostly in the developing countries, will be reduced, not to mention that global warming will force severe hardships on them.

Viewing the functionings–capability approach as a theory of justice, we may even say that differential impacts will be unjust; but we could not say that from within the framework of welfare economics. In fact, we now have a theory which can incorporate market, non-market, and other observations of personal states, and use this information to assess functionings. The pollution indexes, the indexes of the increase in cancer rates due to pollution, now all have a theoretical legitimacy in the interpersonal comparisons of well-being. Anything that alters entitlements will alter functionings and capabilities, which will, in turn, change well-being. A new valuation will show in which direction well-being has changed.

Conclusion

As a theory of public policy and public action, welfare economics and Walrasian general equilibrium theory now dominate not only trade policy, but also taxation, regulation, and environmental policy. However, income support programs characteristic of most developed countries have no theoretical support in conventional welfare economics, since there is no concept of "deservingness" or of "justice" in the theory.[10] The income support programs that exist in Canada and Western Europe have to be explained away as "government preferences or value judgements." However, the theory of functionings and capability does not shy away from serious questions of public ethics. One can only hope that, one day, this new theory will serve as a possible cornerstone of a theory of collective choice and collective action.

Notes

1   This research was financed in part by a grant from the Social Sciences and Humanities Research Council of Canada, grant #410-94-1121. I am grateful to Ken Binmore, Duane Chapman, and Tony Ward for comments and discussions on an earlier draft, but I remain responsible for any remaining errors.

2   The second tenet, ordinalism, states that for a given individual, welfare economics can only distinguish between "higher" and "lower" utility, but nothing can be said about how much higher or lower than a given initial level. Hence only "ordinal" statements about utility levels can be made, as there is no invariant utility scale.

3   Sen (1993, p. 31, especially the references provided in his footnote 3) gives a partial list of references to what he calls the "functionings literature"; see also Balestrino (1991) and Balestrino and Petretto (1994).

4   The net gain proposition can, in principle, be established by standard cost-benefit calculations, where prices reflect competitive prices.

5   For Benthamite utilitarians, this is *all* that matters. For them, there can be *no* valuation index other than a personal happiness index; and any other approach would be an *ipsedixist* error.

6   If each individual ordering is complete, then it is reflexive and transitive. The reflexivity and transitivity carries over to the intersection orderings; see Sen (1973, p. xx).

7   Sen (1970, chapters 7 and 7*) shows that under the assumption of "weak symmetry," one can define a measure of the degree d of partial comparability between 0 and 1, such that $d = 1$ implies complete comparability of the units of the individual orderings, and $d = 0$ implies noncomparability. Thus, there exists a hierarchy of partial orderings, starting with the Pareto partial ordering under noncomparability and ending up with a complete ordering under full comparability of units. A complete ordering can, of course, be reached for degrees of comparability less than 1.

8   In this case, we can say that the price vector $\mathbf{p}$ is strongly supervenient on the matrix pair $(\mathbf{A}, \mathbf{B})$; see Hare (1989, pp. 66–81).

9   Sen (1985, p. 57) refers to this property as "weak supervenience." This property is a consistency requirement, comparable to some "rationality" property of choice orderings. It avoids contradictory orderings. "Strong supervenience" would lead to an objective and complete ordering, without reference to an individual ordering, and the ordering would make well-being directly interpersonally comparable. Week supervenience does not carry this implication. The valuation is merely contingent on functionings. With strong supervenience, well-being of two personal states will be different if and only if their functionings differ.

10   The earlier attempt to introduce "merit wants" into the public finance literature was entirely *ad hoc* and did not catch on. Now the public economics literature distinguishes "public goods" from private goods, but with technological advances that now permit excludability, the set of public goods is shrinking. For reasons of space, this line of reasoning is not pursued here. Suffice it to say that the modern "welfare state" does not have a theretical foundation in neoclassical welfare economics, unless things like a miminum standard of living, healthcare education, etc. are defined in some *ad hoc* way as "merit wants", or "quasi-public goods."

References

Arrow, K. (1951) *Social Choice and Individual Values*. New York: Wiley. 2nd edn 1963.

Balestrino, A. (1991) Some suggestions for the identification of poverty in a non-welfarist framework, *Economic Notes: Monte dei Paschi di Siena*, 20 (2), 335–53.

Balestrino, A. and Petretto, A. (1994) Optimal tax rules for "functioning"-inputs. *Economic Notes: Monte dei Paschi di Siena*, 23 (2), 216–32.

Boadway, R. W. (1974) The welfare foundation of cost-benefit analysis. *Economic Journal*, December, 84, 926–39.

Broome, J. (1991) *The Intergenerational Aspects of Climate Change*. University of Bristol for the Economic and Social Research Council.

Chipman, J. (1987) Compensation test. In J. Eatwell, M. Milgate and P. Newman (eds) *The New Palgrave: A Dictionary of Economics*. London: Stockton Press.

Gorman, W. M. (1956) A possible procedure for analysing quality differences in the egg market. Journal paper no. 3129, Iowa Agricultural Experiment Station, and also *Review of Economic Studies*, 1980, 47, 847–56.

Hare, R. M. (1989) Supervenience. In R. M. Hare (ed.) *Essays in Ethical Theory*. Oxford: Clarendon Press.

Lancaster, K. J. (1966) A new approach to consumer theory. *Journal of Political Economy*, 74, 132–57.

Mitchell, R. C. and Carson, R. T. (1989) *Using Surveys to Value Public Goods: The Contingent Valuation Method*. Washington, DC: Resources For the Future.

Sen, A. K. (1970) *Collective Choice and Social Welfare*. San Francisco: Holden-Day.

Sen, A. K. (1973) *On Economic Inequality*. Oxford: Clarendon Press.

Sen, A. K. (1979) Utilitarianism and welfarism. *Journal of Philosophy*, 76, 463–89.

Sen, A. K. (1985) *Commodities and Capabilities*. Amsterdam: North-Holland.

Sen, A. K. (1987) *On Ethics and Economics*. Oxford: Basil Blackwell.

Sen, A. K. (1992) *Inequality Reexamined*. Oxford: Clarendon Press.

Sen, A. K. (1993) Capability and well-being. In M. C. Nussbaum and A. Sen (eds), *The Quality of Life*. WIDER Studies in Development Economics, Oxford: Clarendon Press.

2

Bequeathing Hazards: Security Rights and Property Rights of Future Humans

Henry Shue

Little surprises

My hobby is building model land-mines. Like model electric trains, my little land-mines are miniaturized but functioning replicas of the originals. When I was young, I just played with matches like everyone else. Now, in the summer-time, I take a few of the model land-mines I have assembled during the winter along with me in my backpack and bury some along a different section of the Fingerlakes Trail each weekend. I call them my "Little Surprises." You do not need to worry, though, even if you are an avid hiker and use the Fingerlakes Trail, because I install over the detonator a special metal cover that will not deteriorate for several generations. So not even your grandchildren need to worry about my little surprises because, by the time the mines become active through the deterioration of the detonator cover, the people who will then be alive will be some totally unknown people of a distant generation – probably with very different preference schedules from ours (Who knows what they will want?) and certainly with much better technology (They will probably have terrific prosthetic limbs by then.) And won't the Boy Scouts (if they still have Boy Scouts) be surprised the summer that my little mines start exploding all along the Trail – it will be a riot! I wish I could actually still be around, but I get a lot of satisfaction from just imagining the chaos.

Now, the criminality and possible insanity of the project just described, had I been serious, are evident. The possible insanity derives from the sheer maliciousness of the project, and the delight in other people's injury, shock, and dismay. However, we could imagine different activities in which the devices I was leaving scattered through the world were not designed precisely so that they would injure and shock others, but were instead designed primarily to provide some benefit now, and would cause the future damage and dismay only as a by-product – as what, in war, we call "collateral damage."

Of course, we do not need to imagine such activities, which combine present benefit with future damage, because we are in fact engaged in them left and right: our nuclear power plants create a previously non-existent hazard in the form of spent fuel that we do not have a clue how to dispose of safely,[1] our fossil-fuel-driven power plants inject long-resident CO_2 into the upper atmosphere in constantly increasing amounts that will lead to rises in surface temperature sufficient to disrupt agriculture, and so on. These real activities differ from my imaginary land-mines in having good intentions, not malicious intentions. In general, however, good intentions do not carry a lot of weight in cost-benefit analyses or other economic calculations, so there is no reason to think they should save anyone here.

Before we leave behind the simple land-mines of imagination for the complex land-mines of reality, we might pause to see what we can learn from the clarity of the simple case. Why is it so obviously totally wrong for anyone to have a hobby of planting even land-mines that would explode only in the distant future? Because the bodies of human beings will be damaged. Some people sometimes engage in the intellectual exercise of denying that there is any such thing as a right at all; certain types of utilitarians, for example, like to deny rights. It is, of course, perfectly possible in theory to deny consistently the existence and even the meaningfulness of all assertions of rights, including the right to physical security – to the integrity of one's body. One can try to imagine, say, a "state of nature" in which assault, beating, rape, torture, and mayhem violate no rights and break no rules, because there are no such rights or underlying rules. If, however, one approaches a person engaged in general theoretical skepticism about the existence of rights with an instrument well-designed to do damage to his body, e.g. a butcher knife, it quickly turns out that, however reluctant on theoretical grounds the person may be to use the word "right," the person has no doubt whatsoever that it is unacceptable for a person's body to be damaged. It is simply not possible for a sane person to act in practice as if he or she believes that his or her body is not entitled to the kind of special protection against the depredations of others that a right constitutes, whatever intellectual doubts he or she may have about concepts of rights.

I think we would consider a person who genuinely acted as if there were no good reason why his or her body should not be used by other people for those other people's purposes to be suffering from a serious psychological problem, perhaps involving a pathological deficiency in self-esteem. A surgeon may be given permission to cause temporary damage to one's body when there is good reason to believe that this temporary damage is the best available means to longer-term benefit. Yet it is precisely because we do in practice think that we ought to be immune to assaults upon our bodies that surgeons must have permission, must be prepared to defend in court any deviations from standard practices, and so on. We have no serious – non-academic – doubt that a person has a right to physical security (and that one of the minimal police functions of government is to provide a high level of protection for our bodily integrity).

The preceding no doubt says more than enough about the obvious. I have belabored the obvious to this extent because I think this practically undeniable basic right to physical security has more implications – even for environmental policy – than it may seem to have. For a start, it seems evident that we should operate on the assumption that all the people who will in future actually exist will have this same fundamental right to bodily integrity. Once again, one can, as always, play logical conceivability games: one can imagine a possible world in which, perhaps through genetic engineering, people have come to have, in effect, bodies of teflon, such that however much others stab at or beat upon them, no damage can be done. In that imagined world, the right to physical security would have lost its point, and the police could cease to concern themselves with physical attacks. It would remain the case that insofar as it remained possible for any person to damage the body of another, every person would retain a right not to suffer the damage that remained possible; in that imagined case, however, I see no objection to saying that the right to bodily integrity had disappeared, along with the function it had served (protecting once highly vulnerable bodies against damage).

However, this imagined case, with its bare logical possibility that the right to physical security could someday lose its point, has zero implications for how we should actually conduct ourselves for the indefinite future, and toward the indefinite future. Absolutely nothing follows from the mere conceivability of change. What we know now is that human bodies are extremely easy to tear, fold, and spindle; consequently, it is extremely important that they be protected. When, and if, we have genuine reason to believe that the human apparatus has become less vulnerable, we can provide it less protection; if invulnerable, no protection at all. Yet, until we have real evidence that things are in fact going to change, it is reasonable to assume only that people in the future – all foreseeable ones – will have the same right to physical security that we have. If, in defense of planting mines along the Fingerlakes Trail, someone offered for no good reason the bare hypothesis that future people might have feet of steel, we would lock him up just as fast.

Surprise annuity

All right, then, human beings have basic rights to physical security, which I will have to take into account if I want to pursue my model land-mine hobby. Still, I cannot help laughing out loud when I think how amazed those little Boy Scouts would be in around 2098 suddenly to hear those explosions going off all up and down the Fingerlakes Trail, when they thought they were all alone communing with nature. This is too good a scheme to abandon. So, here is what I will do. I will endow an annuity – let us call it the "Surprise Annuity" – with enough principal now so that the compounded interest will, by 2098 or so when the mines are likely to become active, have added up to a large enough sum to pay for all the medical expenses and prosthetic limbs and what-not needed by those who suffer from my little joke. No one will end up out-of-pocket by any amount, and whoever needs one will get a nice new high-tech foot. We could discuss the criteria for adequate compensation; perhaps "making them whole," as the lawyers call it, by paying all their expenses in restoring normal functioning would not be sufficient compensation, and I should throw in, say, a college scholarship. I am willing to pay what it is worth.

This scheme is becoming more and more insane, but it is important to understand exactly the reason why. The reason, in old-fashioned terminology, is: inalienability. That means: some things are not for sale – especially not some

rights. This is not a feature of many rights, of course. Property rights, in particular, are mostly transferable for compensation; marketability is their main
function. Not all rights are property rights, however, and the right to physical
security is a prime example of a right that is not a property right. This is the main
reason why, in the USA, it is illegal to sell bodily organs for use in transplants.[2]
Kidneys, hearts, corneas, etc. are non-marketable: there is, by Federal statute, no
legal way to buy or sell a part of a – or, since the abolition of slavery in 1865, a
whole – human being.[3] I cannot transfer the ownership, or use,[4] of a part of my
body and – with regard to the imaginary land-mine example – I cannot sell
anyone the right to inflict damage on my body. By "cannot," I naturally mean
legally and morally cannot; there is usually someone who will in fact trade in just
about anything.

If no one can buy a right to inflict damage upon someone else's body, even in
the case of people who are currently alive and therefore able to agree to the sale,
no one can buy the same right in the case of people of future generations.
Someone who thought, for example, that surrogate motherhood is an acceptable
practice now could go through the usual exercises and come up with some
calculations about, for example, how much in current funds would have to be set
aside to pay for a certain amount of surrogacy at some future date. Any given
woman at that future date would of course still have to agree – assuming for the
sake of argument that surrogacy is the performance of a service, not the sale of a
child – to perform the service (at the rate made possible by the amount set aside
today). Even if the transaction is permissible, it is permissible only on condition
that the service is performed voluntarily. In the imaginary land-mine case, the Boy
Scouts of 2098 would presumably not voluntarily walk a trail containing active
land-mines. However, that is not the point.

The point is that it does not matter whether some Scouts could be found in
2098 who would agree to walk the Trail for a large enough package of compensation. A society that still acknowledged a right to physical security would not
permit such a transaction then, just as we would not permit it now. Submitting
your body to the risk of this kind of injury is a "service" that we do not allow to
be performed; that someone would be willing to perform it has no effect legally
or morally.[5] To repeat: the problem for the land-mine scheme is not that one
cannot get the voluntary agreement (because the people whose agreement would
be needed do not yet exist); the problem is that voluntary agreement is imma-
terial because such agreements are ruled out by our fundamental attitude to the
human body.

Do we not only permit but also require financial compensation for bodily
injury? What about all the lawsuits following automobile accidents? Why did
Dow Chemical agree to set aside billions (without technically acknowledging
having done anything wrong, of course) to compensate women who received
breast implants made of material created by Dow and who are now suffering
various kinds of physical distress? Of course, we do require compensation for
physical injury. However, there is, in both legal and moral terms, an absolutely
fundamental distinction between compensation for injuring something, e.g. an
eye, and the purchase of a right to injure it. If I negligently knock your eye out,

I will have to compensate you for the loss of sight, but I cannot make a contract with you to pay you that same amount in advance to purchase the right to knock your eye out. In reality, either way you lose your eye and I pay, but one should not underestimate the magnitude of the legal and moral difference between *ex-post* compensation and *ex-ante* purchase. Compensation is a distinct second-best after the best has become impossible; purchase would be the legitimated rejection of the fully possible best.

The difference may seem to lie in voluntariness: in the accident, you lose your eye involuntarily while, in the sale, you would lose it, if you were to agree to the transaction, voluntarily. However, as I indicated already, the deeper element of our legal and moral structure is that voluntariness does not come into it. Voluntariness is ruled out, because the sale of such rights in one's body is disallowed, even for – especially for – those who would agree to such transactions. The traditional way to describe the conceptual structure here was to say that the basic right to physical security is inalienable. Now we would probably say simply that the right in question is non-marketable.

Why discounting is not the primary issue

The moral position adopted by economist Richard N. Cooper is to recommend the following principle: "An appropriate minimum standard is to leave a world no worse than ours in terms of income, and with more options for action, and more knowledge about the implications of these options" (Cooper, 1992, p. 301). I will call this Cooper's minimum standard. Although in the chapter I am citing he simply announces it as if it needed no justifying arguments, Cooper's minimum standard is in itself intuitively appealing. Cooper goes on immediately to say: "That standard requires comparing mitigation actions with alternative forms of investment, and choosing investments with the highest returns, appropriately measured. What discount rate should be applied?" However, although we certainly have to compare, in the case of climate change that he is discussing, mitigation actions with alternative forms of investment, we certainly do not have simply to choose the investments with the highest returns. To assume that we either must, or even may, choose the investments with the highest returns is to assume that we must or may maximize returns *without* constraint and that is to assume, without argument, that no one has any non-marketable rights that stand in the way of maximization. The assumption that there are no non-marketable rights that might constrain our maximization of returns is, to say the least, extremely controversial – it is in fact flatly contradicted by the widespread assumption that all persons have non-marketable rights to physical security.

Let us back up a little. First, it is essential to be absolutely clear that Cooper's minimum standard is a moral principle, whatever else it may be in addition. To say "an appropriate minimum standard is to" means "we must do at least" – a requirement for our (economic) behavior is being laid down. I am not complaining because a moral principle has been ventured. Life is complicated and we need well-grounded guiding principles; since guiding principles have economic assumptions and economic implications, we need the help of economists (certainly not exclusively of philosophers) in formulating reasonable principles. While principles like Cooper's minimum standard have economic grounds and economic implications, they nevertheless also tell us how we *may* or *must* conduct ourselves. Consequently, they need to mesh with our other considered judgments about morality as well as our other considered judgments about economics; and one of our most unshakable moral judgments is that people have a (non-marketable) fundamental right not to have their bodies damaged by the actions of others, when the damage is preventable. When bodily damage is unavoidably done, compensation must be paid *ex post*; this does not mean that one may plan to do the damage *ex ante* as long as one also plans to compensate, because that would be equivalent to buying what may not be sold. It is not acceptable for me to plant land-mines provided only that I also establish an annuity for the medical expenses of my victims.

Cooper's proposed standard is, therefore, too weak a requirement to be a *minimum* standard. It may be that we ought not to do anything that would violate Cooper's standard, but there are activities that would not violate Cooper's standard that we nevertheless ought not to engage in. One kind of such activities that ought to be ruled out is activities that will predictably inflict physical damage upon other human beings, including human beings who happen not yet to be alive.

Cooper's minimum standard runs into difficulty in part because it is stated with too much generality and consequently covers too many kinds of cases that are significantly different from each other. Brian Barry has argued for a superficially similar-seeming principle, but Barry's principle is in fact quite different because he restricts it specifically to resource depletion. Here is Barry's minimum standard: "We can now venture a statement of what is required by justice toward future generations. As far as natural resources are concerned, depletion should be compensated for in the sense that later generations should be left no worse off (in terms of productive capacity) than they would have been without the depletion" (Barry, 1983).[6]

The fundamental idea that, I suspect, both Cooper and Barry are attempting to capture is what is often called the "no-harm principle:" one ought not to harm others; and, therefore, one ought not to leave others any worse off than they would have been but for one's actions, with regard to any of their rights.[7] In one respect, Cooper's minimum standard is stronger than Barry's minimum standard, but in another respect Cooper's is weaker than Barry's. On the one hand, Cooper's standard is stronger in that while Barry's principle is strictly negative – "be left no worse off" – Cooper's requires improvements in both options for action and knowledge and settles for the purely negative requirement of no-harm only in the case of income. On the other hand, Barry's principle is tightly drawn to apply only to depletion of natural resources – and he makes clear that he is not willing to have everything homogenized into "utility" – while Cooper's, through being formulated with maximum generality in terms of "returns," allows any trade-offs among more specific categories that would yield the highest overall "returns." Implicitly Cooper's standard allows – because it does not prohibit, in what is explicitly put forward as a "minimum standard" – trade-offs between

1   possible current expenditures to prevent, or mitigate, climate change, and
2   investments to provide future generations with greater resources, which they could, if they choose at the time, use for adapting to the effects of unmitigated climate change.

My thesis is that any of those predictable effects that would constitute physical harm to human beings must be prevented and may not be merely compensated for, no matter how great the proposed compensation, if prevention is possible. Before returning to climate change, let us glance at a relatively simpler case, ozone depletion, which, I am assuming, Cooper might approach in a similar fashion.

Emissions of chlorofluorocarbons (CFCs) damage human bodies by causing skin cancer, for one thing – cornea damage is also done. The causal process has only three basic steps, making it extremely simple and clear as disease etiologies go.

1   Having risen into the Earth's atmosphere, molecules of the various CFCs spend decades destroying molecules of ozone.
2   The progressively thinner layer of atmospheric ozone allows progressively increased levels of ultraviolet-B (UVB) radiation from the sun to penetrate to the Earth's surface.
3   The increased levels of UVB produce human skin cancer (as well as impaired sight, plus damage to other animals and to plants) that would otherwise not be expected to occur, including highly dangerous malignant melanomas.

This is about as straightforward as it gets, and the mechanisms are relatively well-understood:

> The E.P.A. [US Environmental Protection Agency] estimates that every 1 percent depletion in ozone will cause something like a 2 or 3 percent increase in UV-B and a 5 percent increase in skin cancer, including a 1 percent increase in malignant melanomas. In our lifetimes, the thinning of the ozone shield may lead to a 60 percent rise in the incidence of skin cancers of all kinds in the United States.[8]

A report by the Japan Meteorological Agency (Bureau of National Affairs, 1994, p. 302) found continuing thinning in the Northern Hemisphere, over Japan. Creating CFCs, which are entirely man-made and are a compound not found in nature, creates human cancers, through a long-distance but well-grasped set of reactions.

The production of CFCs is, as everyone knows, gradually being phased out under the *Montreal Protocol on Substances that Destroy the Ozone*, although it will be a long time before all the "freon" (one kind of CFC) from all the air-conditioners and refrigerators already filled with it has drifted into the sky to begin its long period of ozone-eating. Thus ozone destruction will continue for decades after the end of CFC production. Cooper's minimum standard, if applied to ozone destruction (he was writing about climate change), would require us to choose, using discounting, between

1   expenditures on the prevention, or mitigation, of CFC-caused future skin cancers, and
2   investments that would provide future generations with greater resources, which "they" could, if "they" choose, use for treating un-prevented skin cancers (or, if "they" choose, use some other way).

Our choice now is to be made by "comparing mitigation actions with alternative forms of investment, and choosing investments with the highest returns, appropriately measured." In contrast, our commonsense conviction, that no one is free to inflict cancer upon other people, requires that we not trade-off prevention measures for the sake of some nebulous overall highest returns to be controlled by an unspecified "they." This conviction actually contains two points.

First, a person's right to physical security against, among other things, anthropogenic malignancies is non-marketable and can, therefore, not be purchased for any amount of returns from alternative investments. Physical security is not for sale; one cannot buy rights to inflict disease on humans any more than one can buy rights to blow off the left feet of Boy Scouts.[9] It is, for example, the realization that "second-hand" tobacco smoke causes cancer that is beginning to put tobacco companies on the defensive. The right to physical security is slowly triumphing in this case over an alleged right to liberty, the "right to smoke" i.e. the right to force others to inhale your carcinogenic second-hand smoke; the difficulty for the "right to smoke" is that liberties are conditional upon fulfillment of the no-harm principle, but smoking clearly harms other people in addition to the smoker.

Second, Cooper's proposal is severely weakened by the indeterminateness of the future "they" who would control the returns from our choice not to mitigate but to invest. Some people in the future will get skin cancer, and some people will control the returns from our current investments on "their" behalf, but will the people who control the returns know the people who get the cancer? Will they even be in the same nations? Will they care? Here is one place not to ignore property rights. Will the specific "they" who control the returns from investment, who have the relevant property rights, be willing to spend those returns on the specific "them" who have the skin cancer? Is there any reason to think they would? To ignore this problem is to ignore property and politics, that is, to ignore both the distribution of wealth and the distribution of power. That is hopelessly apolitical.

Because the institutions created under the *Montreal Protocol* have already been in operation for a while, ozone destruction is a less interesting case than climate change, to which we will presently return. First, one implication is worth drawing so as to bring out more fully the meaning of the right to physical security in this case: the reduction of ozone production ought to be proceeding as rapidly as possible. If I discover that, somehow unknown to me, I am standing on someone's neck, my duty is not to get off his neck sometime soon – my duty is to get off his neck now.[10] Roughly the same is true of ending the production of CFCs. Such a move cannot, of course, literally be taken immediately, but it could have been taken much faster than it was and could still be greatly speeded up. As is well-known, the negotiations on the Montreal Protocol stalled until after some firm (as it happened, Dupont) came up with a (relatively) safer substitute; this is like my keeping my foot on your neck until I find somewhere else equally soft and comfortable to rest it. To my knowledge no one has been forced, against his wishes, to spend a single summer night uncomfortably warm due to lack of air-conditioning for the sake of reducing the ultimate total accumulation of CFCs in the atmosphere, although there is every reason to think that additional skin cancers have been caused by our continuing purchases of CFC-filled air-conditioners for cooling-as-usual. Similarly, the phase-out of production of CFCs appears to be moving at a leisurely pace designed to avoid causing any manufacturers any problems. If we genuinely believe we are not entitled to inflict cancer on others, the phase-out – and the crackdown on the mushrooming black market in freon – ought to be proceeding with more urgency.[11]

Does a respect for rights, then, mean throwing efficiency to the winds? No, but it does challenge the conventional way, typified by Cooper's treatment of climate change, of setting up our decisions. Any pursuit of highest returns that is to be acceptable, I have argued above, must be conducted within the constraints set by established non-marketable fundamental rights.[12] Since the non-marketable rights have no price, they cannot without distortion be incorporated into a single comprehensive efficiency calculation. Their having no price does not mean, as is often suggested, that they have an infinite price – that suggestion is another attempt to insist on incorporating into a single set of calculations what cannot be incorporated.[13] Non-marketable rights are constraints that must be honored, even during the pursuit of highest returns.

Therefore, one may not calculate the path with highest returns by throwing potential expenditures for ceasing, preventing, and correcting violations of non-marketable rights into a single soup with potential expenditures for the satisfaction of ordinary preferences. Decisions need instead to be partitioned into at least two sets:

1   alternative ways of ceasing, preventing, and correcting violations of non-marketable rights, and
2   alternative paths to the highest returns using resources not allocated to the best choice from set 1.[14]

Discounting then becomes a secondary, although still important, issue within each set, but not between the two sets, because trade-offs are not routinely made between sets. What is primary is the partition between

1   resources for the prevention of new violations of non-marketable rights
    and for the restoration of non-marketable rights already violated, and
2   resources not required by respect for non-marketable rights.

Do rights belong, then, to some ethereal realm in which costs, including opportunity costs, somehow do not matter? No; if an attempt to honor a particular putative right can be known to be excessively costly, we do not acknowledge it as a right. Ascertaining whether a proposed right is "excessively costly" does indeed involve considering its opportunity costs, in a general sense – that is, comparing the importance of securing the right in question to the importance of the next best use of the same resources.[15] The judgment about whether we can afford to treat something as the content of a right, however, is a prior, stable judgment that is not re-opened every time that we must choose between consuming resources in the enforcement of the right and consuming the same resources in some other way. Usually, it is a judgment that cannot be quantitatively calculated. In principle, the question whether we can afford to treat any given matter as the content of a right can be re-opened at any time. However, if the question of the affordability of something simply stays open all the time, that matter is being treated merely as the content of one more preference, not treated as the content of a right.[16] We do have to allocate resources between fundamental rights and ordinary preferences, as well as to make allocations within the sphere of rights and within the sphere of preferences. Yet the allocation between spheres takes precedence. First, we provide for basic rights; then, preference-satisfaction uses whatever resources are left.[17]

Efficiency of allocation among alternative uses of resources remains important within each of the two segregated sets of decisions. Inside the first set, the rights-fulfilling set, allocations need to be made as efficiently as anywhere else: it is no more rational to waste resources partitioned off to provide for rights than to waste any other resources. What kind of discounting, if any, is appropriate then becomes the next issue. Within the second, or return-maximizing, set, appropriate kinds of efficiency are also called for. What kind of discounting, if any, is appropriate becomes the next issue there too.

Discounting and property rights

Daniel W. Bromley (1991, pp. 84–103) in a chapter called "Property rights, missing markets, and environmental uncertainty," has reflected on one truly bizarre feature of conventional discounting: it allocates *all* property rights to the current generation.[18] Observing that between generations what one has is not market failure but an entirely missing market, Bromley says: "The economic analysis has implicitly assumed that the present generation has a right to impose costs on the future and can only be denied that right if it is more efficient to do otherwise" (Bromley, 1991, p. 88). The present "has a right" to impose the costs in the sense that it has no property-rights-based duty not to impose them; and the present has no property-rights-based duty not to impose them only if future generations have no property rights at all. Bromley (1991, p. 93) goes on to note that this sharp dichotomy of all-rights and no-rights defines a very specific decision environment and specifies a completely asymmetrical benchmark:

> Notice that the structure of property rights not only determines how decisions are framed and choices made, but also determines how we shall assess the impacts of those choices. If the future is regarded as having no legitimate case to have its losses covered by the present[,] then one might be tempted to view the problem as one of the present generation having to sacrifice present and future income in order to make the future better off. On the other hand, if the future is regarded as having a *right* not to incur losses at the hands of the present, then those now living will be viewed as doing what is correct – giving up ill-gotten income – in order not to impair the well-being of the future.

Now, I have attempted in the bulk of this paper to show that future humans, just like current humans, have non-property rights, most notably non-marketable rights to physical security. Bromley, by contrast, is discussing property rights and suggesting that future humans have property rights too, or at the very least that it is passing strange that absolutely all property rights should happen to belong to the humans who happen to be alive at any given time. This assignment of property rights, Bromley notes, pre-determines the outcome of any discounting.

It is important to distinguish between control and benefit.[19] Insofar as property rights are construed as a matter of control, they must be assigned entirely to the current generation. For better or for worse, any given current generation does in fact exercise control. Control by the living is inevitable. Benefit, however, is a different matter. The living need not exercise their exclusive control for their own exclusive, or even primary, benefit, which is what is done when one maximizes net present value. The technique of discounting values everything from one's own point of view exclusively, which seems to be roughly the opposite of morality, which mandates somehow including the points of view of others, presumably not excluding future generations, along with one's own. Maximizing net present value utterly ignores all rights, property rights as well as non-marketable rights, of every person who will ever live after the present. Whatever may be the correct approach, simply maximizing net present value is certainly not it.

Suppose we grant that all persons, including persons yet to be born, have at least basic security rights – and some (unspecified) property rights, although nothing in my positive argument turns on the property rights. What are the implications of this proposition about minimum universal rights for our current policies regarding climate change? Obviously space here permits merely a couple of hints toward a full answer, but it turns out that what we can establish fairly easily does a great deal to set the direction for policy. First, if all persons universally share some rights, then we in the current generation have those rights too. Those of us now alive are living the only life we will ever get, so we ought to have now everything that everyone is entitled to. This immediately establishes an ultimate ceiling on how much we can be expected to sacrifice for future generations no matter how many more of them than of us there will be.[20] The most that can be demanded of us is a level of sacrifice that does not compromise our secure enjoyment of the same rights that, we are acknowledging, belong as well to persons in the future. To deprive ourselves of basic rights in order to guarantee those same basic rights to people in the future would be in effect to treat our generation as inferior – as somehow entitled to less than equal minimum rights.[21]

Ironically, this undercuts one of the main reasons often given to justify the alleged need to discount future generations: we ought not to have to make excessive sacrifices for the sake of future generations; therefore, we ought to discount their welfare.[22] The premise is true, but the inference is invalid. It is the case that the presumably indefinitely large numbers of persons in all future generations will completely swamp the numbers in any one current generation if one engages in simple aggregation without discounting, and discounting is indeed one method for (radically) reducing the weight given to people in the future even where several generations are aggregated. It is, however, certainly not the only one. Another is to respect universal basic rights, including the rights of people in the present. That is the immediate good news for the current generation.

The bad news is that we are prohibited from engaging in any practices that will make it impossible for people in the future to enjoy their basic rights when, but for our choosing to engage in those practices rather than other practices open to us, they could have enjoyed their basic rights too. The doubtlessly obvious reason for the qualification, "when, but for our engaging in those practices rather than other practices open to us", is to rule out the following: it was what we did that closed the option for them, but we had no alternative. For example, we consumed the last energy available to the planet, but we ourselves could not have survived without consuming that much energy: we have the same basic rights as people in the future, and no alternative way to enjoy our rights was open to us. If there were such an absolute, irremediable scarcity of something vital like energy, it would not be wrong for some people – like us – to consume minimum shares of it even though this would cause other people to be forced to do without it. If the supply of something vital actually were zero-sum and the total were grossly inadequate for everyone to have their minimum share, it would not be wrong to go ahead and consume your own minimum share. Any alternative view would entail a general duty to commit suicide.[23]

However, while this may be a moderately interesting theoretical possibility, it does not even remotely resemble what is in fact happening. Far from only reluctantly and sadly (because we were so sensitive to the fact that we were tragically dooming others with the same rights as we) consuming precisely our minimum share of the planet's resources and pollution-sinks, many of us in the rich countries are, I would think, more nearly engaged in an orgy of self-indulgent consumption and unbridled pollution with little or no thought about the fate of anyone more than approximately two generations after us. The bad news, then, is that we ought to be avoiding consumption and pollution that are superfluous for us and are threatening to basic rights of people in the future.

And exactly which consumption and pollution is that? Obviously, one cannot establish concretely what this limitation means entirely through the kinds of purely theoretical argument with which economists and philosophers feel most at home, and which constitute this chapter. Factual information is, unfortunately for us theorists, needed in addition to theoretical argument. However, uncertainties about anthropogenic climate change are being reduced (Houghton et al., 1996). The not-so-unlikely threats to the physical security of people in the not-so-distant future from fossil fuel consumption by people in the present include:

- the migration away from the equator toward both poles of semi-tropical habitats suitable for mosquitoes and consequently of the mosquito-borne diseases that currently wreak havoc only in the tropics;
- the infiltration by salt-water of the fresh ground-water supplies of gigantic population centers like Shanghai;
- the modification in some impoverished regions of the crucial parameters for agriculture like rainfall patterns and length of growing season, in addition to temperatures themselves, more rapidly than seed-types, irrigation, and fertilizer can in fact be adjusted with the resources likely to be available to many of the people affected;
- and much else.

Uncertainties remain and research needs to continue. But where present practices that are superfluous, trivial, or frivolous – and could consequently be changed at the sacrifice only of preferences of no intrinsic value – are likely to contribute to the infliction of physical harms on people who will live later, we are bound to change our practices to protect their rights. This is an essential element in any minimum standard to guide our behavior where it will affect the physical security of people who will succeed us in this environment.

Notes

1   The best discussion of the follies in current US management of nuclear waste is given by Kristin Shrader-Frechette (1993). We always have new schemes, of course. One is to pay ethnic minorities, who so badly need the money because they have become impoverished as a result of decades of discrimination and violations of treaty agreements, to let us store it near them instead of near us; see Erickson et al. (1994).
2   If we did allow the purchase in the Third World, and then the import, of human organs for use in transplants, the implication would be clear: people here are human beings in a sense that is incompatible with the sale and purchase of their physical parts, but people in the "source" [!] countries are something else deserving less respect. In 1994, a US tourist was beaten to death in a small town in Guatemala (as reported on National Public Radio). When the local people were asked why, they said they had heard that people in the USA were adopting Guatemalan children and, once getting them to the USA, cutting them up to use their vital organs for transplants into ill US children. They suspected the woman they beat to death was there to adopt a child for this purpose. This woman was in fact a completely innocent tourist, not even inquiring about adoption, and the general rumor was not only false but was being calculatedly spread by an

exceptionally virulently anti-US political party. It is still noteworthy how believable the rumor turned out to be.

3   In the states in which contracts for surrogate motherhood are legally enforceable, their enforceability rests on a legal fiction that what is occurring is not the sale of a baby but the performance of a service (which happens to result in a baby) by the surrogate mother. Whether surrogate motherhood is a violation of our basic views about rights remains to be settled. The payments involved in old-fashioned adoptions are also treated as compensations for adoption services, not payments for the purchase of a baby. Lots of illegal payments change hands, of course.

4   Prostitution, where legal, is treated – correctly or incorrectly – as payment for services, not as rental of body parts.

5   Professional boxing could be argued to come very close.

6   See Barry (1983, p. 23). Josh Farley (1998) has persuasively suggested that no compensation could be adequate for the avoidable complete destruction of a renewable resource.

7   John Locke is customarily credited with the no-harm principle, and he certainly embraced it, but what about Hippocrates? The Hippocratic Oath contains a no-harm principle for medical people. I would have thought most morality was at bottom about taking other people seriously and at least, therefore, not inflicting harm on them.

8   Jonathan Weiner (1990, p. 155) cites John S. Hoffman (1987).

9   Here is a possible exception: although medical experimentation may normally be conducted only upon diseases that people already have, not by purposely infecting them with disease for the sake of experimentation, people do sometimes volunteer to have a disease inflicted upon them. This appears to make this case a matter of permission (which we do not have from future generations for the infliction of skin cancer), not exactly traditional inalienability. On the other hand, such people would normally volunteer and be honored, but not be paid; so it is not marketability either.

10   I have discussed such "extrication ethics," as Tony Coady has called it, in Shue (1996a).

11   I am inclined to think that no nation has a right to refuse to do its fair share in a task of this kind, namely the prevention of the severe physical harm to humans that will be caused by a nation's failure to do its share. The existence of a black market, of course, demonstrates anew the difficulty of state prohibitions on purchases of commodities that people with the money strongly desire to buy, but if the nation-state system fails to protect our physical health wherever it is profitable for someone to inflict disease, we need new political structures.

12   Are rights simply side-constraints? No, they are side-constraints upon the pursuit of preferences, but they are also goals to be attained. The provision of adequate security for basic rights is a goal that takes priority over the satisfaction of preferences, which is why rights function as side-constraints on the satisfaction of preferences.

13   In a somewhat similar instance, that kidneys for transplant are non-marketable does not mean that they are very expensive; it means one cannot legally or morally buy them. Period. Insofar as the legal and moral prohibition fails, there will be a "black" market, in which organs for transplant will indeed be expensive. This black-market price is a violation of their status as non-marketable, however, not an illustration of what their status means.

14   For the distinction among ceasing, preventing, and correcting, see Shue (1996b, chap. 2).

15   The clearest account of how the consideration of costs should come into accounts of human rights that I am aware of is given by James W. Nickel (1987, pp. 120–30).

16   I have argued against the "homogenization" by economists of all considerations as so-called preferences – in a misguided effort to create a single, comprehensive calculation about climate change – in Shue (1993, pp. 39–59).

17   This does not mean that no further normative issues arise once provision has been made for basic rights. The provision for basic rights will include provision for urgent needs, but questions of distributive justice still arise as we choose the mechanisms that determine whose preferences will in fact be satisfied to what extent.

18   I am grateful to Josh Farley for this reference and for provocative discussions of discounting.

19   The value of carefully separating control and benefit is emphasized by Thomas W. Pogge (1989, pp. 251–2), in a critique of Beitz's resource redistribution principle. I think, however, Beitz observes the distinction to a greater extent than Pogge allows – see Charles R. Beitz (1979, p. 138).

20   The final ceiling, all things considered, on the extent of our sacrifice may be still lower than this initial ceiling, but it will not be any higher.

21   This is not to say that it is not the case that an earlier generation could ever be expected to make sacrifices in its overall quality of life, where the quality was well above the minimum, so that later generations could have a still higher quality of life. My point is about the minimum guaranteed by basic rights: an earlier generation cannot be expected to accept less than the minimum so that later generations can have more than the minimum. The minimum is the minimum for everyone. Where the earlier generation and the later generations are all above the minimum, the theoretical issues become much more complex, especially if moderate sacrifices by a few early generations would produce vast improvements for indefinitely many later generations. At present, given the extent of the threats to the environment, the health of which is necessary to sustaining minimum quality of life, one can be forgiven for thinking that the practically relevant questions are, not about a "just saving rate" to make future generations better off, but about a just pollution rate to prevent future generations from being worse off or indeed falling below the minimum.

22   Derek Parfit (1983, pp. 31–7) calls this "the argument from excessive sacrifice;" Parfit also refutes five other principal justifications for discounting. The same arguments and examples are repeated, with additional material, in Cowen and Parfit (1991, pp. 144–61).

23   It is not even clear that there is a coherent alternative consisting of a general duty for a whole generation to commit suicide. Duty to whom? Future generations? What future generations! Anyway, as I next indicate in the text, this is hardly our immediate problem, however tantalizing theoretically.

References

Barry, B. (1983) Intergenerational justice in energy policy. In MacLean and Brown (1983); reprinted as: The ethics of resource depletion. In Barry, B (1991) *Liberty and Justice, Essays in Political Theory*, vol. 2, Oxford: Oxford University Press at the Clarendon Press.

Beitz, C. R. (1979) *Political Theory and International Relations*. Princeton: Princeton University Press.

Bromley, D. W. (1991) *Environment and Economy: Property Rights and Public Policy*. Cambridge, MA: Blackwell Publishers.

Bureau of National Affairs, Washington (1994) Report cites largest ozone hole ever as thinning occurs at "significant pace". *International Environment Reporter: Current Reports*, 17 (7) April 6.

Cooper, R. N. (1992) United States policy towards the global environment. In A. Hurrell and B. Kingsbury (eds) *The International Politics of the Environment: Actors, Interests, and Institutions*. Oxford: Oxford University Press at the Clarendon Press.

Cowen, T. and Parfit, D. (1991) Against the social discount rate. In P. Laslett and J. S. Fishkin (eds) *Justice between Age Groups and Generations*. New Haven: Yale University Press.

Erickson, J. D., Chapman, D. and Johnny, R. E. (1994) Monitored retrievable storage of spent nuclear fuel in Indian country: Liability, Sovereignty and Socioeconomics. *American Indian Law Review*, 19 (1), 73–103.

Farley, J. (1998) "Optimal" deforestation in the Brazilian Amazon – theory and policy: The local, national, international and international viewpoints. Ph.D. dissertation Cornell University.

Hoffman, J. S. (ed.) (1987) *Assessing the Risks of Trace Gases that can Modify the Stratosphere*. Washington, DC: Office of Air and Radiation, US Environmental Protection Agency, December.

Houghton, J. T., Meira Filho, L. G. et al. (1996) Climate change 1995: The science of climate change. Contribution of Working Group 1 to the Second Assessment Report of the Intergovernmental Panel on Climate Change. Cambridge and New York: IPCC.

MacLean, D. and Brown, P. G. (eds) (1983) *Energy and the Future*. Lanham, Md: Rowman and Littlefield.

Nickel, J. W. (1987) *Making Sense of Human Rights: Philosophical Reflections on the Universal Declaration of Human Rights*. Berkeley: University of California Press.

Parfit, D. (1983) Energy policy and the further future: The social discount rate. In MacLean and Brown (1983).

Pogge, T. W. (1989) *Realizing Rawls*. Ithaca, NY: Cornell University Press.

Shrader-Frechette, K. (1993) *Burying Uncertainty: Risk and the Case Against Geological Disposal of Nuclear Waste*. Berkeley: University of California Press.

Shue, H. (1993) Subsistence emissions and luxury emissions. *Law & Policy*, 15 (1), January, pp. 39–59.

Shue, H. (1996a) Environmental change and the varieties of justice. In F. O. Hampson and J. Reppy (eds) *Earthly Goods: Environmental Change and Social Justice*. Ithaca, NY: Cornell University Press, pp. 9–29.

Shue, H. (1996b) *Basic Rights: Subsistence, Affluence, and US Foreign Policy*, 2nd edn. Princeton, NJ: Princeton University Press.

Weiner, J. (1990) *The Next One Hundred Years: Shaping the Fate of our Living Earth*. New York: Bantam Books.

3
Non-use Values and the Limits of Cost-benefit Analysis

Marc Willinger

Kornai (1980) defined cost–benefit analysis (CBA) as an "enlightened" orthodoxy. While grounded on the orthodoxy of the neoclassical paradigm, CBA simultaneously recognizes its limitations as a useful guide for public decision-making. CBA actually provides a set of methodologies that are essentially designed to "correct" the existing prices prevailing in a market economy, because these prices are suspected to induce significant distortions in the allocation of resources. Indeed, missing markets and other types of imperfections may be responsible for the failures of a market-based economy to allocate resources efficiently. According to the standard economic view, market prices reflect only market interdependencies because, if the market system is unregulated, non-market interdependencies (externalities) will not be spontaneously incorporated in relative prices. Therefore, the unregulated price system is generally biased in the sense that too much negative – and too few positive – externalities are being produced with respect to the socially optimal level.[1]

CBA is, in many cases, a useful guide for public decision making, especially when market data are not available, decisions have large-scale and long-lasting effects, and several conflicting alternatives exist. Constructing a new airport on existing fields, erecting a dam in a pristine valley, building a nuclear power plant on a no man's land or simply increasing taxes on cigarette consumption, are examples of public decisions where CBA is relevant. For example, even if the construction of the airport can be grounded on reliable cost and benefit data that are provided by existing markets (cost of land, agricultural production, etc.), there are other factors relevant for the decision-maker for which such data is not directly available (e.g. induced costs of "noise" and other types of pollution, consumers benefits of the new facility, etc.). In the dam example, one may argue that the value of the dam is equal to the net present value of future benefits generated by additional electricity consumption and production, but what is the value of preserving the pristine valley that will be lost? Even if there is no current demand for the piece of land on which the nuclear power plant will be built, what is the cost of the foregone option to use it at some future date for another economic activity? How do we evaluate the consumer's benefit of sacrificing the tobacco industry? CBA has developed a conceptual and a methodological apparatus to answer these types of questions. Although CBA has been successfully applied to many cases, there are some important areas of application, such as environmental protection, where the use of CBA raises fundamental methodological questions. The main issue, that I discuss in this chapter, is how to measure costs and benefits for preserving natural assets. Instead of preserving natural assets, one could instead use them in the economic process to generate benefits, but preserving these assets may be valuable if preservation generates other types of benefits. These benefits, usually called "non-use values," can be assessed by CBA.

The fundamental assumption behind CBA, which I discuss, is that well-defined preferences exist. Various measures of welfare change have therefore been adopted by CBA for assessing the unobservable values. Following a tradition going back to Dupuit (1844) these measures are based on the concept of surplus, which was developed by Marshall and Hicks. Although CBA applies to a large variety of "projects," we shall focus on valuation of environmental assets, which is one of the most questionable domains of application. An important debate surrounds the utilization of CBA methodology for environmental issues. One of the reasons is that environmental assets have particular features (e.g. uniqueness, absence of close substitutes, uncertainty about future use) which require a special methodological treatment. Moreover, according to several economists, environmental assets generate a particular type of values – non-use values – which need to be considered by CBA and require special measurement techniques such as contingent valuation (CV). The aim of this chapter is not to discuss the relevance of CBA in general, but to provide an alternative interpretation of the values that are measured when CBA is applied to environmental preservation.

Non-use values are of special interest for providing the missing information due to failures of the price system. It is well-known that if future markets are missing, the prevailing price-system may convey incorrect signals for the intertemporal allocation of resources within the economy. Similarly, whereas use values for environmental assets may be reflected in market price, non-use values are usually not incorporated in relative prices. To overcome the difficulty, we may admit that a positive valuation may be induced by the existence (or non-use) of resources. For example, the current generation may value natural assets not for itself but for future generations. While there are several reasons to rely on the concept of non-use value, which seems at odds with the concept of utility, there is a major difficulty with this concept since non-use values, unlike use-values, do not generate a market demand. Non-use values are generally non-market values. To measure such values on a monetary scale, one has to design some kind of artificial market in which people can express a demand for not using an item. Therefore, there is no guarantee that the estimated value will not be influenced by the design of the artificial market. In other words, the true value cannot be observed unless one is able to give a non-controversial design of an artificial market. We are therefore confronted with the following dilemma: in a market-based economy in which some markets are missing, prices are usually biased. However, no available method is able to provide unbiased estimates to correct the biased market prices!

To escape this dilemma and to provide a basis for corrective policy, I suggest that one can provide a different interpretation of observed preferences for CBA. Usually we assume that agents evaluate their available options and make decisions in a way that is consistent with their preferences. I will argue that, in many cases in which impacts on natural assets are assessed relying on non-use values, one has to relax the central hypothesis of CBA and demand theory: the existence of an invariant preference relation defined on a set of possible choices. Although for most goods we can reasonably assume the postulate that well-defined preferences do exist, we must admit that for other types of goods, including most environmental assets, preferences are not well-defined. Generally, the more experience a consumer has with a type of goods, the more accurately defined his preferences will be. Markets provide a type of context in which preferences are constructed on a monetary scale, on the basis of monetary incentives. The same measure is not available for non-marketed goods and can hardly be achieved. Preferences are partly constructed by the elicitation-method used to "capture them." If this is true, as I will try to show, one must take a radically different view on the actual purpose of CBA.

In the next section I define the properties of an invariant system of preferences. Then I discuss recent experimental evidence, demonstrating that the invariance principle is violated to a large extent, leading to strong disparities in the assessment of values in CBA. This is followed by a discussion on the implications of invariance failures. I then apply the findings to the case of non-use values, before proposing a "constructivist" interpretation of observed preferences in CBA.

The invariance principle

According to the invariance principle, the most fundamental postulate of decision theory, an individual's preferences should depend solely on the underlying attributes of the objects of choice. Irrelevant factors, such as the availability of other options, the framing of the options, or the choice of elicitation method, should not affect the agent's preferences. For example, when we try to estimate the loss of value due to degradation of the quality of some public good, we should collect the same answer from an individual whether we ask for the amount he is prepared to pay for improving the quality to its previous level, or for the monetary compensation he would require to accept the new quality level. If these amounts differ significantly, one must conclude that the agent is influenced by other factors than the quality change of the public good.

More formally, let a, $b \in A$ be choice options, and $\geqslant$ a preference relation defined on the choice set A, where a may represent a consumption plan, a sequence of future choices, or a probability distribution over a set of consequences. We define the invariance principle of the preference relation $\geqslant$ by three properties:

- Property 1: **Context-Free Preferences (CFP)**
  Assume that

$$a, b \in A \qquad \text{and} \qquad a, b \in B$$

  Then

$$a \succcurlyeq b \text{ for } A \text{ if } a \succcurlyeq b \text{ for } B$$

- Property 2: **Procedural Invariance (PI)**
  Assume that $\succcurlyeq^*$ admits a representation $v(\cdot)$, i.e.

$$a \succcurlyeq b \Leftrightarrow v(a) \geq v(b)$$

  Suppose $w(\cdot)$ is another representation of $\succcurlyeq$, i.e.

$$a \succcurlyeq b \Leftrightarrow w(a) \geq w(b)$$

  Then one should have $w(\cdot) = f(v(\cdot))$, where $f(\cdot)$ is an admissible transformation for the representation of $\succcurlyeq$.
- Property 3: **Neutral Framing (NF)**
  Assume that a and a^* are two equivalent descriptions of the same basic option. Neutral framing means that for any two options, $a, b \in A$, and a^*, $b^* \in A^*$:

$$a \succcurlyeq b \Leftrightarrow a^* \succcurlyeq b^*$$

The CFP hypothesis implies that the preference relation does not depend on the set of available options. In other words, $\succcurlyeq_A \equiv \succcurlyeq_B$, where $\succcurlyeq_X$ means preferences on X. In particular, CFP applies when $B \supset A$. The interpretation is that adding new options to the initial choice set should not alter the previously existing ordering on A. Similarly when $A \supset B$, a contraction of A should not modify the relations among the remaining options. In this case, the context is simply defined as the set of available options. The PI hypothesis implies that the response-mode does not affect preferences. If one is allowed to choose the measurement unit for assessing preferences, the resulting ordering should not depend on the choice of the measurement unit or the origin. More generally, if there are several possible methods for eliciting preferences, the resulting ordering should not depend on the particular method that is chosen. For example, one may ask to rank choice alternatives from the most preferred to the least preferred. Alternatively, the method may consist in assigning a value between 0 and 100 to each of the alternatives. Both orderings should coincide. Finally, the NF hypothesis implies that the preference ordering should not depend on the framing of the options. For example, if A is a set of probability distributions on some interval of the real line, the preference ordering should be the same whether the options are defined as cumulative or as decumulative distributions. More generally, preferences should depend only on the basic consequences of the options. The fact that the options can be described as "reduced forms" or "extensive forms" should be irrelevant. This basic requirement of rational behavior has been called "consequentialism" in the case of dynamic choices (Hammond, 1988). Preferences over sequences of choices should depend only on the final consequences, or final asset positions, and not on the sequence itself. Hammond showed that consequentialism was necessary to avoid dynamically inconsistent behavior, such as myopia (Strotz, 1956).

Another definition of CFP can be given by introducing the choice function $C(\cdot)$ defined on the set of available options. Formally, the choice function identifies the chosen option from the set of available options. In terms of the choice function, CFP is equivalent to two properties:

- **Basic contraction consistency**

$$a \in \bigcap_{j=1}^{n} C(A_j) \text{ implies } a \in C\left(\bigcap_{j=1}^{n} A_j\right)$$

- **Basic expansion consistency**

$$a \in \bigcup_{j=1}^{n} C(A_j) \text{ implies } a \in C\left(\bigcup_{j=1}^{n} A_j\right)$$

In the case of finite sets, basic contraction consistency and basic expansion consistency are necessary and sufficient properties for binariness of the choice function (Sen, 1993). Binariness of the choice function is therefore a fundamental property that guarantees that comparisons between choice options are context-free.

The choice function is the basic concept that links the empirical and the theoretical world. CBA, and more generally, demand theory, must rely on some observables. Since demand relations cannot be directly observed, we have to rely on observed choices made by agents, i.e. the choice function. The individual demand function can therefore be constructed by linking the observable choices and the non-observable preference relation. The revealed preference axiom provides the necessary connection between preference and choice, i.e. the unobservables and the observables. Loosely speaking, the revealed preference axiom simply states that the agent always chooses the most preferred bundle of goods, for any set out of which he may have to choose.[2] The revealed preference axiom implies existence of a unique demanded bundle of commodities by the consumer for given income and relative prices. Binariness and the revealed preference axiom together are the most fundamental properties on which welfare measures applied in CBA are based. Therefore, it is an important task to evaluate the consistency of these properties with respect to observed behavior.

Failures of invariance: Experimental evidence

There is growing evidence in the psychological literature on failures of invariance. The three basic requirements of invariance, context-free preferences (CFP), procedural invariance (PI) and neutral framing (NF) have been contradicted by observed behavior. I will comment briefly on the nature of each of these invariance failures.

The WTP–WTA disparity

CBA is based on two alternative measures of welfare: maximum willingness to pay (WTP) to retain an entitlement, and minimum compensation demanded – or willingness to accept (WTA) – to forego the entitlement. Both concepts can be applied either to price changes, quantity changes or quality changes. The fundamental difference between the two measures depends on an assumption about property rights. Consider, for example, the case of a price change with the consequence that the utility level of some individual will change from u_0 to u_1, with $u_0 < u_1$. If we assume that the individual has a right to his initial utility level, WTP for receiving level u_1 is the correct measure. On the other hand, if we assume that he has a right to the level u_1, WTA to forego that level (and stay at u_0) should be used instead.

A large WTA/WTP ratio has been observed, both in experimental studies and survey studies, suggesting that the two measures of welfare will usually reflect quite different values. According to conventional CBA, both measures of welfare should differ only by a negligible income effect, although WTP is usually bounded by the available income, while WTA is unbounded. Willig (1976) showed that, in the case of a price change, the two measures of welfare, called compensating variation and equivalent variation in this case, are fairly close if income effects are negligible. Since corresponding measures of welfare can be defined in the case of a quantity change (Randall and Stoll, 1980), the same observation applies to the quantity dimension. However Hanemann (1991) argued that for quantity changes, the difference between WTP and WTA depends not only on the income effect but also on a substitution effect. If one measures the welfare gain for some change in the supply of a public good, Hanemann shows that WTP = WTA only for the case in which a perfect substitute for the public good is available. However, WTA can be unbounded if there is zero substitutability for the public good, even though WTP is finite. Hanemann's conclusion is that: "large empirical divergences between WTP and WTA may be indicative not of some failure in the survey methodology but of a general perception on the part of the individuals surveyed that the private-market goods available in their choice set are, collectively, a rather imperfect substitute for the public good under consideration."

Therefore, large differences may be expected whenever the loss of a public good has irreversible consequences. This is the case for most irreplaceable assets. Furthermore, it is sometimes difficult to define the entitlement for such goods.

There are several examples of observed disparities in CV studies. One of the first is the study by Bishop and Heberlein (1979) about the valuation of hunting licenses. They found that goose hunters were willing to pay $21 on average for the hunting license, but that the WTA for giving up the license was equal to $101. Another example is given by the study of Brookshire and Coursey (1987) concerning the valuation of additional trees planted in a neighborhood park (Ft Collins, Colorado). While average WTP for 25 additional trees was $14, the mean WTA to forego the additional trees was $855! Such large disparities represent a major challenge for the credibility of CV studies. Therefore, an important question was whether the observed disparity was akin to the CV methodology itself or could be explained by some deeper behavioral patterns. Several experiments tried to answer this question.

Knetsch and Sinden (1984) have provided experimental evidence on the existence of a significant disparity between WTP and WTA measures of welfare. In their experiment, subjects could participate in a lottery whose prize was either $50 in cash or a $70 merchandise voucher redeemable at a local store. Participants were randomly assigned to one of two groups. In the first group, they could participate in the lottery by paying $2 (with credit). In the second group, they were free to participate in the lottery, and were offered a compensation of $2 for not participating. Because of the random allocation of subjects between the two groups, one should observe approximately the same number of subjects willing to participate in the lottery in both groups. However Knetsch and Sinden found a significantly larger number in the second group (75 percent) than in the first group (50 percent). The conclusion is that on the aggregate level the equivalence between WTA and WTP should be rejected.

The compensation demanded to forego some entitlement is usually larger than the WTP for receiving the entitlement, by a factor at least equal to two. Although Hanemann showed that the disparity may be consistent with standard utility theory, his argument does not apply to situations for which only private goods are involved, which describes most experimental studies. Since one observes large disparities even in experimental studies involving only private goods, a major issue would be to know the real magnitude of the income effect, which is the only rational explanation for the disparity.

Another possible explanation for the observed disparity is the "endowment effect," an expression coined by Thaler (1980). People are reluctant to give up a given entitlement because it belongs to their endowment. They place a higher value on the good when they own it than in the situation where they are considering its acquisition. Therefore, they require a larger compensation for giving up the good compared to the amount that they are willing to pay for the good.

The experiment performed by Knetsch and Sinden involved lotteries, and therefore a possible explanation for the disparity could be due to a violation of the axioms of expected utility. Furthermore, subjects could not learn from their choices, contrary to real market situations. Coursey et al. (1987), tried to show that the disparity would not survive in a market environment for a certain good. In market contexts, agents can learn and have incentives to avoid mistakes because selective pressures come into play. They conjectured therefore that the disparity would be negligible in a market context. Coursey et al. showed that, in a repeated auction market in which subjects had to trade "sure things," the WTA converged to WTP, although a large difference (a factor of 2) remained after several iterations. They suggest that their experiment provides evidence towards a tendency of the market to eliminate behavior that is based on strategic misrepresentation. Therefore, the authors concluded that "economic theory is correct in predicting that WTA and WTP will usually be close in a mature market setting", although a disparity may well persist outside the market area. The experiment performed by Coursey et al. was designed as an auction for a "public bad." The choice of a public bad could possibly explain the remaining disparity. Harless (1989) further examined auction for lotteries, which could be "good" or "bad."

In CBA, we are typically in a situation where markets are missing, and therefore one cannot eliminate the disparity. Agents have few opportunities to learn, and therefore disparities are likely to persist. The conclusion of Coursey et al. stands also in conflict with the repeated market experiment for "sure things" of Kahneman et al. (1990), in which the endowment effect persists despite the opportunity to learn through repetition of the market. Furthermore, they show that the disparity is smaller for induced-value markets than for "real-value" markets. Therefore, the conjecture that, in a market context in which people can learn to be rational, the disparity would become irrelevant has not yet been firmly established.

The disparity does not necessarily reflect irrational behavior. According to prospect theory, losses have a higher psychological weight than gains of the same magnitude. In the case of environmental goods, people may think that they are endowed with an entitlement to the good. Therefore, the agent asks both for the loss of the entitlement and for the loss of the good itself. On the other hand, in the case of an acquisition people may think that they have already an entitlement although the good has not yet been acquired. The WTP–WTA disparity remains a major difficulty for CBA, since the value of a given environmental change can be worth twice or thrice some base value, depending on the welfare measure that is chosen.

The disparity has also important consequences when CBA is conceived as a public decision aid. On the aggregate level, CBA is based on the Hicks–Kaldor (HK) compensation test. A prospective change in the resource allocation is socially desirable if the benefits of the winners exceed the costs of the losers. Therefore, the benefits of the winners could potentially compensate the losses of the losers. This criterion is based on the notion of "potential Pareto improvement." It is well-known that the HK criterion does not provide a complete ordering of the set of possible allocations. As shown by Scitovsky (1941), a change from situation X to situation Y may be socially desirable if seen from X, and a change in the opposite direction may be desirable when seen from Y. The disparity between WTP and WTA is evidence that the paradox raised by Scitovsky is probably more common than we thought, which would mean that compensation tests are not well-defined.

Framing effects

Framing effects represent a major failure of invariance. The main consequence for CBA is that one can no longer meaningfully predict hypothetical choice from observed choices, although this is exactly what we usually expect from CBA. For example, the transportation cost method may be useful in estimating the WTP for preserving some natural site. Similarly, wage differentials, reflecting different mortality risks between jobs, are sometimes used as estimates for the value of risk to life. However, framing effects show that preferences and behavior may change with the framing of the choice options, and that people may reverse their preferences.

Framing effects are due to a varying perception of the options. According to neutral framing (NF), preferences and values should not depend on the manner in which choice options are framed. However, Tversky and Kahneman (1986) showed that, in many instances, framing of options plays a significant role for assessing an individual's preferences.

A well-known example of the framing effect is provided by an experiment performed by McNeil et al. (1982). In the experiment, subjects had to choose between two alternative treatments for a particular disease: therapy A or therapy B. All subjects were provided exactly the same available statistical information about the two therapies. However, two different framings were used and subjects were randomly assigned to one or the other. The "survival framing" presented the statistical information in terms of survival probabilities for each of the two therapies, while the "mortality framing" presented the same information in terms of mortality probabilities.[3] Of course, the mortality probability is equal to one minus the survival probability. However, in the survival framing, 18 percent of the subjects preferred therapy B while, in the mortality framing, 44 percent preferred therapy B, a significant difference.[4] In this example, the reduction in mortality probability (during therapy) obtained by using therapy B rather than A, loomed obviously larger than the equivalent increase in survival probability.

Violations of NF contradict one of the basic requirements of rational behavior, called "extensionality" by Arrow (1982). Since observed behavior varies with the framing, one can no longer draw meaningful inferences from observed behavior to assess the desirability of a given change. This is a rather strong criticism against CBA, if CBA is intended to be a guide for public choice.

Preference reversals

Preference reversals show that the ordering of the alternatives may depend on the response mode that is used to express preferences, in contradiction with procedural invariance (PI). Preference reversal was first shown by Lichtenstein and Slovic (1971) and by Lindman (1971). In the standard experiment, subjects are presented two lotteries, called P-bet and $-bet, having the same expected value. The P-bet offers a high probability of winning, while the $-bet offers a larger gain. When asked to choose one of the options, most people express a preference for the P-bet, but when they are asked for their reservation price (buying or selling price), they prefer the $-bet. One typically observes a reversal of preference between choice and valuation, which is inconsistent with the basic axioms of expected utility theory. Although people were skeptical about the experiment, future repetitions and variations did not succeed in eliminating the observed reversals.[5]

According to Grether and Plott (1979), the preference reversal reveals a strong inconsistency with optimizing behavior since, according to them, it contradicts the transitivity axiom. On the other hand, for psychologists, the preference reversal can be explained by the fact that "choice" and "judgment" are based on different cognitive processes.

A large debate developed over the implications of preference reversal. For example, Holt (1986) and Karni and Safra (1987) have shown that because of the incentive scheme which was used in the experiment, the ordering axiom is not directly contradicted.[6] They showed that the independence axiom, which is the basic axiom of expected utility theory, may be contradicted, and that preference reversals may be rational for non-expected utility maximizer.[7] Loomes and Sugden (1982, 1983) took a different approach by relying on regret theory (Bell, 1982) to rationalize intransitivities. The idea is that people assess the attractiveness of a choice option with respect to the set of existing options. Regret theory is therefore not context-free, but assessments depend on the available set of options. If one expands or contracts the choice set, the ordering may change, in contradiction with context-free preferences (CFP). Although regret theory accounts for some reversals, it does not explain all of them.

Psychologists propose a different interpretation of the preference reversal, since they make a distinction between the task of choosing and the task of evaluating. According to Lichtenstein and Slovic (1971), the expression of preferences is a matter of choice, while the expression of values is a matter of judgment. There is no reason to observe the same ordering resulting from two distinct processes. Goldstein and Einhorn (1987) showed furthermore that one should make a distinction between expression and response-mode. They define expression as a dimension of choice or of value, and response-mode as a dimension of price, ordering or desirability. Since most experiments on preference reversals confounded expression-mode and response-mode, they conducted an experiment in which they showed the existence of several types of reversals, based on each distinction.

Preference reversal is a good indication of how preferences may be influenced by factors other than the intrinsic properties of the choice options, and which are usually neglected by standard economic analysis. One may argue that ignorance of such factors is not misleading, as long as they can be assimilated to random error in preference assessment. Economists are less interested in the individual value or choice of an agent than in the values or choices of a group of agents. On an aggregate level, errors may cancel out. However, the random error hypothesis must be rejected in many cases since very often one observes systematic errors, even when relying repeatedly on the same cognitive process. This is further evidenced by response-mode effects.

Response-mode effects

Several experiments on response-mode effects (Hershey, Kunreuther and Schoemaker, 1982; Hershey and Schoemaker, 1985; Delquié, 1993), showed that subjects' responses were "biased" in several ways.

In the matching-task experiment, subjects have to adjust one dimension, so as to match a difference on another dimension. Assume that options are represented by two dimensions, $a = (x_1, y_1)$. In the first stage of the matching-task, subjects are asked to give the value y_2^* that compensates for a given difference in the x-dimension, such that they will be indifferent between (x_1, y_1) and (x_2, y_2^*); in the second stage, the subjects give the value x_1^* that compensates for the difference on the y-dimension, to have an indifference between (x_1^*, y_1) and (x_2, y_2^*). As shown by Johnson and Schkade (1989) and Delquié (1993), the observed difference between x_1 and x_1^* is not a random error, since there is usually a significant difference, and of the same sign for all subjects. There is a strong tendency for the answer to be biased towards the value of x_2, which is sometimes defined as the stimulus. In the case of the matching-task, a possible explanation of the observed bias is "anchoring and adjustment." Suppose $x_1 > x_2$, then $y_2^* > y_1$, and $x_1^* > x_2$. As shown by P. Delquié, $x_1^* < x_1$ because the x-response is attracted by the stimulus x_2. This is consistent with "anchoring and adjustment:" in the case of y-matching, the subject increases the value of y_1, and in the case of x-matching, he or she increases the value of x_2. Since the "anchor" differs, the matching task shows that the reference point matters.

Response-mode effects also provide an additional explanation for the WTP–WTA disparity. Assume that prices (p) and income (y) are constant. Let q represent the quantity (or quality) of a public good. WTP is defined as the variation in income that compensates a change in q, leaving the agent at his or her current utility level, i.e. the algebraic solution of

$$(q^*, p, y - \text{WTP}) \sim (q, p, y)$$

where $q^* > q$. $\sim$ means "indifferent". Similarly WTA is defined as the variation in income that compensates the individual for resigning to the change in q,

$$(q^*, p, y) \sim (q, p, y + \text{WTA})$$

Although matching for surplus measures is only defined on the income dimension, the reference point is not the same for WTP as for WTA. For WTP, the reference point is the initial level of q, and therefore the agent is adjusting downwards. On the other hand, in the case of WTA, the reference point is q^* and the agent adjusts upwards to match the difference between q^* and q. The disparity may be due to a tendency of reluctance to adjust downward.

Status-quo bias

Samuelson and Zeckhauser (1988) tried to show that many economic decisions are actually taken with respect to a "benchmark," defined as the initial endowment position or "status quo." Choices are strongly influenced and "biased" towards the status quo position. The status quo bias is a special type of framing effect, in which subjects make a choice or express their preferences among two options, X and Y. One of the options is defined as the initial position or endowment position. A status quo bias is observed if a subject chooses alternative Y when X is available in a "neutral framing," but decides to retain alternative X instead of Y whenever X is defined as the endowment option. Samuelson and Zeckhauser submitted a questionnaire to several groups of subjects. One of the groups had a questionnaire with a neutral framing, whereas the other groups had a questionnaire in which one option was identified as the status quo. In the first group, options are perceived as alternative choice possibilities, which can be distinguished by their consequences. In the other groups, options are perceived not only as choices leading to different consequences, but also as possible alternatives to the status quo position. Although subjects were assigned randomly to groups, one typically observes a larger proportion of subjects choosing a given option when it is defined as the status quo.

Samuelson and Zeckhauser discussed three possible explanations for the status quo bias: transition costs, loss aversion, and psychological commitment. The transition costs hypothesis assumes that agents take into account the cost of changing from one situation to another in maximizing their utility. Subjects compare the marginal cost with the marginal benefit of a change. Since the status quo has zero transition costs, the possible gain of a change must also compensate for the cost of changing. Loss aversion, which is based on Kahneman and Tversky's "prospect theory," provides another rationale for the status quo bias. There is a behavioral asymmetry in the value function: losses loom larger than gains of the same magnitude. Reluctance to change may be due to the overweighting of costs compared to benefits. Psychological commitment defines the status quo as the result of past investments. There are "psychological sunk costs" in the status quo that induce people to retain the current situation to avoid cognitive dissonance.

An important consequence of the status quo bias is reluctance to trade. The willingness to trade depends not only on the agent's preferences but also on the agent's endowment. The status quo endowment provides two different kinds of information to the decision-maker. It provides information on the budget set and a bench mark for evaluating alternative possible situations that lie in the boundaries of the budget set. Thus this bias contradicts the neutral framing (NF) hypothesis of the invariance principle, and gives a possible explanation for the WTP–WTA disparity.

Contextual rationality

Failures of invariance with respect to procedure, framing, and context suggest that preferences are partly determined by the context with which they interact. Economists usually rely on several different sources of information for estimating values: market data, experimental data, and survey data. Market information is extracted directly from market indicators, such as prices and quantities, or directly from consumer choices. These indicators are assumed to reflect correctly the underlying system of values. The revealed preference axiom is the essential link between the theoretical level and the empirical level, which allows one to induce the preference structure that generates an agent's observed market behavior. One can also observe an agent's preferences by using artificial markets, allowing for precise control on the part of the experimenter, especially with respect to the incentive structure. Experiments should reduce the noise that surrounds real market data, since observed behavior in experimental markets stands closer to the *ceteris paribus* assumption that one usually postulates to define supply and demand relations. Observed prices and buying and selling decisions in real markets do not correctly reflect the supply and demand schedules, since this data is usually collected under changing market conditions. Finally, one can also assess the individual's preference structure by asking subjects to respond to a questionnaire, as in CV studies.

Because of invariance failures, a typical subject may behave differently in each of the three contexts, and therefore one can observe a different preference structure under each assessment context. One may ask, of course, which one is the "true" one. The usual answer is that correct preferences are the ones observed under real market conditions, a context in which agents have real incentives to reveal their true preferences. In comparing market data and experimental data, a classical criticism is that experiments produce artifacts that one would hardly observe in real markets. The justification is that experimentally observed patterns of behavior may not survive in the context of a real market in which competitive and selective pressures operate. However, this raises two difficulties. The first is that preference theory makes no assumption about the relevant context for observing the most reliable preferences, since preferences are assumed to be context-free; nor does the theory rely on the selection argument to identify a kind of "dominant preference." The second difficulty is the question of observability. If one assumes that intrinsic preferences do exist for most goods, then one should be able, at least in principle, to observe them by a carefully designed assessment methodology. At least it lends credibility to a research program on preference assessment, since a meaningful objective exists. One could even assume that there is no difference between a real and an experimental market since, in both types of markets, final asset positions depend on individual performance, which makes incentive schemes comparable. The experimental market has the distinguishing feature of being a small market with limited access in time and restricted to a few selected participants. If we accept the invariance principle, then we must also be ready to accept that preferences are not affected by the size and duration of the market on which they are expressed.

In many circumstances, one observes that preferences are shaped in part by the market. The increasing role of advertising in most economies is not just evidence of a coordination failure, but also of the potential to manipulate values to a certain extent. As we shall argue, preferences are not always well defined, but are partly constructed by the interaction with the context. Therefore, it is quite clear that if one tries to observe preferences that are incompletely defined, one may actually contribute to their formation through this interference of the surveyor with the observational context.

Non-use values and contingent valuation

Contingent valuation is a particular methodology of CBA that was developed during the last 25 years, mainly for assessing the non-use values of natural assets and resources. A CV study is basically a hypothetical market in which people can express values, usually willingness-to-pay (WTP), for various types of changes that may affect their well-being. First I will define the concept of non-use values and then I will discuss to what extent CV studies can assess them meaningfully.

Non-use values

The concept of non-use value captures the idea that rational economic agents may value a commodity, or a natural asset, even if they do not use it. At first, the concept seems at odds with economics, which primarily deals with consumption of valuable scarce resources. Since Adam Smith, relative scarcity and use-value are considered to be the main determinants of the relative prices of goods. While both arguments together explain, for example, the well-known water-diamond paradox, they do not explain the apparent conflict between the value that agents reveal for most environmental resources and the claim that the market price of most of them is underestimated. Since many environmental resources are becoming scarce (though they have a high value), the concept of non-use value may be useful in solving this contemporary paradox. Non-use values, unlike use values, are not reflected in current market prices. Therefore the "true value" of a commodity having a large non-use value may significantly differ from its market price. For example, despite international trade restrictions, there are still markets (usually black markets) for many endangered species in which prices are quoted below their value (fur, ivory, etc.).

There are many possible causes for the existence of a positive non-use value, including religious, philosophical and moral reasons. However, I will consider only non-use values that are explained by economic factors that affect rational behavior. Of course, the other reasons may also affect the agent's behavior, but these reasons are beyond the scope of this paper.

The economic literature distinguishes between three main concepts of non-use values: option value, bequest value, and existence value. All of these values imply a higher WTP for the preservation of natural assets. Therefore, we speak about "preservation values." Strictly speaking, the only "true" non-use value is the existence value, which is not based on any consumption prospect. Option value is measured by WTP to preserve a natural asset for a future possible consumption. Since future consumption is uncertain, a rational agent may be willing to preserve the option to consume the asset at some future date, even if he or she does not use this option in the future. Usually, there is some future state for which consumption would be the most profitable action, and some other state for which it would be more profitable to preserve the resource. In any case, the option for future consumption usually has a positive price.

Bequest value measures the WTP to preserve a natural asset for future genera-tions. A rational agent may be willing to preserve a natural asset, by reducing his or her own current consumption, because he or she cares about his or her children's welfare. In other words, the bequest of a good both for his or her children's as well as for his or her own consumption can have positive value, so that the optimum amount to be consumed will be affected by his or her children's utility. In this case, the preservation value reflects a positive externality in the agent's current utility, generated by the amount of resource preserved for his or her children. There are several reasons why a rational agent may have a bequest value, in particular, altruistic preferences. We may simply assume that preferences are to some extent interdependent, and therefore, agents may value resources not only for their own purposes, but also for the consumption of other agents. It is important to realize however that the agents need not necessarily be altruistic. Parents, for example, may save resources for their children's future education, and have a positive utility for this action, although their children have a negative utility for the education that their parents decided.

Finally, existence value is defined as the WTP to preserve a natural asset, without any expectation about future use, either by the agent or by somebody else. Existence value is not linked to any identifiable use of the resource. There-fore, existence value is the most questionable concept of non-use value, although it is also the only "true" instance of non-use value. Existence value is only based on the knowledge that the resource does exist, even if the agent would never experience it. For example, one may be willing to pay something for preserving the white whales, even though one would never see one. In this case, the precise meaning of not consuming is difficult to define, but it is also difficult in some instances to define the exact meaning of consumption as well.

Contingent valuation of non-use values

CV surveys define a hypothetical market in which subjects can express their WTP. Observed WTP usually does not perfectly reflect the true unobservable WTP, because there are several potential biases: strategic, hypothetical, instrumental, etc. The strategic bias is due to the absence of an incentive scheme that would induce respondents to answer truthfully. Stated preferences and values are biased because of strategic misrepresentation. The hypothetical bias is due to the hypo-thetical nature of the proposed transaction, and instrumental bias to the particu-lar payment vehicle that is used. Mitchell and Carson (1989) provide a detailed list of possible sources of bias in CV studies.

However, one can go further and ask to what extent one may assume that the true WTP really does exist, independently of the questionnaire. We must ask ourselves whether preferences are recalled from the agent's memory, or if they are framed simultaneously with the questioning itself. Since in a questionnaire, there is neither a contract nor a transaction by which property rights are transferred, we cannot assume that people will behave as if they were making transactions in real markets. Furthermore, questionnaires can only reveal values, not actual decisions.

This is not the usual conception about CV. According to Kahneman (1986), the methodology is founded on the presupposition that "there exists a set of coherent preferences for goods, including non-market goods such as clean air and nice views; that these preferences will be revealed by a proper market; and that these preferences can be recovered by CV."

However, we cannot reject the hypothesis that most people have well-defined values only on a limited domain of their choice set. Outside the relevant domain, values are weakly defined and sometimes even undefined. If this is the case, any questionnaire format which is designed to provide information about a public good will usually interfere with the undefined values. The process of assessing preferences will simultaneously build a preference structure which does not necessarily exist. In other words, in some cases, preferences are constructed rather than observed. It is reasonable to assume that the more weakly they are defined, the more likely they will be constructed. Therefore, the CV method is more likely to structure preferences when they are weakly defined, and more likely to assess existing values in the case when they are well defined. Although well-defined preferences may exist for non-use, it is more likely in many cases that non-use values are less accurately defined than use-values. Since most CV studies are specially designed to elicit those values, they are more exposed to a "criticism" of artificial construction of preferences, than are other methods.

However, the standard conception leads to the rejection of CV studies, because the observed values are strongly dependent on irrelevant factors, such as questionnaire framing, payment vehicle, etc.; see Hausman (1993). Although the sensitivity of CV to methodological factors is consistent with the observed violations of the invariance principle in experiments, the behavior of decision makers is influenced by the task and the context. Schkade and Payne (1993, p. 278) therefore conclude "the literature on the psychology of preferences suggests that the susceptibility of CV results to various influences is just one example among many of how expressed preferences, in general, are sensitive to task and context factors. . . ."

Schkade and Payne identify several reasons which may explain procedural invariance in CV studies, namely, conflicting dimensions in matching, complexity of decisions, and uncertainty about preferences. Uncertainty is certainly a major reason for PI failures. The more uncertainty and ambiguity in preferences, the more likely the violation of PI. Therefore, CVs are clearly more exposed to such failures of PI than are other methods for assessing private values, since CV studies are primarily designed to measure non-use values, which are not well-defined values.

A "constructivist" view on values in CBA

If we admit that observed values are partly constructed, we have to answer a new type of question. The traditional view is that well-defined preferences exist, which means that the analyst can design a suitable methodology to observe them. But what is the purpose of the elicitation of preferences, if the assessment methodology is simultaneously a process through which preferences are constructed? What method of construction should be recommended? What are the relevant criteria to select such a method?

We have to admit that the answer to such questions cannot be based purely on economic justifications. One needs to take into account values that are usually considered external to the economic domain, such as ethical values. According to Sen (1993), "there is no 'internal' way – internal to the choice function itself – of determining whether a particular behavior pattern is or is not consistent." Sen argues in favor of referring to something external to choice behavior that would entail internal consistency, not impose it. Since we observe that the lack of internal consistency of preferences becomes rational if we take into account external factors, we know the way towards the solution. The assessment of individual values must be focused towards the direction of some "meta-value," that is defined on another level than the level of basic preferences.

Building external factors into individual preferences has many unsatisfactory features however. First, it contradicts the traditional principle of consumer sovereignty, which is a basic requirement of liberal economics. According to the principle of consumer sovereignty, the agent is a better judge than anyone else for assessing his or her values. This principle dominates other possible rules for stating values, such as "paternalism," minimum standard of living, minimum entitlement for other species, etc., but the principle of consumer sovereignty also has serious limitations. For example, considerations of fairness are not taken into account. Moreover, consumers can make mistakes, because their information is poor, or because they have little experience with certain kinds of decisions. Therefore, in practice, consumers' freedom needs to be regulated and has actually been regulated, either in markets or in other areas; see Milgrom (1993).

Regulation may be even more necessary if we admit that preferences are ill-defined in some domains, since there is an obvious danger of manipulation. If such a danger exists, it is certainly "more desirable" to rely on some explicit manipulation scheme of preferences, by reference to some publicly expressed focus values, rather than leaving a state of tacit manipulation. Otherwise, private uncontrolled forces could orient individual preferences towards socially undesirable goals.

Taking into account ethical values may be a solution if there is a social consensus about such values. It appears that, in many CV studies, respondents actually express ethical values. According to Kahneman and Knetsch (1992), the "embedding effect" is evidence that people actually "buy a moral satisfaction" in their response to CV studies, rather than expressing a true preference. Diamond and Hausman (1993) strongly criticized the possible presence of ethical or moral values in CV responses, by showing that it was inconsistent with basic economic theory. According to value theory, economic agents are primarily motivated by self-interest, and not by ethical values. For example, if one measures the required compensation for a damaged environment, a theoretically consistent method should only assess the compensation required for the individual loss, but not the ethical values which are linked to the loss for society. Instead, Diamond and Hausman argue that in CV, respondents express "charitable giving," and do not only take into account their personal interest. According to them, CV studies should be rejected because they mix up both types of values. We claim that exactly the contrary should be done, but instead of leaving respondents without any ethical reference, we should make the ethical reference explicit. Because ethical and individualistic values are entangled, making the ethical reference explicit would minimize the variability of assessed values, because all respondents would rely on the same ethical reference instead of giving an answer that would be based on an unobservable personal reference. Although making ethical references explicit does not disentangle ethical values from other values, the evaluation process should nevertheless provide an even basis of assessment, since all respondents would use the same reference. This could, one hopes, also provide a better control over the data. Of course, the choice of an adequate reference point is an essential issue, since it affects the assessed values, especially if they are not clearly defined. Furthermore, in choosing the referent, we may need to take into account not only economic arguments, but also other dimensions as well. How to choose an adequate reference remains therefore an open question closely related to policy objectives.

The above argument is particularly relevant for the assessment of existence values. Milgrom (1993) expressed a strong skepticism against the possibility of assessing such values with CV studies. The existence value is related only to the information that an agent has for the good. The value comes from the information and not from the good itself. Milgrom points out correctly that the real damage is done by the first journalist who reports on the damage. The background provided for the CV question is therefore the fundamental information for the respondent. Milgrom proposes replacing subjective values by a public policy definition and public regulation for the good. The reason is that if we rely on individual values, we may overestimate the "real" value of the good. Because of altruistic preferences, we may double count some values. As a rule of public choice, we should retain a public project only if it is a "potential Pareto improvement" excluding altruistic values. Although I share Milgrom's view on the necessity of some external reference – in his case a public policy definition – I think that the role of the external reference should be exactly the opposite one: providing a reference point, or a guideline, for assessing individual values.

Conclusion

Gregory et al. (1993) recently expressed a position with respect to CV that is comparable to the one expressed in this chapter: "we believe, the designers of a CV study should function not as archeologists, carefully uncovering what is there, but as architects, working to build a defensible expression of value." They assume, however, that people have nevertheless "strong feelings, beliefs, and values for many things that are not sold through markets." Basically, they face the same problem that we faced in this chapter, namely, designing a sensible method for constructing values. The main difference is that they consider values that are already "framed" in the respondent's mind, but that are not usually expressed on

a monetary scale. Therefore, the choice of scale and reference values will affect
the observed values. The problem is even more difficult if preferences are not well
defined, as in the case of non-use values for environmental preservation. In this
case, one must admit that methods designed for assessing true values no longer
provide the expected data, since "true values" do not even exist. This does not
imply that these methods become useless, but that a different interpretation of the
"observed" data must be given. As I argued in this chapter, since CV can also
be used as a tool for constructing values, one should rely on some explicit
reference values (e.g. ethical values) that are external to the agent's system of
preference and chosen on a collective basis. This would provide a common
"yardstick," or convention, with respect to which individual values can be
properly constructed.

Notes

1 This proposition is generally stated as an assumption. However C. Plott (1983) showed
that experimental market subjects do not take into account the external cost in their
buying or selling decisions.
2 Formally, assume that the agent's choice possibilities are constrained to be in the set A
and that $a, a^* \in A$. If the agent chooses a^* we infer from this choice that a^* is *revealed
preferred* to a if $a \neq a^*$. Define $\geq$ the revealed preference relation, and assume that there
exists a utility function $u(\cdot)$ that represents the decision-maker's preference on A. This
implies that $u(a^*) \geq u(a)$. The weak axiom of revealed preference states: if $\alpha^* \geq \alpha$ and
α^* is not equal to α, then not $(\alpha \geq \alpha^*)$.
3 *Survival framing*: In therapy A, 90 percent of the patients survive the therapy, 68
percent are alive after one year and 34 percent after five years. In therapy B, 100 percent
of the patients survive the therapy, 77 percent are alive after one year and 22 percent
after five years.
   Mortality framing: In therapy A, 10 percent die during the therapy, 32 percent in the
first year and 66 percent die within five years. In therapy B, 0 percent die during the
therapy, 23 percent in the first year and 78 percent die within five years.
4 The experiment, carried out with subjects from a hospital, including doctors and
patients, produced the same effect among the different categories of subjects; 247
answered the survival framing and 336 the mortality framing.
5 See D. Grether and C. Plott (1979), W. Pommerehne, F. Schneider and P. Zweifel
(1982), R. Reilly (1982), P. Slovic and S. Lichtenstein (1983) and J. Cox and S. Epstein
(1989).
6 Becker, DeGroot, Marschak.
7 However, Cox and Epstein (1989) showed that the preference reversals may contradict
more fundamentally anti-symmetry which is more fundamental than transitivity.

References

Arrow K. (1982) Risk perception in psychology and economics. *Economic Inquiry*, 20, 1–
9.
Becker, G., De Groot, M. and Marschak, J. (1964) Measuring utility by a single-response
sequential method. *Behavioral Science*. 9, 226–32.

Bell, D. (1982) Regret in decision-making under uncertainty. *Operations Research*, 30, 961–81.

Bishop, R. and Heberlein, T. (1979) Measuring values of extramarket goods: are indirect measures biased? *American Journal of Agricultural Economics*, 61, 1979, 926–30.

Brookshire, D. and Coursey, D. (1987) Measuring the value of a public good: an empirical comparison of elicitation procedures. *American Economic Review*, 77, 554–66.

Coursey, D., Hovis, J. and Schulze, W. (1987) The disparity between willingness to accept and willingness to pay measures of value. *Quarterly Journal of Economics*, 679–90.

Cox, J. C. and Epstein, S. (1989) Preference reversals without the independence axiom. *American Economic Review*, 79, 408–26.

Delquie, P. (1993) Inconsistent trade-offs between attributes: new evidence in preference assessment biases. *Management Science*, 39, 1382–95.

Diamond, P. and Hausman, J. (1993) On contingent valuation measurement of nonuse values. In J. A. Hausman (ed.), *Contingent valuation: a critical assessment*, North-Holland, 3–38.

Dupuit, J. (1844) On the measurement of the utility of public works. *Annales de Ponts et Chaussées*, 2nd series, vol. VII.

Goldstein, W. and Einhorn, H. (1987) Expression theory and the preference reversal phenomena. *Psychological Review*, 94, 236–54.

Gregory, R., Lichtenstein, S. and Slovic, P. (1993) Valuing environmental resources: a constructive approach. *Journal of Risk and Uncertainty*, 7, 177–97.

Grether, D. and Plott, C. (1979) Economic theory of choice and the preference reversal phenomenon. *American Economic Review*, 69, 623–38.

Hammond, P. (1988) Consequentialism and the independence axiom. In *Risk, Decision and Rationality*, Munier B.D. Reidel Publ. Co. 1988, 503–16.

Hanemann, M. (1991) Willingness to pay and willingness to accept: how much can they differ. *American Economic Review*, 81 (3), 635–47.

Harless, D. (1989) More laboratory evidence on the disparity between willingness to pay and compensation demanded. *Journal of Economic Behavior and Organization*, 11, 359–79.

Hausman, J. A. (ed.) (1993) *Contingent valuation: a critical assessment*, North-Holland.

Hershey, J., Kunreuther, H. and Schoemaker, P. (1982) Sources of bias in assessment procedures for utility functions. *Management Science*, 28, 936–54.

Hershey J. and Schoemaker, P. (1985) Probability versus certainty equivalence methods in utility measurement: are they equivalent?. *Management Science*, 31, 1213–31.

Holt, C. A. (1986) Preference reversals and the independence axiom. *American Economic Review*, 76, 508–14.

Johnson, E. and Schkade, D. (1989) Bias in utility assessments: further evidence and explanations. *Management Science*, 35, 1213–31.

Kahneman, D. (1986) Comments. In R. Cummings, D. Brookshire, W. Schultze (eds). *Valuing Environmental Goods: an Assessment of the Contingent Valuation Method*. Rowman & Allen: Totowa, NJ.

Kahneman, D. and Knetsch, J. (1992) Valuing public goods: the purchase of moral satisfaction. *Journal of Environmental Economics and Management*, 22, 57–70.

Kahneman, D., Knetsch, J. and Thaler, R. (1990) Experimental test of the endowment effect and the Coase theorem. *Journal of Political Economy*, 98, 1325–48.

Karni, E. and Safra, Z. (1987) Preference reversals and the observability of preferences by experimental methods. *Econometrica*, 55, 675–85.

Knetsch, J. (1989) The endowment effect and evidence of nonreversible indifference curves. *American Economic Review*, 79, 1277–84.

Knetsch, J. L. and Sinden, J. A. (1984) Willingness to pay and compensation demanded: experimental evidence of an unexpected disparity in measures of value. *Quarterly Journal of Economics*, 99, 507–21.

Kornai, J. (1980) *Economics of shortage*. New York: Elsevier North-Holland.

Lichtenstein, S. and Slovic, P. (1971) Reversals of preferences between bids and choices in gambling decisions. *Journal of Experimental Psychology*, 89, 46–55.

Lindman, H. R. (1971) Inconsistent preferences among gambles. *Journal of Experimental Psychology*, 89, 390–7.

Loomes, G. and Sugden, R. (1982) Regret theory: an alternative of rationale choice under uncertainty. *Economic Journal*, 92, 805–24.

Loomes, G. and Sugden, R. (1983) A rationale for preference reversal. *American Economic Review*, 428–32.

McNeil, B., Pauker, S., Sox, H. and Tversky, A. (1982) On elicitation of preferences for alternative therapies. *New England Journal of Medicine*, 306, 1259–62.

Milgrom, P. (1993) Is sympathy an economic value? Philosophy, economics and the contingent valuation method. In Hausman (1993) 417–35.

Mitchell, R. and Carson, R. (1989) *Using Surveys to Value Public Goods: The Contingent Valuation Method*. Washington DC: Resources For the Future.

Pommerenhe, W. W., Schneider, F. and Zweifel, P. (1982) Economic theory of choice and the preference reversal phenomenon: a reexamination. *American Economic Review*, 72, 569–74.

Plott, C. (1983) Externalities and corrective policies in experimental markets. *The Economic Journal*, 93, 106–27.

Randall, A. and Stoll, J. (1980) Consumer's surplus in commodity space. *American Economic Review*, 71, 449–57.

Reilly, R. J. (1982) Preference reversal: further evidence and some suggested modifications in experimental design. *American Economic Review*, 72, 576–84.

Samuelson, W. and Zeckhauser, R. (1988) Status quo bias in decision making. *Journal of Risk and Uncertainty*, 1.

Schkade, D. and Payne, J. (1993) Where do the numbers come from? How people respond to contingent valuation. *Contingent Valuation: a Critical Assessment*. In J. A. Hausman (ed.), North-Holland, 271–93.

Scitovsky, T. (1941) A note on welfare propositions in economics. *Review of Economic Studies*, 9, 77–88.

Sen, A. (1993) Internal consistency of choice. *Econometrica*, 61, 1993, pp. 495–521.

Slovic, P. and Lichtenstein, S. (1983) Preference reversals: a broader perspective, *American Economic Review*, 73, 596–605.

Strotz, R. H. (1956) Myopia and inconsistency in dynamic utility maximization. *Review of Economic Studies*, 23, 165–80.

Thaler, R. (1980) Towards a positive theory of consumer choice. *Journal of Economic Behavior and Organization*, 1, 39–60.

Tversky, A. and Kahneman, D. (1986) Rational choice and the framing of decisions, In R. Hogarth, M. Reder (eds), *Rational choice: the contrast between economics and psychology*, University of Chicago Press, 67–94.

Willig, R. (1976) Consumer's surplus without apology. *American Economic Review*, 66, 4, 587–97.

II

Equity and Environmental Options

4
Environmental Uncertainty and Future Generations[1]

Alessandro Vercelli

Although the environmental problems induced by economic development became more acute in the last part of this century, public opinion and government authorities did not achieve a sufficient determination to change the current model of development. This failure depends in part on the fact that the environmental damages, as well as the effects of environmental policies, become evident only in the medium or long term, while the time horizon of decisions is very often confined to the short term. Public authorities are obsessed by very short electoral terms, while private agents are often over committed to short-run returns. Generally speaking, economic agents appear to be victims of a distorted conception of rationality confined within the limits of a short-term horizon. A consequence of this attitude is an almost complete neglect of the needs of future generations. Responsibility of current generations for future generations is even denied, mainly because the consequences of current decisions are very uncertain, and the preferences of future generations are unknown. This paper intends to show that the deep uncertainty which characterizes the interaction between the process of economic development and the environment does not justify a lack of concern for the well-being of future generations. The underlying arguments point the way towards a new conception of sustainable development based on a more comprehensive conception of rationality.

The structure of the argumentation is as follows: Mainstream economic theory assumes that historical time is substantially irrelevant from the descriptive point of view, and crucially relevant from the normative point of view (pages 78–80). This attitude towards time is based on a conception of economic rationality which is very restrictive, since it assumes that the environment is invariant with respect to the decisions of economic agents and policy authorities. In particular, such an assumption prevents serious analysis and control of the environmental problems induced by economic development (pages 80–1).

To face the environmental problems of development, economics should reverse its attitude towards time by assuming that time is substantially relevant from the descriptive point of view, but irrelevant from the ethical point of view. This reversal of the traditional attitude towards time presupposes a paradigm of economic rationality, more comprehensive than that of orthodox economics, and capable of inspiring a far-sighted design of the institutional and natural environment. One of the main targets of this point of view is the outline and implementation of a model of sustainable development which duly takes into account the complex interaction between economic development and environment.

The definition of sustainable development suggested here is based on the principle of equal opportunities for different generations. This is assured by the condition that the extension of the set of options at the disposal of future generations should be at least as large as that at the disposal of the current generations. Contrary to the appearance, this criterion is not less operational than the alternative ones suggested in the literature (pages 81–5). Its implementation realizes a fundamental deontological principle: the preservation of liberty of choice for all generations. The stress on this principle is consistent with the recent revival of the analysis of the *deontological* implications of economic decisions, concerning the evaluation of their conformity with universal ethical values. The recent evolution of ethical theories has undermined the illusion, typical of classical utilitarianism, that the ethical questions may be completely reduced to their *teleological* aspects, i.e. to a mere evaluation of the utilitarian consequences of the actions. In this perspective, it has been pointed out that the traditional use of a discount rate for intertemporal optimization violates *prima facie* the deontological principle of ethical irrelevance of time. However, it can be shown that this principle is not necessarily violated by discounting if proper foundations, more solid than the traditional utilitarian ones, are provided (pages 85–8).

Contrary to a widespread opinion, the responsibility of current generations for future generations is not jeopardized by the acknowledgment of the profound uncertainty that characterizes the interaction between economic development and natural environment. In fact, taking account of the high degree of uncertainty and irreversibility which characterizes this interaction, it is rational to intervene so as to preserve a set of options at least as large as the present one (pages 88–9). A few concluding remarks follow (page 89).

Time and economic theory

Mainstream economic theory maintains that historical time is substantially irrelevant for economic analysis from the descriptive point of view, and crucially relevant from the normative point of view. From the descriptive point of view, historical time is deemed irrelevant for economic analysis since the set of options faced by the economic agent is not allowed to change over time. Therefore, no decision of the economic agents and of the economic policy authorities may have irreversible effects in this crucial sense. In the extreme version of orthodox economic theory, even long-term investment is not seen as irreversible, since it is seen as a sort of "putty" which can always be molded and remolded at the wish of the owner. Innovation itself is seen as the choice of a "new" technological option, belonging to a given set of technological options, which is invariant over time. Of course, this does not imply that time has no role to play in orthodox economic theory. In traditional economic dynamics (the theory of stability, growth, and business cycles), time plays an essential role, as was clarified long ago by Frisch (1933) Hicks (1939), and Samuelson (1947); however, this role is a purely quantitative one, exactly because the set of options faced by the economic agents does not change over time. This precludes genuine structural changes which affect the qualitative characteristics of equilibrium: in traditional economic theory, disequilibrium dynamics does not affect the existence, stability, uniqueness or multiplicity of equilibrium. The economy expands like a crystal without changing its proportions, and it oscillates like a pendulum according to a regular pattern which can be disturbed only by exogenous shocks.

In the orthodox economic theory, which is based on the model of general equilibrium, time is fully reversible, exactly as in classical mechanics from which it drew inspiration. On the contrary, historical time plays a crucial role only when its asymmetry is essential (Newton-Smith, 1980). The irreversibility of time was introduced into modern physics in the nineteenth century, mainly through thermodynamics, and it has acquired an increasingly important role since; see, for example, Prigogine and Stengers (1984). Unfortunately, mainstream economic theory, being still heavily influenced by the paradigm of classical mechanics, did not consider in a systematic way the implications of thermodynamics and of the recent advances in physics which stress the importance of irreversibility of time, instability, structural change, and complex dynamics (Faber and Proops, 1990; Vercelli, 1995).

The second law of thermodynamics implies that time is irreversible, though only in the very long period. This is true not only for physical time but also for economic time, since the set of economic options progressively tends to shrink due to the irreversible process of degradation of energy (Georgescu-Roegen, 1971). The set of options available for economic agents can also be modified in an irreversible way by the action of other natural laws (which produce, e.g., sizeable climatic changes), as well as endogenously by the economic agents' decisions. In this paper, I focus on this last case which involves in the most direct and deep way the moral responsibility of decision makers.

From the prescriptive point of view, on the contrary, in mainstream theory, time plays a crucial role, as is clearly revealed by the usual practice of discounting future values in normative models. The discount rate gives different "weights" to future costs and benefits according to the time of their expected occurrence. This practice is so common among economists that it is taken for granted; therefore its foundations and its implications are almost never discussed in the current literature. However, the practice of discounting was often challenged in the past, and often altogether rejected for ethical reasons. In particular, in Cambridge (UK), at the turn of the century, Sidgwick (1901) initiated a tradition of thought which considered discounting as inconsistent with the deontological principle of ethical irrelevance of time. This was considered self-evident since an action producing the death or the suffering of a person should be considered immoral whenever this consequence occurs. The same point of view was confirmed a few years later by Ramsay, who said that discounting "is ethically indefensible and arises merely from the weakness of the imagination" (Ramsay, 1928). Analogously, Harrod observed that discounting is "a polite expression for rapacity and the conquest of reason by passion" (Harrod, 1948). This critical attitude towards discounting is not groundless, since discounting quickly makes future benefits unimportant; see Heal (1991, p. 25) and literature there cited. Therefore, the usual practice of discounting implies an embarrassing ethical relevance of time. This implication is not clearly rejected by classical utilitarianism, which lies at the foundations of mainstream theory, as this school of thought aimed to substitute a teleological conception of ethics for the deontological conception which had until then prevailed. However, while the traditional practice of mainstream economics, in principle, violates the basic deontological principles of ethics, this is not necessarily true if a different approach is adopted; see pages 85–8).

Economics, rationality, and time

The attitude towards time which characterizes mainstream economics – descriptive irrelevance and ethical relevance of time – is based on a conception of rationality which is extremely restrictive (Simon, 1982; Vercelli, 1991). In mainstream economics, rationality from the point of view of the normative values – in the sense of Max Weber (1922) – is completely neglected, so that it has substantially neglected the deontological dimension of human behaviour. Rationality from the point of view of the ends, always in the sense of Max Weber, is considered as the central and unifying principle of economic theory, which is conceived in a reductionist manner as the science that studies the optimal allocation of scarce resources so as to maximize the welfare of economic agents. In addition, rationality from the point of view of the ends is conceived, in its turn, in a very reductionist manner as exclusively concerned with the optimal adaptation to a given environment. Notwithstanding a growing formal sophistication, the paradigm of economic rationality remains that of Robinson Crusoe who does his best with the resources of his island to adapt himself as well as possible to the environment. It can be argued that the mainstream conception of economic rationality is even more restrictive. Robinson Crusoe cannot escape a gradual and tiresome process of learning, by trials and errors, how to adapt to his new environment. Mainstream economics, on the contrary, focuses only on the optimum equilibrium of this adaptation process. This is a particularly limited version of teleological rationality, often called "substantive" rationality (Simon, 1982), which assumes that the *telos* (the end of the action) has been already reached (Faucheux et al. 1993).

Substantive rationality implies a given environment and a given set of options with the result that historical time is condemned to be fully irrelevant for descriptive economic theory. On the contrary, from the normative point of view, time is important because reversible time has to be telescoped into the present period, to allow the choice of the best available intertemporal strategy.

The reduction of ethics to its teleological aspects was introduced in economics by the classical utilitarianism founded by Bentham (1789). However, the impor-

tance of the deontological aspects of ethics has been progressively recognized in
the recent years also in economics. The purely teleological conception of ethics
has been recently abandoned also by the neo-utilitarian stream of thought; see
pages 85–8. This is connected with a progressive recognition of the importance of
structural change and of structural comparisons between different environments
and sets of options. As a matter of fact, a purely teleological point of view
presupposes a merely quantitative approach to ethical values and a complete
neglect of the relevance of "qualities" or structures. This process of conceptual
revision has a crucial bearing on the analysis of environmental problems which
requires, by definition, the assumption of a changing environment and of a
variable set of options. Analogously, the analysis of sustainable development
raises deontological problems which cannot be avoided, in particular, the choice
of a satisfactory criterion of intergenerational equity.

Designing rationality, structural invariance and sustainable development

As we have seen, the mainstream conception of economic rationality, adaptive
and substantive, is not appropriate for the analysis and control of the environmental problems raised by economic development. A possible way out consists in
endogenizing the economic effects of the feedback between economic development and environment. This is the research line pursued by economic theory at
least since Pigou (1920). The basic approach of this research strategy, based on
the concept of external effects (also called external economies or diseconomies),
acknowledges the limits of the market and suggests how to internalize these
effects so as to restore the sovereignty of the market and the basic premises of
orthodox economic rationality.

Unfortunately, this strategy comes into collision with the insuperable barriers
of observability and controllability of complex dynamic systems, such as the
interactive system economy and the environment. The so-called external effects
are consequences of the interaction between the economic system and the environment which are not registered by the market price system. The allocation of
resources, that a perfectly competitive market would have optimized in the
absence of external effects, becomes distorted. The Pigouvian solution is that of
correcting these distortions through an apparatus of taxes and subsidies which
modify the system of prices in such a way as to register the external effects.
Unfortunately, this solution works only very imperfectly: first, because it is very
difficult to discover the external effects and to measure their impact; second,
because, in most cases, this can be done only *ex post* (Hanley and Spash, 1993).
Moreover, the precarious observability of external effects implies an analogous
degree of controllability, since the theory of systems makes clear that the conditions of controllability are analogous to those of observability (Perrings, 1987).
Even if we assume that external effects may be controlled in principle, the
effective implementation of the correction measures (taxes and subsidies) must

rely on the intervention of public authorities, whose far-sightedness, equity, and efficiency have been increasingly questioned by the theory of public policy and by the historical record (Dietz and van der Straten, 1992).

To overcome these problems, it is necessary to study systematically the interaction between the economic system, examined in all its institutional aspects without reducing the analysis exclusively to the market, and its natural environment. This implies a different conception of rationality, not purely adaptive but with a much broader scope. The rejection of the postulate of structural invariance implies that the choice set has to encompass also the structure of the environment and that of the economic system. A rational choice must involve a design including change or conservation of certain structural properties of the system, the economy and the environment. Therefore, the basic guidelines of our choices should conform to a criterion of rationality which could be called "designing" (Vercelli, 1991) because it must involve a design (or project) of harmonious coexistence between the process of economic development and the evolution of the biosphere. In this framework, the decisional problems become much more complex since the option set can change over time as a consequence of the interactions between the economic system and the environment; it may also change endogenously owing to the effects of past decisions. The historical time becomes crucial because it implies irreversible changes in the extension and contents of the set of viable options.

The conceptual shift from the theory of growth to the theory of sustainable development further clarifies the need for a transition towards a new paradigm. The theory of economic growth, as developed in the 1950s and 1960s, assumed the invariance of the economic structure and the irrelevance of the natural environment. However, it was recognized that developing economies were characterized by profound structural changes and that the theory of growth could not apply to them. Therefore, the distinction was introduced between growth theory – abstract and formalized, characterized by structural invariance and applied to mature economies (see, for example, Barro and Sala-I-Martin, 1995) – and theory of development, more historical and sociological, directed to the study of the structural transformations which characterize the process of development; see, for example, Todaro (1994) or Ghatak (1995).

The natural rate of growth which characterizes the standard growth model is indefinitely sustainable, given the structure of the model and the exogenous influences analyzed: technical change and growth of population. However, since the early 1970s, it was increasingly understood that no growth process may be considered really sustainable without considering the interactions between the evolution of the economic system and the evolution of the natural environment (Meadows et al., 1972). It became increasingly clear that no process of growth can go on without profound structural transformations of both the economic system and the natural environment, even in the most industrialized countries. The emerging concept, which aims at a synthesis and a generalization of both growth theory and development theory, is the theory of sustainable development that studies the interaction between the structural evolution of the economic system and the structural evolution of its natural environment in both mature and developing economies, as well as at the world level; early contributions came from Pirages (1977), Cleveland (1979), Coomer (1979) and IUCN (1980).

The success of the concept of sustainable development, which was soon adopted by important official documents such as "the Bruntland Report" (WCED, 1987) and Pamphlet 14 of the World Bank (1987), lies in its ability to evoke at the same time an implicit critique of the limits of the traditional theories of growth and development, and of the catastrophic collapse predicted by early environmentalism. Unfortunately, though the concept of sustainable development is very appropriate to express in a synthetic way a set of contrasting exigencies, and is also able to point out a direction of fruitful research, it has so far escaped a rigorous definition; for some recent discussions, see, for example, Pearce and Turner (1990), Costanza (1991) and Turner (1993).

According to one of the most popular definitions (Pearce, 1988, p. 58) development may be considered sustainable when the rate of exploitation of natural resources does not exceed their rate of regeneration, and the rates of polluting emissions do not exceed the rates of assimilation of the receiving ecosystems. This definition, like the others suggested so far, raises more problems than it is able to solve. In particular, it does not clarify which criterion of intergenerational equity is adopted. This problem is crucial since any definition of sustainability is relative to a well-specified criterion of intergenerational equity. The more popular criteria require that the flow of consumption does not shrink through time (Solow, 1974, 1986), or that utility per capita does not diminish in the future (Pezzey, 1989).

I think it preferable to adopt a criterion which can be considered more general than those mentioned above and which may avoid any charge of paternalism towards future generations; see pages 88–9. According to this criterion, development may be considered sustainable only when future generations are guaranteed a set of options at least as wide as that possessed by the current generation.

A criterion of sustainability very close to the one suggested here is based on the preservation over time of the current stock of produced and natural capital – see, for example, Pearce, Markandya, and Barbier (1989) and Victor, Hanna, and Kubursi (1996) – allowing some degree of substitution ("weak sustainability criterion") or no substitution at all ("strong sustainability criterion"). This criterion rightly stresses that intergenerational equity should be concerned with the economic potential of future generations rather than with the modalities and characteristics of its actualization which must be fully left to their autonomous choices. However, this formulation stresses mainly the productive aspect and only in aggregate terms. Therefore, such a criterion, besides forbidding measurement problems (discussed in the next section), is unable to focus on the full range of options, concerning both production and consumption, which is actually "sustained" by a certain stock of capital. The formulation in terms of option sets advocated here seems thus preferable, because it focuses the attention on the magnitude most relevant for assuring the liberty of choice of future generations. In addition, this magnitude is more suitable for bridging the gap between economic and ethical considerations.

Operational measures of sustainability

To give an operational meaning to the criterion of sustainability suggested here, it is necessary to compare the extension of option sets belonging to different generations. This raises difficult problems of measurement which however, contrary to a first impression, are not more difficult than those raised by the alternative criteria of sustainability mentioned above. What, in operational terms, does the criterion of non-decreasing utility (welfare) through time really imply, if the tastes of future generations, particularly those in the distant future, are unknown? Analogously, the criterion of non-decreasing consumption through time has no operational meaning without knowing the preferences of future generations. Any aggregate index of consumption requires a knowledge of prices which depend on the tastes of future generations; moreover, even a physical index cannot be worked out without knowing their preferences. As for the criterion based on the stock of capital, as is well known, the stock of produced capital goods cannot be reliably measured, even knowing the preferences or relative prices; the stock of natural capital could be measured only knowing the value of all the relevant externalities, a condition which is not at all realistic even for the current economy (see pages 81–3), and which is certainly not met by future economies characterized by unknown parameters.

Let us consider first the sustainability criteria based on consumption and utility. Since we do not know the tastes of future generations, we are concerned with the preservation not only of the goods which are currently considered consumer's goods but also of the goods which might be considered consumer's goods by future generations. Virtual consumer's goods are either artificial (produced) or natural (non-produced environmental goods). The availability of artificial goods depends on the extension of *implementable* technological options which depends, in turn, on the extension of *virtual* technological options (realizable on the basis of existing technological knowledge) and on the availability of productive factors required by the implementation of the virtual technological options. The presumable future evolution of the set of virtual technological options does not raise worries for the sustainability of development since there is a legitimate hope that technological progress will further enlarge the set of virtual technological options. The crucial problem lies in the availability of productive factors, particularly as far as natural resources are concerned. Therefore, unless we believe in the full substitutability of artificial products for natural resources, it is necessary to preserve a stock of natural resources sufficient to keep an extension of the productive option set at least as large as that of current generations.

As for natural consumer's goods (clean air, clean water, environmental amenities, etc.), their availability is currently jeopardized by over-exploitation and pollution. It is therefore necessary to intervene so as to preserve as much as possible the set of consumption options. Very often, the availability of environmental goods affects both the productive options and the consumption options. This is the case of biodiversity whose progressive loss reduces the set of implementable technological options (e.g. in the pharmaceutical industry) as well as the direct utility which may be drawn from natural amenities (e.g. in natural parks).

If intergenerational ethical equity is referred not only to the choices directly affecting the welfare of existing and future generations, but also to the other economic choices, the criterion suggested here permits a full-scale analysis without the intrinsic limitations of the alternative criteria centered on utility or consumption. As for the criterion based on the capital stock, there is no reliable way to make it operational. Summing up the argument, to preserve the liberty of choice of future generations, we have to preserve a set of options at least as large as that available to current generations, and this requires an environmental policy aimed at preserving environmental goods.

In formal terms, sustainable development requires that the set of options of current generation is a subset of the set of options of future generations. This is the standard measure utilized in the theory of option values. It has a few shortcomings pointed out in the literature (see Basili-Vercelli, this volume, Chapter 5) but it allows a qualitative ordering of option sets which, at first sight, seems good enough for our purposes. However, there is a further shortcoming, neglected in the literature, which forbids a sound application of this measure to our very long-run problem of intergenerational equity. As the loss of biodiversity clearly suggests, in the long run, relevant for intergenerational equity, we cannot neglect an irreversible leakage from the option set. Whatever policy of environmental conservation will be implemented, there will always be an unavoidable residual process of option destruction. In this case, the measure mentioned above cannot be applied. How can we compare the extension of two sets, neither of which is a subset of the other? Certainly not counting the elements of the two sets, because many of them could be irrelevant. Fortunately, there is a possible way out. If the main target of sustainable growth is that of preserving the liberty of choice of future generations, the crucial aspect to be preserved is a variety of options at least as large as that of current generations. Therefore, it is sufficient to compare the degree of option diversity characterizing the option sets available to different generations, and this can be done by means of measures of diversity similar to those already applied in the analysis of biodiversity. In particular, the degree of option diversity is a function of biodiversity, cultural diversity, and availability of irreplaceable natural resources which are confirmed to be the crucial magnitudes to be preserved to assure the sustainability of development; see Vercelli (1994).

Ethical irrelevance of time and discounting

There is a growing consensus among economists on the thesis that economics cannot neglect the ethical implications of economic decisions, and that ethics cannot leave out of consideration its deontological dimension. The theory of "natural rights," which was very popular in the Enlightenment, was progressively abandoned because no one had succeeded in providing satisfactory foundations capable of reconciling conflicting rights which appeared equally "natural" or inalienable. Bentham believed that his version of utilitarianism could solve the conflict between inconsistent rights by reducing ethical evaluations to a homogeneous measure (Bentham, 1789, p. vii). This gave the illusion to early utilitarians that the deontological aspects of ethics could be reduced to the teleological aspects. This sort of "strict" utilitarianism became very influential also in the development of economic theory.

Strict utilitarianism began to be seriously challenged long ago, with particular rigour since the end of last century, in ethics (Sidgwick, 1901) and in the philosophy of law; but it managed to survive in economics. At first, "welfare economics" appeared to be able to give appropriate foundations and operationalize Bentham's dream of a scientific calculus capable of measuring social "values" under any circumstances. However, the grand design of welfare economics was soon undermined by difficulties and paradoxes (as the famous "impossibility theorem" pointed out by Arrow, 1951); this accelerated the crisis of classical utilitarianism and eventually convinced many economists that the deontological dimension of ethics cannot be reduced to its teleological dimension (Sen, 1979). This has been recognized also by a few recent supporters of utilitarianism who modified its axioms in such a way to give a crucial role to deontological principles; a few distinguished scholars, such as Harsanyi (1988) and Hare (1981), tried to work out versions of the utilitarianism, often called "neo-utilitarianism," which combine some of its original postulates with Kantian deontological principles.

A radical break with utilitarianism came with the influential *Theory of Justice* by J. Rawls (1971) who adopted a deontological perspective in open opposition to the teleological point of view of utilitarianism. The process, initiated by Hume, which had progressively reduced the notion of justice to that of utility was reversed by Rawls: justice again became a concept completely autonomous from that of social utility. This triggered an authentic revival of the theory of moral rights. Nowadays, both main doctrinal streams on the subject, neo-utilitarianism and the theory of moral rights, share the conviction that ethical principles must be conceived as universal and that, therefore, time should be ethically irrelevant.

As we have seen before, the principle of ethical irrelevance of time collides *prima facie* with the traditional practice of discounting which is routinely used for comparing economic values referring to different dates. However, though discounting is utilized with increasing embarrassment, it is still routinely used in normative economic models. This depends in part on the difficulty of finding alternative solutions which are fully operational (Heal, 1991, pp. 25–8), but this justification is clearly unacceptable from the ethical point of view. However, it is possible to get round this dilemma by showing that proper foundations to the discounting method, different from the traditional utilitarian ones, may be given and may rescue the deontological principle of ethical irrelevance of time.

A first step in this direction may be made by observing that the discounting of future utility should not be confused with the discounting of future benefits (Heal,

1991, pp. 34–7). The assumption that future utility should have a smaller weight than the present one does not imply that future consumption should have a smaller weight than the present one (p. 26). Therefore, by applying the discounting procedure to utility, it is possible to work out a model of sustainable growth such that the consumption of future generations is preserved.

A second step may be made by observing that, in any model of growth, the discount rate is strictly related to the interest rate. In the most simple models, the two rates must be equal; in most models, the two rates move together. To study the ethical implications of discounting, it is necessary to study its implications on the interest rate, and through the interest rate on the other main economic variables. The relationship between the interest rate and the sustainability of development is an ambiguous one; see Lind (1982) Hanley and Spash (1993) and Price (1993). Whenever the rate of interest is used for discounting, a lower rate of interest in principle enhances the long-run sustainability of growth as the weights of future benefits decrease less rapidly with time; but, generally, a lower rate of interest induces more investment and a higher rate of growth of real output, and this *ceteris paribus* increases pollution and the exploitation of natural resources and makes development less sustainable (Norgaard-Howarth, 1991). This argument may be generalized by taking account of other influences exerted by the social discount rate on the variables of a development model.

In principle, in any model of development, it is possible to calculate the value of the social discount rate which maximizes an index of its sustainability. In a model of sustainable growth, where sustainability is assured by well-specified constraints, it should be chosen at the rate of discount that maximizes the rate of growth. The choice of the "optimal" (from the point of view of sustainability) level of the social discount rate seems able to reconcile the consequentialist point of view with the deontological point of view, since the sustainability of development was defined according to a deontological criterion of equity for intergenerational distribution. Therefore, the principle of ethical irrelevance of time does not necessarily imply that discounting is inadmissible. Obviously, the "optimal" (from the point of view of sustainability) rate of discount is a magnitude which is extremely sensitive to the specification of the model, and in particular to the very definition of sustainability, so that its choice for practical purposes should be very careful.

In more abstract terms, in a model of sustainable growth any value of the rate of discount has a set of ethical implications. The optimal value of the rate of discount does not need to be zero for any of the possible ethical implications, and it may be different for each of them. The choice of the optimal rate of discount depends on the hierarchy between the ethical implications of different values of the rate of discount and their trade-offs. Therefore, the discount rate which is most consistent with the full set of deontological values and their hierarchy cannot be zero in most cases; on the contrary, it is likely to be positive, though only moderately so (Heal, 1991). In other words, the principle of ethical irrelevance of time cannot find a mechanical application to the rate of discount and does not exclude the opportunity of discounting, provided that the discount rate is chosen on the basis of a criterion which does not leave out of consideration the deontological aspects of ethics.

Responsibility towards future generations and uncertainty

The unpredictability of the future is often considered a good reason for giving a bigger weight to present utility than to future utility. There are three basic arguments.

First, it is claimed that, owing to the permanent risk of extinction of the human race, each generation is slightly more likely to exist than the subsequent one, and this progressively reduces the commitment of a rational agent to save resources for the well-being of future generations.

Second, it is claimed that, in any case, it would be paternalistic, or devoid of any content, to assume that we have any moral responsibility concerning the welfare of future generations, since it is clearly impossible to foresee their tastes and values (Pontara, 1988).

Third, since the further into the future costs and benefits are expected to occur, the more uncertain they are, it is claimed that a "risk premium" should be added to the discount rate which increases with the degree of risk for a risk-averse individual.

Taking account of one or more of the preceding arguments, many jump to the conclusion that, given the profound uncertainty surrounding the tastes of future generations and the characteristics of the future interactions between the economic system and the environment, it is not advisable to adopt any environmental policy which involves sizable economic costs in the present. However, it is possible to show that this thesis is not a sound one.

First, the extinction of human race is not independent of our choices. In any case, since we cannot exclude the existence of future generations even in the distant future, there is no reason to deny the principle of equal opportunities for different individuals and generations.

Second, whatever effect a positive discount rate may have on the current evaluation of future costs and benefits, future generations should be allowed to decide for themselves. This is possible only if we make sure that the set of options inherited by future generations will be no more restricted than the current one. Otherwise, it is not so sure that future generations will succeed in all cases to take care of themselves. If the set of available options is too small, their survival could be jeopardized, or their life could be of a very low quality, as is suggested by what happens today in the poorest areas of the world. In addition, any reduction in the available set of options would imply a reduction in the liberty of choice. From the deontological point of view, it is an inescapable duty that the current generations should leave to future generations a chance of survival and a degree of freedom not inferior to its own. The fact that the tastes and values of future generations are unknown cannot diminish our concern for their liberty of choice.

Third, as is well known, a wide and rigorous literature, initiated by Arrow and

Fisher (1974) and Henry (1974), has proved that it is rational to react to an increase in uncertainty by increasing the intertemporal flexibility of the decision strategy; see Basili and Vercelli, this volume (Chapter 5). In fact, under quite general conditions, an increase in uncertainty concerning the outcome of an irreversible process implies an increase in the economic value of future options. Therefore, whenever there is the risk of an irreversible loss of some future options, it is rational to intervene to reduce this risk. It is not sufficient to wait, nor to learn, before acting. A case in point is that of biodiversity: it is rational to intervene immediately to avoid, or at least to reduce, any risk of a further loss in biodiversity, since any regret for the extinction of a living species could not be remedied *ex post*.

Conclusion

As we have seen, the uncertainty concerning the actual existence of future generations is not a good excuse for evading the ethical responsibility concerning their coming into existence, their survival, as well as the quality of their life, but it should be a good reason for increasing the efforts directed to establish a sustainable development capable of guaranteeing their rights. Analogously, the ignorance of the preferences and values of future generations is not a good excuse for evading the ethical responsibility for their well-being but it should be a good reason for preserving their freedom of choice.

The accommodation of the above deontological principles concerning future generations within the paradigm of economics requires a more comprehensive criterion of economic rationality that abandons the traditional bias towards the mere adaptation to a given environment, which in fact opened the door to its uncontrolled transformation, and explicitly recognizes the unavoidable mutual influence between the process of economic development and the evolution of the environment, so as to induce a sustainable co-evolutionary interaction between them. The very long-run horizon of this perspective does not exclude, indeed involves, a more detailed analysis of the economic processes and of their short-run effects on human welfare and on natural environment.

The insights coming from the above approach to sustainable development will affect also the decisions having a short- and medium-run time horizon, because they have to respect the constraints fixed within the long-run time horizon. In particular, taking into account the deep uncertainty and ubiquitous irreversibility which characterize the interaction between economic development and natural environment (Funtowicz and Ravetz, 1990, 1994), environmental policy should shift from the traditional use of therapeutic instruments (such as environmental insurance or legal liability) which seek to compensate the environmental damages *ex post*, towards the systematic use of "preventive" instruments able to avoid, or at least reduce, the environmental risks *ex ante*; see Faucheux and Froeger (1995) and Vercelli (1995). On the success of these policies depends the survival of future generations and the preservation of their effective liberty of choice.

Note

1   The content of this paper is complementary to, and partially overlaps with, that of a companion paper (Vercelli, 1996) which recalls in a more concise way the general conceptual framework here developed, and extends the analysis of the rationality criterion involved in it. Part of the underlying research was developed within the project SUSTEE coordinated by the OIKOS Foundation of Siena.

References

Arrow, K. J. (1951) *Social Choice and Individual Values*. New York: Wiley.
Arrow, K. J. and Fisher, A. (1974) Environmental preservation, uncertainty and irreversibility. *Quarterly Journal of Economics*, 89, 312–19.
Barro, R. J. and Sala-I-Martin, X. (1995) *Economic Growth*. New York: McGraw Hill.
Bentham, J. (1789) *An Introduction to the Principles of Morals and Legislation*. Reissued 1970. J. H. Burns and H. L. A. Hart (eds) London: Athlone Press. 1970.
Cleveland, H. (ed.) (1979) *The Management of Sustainable Growth*. New York: Pergamon Press.
Coomer, J. C. (ed.) (1979) *Quest for a Sustainable Society*. New York: Pergamon Press.
Costanza, R. (ed.) (1991) *Ecological Economics: The Science and Management of Sustainability*. New York: Columbia University Press.
Dietz, F. J. and van der Straten, J. (1992) Rethinking environmental economics: missing links between economic theory and environmental policy. *Journal of Economic Issues*, 26, 27–51.
Faber, M. and Proops, J. L. R. (1990) *Evolution, Time, Production and the Environment*. Berlin: Springer-Verlag.
Faucheux, S. and Froger, G. (1995) Decision-making under environmental uncertainty. *Ecological Economics*, 15, 29–42.
Faucheux, S., Froger, G. and Noël, J. F. (1993) Quelles hypothèses de rationalité pour le développement soutenable? *Économie Appliquée*, 46, 59–103.
Frisch, R. (1933) Propagation problems and impulse problems in dynamic economics. *Economic Essays in Honour of Gustav Cassel*. London: Allen & Unwin.
Funtowicz, S. O. and Ravetz, J. (1990) *Uncertainty and Quality in Science for Policy*. Dordrecht: Kluwer Academic Publishers.
Funtowicz, S. O. and Ravetz, J. (1994) The worth of a songbird: ecological economics as a post-normal science. *Ecological Economics*, 10, 197–207.
Georgescu-Roegen, N. (1971) *The Entropy Law and the Economic Process*. Harvard: Harvard University Press.
Ghatak, S. (1995) *Introduction to Development Economics*. London: Routledge.
Hanley, N. and Spash, C. L. (1993) *Cost-benefit Analysis and the Environment*. Aldershot: Edward Elgar.
Hare, R. M. (1981) *Moral Thinking: Its Levels, Method and Point*. Oxford: Oxford University Press.
Harrod, R. (1948) *Towards a Dynamic Economics*. London: Macmillan.
Harsanyi, J. C. (1988) *Essays on Ethics, Social Behaviour, and Scientific Explanation*. Dordrecht: Reidel.
Heal, G. (1991) The optimal use of exhaustible resources, First Boston Working Paper Series.
Henry, C. (1974) Option values in the economics of irreplaceable assets. *Review of Economic Studies*, 41, 89–104.

Hicks, J. L. (1939) *Value and Capital*. Oxford: Clarendon Press.

IUCN (1980) *World Conservation Strategy: Living Resource Conservation for Sustainable Development*. Gland (Switzerland): IUCN-UNEP-WWF.

Lind, R. C. (ed.) (1982) *Discounting for Time and Risk in Energy Policy*. Baltimore: Johns Hopkins University Press.

Meadows, D. H. et al. (1972) *Limits to Growth*. New York: Universe Books.

Newton-Smith, W. H. (1980) *The Structure of Time*. London: Routledge and Kegan Paul.

Norgaard, R. B. and Howarth, R. B. (1991) Sustainability and discounting the future, in Costanza (1991) 88–101.

Pearce, D. W. (1988) The sustainable use of natural resources in developing countries. In R. K. Turner (ed.), *Sustainable Environmental Management: Principles and Practice*. London: Belhaven Press.

Pearce, D. W. and Turner, R. K. (1990) *Economics of Natural Resources and the Environment*. Baltimore: John Hopkins University Press.

Pearce, D. W. Markandya, A. and Barbier, E. B. (1989) *Blueprint for a Green Economy*. London: Earthscan Publications.

Perrings, C. (1987) *Economics and Environment*. Cambridge: Cambridge University Press.

Pezzey, J. (1989) Economic analysis of sustainable growth and sustainable development, Environment Department Working Paper no. 15, The World Bank, Washington.

Pigou, A. C. (1920) *The Economics of Welfare*. London: MacMillan.

Pirages, D. C. (ed.) (1977) *The Sustainable Society. Implications for Limited Growth*. New York: Praeger.

Pontara, G. (1988) Responsabilità per le generazioni future? *Linee d' Ombra*, 31–6.

Price, C. (1993) *Time, Discounting and Value*. Oxford: Blackwell.

Prigogine, I. and Stengers, I. (1984) *Order Out of Chaos. Man's New Dialogue With Nature*. London: Fontana Paperback.

Ramsey, F. (1928) A mathematical theory of saving. *Economic Journal*, 38, 543–59.

Rawls, J. (1971) *A Theory of Justice*. Cambridge: Cambridge University Press.

Samuelson, P. A. (1947) *Foundations of Economic Analysis*. Harvard: Harvard University Press.

Sen, A. (1979) Utilitarianism and welfarism. *Journal of Philosophy*, 76, 463–89.

Sidgwick, H. (1901) *The Methods of Ethics*. New York: Dover Publications.

Simon, H. (1982) *Models of Bounded Rationality*. Cambridge, Mass.: MIT Press.

Solow, R. M. (1974) The economics of resources or the resources of economics. *American Economic Review*, 64, 1–21.

Solow, R. M. (1986) On the intergenerational allocation of natural resources. *Scandinavian Journal of Economics*, 88, 141–9.

Todaro, M. P. (1994) *Economic Development*. (5th edn): New York: Longman.

Turner, K. (ed.) (1993) *Sustainable Environmental Economics and Management: Principles and Practice*. London: Belhaven Press.

Vercelli, A. (1991) *Methodological Foundations of Macroeconomics: Keynes and Lucas*. Cambridge: Cambridge University Press.

Vercelli, A. (1994) Operational measures of sustainable development and the freedom of future generations. Report for the SUSTEE Project, Oikos Foundation, Siena.

Vercelli, A. (1995) From soft uncertainty to hard environmental uncertainty. *Économie Appliquée*, 48, 251–69.

Vercelli, A. (1996) Sustainable development, rationality and time. In S. Faucheux, M. O'Connor and van der Straten (eds) (1996) *Sustainable Development: Analysis and Public Policy*. Dordrecht: Kluwer Academic Publishers.

Victor, P. A., Hanna, J. E. and Kubursi, A. (1996) How strong is weak sustainability?

WCED, The World Commission on Environment and Development (1987) *Our Common Future*, ("The Brundtland Report"). Oxford: Oxford University Press.

Weber, M. (1922) *Wirtschaft und Gesellschaft*. Tübingen: Mohr.

World Bank (1987) Environment, growth and development, *Development Committee Pamphlet 14*, Washington, DC: World Bank.

5

Environmental Option Values: A Critical Assessment[1]

Marcello Basili and Alessandro Vercelli

Environmental conservation is advocated for a host of reasons, many of which are non-economic: ethical, aesthetic, religious, and so on. These motivations have an economic impact which should not be neglected since many people would be prepared to pay a sizeable amount of money to conserve certain environmental goods. However, environmental conservation is also advocated for strictly economic reasons, some of which have often been neglected by mainstream economic theory. Whenever there is uncertainty and the choice of a decision maker may have irreversible consequences, the conservation of an environmental good may be justified, irrespective of any non-economic consideration, by virtue of its implicit intertemporal option value (or quasi-option value), i.e. by virtue of the fact that by preserving the environmental good, one gains the possibility of exploiting subsequent information on the pros and cons of existing alternative choice strategies. In other words, the choice of preserving an environmental good gives time to learn and eventually to discover a more profitable choice strategy.

The preference for intertemporal flexibility revealed by (quasi-)option values have been analyzed in monetary and financial theory at least since Keynes (1936), who called it (speculative) liquidity preference. The idea was subsequently developed by Hart (1942), Marschak (1938, 1949), Marschak and Nelson (1962) and others. Similar ideas have been introduced in environmental economics since the seminal contributions by Weisbord (1964) and Krutilla (1967). Rigorous treatments were suggested by Arrow and Fisher (1974) and Henry (1974a, b) which are starting points for the recent debate.

This paper surveys a few crucial aspects of the literature on environmental option values (and quasi-option values), taking into account the parallel literature on liquidity preference and financial option values. In the next section, the concept of quasi-option value is clarified with reference to other partially overlapping concepts, emphasizing its crucial role in measuring the preference for intertemporal flexibility. In the following section different measures of intertemporal option values are briefly presented and discussed. A few concluding remarks follow.

Option value and intertemporal flexibility

The recent environmental literature has stressed the importance of a family of values which depend, at least in part, on non-user benefits: existence value, bequest value, waiting value, option value, quasi-option value, flexibility preference, etc. A close affinity among these concepts is readily recognizable, but the exact nature of their mutual relationships has not yet been sufficiently clarified. In this section, we will try to put some order in this conceptual web so as to orientate the ensuing discussion. The main thesis that will emerge from this short critical survey is the following: the basic concept for an economic analysis of environmental conservation is that of "intertemporal" option value, or "quasi-option value" whose existence and degree rests on preference for intertemporal flexibility.

Non-use value and (quasi-)option value

Krutilla (1967) was the first to emphasize the importance of non-user benefits so as to allocate natural resources efficiently. Mitchell and Carson (1989) proposed a way to measure these benefits. The former defined "existence" value, as the desire to preserve certain natural resources, and "bequest" value, as the propensity to leave a certain amount of natural resources to future generations. Both these categories of value depend mainly on non-economic motivations, such as aesthetic and ethical considerations, but they have potential economic impacts because people are prepared to pay for them.[2] In other words, the environment appears in the utility function not only indirectly as use value (which depends directly on the consumption of different kinds of natural resources), but also directly as non-use value. Existence and bequest values also depend on economic considerations based on the prospective use value of certain natural resources due to possible future changes in the conditions of economic activity (change in tastes, in the choice set, in the consequences of actions, in the quality of goods, etc.).

   The economic aspects of environmental conservation under uncertainty have recently been studied in terms of option values and quasi-option values.[3] In the recent debate,[4] Weisbrod (1964) was the first to relate environmental conservation to option value. Considering, for example, an action with irreversible consequences such as the closure of a national park, he argued that many people would be willing to pay something to preserve the option of visiting the park in the future. Under uncertainty and risk aversion, it is generally rational to keep open an option which could turn out to be useful in the future.

   Later on, Arrow and Fisher (1974) and Henry (1974a, b) independently pointed out that under uncertainty, when a given decision may have irreversible effects (at least in part) and learning is possible before future decisions, it is generally valuable to keep open an option, even in the case of risk neutrality. Arrow and Fisher called "quasi-option value" the extra value attached to the preservation of the reversible option to stress the crucial role played in their analysis by irreversibility and learning (neglected in the preceding analysis of option value), and stressed its independence of risk aversion. Notwithstanding the misleading name, we should consider the theory of environmental quasi-option values as the most general approach to intertemporal flexibility and environmental conservation under uncertainty, since it is relevant whenever there are at least two options the consequences of which have different degrees of irreversibility[5] (perfect temporal symmetry would obviously be an extreme case), and whenever learning is possible before future choices are made (the impossibility of learning would be a very extreme hypothesis).[6]

To avoid confusion, not absent in the literature even after the illuminating contributions by Arrow and Fisher (1974) and Henry (1974a, b), we have to distinguish sharply between two concepts of option value. Although both refer to rational behaviour under conditions of uncertainty and assume different degrees of reversibility of available choices, the conceptual differences are quite radical.

The *plain* option value is an expression of rational behaviour towards soft uncertainty (or "risk"). The intertemporal option value ("quasi-option value") is an expression of rational behaviour towards hard uncertainty (Jones and Ostroy, 1984, p. 26). This second concept of option value is defined as intertemporal because the intertemporal decision problem cannot be reduced, even in principle, to the choice in the first period of the optimal contingent strategy, unlike in the first case. In this second case, learning before a subsequent choice is the crucial factor. In the first case, learning intervenes only in the very weak sense of prompt recognition of the contingencies to which to adapt the optimal strategy. In the case of intertemporal option value, learning plays a strategic role as new information may be used to detect systematic mistakes produced by the existing strategy so that it can be replaced with a better one. Option value is a sort of "risk premium," the value of which is mainly precautionary and related to different adjustment costs, e.g. transaction costs. The value of an intertemporal option is mainly strategic and reveals a preference for intertemporal flexibility which is related to the reversal costs of a given strategy and is the higher the larger the choice set available for the future.[7]

The main results of the contributions of Arrow and Fisher (1974) and Henry (1974a, b) were that:

- the sign of the intertemporal option ("quasi-option") value is positive under quite general assumptions
- an increase in uncertainty induces an increase in the intertemporal option value and therefore encourages environmental conservation.

Both these conclusions were challenged in the ensuing debate. The debate on the importance and the sign of quasi-option value clarified the dependence of the intertemporal option value on the shape of the benefit function, the relationship with different types of uncertainty, etc. Today, there is a wide agreement that option value should be regarded not as the "unrecognized son of that old goat, consumer surplus," as argued by Long (1967), but rather as an extra component of the benefits associated with preservation.

As for the sign of intertemporal option value, Schmalensee (1972) and Bohm (1975) claimed that the sign of option value is undetermined as it depends on the particular shape of utility functions. Plummer and Hartmann (1986) found an undetermined sign when uncertainty is related to a change of preference but were able to prove that when uncertainty is relative to the quality of an environmental good, the sign of option value is generally positive. As soon as we consider irreversibility, neglected by the preceding models, a positive quasi-option value becomes likely (Smith, 1983). However, also in this case, it has been maintained (notably by Freeman, 1985) that the sign of quasi-option value need not be positive. On the contrary, Fisher and Hanemann (1987, p. 189) proved that if information about future benefits and costs of development is independent of the current development decisions, the quasi-option value of preservation must be positive. Assertions to the contrary are based on the confusion of quasi-option value with the net benefit of preservation which need not be positive.

These results were recently confirmed by Hanemann (1989), but have been criticized by Olson (1990), who claimed that when the developed resource is utilized as an input to production, an unambiguous bias toward preservation does not exist. In his opinion, preservation, by reducing current production, may jeopardize future consumption opportunities. However, Moretti (1993b) has proved that Olson's conclusions depend on very restrictive assumptions and collapse in a more general model. At this stage of the ongoing debate, it may be concluded that the sign of a quasi-option value is likely to be positive under quite general circumstances.

As for the effects of an increase in uncertainty on the intertemporal option value, the results obtained by Arrow and Fisher (1974) and Henry (1974a, b) have been confirmed in a different analytical setting by Jones and Ostroy (1984). Generally speaking, an increase in uncertainty tends to increase the intertemporal option value, inducing a more conservationist environmental policy. However, this statement is quite sensitive to different assumptions on the nature of prospective information and viable learning processes. Generally speaking, the more it is possible to learn in subsequent periods, the more it is rational to increase intertemporal flexibility, which allows the exploitation of expected learning (Epstein, 1980). However, if prospective learning depends on the choice made in the first period, the above conclusions may be altered (Viscusi and Zeckauser, 1976; Miller and Lad, 1984). If uncertainty refers to the benefits of development, learning might depend on the effective implementation of the development project, so that the desirability of a policy of environmental conservation would be weakened. If uncertainty refers to the conservation benefits, learning is fostered by a conservation policy. In addition, when information is dependent on development, a very slow and cautious process of development could be sufficient to make learning possible (Fisher and Hanemann, 1987, p. 190).

The consequences of an increase in uncertainty on quasi-option values are ambiguous because we have assumed uncertainty neutrality[8] so far. As soon as we assume uncertainty aversion, an increase in uncertainty generally increases the intertemporal option values (Caballero, 1991). Whenever uncertainty neutrality is assumed, the option values are sensitive not to the degree of "risk," but to the amount and characteristics of expected learning which depend not only on the amount of missing information, but also on the actual viability and timing of learning and its dependence on different categories of actions.

We cannot say much *a priori* about the degree of uncertainty aversion (as is usual with individual tastes); however, psychological considerations provide some insights. A few authors have observed that ignorance of relevant information that could be possessed by someone else is particularly upsetting. This may explain why hard uncertainty may restrain people from betting, particularly when they feel incompetent in the field to which the bet relates (Heath and Tversky, 1991; Frisch and Baron, 1988). Further insights come from experimental economics. Generally speaking, economic agents are uncertainty averse, though a limited degree of uncertainty preference may emerge for very low gain probability or for very high loss probability (Hogart and Einhorn, 1990; Camerer and Weber, 1992). It is also confirmed that agents prefer to bet on events in which they feel fairly competent (Fellner, 1961, p. 687; Keppe and Weber, 1991), or on events whose occurrence is affected by their ability rather than on purely random events (Langer, 1975). Similarly, they prefer to bet on future events rather than on past events which might be known to others (Brun and Teigen, 1990). These experimental results also depend on the fact that competence affects the social attitude towards the choices of an agent: competent people may be praised for having chosen the right bet, while incompetent people may be only blamed for having chosen the wrong bet (Heath and Tversky, 1991). Finally, uncertainty aversion increases when the bet is adjudicated in public (Curley, Yates and Abrams, 1986).

Summing up, the recent literature clarifies that the value of an intertemporal option under uncertainty and irreversibility depends on two basic factors: the value attributed by the decision-maker to prospective learning, and the degree of uncertainty aversion which depends crucially on the stock of past learning or competence.

Quasi-option value and intertemporal flexibility

The analysis of quasi-option values is founded on the assumption of a preference for what we have called "intertemporal flexibility," whenever the choice is characterized by uncertainty, irreversibility, and potential learning before subsequent decisions. The trouble is that intertemporal flexibility preference is itself in need of solid foundations as it is inconsistent with the mainstream decision theory under uncertainty based on the maximization of expected utility (EU) – see, for example Arrow (1971) and Cohendet and Llerena (1989) – since one of its fundamental axioms, the axiom of independence, implies the dynamic coherence of choices (Strotz, 1956; Hammond, 1988). In this view, a rational agent makes the optimal choice in the initial period, taking into account all the final conse-

quences of each possible choice profile. He or she then tries to avoid any change
of choice profile since this would reduce its expected utility, even by adopting
strategies of precommitment, as in the classic case of Ulysses and the Sirens
(Elster, 1979), or of drug addiction (Hammond, 1976). According to Strotz
(1956), a rational agent is prepared to pay so as to avoid intertemporal
incoherence. In other words, the intertemporal coherence of choice by EU decision theory implies a preference for intertemporal rigidity, or a negative preference for flexibility, which would exclude the existence of positive quasi-option
values.

However, EU decision theory is not applicable in situations characterized by
hard uncertainty[9] and irreversibility, as it requires that the decision-maker knows
all the possible choices and states of nature at any date and all the possible
consequences of actions, as well as their utility and probability. These hypotheses
are acceptable only in cases of soft uncertainty, when the relevant probability
distributions are known and stationary. This is clearly excluded by the joint
assumptions of hard uncertainty and irreversibility which underlie intertemporal
option values, for a host of reasons:

- Preferences may change, and we do not know when and how.
- The set of possible actions may change as a consequence of irreversible
  actions, but we cannot forecast when and how.
- The consequences of the choices are partly unknown and the probabilities
  of those which are known are unreliable.
- A rational agent has a preference for the early resolution of uncertainty.[10]

Strotz himself had a clear intuition of the limits of his suggested strategy of
precommitment:

> What needs to be explained is not that people do precommit their future actions, but
> that the practice is not still more wide-spread. The reason it is not, I believe, is
> because of the presence of risk and uncertainty, both as to future tastes and future
> opportunities. Because of risk and uncertainty people are also willing to pay
> for options permitting them a greater range of choice at future dates and this is
> of overwhelming importance, especially as it affects the detailed aspects of
> future behaviour.

It should be emphasized that the concepts of rationality underlying mainstream
decision theory and that underlying the existence of positive quasi-option values
are quite different. EU theory rests on *substantive* rationality, as the decision
maker is able to choose the optimal choice profile which, by definition, will never
be regretted in the future; intertemporal coherence is nothing but a corollary of
such a conception of rationality. However, as soon as we assume hard uncertainty
and irreversibility, substantive rationality does not apply; we may only adopt
a conception of *procedural* rationality, since the optimal decision strategy
may change as a consequence of learning and can only be approximated by
periodically revising the sequence of choices according to a rational rule
(Favereau, 1989).

Rigorous foundations for a theory of intertemporal option values and of their measurement require a theory of decision under hard uncertainty based on axioms different from those of EU decision theory. The first to suggest a new set of axioms for decision theory under hard uncertainty, incorporating the hypothesis of (intertemporal) flexibility preference, was T. Koopmans (1964). The fundamental axiom suggested by Koopmans establishes a correlation between the relation of inclusion among sets and preference relation: a set of choices is always preferred to any of its subsets, unless their complement is characterized by "redundant flexibility." Kreps (1979) generalized Koopmans' set of axioms obtaining a representation theorem for flexibility preference based on the idea that more flexibility is preferred only if the extra choices are associated with a larger set of non-redundant information. Further generalizations have been provided by Freixas and Laffont (1984), Freixas (1986), and Suppes (1987). All these contributions still suffer from a few restrictive assumptions. In particular, it is assumed that uncertainty is fully resolved before future choices. The next step is that of generalizing this sort of decision theory to model learning in a satisfactory way.[11] This is particularly important because learning may be properly modelled only in the framework of a decision theory incorporating preference for intertemporal flexibility. In a decision framework characterized by full irreversibility or precommitment, learning is deprived of any strategic value. In the meantime, the existing measures of intertemporal flexibility must be further refined and better founded.

Measures of option value

In the preceding section we identified a wide variety of definitions of option value, with or without modifiers. Sometimes these concepts appear to be close relatives, but sometimes we cannot detect more than a vague kinship. To create some order in this tangled matter, we distinguished two "ideal-types" at the extremes of the spectrum: the plain option value and the intertemporal option value.

The plain option value is the expression of a rational valuation under soft uncertainty ("risk") and depends on the attitude towards (soft) risk, while intertemporal option value (often called "quasi-option value" in the environmental literature) is the expression of a rational valuation under hard uncertainty and is independent of the attitude towards (soft) risk, although it is sensitive to the attitude towards hard risk (or "uncertainty" in the Knightian sense). The option value so defined is basically a static concept although its use may be extended to dynamic problems whenever markets are complete and the decision problem is not a genuinely intertemporal one. The intertemporal option value is an intrinsically dynamic concept as it presupposes incomplete markets and a sequential decision problem which cannot be reduced to an equivalent non-sequential problem. Most definitions of option value suggested so far may be classified in a grey zone between these two ideal-types. We will examine some of them in more detail to assess the robustness of the measures of option value suggested so far.

Marschak and Nelson's measures of flexibility

The seminal contribution of Marschak and Nelson (1962) is the first to suggest a rigorous measure of intertemporal option value and to identify the main problems raised by this attempt. They formulated three alternative measures of flexibility which are at the root of much of the subsequent literature on option value measures. Flexibility is seen as "that characteristic of early decisions in a sequential chain which permits the decision-maker to adjust and take advantage of the information he perceives as time elapses" (Marschak and Nelson, 1962, p. 56). Therefore the measures of flexibility analyzed by Marschak and Nelson may be interpreted as measures of option value.

The first measure explored is connected with the size of the second-stage choice set (Λ_2) feasible in ($t + 1$), when a choice a_1 is made in t. Given this $\Lambda_2(a_1)$ subset, they define "an initial action $a_{1'}$ as more flexible than another action $a_{1''}$ if $\Lambda_2(a_{1''}) \subset \Lambda_2(a_{1'})$" (Marschak and Nelson, 1962, p. 45). In this case, the measure of flexibility depends exclusively on the size of the second-stage choice set: the wider the second-stage set of feasible choices, the more flexible the initial choice. This is fully consistent with intuition. Unfortunately, this measure is not fully satisfactory, since it does not permit a unequivocal ranking of the initial actions according to the degree of flexibility so defined. In fact, although $\Lambda_2(a_{1''}) \subset \Lambda_2(a_{1'})$, many actions in $\Lambda_2(a_{1'})$ may be "more expensive if $a_{1'}$ is taken initially than if $a_{1''}$ is taken" (Marschak and Nelson, 1962, p. 45).

The second measure is based on the payoff of a given initial action a_1 and on second-stage actions. In this case, the payoff π is given by the difference between the revenue R, depending on the state of the world w and the second-stage action a_2, and the cost C of switching from a_1 to a_2.

$$\pi = R(w, a_2) - C(a_2, a_1)$$

Then, given two initial actions, $a_{1'}$ is more flexible than $a_{1'}$ if

1   given any number $\alpha > 0$, there exists an action a_2 such that

$$C_2(a_2, a_{1''}) - C_2(a_2, a_{1'}) > \alpha$$

2   there exists a number $\alpha^* \geqq 0$ such that for all a_2

$$C_2(a_2, a_{1'}) - C_2(a_2, a_{1''}) \leqq \alpha^*$$

From these inequalities "the amount by which the more flexible action can turn out to have the lower cost is unbounded; the amount by which the less flexible action can turn out to have the lower cost is bounded" (Marschak and Nelson, 1962, p. 46).

The third measure extends the logic of the second measure to situations in which the payoff function cannot be expressed as a difference between a revenue and a cost. An initial action $a_{1'}$ is more flexible than $a_{1''}$ if

1   given any number $\beta > 0$, there exists a signal z_2 such that

$$\pi^*(z_2, a_{1'}) - \pi^*(z_2, a_{1''}) > \beta$$

2   there exists a number $\beta^* > 0$ such that for all z_2

$$\pi^*(z_2, a_{1''}) - \pi^*(z_2, a_{1'}) \leqq \beta^*$$

Therefore "the amount by which $a_{1'}$ can turn out to be better is bounded from below but not from above" (Marschak and Nelson, 1962, p. 46).

All these measures are ordinal and they have partial applicability, since "they permit ranking of some pairs of initial actions with respect to flexibility but not all pairs" (Marschak and Nelson, 1962, p. 45). According to Marschak and Nelson, the second and third measures never contradict the intuitive notion, best captured by the first measure, "that an action which permits all the alternatives that another permits, and more besides, is the more flexible of the two" (p. 57). However, there is a possible tension between the first definition, based on the size of option sets, and the other two, based on the amount of reversal costs, as clearly emerges from the definition of Jones and Ostroy (1984) which combines the two (see page 103). The criterion of the size of option sets must be made relative to a certain maximum reversal cost, but the ranking of options may change with different thresholds. As will become clear in the rest of this paper, none of the existing measures seems able to overcome this problem.

Environmental measures

A further step towards a clear distinction between option value and intertemporal option value comes from environmental economics.

Arrow and Fisher (1974) proved that whenever uncertainty is assumed, "even where it is not appropriate to postulate risk aversion in evaluating an activity, something of the feel of risk-aversion is produced by a restriction on reversibility of decision" (p. 318). Therefore, assuming risk-neutrality, they were able to identify "a quasi-option value having an effect in the same direction as risk aversion, namely, a reduction in net benefits from development" (p. 315).

To define the notion of "quasi-option value," Arrow and Fisher work out a very simple two-period model where the decision-maker is uncertain about the future state of nature and faces two feasible choices, one of which is irreversible while the other is reversible. Then they calculate the net expected benefits of the irreversible and reversible choices, whether a given event, favourable to the irreversible decision, occurs or not. The difference in conditional expected benefits between the irreversible and reversible choice gives the net benefit of the irreversible choice; whenever this measure is positive, it is optimal to choose the irreversible choice (development of the area) in the first period. They repeat the same sort of evaluation procedure assuming that the decision maker replaces the uncertain variables with their expected values and find that "the expected value of benefits under uncertainty is seen to be less than the value of benefits under certainty" (p. 317). The value of this difference is named "quasi-option value" and is related to the possibility, permitted by the reversible choice and not by the irreversible choice, of acquiring and exploiting further information before the second-period decision. This "irreversibility effect" clearly identifies what we have called an "intertemporal option value" although, in the Arrow and Fisher model, soft uncertainty is assumed. This precludes the analysis of further factors which may influence the intertemporal option value, as for example the subjective attitude towards hard uncertainty, which should be sharply distinguished by the attitude towards "risk."

The same year, independently of Arrow and Fisher, Henry (1974a, b) published two seminal articles which further clarify what Arrow and Fisher had called "quasi-option value," although from a slightly different perspective. Henry (1974a) proved that the coexistence of uncertainty and irreversibility prevents the use of the standard certainty-equivalence methods to solve decision problems, even when the payoff function is quadratic. He also clarified that, given an uncertain future, available indivisible decisions and a sequential decision process in which uncertainty may be reduced by incremental information, the "existence of a positive option value is a very general property, true whatever the number of periods, the way of coming to fuller information, the intertemporal shape of utility function and the lesser or greater the uncertainty of the benefits and costs" (Henry, 1974b, p. 94).

The contributions of Henry are an important step in the direction of a clarification of the concept of intertemporal option value. However, the measure suggested suffers from a few shortcomings. In particular, even in this case, the influence of different modalities of uncertainty is not explored. This is unfortunate because the coexistence of irreversibility and learning is hardly consistent with soft uncertainty and, in any case, learning may have different features and a different value with different modalities of uncertainty. Therefore, only the case of independent learning can be considered.

As we have seen already, the subsequent literature on environmental option values has somewhat further developed the seminal ideas of Arrow and Fisher and Henry, but the measures of sequential option value suggested so far are still quite unsatisfactory. In the remaining part of this section, we explore whether some useful suggestions may come from the monetary and financial literature which, in its turn, has tried to develop a measure of sequential option value related to liquidity preference and negotiable financial options.

Monetary and financial measures

As mentioned earlier, monetary and financial theory tried to define measures of option values even before the environmental literature attempted to do so. The monetary and financial measures suggested so far may be classified in two broad categories: objective and subjective measures. The objective measures try to work out an "operational" measure independent of the individual characteristics of the decision maker. This is appealing because it would greatly simplify the application of the theory to actual choices. However, according to a few authors, this target is utopian if not misleading. In their opinion, less ambitious but more robust subjective measures should be worked out. We will now consider in some detail a selected sample of these two categories of measures.

Objective measures

The idea of a measure independent of the subjective characteristics of the decision maker is certainly appealing, because it would avoid ambiguities while improving the robustness of option value theory. It is therefore worthwhile to evaluate the success of the efforts made in this direction.

The important contribution of Jones and Ostroy (1984) is a very comprehensive and illuminating synthesis of the preceding literature on option values and also takes the environmental literature into account. In particular, they establish a connection between an ordering based on the variability of a decision maker's beliefs, and an ordering of current actions, or positions, based on flexibility. In sequential decision problems, a clear behavioral principle emerges: "the more variable are a decision maker's beliefs, the more flexible in the position he will choose. This principle potentially applies whenever (i) there will be opportunities to act after further information is received, and (ii) current actions influence either the attractiveness or availability of different future actions" (Jones and Ostroy, 1984, p. 13).

Jones and Ostroy assume a set of states of the world (S) and a set of messages (Y), each element $s \in S$ and $y \in Y$ having a probability measure. Given the sets of possible probability vectors on states (Ω_S) and messages (Ω_Y), naming $(\Omega_S)^Y$ the set of conditional distributions of s given y, Jones and Ostroy denote a belief conditional on the message y with $\pi(y) \in \Omega_S$. The set of conditional beliefs is termed "information structure" (Γ, q) as in Marschak and Miyasawa (1968). On this basis, Jones and Ostroy compare two information structures and define a partial ordering based on the variability of beliefs. To define a belief more variable than another, they propose using the (gross) value of the information structure or regarding (Γ, q) as an "experiment" in Blackwell's sense (1951, 1953). The gross value of the information structure is the maximum expected utility, and a structure is more informative than another if its gross value is not inferior to that of the other structure. In the second case, the structure is defined by its likelihood matrix (Bohnenblust, Shapley and Sherman, 1949): an information structure Y is more informative than another structure Y' if the convex hull $K(W_Y^W)$ of the set W_Y^W contains $W_{Y'}^W$ for all w.[12] Jones and Ostroy (1984) assume the switching cost function

$$G(a, s, \alpha) \equiv \{b: c(a, b, s) \leqq \alpha\}, a \in \Lambda, b \in B, s \in S, \alpha \geqq 0$$

such that:

1   $G(a, s, \alpha) = 0$, if $\alpha < 0$ for $(a, s) \in \Lambda XS$ (non-negative switching costs);
2   there exists a $g: A \rightarrow B$ such that $g(a) \in G(a, s, 0)\ \forall\ (a, s) \in \Lambda XS$ (zero switching cost alternative).

Using G, they define a partial order on Λ, such that position a is more flexible than a' if, given $a \geqq 0$ and $s \in S$

$$G(a', s, \alpha)\backslash g(a') \subset G(a, s, \alpha);$$

that is "the set of positions attainable from a always contains the set attainable from a', excluding its zero cost option $g(a')$" (ibidem, p. 17).

Combining the two partial orderings, they derive a net payoff function, additive in both costs and returns, that represents the result of a sequential decision process. From the strategy that maximizes the expected total payoff

$$J(\Gamma, q) = \max_{a \in \Lambda}[r^*(a) + \Lambda(a; \Gamma, q)]$$

Jones and Ostroy derive the following order-preserving relation:[13] if $(\Gamma, q) \geq (\Gamma', q')$ and $a \geq a'$ then

$$V(a; \Gamma, q) - V(a; \Gamma', q') \geqq V(a'; \Gamma, q) - V(a'; \Gamma', q')$$

The crucial assumption for the validity of this order-preserving relationship between variability and flexibility, is that the difference of two convex functions

$$v(a; \pi) - v(a'; \pi)$$

is also convex. Therefore "when all positions are perfectly flexible, the optimal initial position is that which offers the highest expected first period return . . . when all positions are economically irreversible, the optimal position depends only on prior beliefs π^* . . . an increase in the variability of beliefs raises the value of any position relative to any economically irreversible position" (ibidem, p. 20).

The approach of Jones and Ostroy engenders a few technical perplexities. The first problem is in regard to the possibility of deriving a net payoff function. In fact, the function that distinguishes between the monetary profit of a decision and the monetary cost associated with a message not only presupposes a linear utility function for money, but may also reverse the preference ordering. In fact, whenever the net payoff w_y is decomposed into gross payoff w and information costs $\mu(y)$, then:

1   $w_y(z, d, y) = w(z, d) - \mu(y)$ such that for any $k \in \mathbb{R}_+$
2   $k > U_y(Y; w_y) - U_{y'}(Y'; w_{y'}) \geq 0$

and "it is always possible to imagine information cost functions $k(y)$, $k'(y')$ that would reverse the second inequality in [2 above]" (Marschak and Miyasawa,

1968, p. 149). That is, another pair of net payoff functions $w_y^\wedge$ and $w_{y'}^\wedge$ exists such that

$$U_y(Y; w_y^\wedge) - U_{y'}(Y', w_{y'}^\wedge) < 0$$

In this way, the preference ordering cannot be preserved. Since the structure of the net payoff function is fundamental in the definition of ordering of alternatives, its rebuttal would have a devastating effect on the model.

The second technical problem is connected with the role of switching costs to determine the objective measure of flexibility. If "an agent is interested in the costs of a change in asset position only for states at which he [or she] will find it optimal to change [then] the agent may regard a chosen a as more flexible than another without satisfying the Jones and Ostroy criterion" (Hahn, 1990, p. 72). In addition, as it was rightly observed by Hahn (1990), the assumption of convexity of the difference between the variability of belief function and the flexibility function looks arbitrary.[14]

Jones and Ostroy show a clear understanding of the need to distinguish between two different concepts of option value (or "liquidity preference"): one expresses behaviour towards "risk" (as in the famous paper by Tobin, 1958), the other (which corresponds to what was called here "intertemporal option value") expresses behaviour toward "uncertainty" (as stressed by Hart, 1942; Hicks, 1974):

> One individual might value flexibility because, by appropriately adapting choices to the information received, it permits a more nearly certain pecuniary reward; but another might value it because it allows the making of informed higher risk bets at the last moment. The way flexibility is used to exploit forthcoming information may be dictated by attitudes toward risk; but flexible positions are attractive not because they are safe stores of value, but because they are good stores of options (Jones and Ostroy, 1984, p. 14).

Therefore, Jones and Ostroy correctly emphasize that the second meaning of option value, intertemporal option value, is "basically unconnected with risk aversion" (Jones and Ostroy, 1984, p. 14). Unfortunately, in Jones and Ostroy's paper, the analysis of the role of hard uncertainty is quite rudimentary. In particular, the degree of hard uncertainty is measured by an index of dispersion of second-order probability distributions, interpreted as an index of variability of beliefs. Even neglecting the criticism raised against this sort of measure of uncertainty (see Vercelli, 1994, and the literature there cited), its application requires the assumption of identical prior beliefs of decision makers, which is a very controversial assumption in the case of soft uncertainty (Kurz, 1993) and appears altogether unacceptable in the case of hard uncertainty.

We now turn to Lippman and McCall (1986). They explicitly look for an operational measure of liquidity, or financial flexibility (interpreted as the expected time to convert an asset into cash), in the framework of a search model. In fact, "in a simple search model (with timeless search), a set of initially available assets with exponential offer distributions and a subsequently available golden asset, the risk-neutral investor improves his [or her] expected return by selecting a more liquid asset for his [or her] initial investment" (Lippman and McCall, 1986, p. 54). In this approach, an agent maximizes the expected discounted value of the net proceeds associated with the sale of the asset. The liquidity of the asset is the "expected time until the asset is sold when following the optimal policy" (p. 44).

If $R(\delta)$ are the discounted net receipts associated with a stopping time δ of the search, the agent chooses a stopping rule δ^* in the set T of all stopping rules such that the expected return (ER) is given by:

$$ER(\delta^*) = \max\{ER(\delta) : \delta \in T\}$$

$V^* = ER(\delta)$ is the value of the asset, and the random variable δ^* is the length of time to convert the asset into money. The variable δ^* determines the liquidity of the asset. Lippman and McCall suggest employing $E\delta^*$ as "the measure of an asset's liquidity with an increase in $E\delta^*$ corresponding to a decrease in liquidity" (Lippman and McCall, 1986, p. 45); therefore, if $E\delta^* = 0$, liquidity is perfect, while if $E\delta^* = \infty$, illiquidity is perfect.

The model shows that:

1   an increase in the market interest rate and the asset holder's time preference (lowest value of the discount rate) leads to an increase in asset liquidity
2   the market thickness for an asset directly influences the liquidity
3   the asset's liquidity is a growing function of its predictability.

When future opportunities differ from current opportunities, the agent avoids investments with high $E\delta^*$ (illiquidity), and prefers to have more flexible assets in his portfolio. Therefore, this model leads to a portfolio behaviour similar to that of Jones and Ostroy.

However, the approach of Lippman and McCall is also not fully convincing. First, the saving decisions are analyzed independently of investment decisions, so that it is restricted to considering the effect of uncertainty on a portfolio's composition, given the saving decisions. Second, they arbitrarily neglect the subjective factors, such as the attitude towards risk and uncertainty. As correctly observed by F. Hahn, it "is the frequent abstraction from risk aversion by (implicitly) assuming that utility functions are linear [that] leads Lippman and McCall to claim that they have found an operational measure of liquidity, i.e. one that is independent of the agent" (Hahn, 1990, p. 64). Third, the statement that all agents face similar costs of search and distribution of offers seems very dubious when we consider that the discount rate of each agent affects $E\delta^*$, and consequently also the measure of liquidity, through the effect on the reservation price and thus on the decision rule.

According to Pindyck (1991), an irreversible investment opportunity can be seen as a financial call option which "gives us the right (which we need not exercise) to make an investment expenditure (the exercise price of the option) and receive a project (a share of stock) the value of which fluctuates stochastically"

(p. 1114). The exercise of this opportunity (investment) is irreversible because it "kills" the option. The comparison between an irreversible investment opportunity and a call option on common stock allows, in some cases, the extension of standard pricing methods to the estimate of the option value of a decision. However, before extending this methodology to the investment decisions, we have to know whether the markets are complete (the decision to invest does not affect the opportunity set that is available to investors) or if there are missing markets.

Assuming complete markets, we can obtain an estimate of option value independent of the agent's preferences and of the expected return of decision by risk arbitrage, given the Black- Scholes conditions (1973). Let us assume that C is the sunk cost of irreversible investment, and $F = F(S, C)$ the project worth, where S (competitive spot price of the single commodity produced) is assumed to follow the exogenously given continuous stochastic process:

$$\frac{dS}{S} = \mu dt + \sigma dz$$

where dz is the increment of a standard Gauss and Wiener process, σ is the instantaneous standard deviation of the spot price and μ is the trend in price.

Since, in this case, the stochastic changes in S are spanned by existing assets, "it is possible to find an asset or construct a dynamic portfolio of assets (i.e. a portfolio whose holdings are adjusted continuously as asset prices change), the price of which is perfectly correlated with S" (Pindyck, 1991, p. 1119). The agent can estimate the value of investment and the option value by applying the method of contingent claims. In fact, by constructing a replicant risk-free portfolio of the investment project, the agent can estimate the option value and find the rule for optimum investment.[15]

The analogy between an irreversible investment opportunity and a call option on a given stock, suggests the extension of financial option pricing methods to the estimate of environmental option value. However, although the use of these measures may be partially extended to problems typically analyzed by intertemporal option values (problems involving irreversibility and learning), this possibility is very limited because a correct application of Pyndick's stochastic methods requires the assumption of complete markets and soft uncertainty.

Subjective measures

The shortcomings of the "objective" measures of option value has led a few authors to regard the search for an "operational" measure of option value as utopian and misleading. They tried instead to define "subjective" measures of option values and work out statements concerning option values as robust as possible, i.e. valid under wide subjective assumptions.

Goldman's (1974, 1978) analysis focuses on variable consumer preferences which depend upon the observation of a random event describing the "state of the world." Goldman (1974) aims to clarify why an agent holds money (without return) when other assets yield higher rates of return. He works out a simple theoretical model in which an agent (consumer) has to decide the allocation of wealth across different assets to maximize expected utility. This model of portfolio selection involves a sequential decision process with learning, uncertainty (since the consumer faces the prospect of stochastic bargains) and switching costs. The consumer has to select a particular allocation of his wealth, between money and interest-bearing assets, before gaining precise knowledge of his preferences.

Goldman analyzes a two-period model where the consumer's preferences depend on the state of the world. The consumer has to allocate his given wealth between money and other assets before learning his exact preferences. Once a choice is made in the first period, the possibility of modifying the allocation depends on the flexibility of his portfolio, as the consumer can revise his consumption flow only "by selling assets subject to transaction costs or by carrying his unspent balances" (Goldman, 1974, p. 213). Given an *a priori* feasible consumption (choice) set, Goldman describes the upper and lower bounds of this flexibility measure by defining total flexibility, a situation in which a coincidence exists between *ex-ante* and *ex-post* choice sets, "no opportunities have been lost by initial allocation," and complete inflexibility when the *ex-post* choice set coincides with the particular choice initially selected (p. 214). The desire for portfolio flexibility, *ceteris paribus*, induces the individual "to raise (lower) his holdings of money where the interest rate is low (high) . . . further, on the average, the desire to maintain flexibility renders the demand for money more sensitive to the interest rate than would be expected from time preferences alone" (p. 213). Goldman shows that flexibility is not the property of a particular asset (such as money), but relates to the "opportunities" (or options) for consumption flow revision.

In 1978, Goldman extended this approach to the case of a multiplicity of assets having different expected returns and transaction costs (for sale prior to maturity). The agent, whose utility function is assumed to have zero elasticity of substitution, has to compromise between immediate return and liquidity. The measure of option value suggested by Goldman suffers from many limitations. First, it cannot be applied to entire portfolios since in this case "the ordering cannot be complete as there will always be noncomparable portfolios" (Goldman, 1978, p. 271). Second, it applies only to soft uncertainty, since the random variable is characterized by a known probability distribution. Third, learning is limited to the observation of the realization of the random variable. Since uncertainty is soft, the sequential nature of the decision problem is not essential. We may conclude that Goldman's measure may be interpreted as a measure of plain option value examined in its intertemporal implications.

While Goldman's model is developed in a partial equilibrium framework, Hahn (1990) works out a subjective measure of option value in a general equilibrium framework.

Hahn postulates a perfect market economy in which, for every state and date, all assets have well-defined prices; these prices are functions of the state and date. The decision maker is assumed to have a three-period time horizon: in $t = 1$, the agent receives a money income $y(s_1)$ and zero assets; he can trade but he sells all assets in $t = 3$, $a(s_3) = 0$. The agent is uncertain about the true future state of the world and he has a separable von Neuman utility function with discount factor δ, $(0 < \delta < 1)$. Let

$k(b, a, s)$ be the switching cost from a to b $(a, b \in R_t^m)$ in, state s, with $k(a', a, s) = 0 \ \forall \ s$ if a' differs from a only in money

$q(s_t) \in R_t^m$ be the price vector of assets at s_t

$c(s_t) \in R_t^l$ be the agent's consumption (l goods) vector at s_t

$p(s_t)$ be the money vector

$\alpha(s_t) = (c(s_t), a(s_t))$

The agent makes his choice by solving a problem of constrained maximization (Hahn, 1990, pp. 66–9). Since the idea of liquidity is related to the cost of reversing a position, "in the present context this suggests that the cost of selling an asset in a second period which was bought in the first should play a [crucial] role" (p. 71). Then Hahn defines an index T of the illiquidity of a portfolio that measures "the maximum an agent would be prepared to pay to escape reversal costs" (Hahn, 1990, p. 71). The value of T will be smaller when the variability of beliefs of the agent is higher. In any case, the value of T depends on the subjective characteristics of the agent.

Hahn shows that, in this model, money commands a liquidity premium σ over any asset. This premium "is due to the possibility that an asset brought at one date and state is optimally sold at a future date and state and so incurs the cost of selling" (p. 77). It is possible to achieve another ordering of assets "by utilizing the premium σ an asset must earn over money if that asset is to be bought in an optimum plan" (p. 74). Using this premium, an asset j is more liquid than an asset k if and only if $\sigma_j < \sigma_k$.

Hahn rightly observes that the recognition of the importance of transaction costs, implied by liquidity considerations "leads us to conclude that agents will maximize, subject to a number of, rather than a single, budget constraints" (p. 65), and this may be used to account for missing markets. However, it is questionable whether this correct observation is consistent with the kind of soft uncertainty assumed in the model (as an event tree characterized by known probability distributions; see p. 66). Climbing this event tree, uncertainty resolves independently of the will of the learning decisions of the agent. This assumption prevents a deeper analysis of the nexus between the value of liquidity (option value) and the modalities of learning. We may conclude by observing that Hahn's measure should be interpreted as a measure of option value rather than of intertemporal option value.

Financial and environmental measures of option values

The study of monetary and financial concepts of option value may be of some interest for the analysis of environmental option values, taking into account the profound conceptual analogies. In particular, the effort of producing an "operational measure" of different varieties of option value is more developed in the monetary and financial field than in the environmental field. Any advance in this direction would also be important for environmental applications. Unfortunately, the recent attempts surveyed in this paper do not seem completely successful. The measures suggested so far are only ordinal and are based on a few arbitrary technical assumptions. In addition, the illusion of an operational measure is obtained only by abstracting from subjective factors which crucially influence option values according to theoretical and experimental considerations. However, the approach in terms of stochastic processes surveyed and developed by Pindyck is a potentially fertile research program as far as plain option values are concerned. Unfortunately, the assumption of complete markets and soft uncertainty precludes an application to genuine intertemporal option values which are crucially important in environmental economics. The only financial measure which clearly assumes hard uncertainty is that of Jones and Ostroy which, unfortunately, is spoiled by a few technical shortcomings and by a rudimentary analysis of hard uncertainty which could not take into account advances made after the publication of their paper.

The subjective measures of financial option values are more robust than the objective financial measures from the theoretical point of view, but this approach is so far limited to soft uncertainty and exogenous learning. Thus, the insights which may be drawn from these measures are not easily transferred to the analysis of intertemporal option values which are particularly relevant to environmental problems.

Conclusion

Environmental option values play an important role in any assessment of environmental values for both theoretical and practical purposes, and provide the ultimate foundations for a rational policy directed towards the conservation of environmental resources.

We have surveyed a variety of definitions and measures of option value which may be classified according to a basic dichotomy between plain option value and intertemporal option value. The first concept is relevant when uncertainty is soft and markets complete, as it essentially reflects risk aversion. In this case, a more flexible option commands a sort of risk premium because it is a safe store of values. The second concept is relevant when markets are incomplete, uncertainty is hard, and the decision problem is intertemporal. In this second case, a more flexible option, even under risk neutrality, commands a premium to the extent that it allows the exploitation of prospective learning before subsequent decisions. In the environmental field, intertemporal option values are particularly important because the uncertainty faced is typically hard, and irreversibility is very serious, involving very delicate intertemporal decision problems. Unfortunately, while fairly precise measures may be assigned to plain environmental option values, particularly through the methods developed in financial theory for financial options, intertemporal option values cannot be easily measured. All the measures suggested so far are only ordinal and, what is worse, the ordering of choices according to intertemporal flexibility, which gives the ordering of intertemporal option values, is very sensitive to the specification of the model.

Notwithstanding all the shortcomings underlined in this paper, the theory of intertemporal option values has obtained a few qualitative results which are quite important for environmental conservation. First, it was established that whenever intertemporal options have a positive value, the traditional techniques for selecting the optimum choice and for analyzing problems characterized by uncertainty on the basis of the certainty equivalence approach cannot be safely used because they underestimate the value of environmental resources. Second, it was proved that intertemporal option values are positive under quite general conditions, whenever hard uncertainty and irreversibility coexist, and learning is possible before future choices. Third, the value of an intertemporal option, given a certain degree of hard uncertainty and of irreversibility of choice, depends crucially on the characteristics of prospective learning, on past learning (competence) and on the attitude towards hard uncertainty. In addition, *ceteris paribus*, it depends on the degree of irreversibility (irreversibility effect). Finally, the intertemporal option value increases, under quite general conditions, with the degree of uncertainty. Therefore, the growing awareness of our deep ignorance about the long-term effects of the interaction between economic development and environment, as well as of their irreversibility, should induce a more cautious environmental policy.

Notes

1 Though this paper was jointly written by the authors, Marcello Basili takes responsibility for pages 99–110, and Alessandro Vercelli for the rest of the paper.
2 Empirical work based on contingent valuation confirms a disposition to pay per adult per year for the conservation of environmental goods as in the following examples:

$8 for the conservation of tropical forests (Markandya, 1991)
$6 for the conservation of the European salmon (*Salmo salar*) in New England (Stevens et al., 1991)
$28 for the conservation of a rare kind of eagle (*Haliaetus leucocephalus*) in New England (Stevens et al., 1991).
A general survey of this sort of empirical estimation may be found in Swanson and Barbier, 1992.

3 Option values and quasi-option values may also be related to possible future changes in non-economic values, but these topics have been neglected so far by the economics literature.
4 A concept similar to that of option value may earlier be found in the concept of "prospective utility" analyzed by Jevons (1888); see Moretti (1993a).
5 Irreversibility is also sometimes considered in the literature on option value, but its role is not clearly spelled out.
6 Another magnitude conceptually close to (quasi-)option value is the "value of waiting"

which is analyzed mainly so as to choose the optimal starting time for a new project or investment. The value of waiting may be regarded as a special case of (quasi-)option value when a subset of two alternatives (to start the investment or to postpone it) is involved; see, for example, McDonald and Siegel (1986).

7   In monetary theory, the distinction was already quite clear in Keynes (1936) who distinguished between precautionary liquidity related to probability ("risk" in the Knightian sense) and speculative liquidity related to the weight of evidence ('uncertainty" in the Knightian sense). In this view, precautionary liquidity plays the role of a risk-premium, when speculative liquidity is best interpreted in terms of preference for intertemporal flexibility (Hicks, 1974). A similar dichotomy was emphasized by Makower and Marschak (1938), who distinguished between two properties of liquidity: safety and plasticity.

8   It is necessary to speak of uncertainty neutrality or aversion rather than of risk neutrality or aversion, since irreversibility implies hard uncertainty. An analysis of a few measures of uncertainty aversion may be found in Montesano (1993).

9   Uncertainty may be defined "hard" whenever it may not be expressed in terms of a unique, additive, fully reliable probability distribution; for a short survey of the recent literature on hard uncertainty orientated towards environmental problems, see Vercelli (1994).

10   This is excluded by EU decision theory which implies indifference to the timing of the resolution of uncertainty; otherwise, the axiom of independence would be contradicted (Willinger, 1990).

11   A first attempt is that of Willinger (1988), who defines preferences directly on the modalities of revelation of information.

12   Given an information structure Y and a payoff function w, we can find the set W_Y^w.

13   An increase in the variability of beliefs never leads to the choice of a less flexible position.

14   On the contrary, it is possible to defend the contribution of Jones and Ostroy from another charge of arbitrariness raised by Hahn (1990). The assumption of linearity of the utility function is justified by the assumption of risk neutrality which is meant to distinguish the intertemporal option value, unrelated to risk aversion, from plain option value which crucially depends on risk aversion.

15   Applying Ito's lemma, we derive a partial differential equation of $F(S, C)$ which together with the constraint conditions gives the solution to the choice problem.

References

Arrow, K. J. (1971) *Essays in the theory of risk-bearing*. Amsterdam: North-Holland.

Arrow, K. J. and Fisher, A. (1974) Environmental preservation, uncertainty and irreversibility. *Quarterly Journal of Economics*, 89, 312–19.

Black, F. and Scholes, M. (1973) The pricing of options and corporate liabilities. *Journal of Political Economy*, 81, 637–54.

Blackwell, D. (1951) The composition of experiments. *Proceedings of the Second Berkeley Symposium on Mathematical Statistics and Probability*. University of California Press.

Blackwell, D. (1953) Equivalent comparison of experiments. *Annals of Mathematics and Statistics*, 24, 265–72.

Bohenblust H. F., Shapley, L. S. and Sherman, S. (1949) *Reconnaissance in Game Theory*, RM 208. The Rand Corporation.

Bohm, P. (1975) Option demand and consumer's surplus: comment. *Am. Econ. Rev.*, 65, 733–7.

Brun, W. and Teigen, K. (1990) Predication and postdiction inferences in guessing. *Journal of Behavioural Decision Making*, 3, 17–28.

Caballero, R. (1991) On the sign of the investment-uncertainty relationship. *American Economic Review*, 81, pp. 279–88.

Camerer, C. and Weber, M. (1992) Recent developments in modeling preferences: Uncertainty and ambiguity. *Journal of Risk and Uncertainty*, 5, 325–70.

Cicchetti, C. and Freeman, A. M. (1971) Option demand and consumer surplus: further comment. *Quarterly Journal of Economics*, 85, pp. 523–37.

Cohendet, P. and Llerena, P. (eds) (1989) *Flexibilité, information et decision*. Paris: Economica.

Curley, S. P., Young, M. J. and Abrams, R. A. (1986) Psychological sources of ambiguity avoidance. *Organizational Behaviour and Human Decision Processes*, 38, 230–56.

Elster, J. (1979) *Ulysses and the Sirens, Studies in Rationality and Irrationality*. Cambridge University Press.

Epstein, L. (1980) Decision making and temporal resolution of uncertainty. *International Economic Review*, 21, 269–83.

Favereau, O. (1989) Valeur d'option et flexibilité: de la rationalité substantielle a la rationalité procédurale. In P. Cohendet, and P. Llerena (1989).

Fellner, W. (1961) Distortion of subjective probabilities as a reaction to uncertainty. *Quarterly Journal of Economics*, 75, 670–94.

Fisher, A. and Hanemann, M. (1987) Quasi-option value: Some misconceptions dispelled. *Journal of Environmental Economics and Management*, 14, 183–90.

Freeman, A. M. (1985) Supply uncertainty, option price, and option value. *Land Econ.*, 61 (2), 176–81.

Freixas, X. (1986) L'effet-irréversibilité généralisé. In M. Boiteux, T. De Montbrial and B. Munier (eds) *Marchés, Capital et Incertitude, Essais en l'honneur de Maurice Allais*. Paris: Economica.

Freixas, X. and Laffont, J. J. (1984) On the irreversibility effect. In M. Boyer and R. E. Kihistrom (eds) *Bayesian Models in Economic Theory*. Amsterdam: North-Holland, 105–44.

Frisch, D. and Baron, J. (1988) Ambiguity and rationality. *Journal of Behavioural Decision Making*, 1, 149–57.

Goldman, M. (1974) Flexibility and the demand for money. *Journal of Economic Theory*, 9, 203–22.

Goldman, M. (1978) Portfolio choice and flexibility. *Journal of Monetary Economics*, 4, 263–79.

Hahn, F. (1990) Liquidity. In F. Hahn and M. Friedman (eds) *Handbook of Monetary Economics*. Amsterdam: North-Holland, 63–80.

Hammond, P. (1976) Changing tastes and coherent dynamic choice. *Review of Economic Studies*, 43, 159–73.

Hammond, P. (1988) Consequentialism and the independence axiom. In B. Munier (ed.) *Risk, Decision and Rationality*. D. Reidel Publ. Co., 503–16.

Hanemann, M. (1989) Information and the concept of option value. *Journal of Environmental Economics and Management*, 16, 23–37.

Hart, A. G. (1942) Risk, uncertainty, and the unprofitability of compounding probabilities. In Lange, F. McIntyre and T. O. Yntema, (eds) *Studies in Mathematical Economics and Econometrics*. Chicago: Chicago University Press.

Heath, C. and Tversky, A. (1991) Preference and belief: Ambiguity and competence in choice under uncertainty. *Journal of Risk and Uncertainty*, 4, 5–28.

Henry, C. (1974a) Option values in the economics of irreplaceable assets. *Review of Economic Studies*, 41, 89–104.

Henry, C. (1974b) Investment decision under uncertainty: the irreversible effect. *American Economic Review*, 64, 1006–12.

Hicks, J. (1974) *The Crisis in Keynesian Economics*. New York: Basic Books.

Hogart, R. M. and Einhorn, H. J. (1990) Venture theory: A model of decision weights. *Management Science*, 36, 780–803.

Jevons, S. (1888) *The theory of political economy*. Harmondsworth: Penguin Books, 1970.

Jones, R. and Ostroy, J. (1984) Flexibility and uncertainty. *Review of Economic Studies*, 51, 13–32.

Keppe, H.-J. and Weber, M. (1991) Judged knowledge and ambiguity aversion. Unpublished working paper no 277. Kiel, Germany: Christian-Albrechts Universitat.

Keynes, J. M. (1936) *The General Theory of Employment, Interest and Money*. London: MacMillan.

Koopmans, T. C. (1964) On flexibility of future preferences. In M. Shelly, and G. Bryan (eds) *Human Jand Optimality*. Wiley, 243–54.

Kreps, D. (1979) A representation theorem for preference for flexibility. *Econometrica*, 47, 565–77.

Krutilla, J. (1967) Conservation reconsidered. *American Economic Review*, 57, 776–86.

Kurz, M. (1993) *Rational Preferences and Rational Beliefs*, Stanford University, mimeo.

Langer, E. J. (1975) The illusion of control. *Journal of Personality and Social Psychology*, 32, 311–28.

Lippman, S. and McCall, J. (1986) An operational measure of liquidity. *American Economic Review*, 76, 43–55.

Long, M. (1967) Collective-consumption service of individual-consumption goods: Comment. *Quarterly Journal of Economics*, 81, 351–2.

Makower, H. and Marschak, T. (1938) Assets, prices and monetary theory. *Economica*, 5, 261–88.

Markandya, A. (1991) *The Economic Appraisal of Projects: The Environmental Dimension*. Interamerican Development Bank.

Marschak, T. (1938) Money and theory of asset. *Econometrica*, 6, 311–25.

Marschak, T. (1949) Role of liquidity under complete and incomplete information. *American Economic Review*, 39, 182–95.

Marschak, T. and Miyasawa, K. (1968) Economic comparability of information systems. *International Economic Review*, 9, 137–74.

Marschak, T. and Nelson, R. (1962) Flexibility, uncertainty and economic theory. *Metroeconomica*, 14, 42–58.

McDonald, R. and Siegel, D. (1986) The value of waiting to invest. *Quarterly Journal of Economics*, 101, 707–27.

Miller, J. R. and Lad, F. (1984) Flexibility, learning and irreversibility in environmental decisions: A Bayesian approach. *Journal of Environmental Economics and Management*, 11, 161–72.

Mitchell, R. C. and Carson, R. T. (1989) *Using Surveys to Value Public Goods: The Contingent Valuation Method*. Washington, DC: Resources for the Future.

Montesano, A. (1993) *Non-Additive Probabilities and the Measure of Uncertainty and Risk Aversion*. mimeo.

Moretti, E. (1993a) Irreversibilià e incertezza nei problemi ambientali. Degree Thesis. Milano: Università Bocconi.

Moretti, E. (1993b) *Environmental Irreversibility and Production: A Multiperiodal Model*. mimeo.

Olson, L. J. (1990) Environmental preservation with production. *Journal Of Environmental Economics and Management*, 18, 88–96.

Pindyck, R. (1991) Irreversibility, uncertainty, and investment. *Journal of Economic Literature*, 29, 1110–48.

Plummer, M. L. and Hartman, R. C. (1986) Option value: a general approach. *Economic Inquiry*, 24, 455–70.

Schmalensee, R. (1972) Option demand and consumer's surplus: Valuing price changes, under uncertainty. *American Economic Review*, 62, 813–24.

Smith, V. K. (1983) Option value: a conceptual overview. *Southern Economic Journal*, 654–68.

Stevens, T. H., Echeverria, J., Glass, R., Hager, T. and More, T. A. (1991) Measuring the existence value of wildlife: what do CVM estimates really show? *Land Economics*, 67 (4), 390–400.

Strotz, R. H. (1956) Myopia and inconsistency indynamic utility maximization, *Review of Economic Studies*, 23, 165–80.

Suppes, P. (1987) Maximising freedom of decision: an axiomatic analysis. In G. Fewer (ed.) *Arrow and the Foundations of the Theory of Economic Policy*. MacMillan Press, 243–54.

Swanson, T. M. and Barbier, E. B. (1992) *Economics for the Wilds*. London: Earthscan.

Tobin, J. (1958) Liquidity Preference as Behaviour Towards Risk. *Review of Economic Studies*, 25, 65–86.

Vercelli, A. (1994) Hard uncertainty and environment, Manuscript, Università di Siena.

Vercelli, A. (1998) Hard uncertainty and environmental policy. In G. Chichiluisky, G. M. Heal, and A. Vercelli (eds) *Sustainability: Dynamics and Uncertainty*. Dordrecht: Kluwer Academic Publishers, 191–221.

Viscusi, W. K. and Zeckhauser, R. (1976) Environmental policy choice under uncertainty. *Journal of Environmental Economics and Management*, 3, 97–112.

Weisbrod, B. (1964) Collective-consumption services of individual-consumption goods. *Quarterly Journal of Economics*, 78, 471–7.

Willinger, M. (1988) The foundations of the theory of choice between experiments. Fourth international conference on the Foundations and Applications of Utility, Risk and Decision Theory. Budapest, mimeo.

Willinger, M. (1990) Irréversibilité et cohérence dynamique des choix. *Revue d'Economie Politique*, 100 (6), 808–32.

6
Risk and Uncertainty in Environmental Policy Evaluation

Tony Ward

This chapter examines received treatment of risk and uncertainty in the cost-benefit analysis (CBA) of environmental issues.[1] The essay argues that, for several reasons, existing approaches to the evaluation of uncertainty are inappropriate. Developments in the theory of risk may ameliorate some of the problems. However CBA was developed for a social objective of growth, whereas those concerned with the environment now seek "sustainable development." Sustainability inherently involves criteria of distribution rather than efficiency, so the utilitarian CBA framework is not appropriate. Fundamental changes to the approach to project evaluation are therefore required to attain this new objective.

The evolution of social objectives

When the technique of CBA was first developed in the 1950s, the consensus was that the needs of society were for the expansion of production, to be engineered primarily through the creation of produced physical capital. This would result in increased per-capita output and income. CBA was developed to appraise the net social impact of such production investment projects, and as such was an appropriate evaluation tool. The technique however ignores questions of equity, on the assumption that they will be dealt with by subsequent redistribution, if at all.[2] The underlying ethic, as for most micro-economic analysis of the time, was utilitarian, aiming only for the maximization of total output.

During the later 1960s and 1970s, the objective of development superseded that of growth, particularly in less developed countries. Satisfaction of human needs became more important, so that the distributive aspects of a project had to be considered at an earlier stage. Decisions were then no longer made solely on the basis of the expected net output of a project. CBA techniques were not ideal for this new perspective, but it was to some extent feasible to measure the distributional implications of each possible project separately from its net benefits, and to rank alternatives accordingly. The Hicks-Kaldor (HK) principle of potential compensation on which CBA is based does not require that this redistribution be carried out, and only rarely is it done.

In the 1990s, the emphasis shifted from "development" to "sustainable development." The implied objective of development was that all people currently directly affected by a project should share in its benefits, and projects were selected because of their contribution to social and economic goals. Sustainable development has a wider perspective. It is inherently a distributional issue – the sharing of resources among both current and future people.

There are many alternative definitions of sustainable development, the simplest and most common of which is that coined in the Brundtland Report, which calls for "development that meets the needs of the present generation without compromising the ability of future generations to meet their own needs"(WCEB, 1990, p. 43). The many versions of this reflect a basic obligation to consider the needs of the future, as well as today's wants. Project evaluation therefore has to incorporate in some "willingness to pay" measure the viewpoints of people who cannot represent themselves directly at the evaluation. The question then is how to reflect these peoples' interests in the CBA. Any framework for doing so has to have explicit ethical foundations. In the past, it has been customary to discount the needs of future people to the point at which any effects that occur after about twenty or thirty years are irrelevant. The criterion of sustainability now inherently precludes us from doing this, and also from discounting outcomes because they are not certain to occur.

This is a fundamental change from the assumptions behind standard CBA, particularly for projects with important environmental implications. In many instances of the exploitation of natural or environmental resources, the stock of the resource is finite. Many renewable resources also have limited sustainable flows. In such cases, there is no way in which all current and future people can share equally in its use. In the past, this intractability was dealt with by discounting future benefits, thereby in effect eliminating future generations from enjoyment of the resource. For reproducible assets or those with good substitutes, this was not totally inappropriate, although there were dissenting voices even on these issues.

However, for environmental resources, particularly ones that provide basic life-support services such as air and water, no ethical criteria that incorporates the rights of future people can support that perspective. The objective of sustainable development therefore prohibits the use of discounting for time or uncertainty in the allocation of environmental resources. Establishment of sustainable development policies therefore inherently requires the establishment of explicit ethical criteria, which have not been present in past applications of CBA.

Risk and uncertainty in CBA

Progression from a social objective of growth to one of development, and now to sustainable development is vital for the future. The transition, however, is very difficult, both for theoretical and practical reasons. The mixed economic system used in most democracies can be justified on the basis of efficiency, in that output is maximized. However, the price of that efficiency is a total disregard for equity. Any point on the contract curve is Pareto optimal. Sustainable development, though, inherently involves considerations of justice. All definitions of sustainability entail the consideration of future generations. Equity between generations and between members of the same generation becomes the primary consideration, with efficiency becoming subsidiary to that. Existing economic paradigms are not pertinent to the evaluation of these objectives, and many researchers are working to revise economic theory to reflect a non-static world that cannot operate in isolation from its surrounding natural environment.

There are many well-documented problems with CBA; see for example the chapter in this volume by Willinger. In the context of environmental issues, one particular problem involves the analytical treatment of capital, which is typically regarded as having acceptable substitutes. Standard CBA tools may be appropriate for evaluating the generation of new human-produced capital goods as substitutes for current capital equipment. The critical difference between environmental "capital" and human-produced capital though is just that – human-produced capital is at least in principle *re*-producible, and the assumption of substitutability is at least feasible. Humans, however, did not create natural and environmental capital and do not have the ability to create more of it, or to regenerate its original quality characteristics if we despoil it.

Current decisions on environmental issues have complex and highly uncertain implications for the future. Typical CBA of such issues is too simplistic, treating what are wholly uncertain issues as being at least conceptually predictable and quantifiable. By their nature, though, we do not know the probabilities to associate with possible future events, the potential existence of which we may be entirely unaware. The general Bayesian approach of guessing possible sequences of complex, poorly understood phenomena tends to generate underestimates of true probabilities, which is highly inappropriate when applied to potentially disastrous environmental events.

Uncertainty enters environmental assessment in three principal ways. First, there is uncertainty about the occurrence and extent of physical events. Second, there is uncertainty over the chemical and biological effects of these events on human and other forms of life. Last, there is uncertainty about the way in which those people affected evaluate the occurrence of biological or other damage to the environment.

The issue of uncertainty in environmental economics is closely related to that of irreversibility. The main problem is that those policy actions today will have unpredictable impacts on the environment of the future, which frequently will be irreversible. Given the potentially disastrous consequences of some of the issues at stake, careful analysis of the risks we take is vital.

Sustainability inherently involves ethical criteria – assessment and judgement on intertemporal comparisons of well-being. The overriding considerations then are rights rather than utilities, so any evaluation mechanism that supports sustainable development has to be based on ethical criteria. Both actual markets and the pseudo-market of CBA derive their justification from utilitarianism, which ignores rights. These, therefore, are not appropriate mechanisms for attaining sustainability.

The different nature of environmental resources therefore calls for innovative approaches. Unsuitable policy prescriptions arise in part from a failure to distinguish the different types of risk and uncertainty that exist, and partly from the utilitarian moral framework underlying standard marginal economic analysis. Government action cannot eliminate risk, but can and should reduce and redistribute it equitably.

Definitions of risk and uncertainty

Little in human life is certain. When making decisions, we have to assess the alternative possible streams of future events affected by the decision, and choose that which *ex-ante* appears the most attractive. Under some conditions, we can reduce or eliminate some individual uncertainty by purchasing insurance or other financial instruments. In such a case, the issue for the individual is that of risk, in that, through the purchase of insurance, the indeterminacy of the outcome for the individual can be reduced or eliminated.

However, when evaluating environmental policies, this is not usually the case: it may not be possible even to identify some outcomes; we may not know the probabilities of those of which we are aware; or there may be no basis on which to estimate those probabilities. The extent of the damage that would occur under some outcomes may also inherently preclude any form of compensation, due to the impossibility of replacing many environmental assets. It is essential to treat such uncertainty far more carefully than insurable risks, since no current decision can be sure of reducing, let alone minimizing or eliminating, future consequences of the problem.

While the theoretical literature distinguishes between risk and uncertainty, practical CBA rarely does so.[3] To some extent this is due to the difficulty of coping with uncertainty in the existing analytical framework. Another problem is that risk and uncertainty frequently are not carefully differentiated. The distinction is of less concern for commercial projects when viewed from the perspective of the investor. In that case, gains and losses are to a large extent under human control, are inherently bounded between private bankruptcy and private riches, and rarely have wider social implications. For projects with environmental implications, uncertainty is a quite different problem. The incidence of uncertainty as opposed to risk is far more extensive, and the extent of the problems it creates is far greater.

Ruckelhaus (1990) notes that the problem of environmental protection is really that of managing risk. He defines risk-management as "adjusting our environmental policies to obtain the array of social goods – environmental, health-related, social, economic and psychological – that forms our vision of how we want the world to be" (p. 110). The formulation of that vision though is problematic if we cannot predict either the probabilities, the physical outcomes, or the economic values to attribute to the outcomes we are trying to evaluate.

The development of economic analysis of risk and uncertainty
Knight

After comparing existing definitions of risk and uncertainty, this essay will seek
to extend our approach to the issue of uncertainty, so as to incorporate critical
ethical aspects of potential threats to human well-being in a more appropriate
manner. The next section summarizes the development of thought on the definition of uncertainty and its distinction from risk.

Current attitudes to risk and uncertainty originate from the work of Fisher
(1906, 1930), Knight (1921, p. 214ff) and Shackle (1949–50). Knight first clarified the terminology, making the crucial distinction between risk and uncertainty.
He used the term "risk" for situations in which an individual may not know the
outcome of an event, but can form realistic expectations of the probabilities of the
various possible outcomes based either on mathematical calculation or the history
of previous occurrences. These situations may present problems to the individual
but, at the aggregate level, the frequency of each possible outcome is entirely
predictable. Individual problems can be eliminated through insurance or other
financial instruments.

Knight (1921) distinguished risk from the type of uncertainty for which
there exists "no valid basis of any kind for classifying instances" (p. 225). In
other words, an uncertain situation is one in which information about what
all the possible outcomes might be is not available and cannot be obtained,
and the probabilities of those outcomes that can be identified are not known.
This is the most typical, and the most problematic, case for environmental
policy analysis. Often, there is no prior experience of a particular environmental
problem, the effects cannot be identified or quantified, and there can be no
meaningful probability attributed to the likelihood of any particular outcome
occurring.

The distinction between risk and uncertainty in the context of a business can
be illustrated using Knight's criterion of insurability. Knight would classify the
possibility that its premises might burn down as a risk, since the frequency with
which buildings of various types burn can be established by reference to past
occurrences. The incidence of one building catching fire is largely independent of
that of other buildings burning, and the probability of a claim can be estimated
with some accuracy by actuarial analysis. It is therefore straightforward to
buy insurance, and risk-pooling can eliminate such commercial risks at the individual level.

A business also does not know the price at which its product will sell next year,
nor its costs. Exogenous factors such as weather or export demand can also create
problems. Against these problems, the business cannot generally buy insurance.
Therefore, Knight would classify these problems as uncertainty.[4] In part, this
occurs because insurers have no information by which to evaluate the probability
that the event will occur.

The commercial context that Knight was considering involves exchanges between private individuals that have no external implications for society at large.
Consequences are therefore private, and are bounded by the wealth of the parties

to the exchange. There is also greater contemporaneous correlation of losses and a potential for "moral hazard." If a business could insure against loss of market share, there is a danger that those responsible for directing the business would stop working, since their well-being would no longer depend on the level of effort they made.

Insurability is not as good a criterion as Knight suggests. Insurance companies do not rely on historical data nearly as much as a statistical purist might want. A large amount of insurance business is, in reality, gambling – assessing the probability of an event's occurring based on "hunches" rather than science. Therefore, insurability is a poor guide for determining whether an issue constitutes risk rather than uncertainty.

Hirshleifer (1992) sees Knight's distinction as sterile; he regards probability as "simply degree of belief," and considers that decision-makers are "never in Knight's world of risk but instead always in his world of uncertainty" (p. 9). This lack of differentiation, pervasive in CBA, oversimplifies the problems faced when evaluating environmental policy, where information on possible outcomes and their probabilities may be entirely speculative. For many environmental problems, such as those created by toxic chemicals or global warming, there is not sufficient information *ex ante* to estimate the probabilities and impacts of the various outcomes or even to identify all possibilities. The only way to identify the value of a bad outcome accurately is to ignore the danger, allow the damage to occur, and count the dead. In contrast, we can quantify most types of commercial risk with an accuracy that is qualitatively different to that encountered in environmental assessment.

Von Neumann-Morgenstern

Most economic analysis of risk and uncertainty has not been concerned with the source and characteristics of the uncertainty. Instead, it has focused on the simpler task of incorporating a multiplicity of possible outcomes into a decision-making framework. Even Finkel (1990), in an excellent analysis of risk and uncertainty, is sure that all factors in uncertainty can be reduced to uncertainty in the parameters, model, decision rules or variability. The existence of instances in which we have no information whatsoever about possible future implications to the environment from current activities is not considered.[5]

The most common approach to evaluating the implications of risk is the von Neumann–Morgenstern (1944) "expected utility" framework. This attributes particular levels of well-being to the various possible outcomes of risky situations, with human life and suffering entering the calculations on a basis similar to any other change in circumstances. It defines expected utility as the sum of the utility of each of the possible outcomes multiplied by the probability of its occurring. Dislike of risk is classified as "risk aversion," demonstrated by an expected utility function that is concave in income.

As with Knight, the focus of the von Neumann and Morgenstern analysis is on individual, static decisions. Generally, no distinction is made for the effects of the ill-defined probabilities that typically are faced by environmental policy makers.

There is also no penalty for, or proscription of, the possibility of "zero utility" outcomes – the utility often ascribed to death.

The Bayesian approach to von Neumann–Morgenstern expected utility maximization allows for a lack of knowledge of historical probability data. It does so, however, by presuming that decision makers assume that they know the probabilities of future states. This may be viable for individual "insurable-type" risks, but it cannot solve issues of uncertainty at the social level, where information about possible states of nature does not exist, let alone information to assess probabilities of each state.

Recent work

Vercelli (1994) discusses recent work on the classification of risk and uncertainty, and seeks to move away from the connotations associated with the word "risk." He effectively dichotomizes uncertainty into two types – soft and hard. "Soft" uncertainty is similar to Knight's risk, with the probability distribution of all outcomes known, fully reliable and additive. For instances of this type of uncertainty, traditional probability theories can be applied. Vercelli contrasts this with "hard" uncertainty. In that case, the probability distribution does not exist and the issue "cannot be properly analysed by relying only on received wisdom" (p. 1). The lower limiting case of soft uncertainty is certainty, and the upper limit of hard uncertainty is complete ignorance (p. 5).

In summary, for the analysis of environmental issues, information on probabilities is neither a necessary nor a sufficient criterion for the determination of whether an issue constitutes risk or uncertainty. Ongoing monitoring and control are required for many natural and environmental resource projects to ensure that state variables such as stock levels remain within desired limits. As Vercelli suggests, even our theoretical ability to monitor and control complex dynamic systems is highly questionable; see Vercelli, this volume chapter 4. That, combined with a lack of financial and political will to carry through expensive monitoring and enforcement programs, often leads to the failure of otherwise feasible projects. A current case in point is that of many ocean fisheries. In 1994, Canada's East coast fishery for example was in ruins, with devastating consequences for the present and future economy of a poor region. The main reason for the disaster is the failure to manage a renewable resource that could have lasted forever.[6]

The distinction between risk and uncertainty

In this chapter, the term risk is defined as the absence of knowledge of the sequence and specific incidence of future events. If all possible outcomes can be identified and their probabilities estimated, a situation involves risk rather than uncertainty. In contrast, uncertainty is defined as the existence of an unquantified possibility that some future event, the prior existence of which may or may not be identifiable, might occur. The known possible events are not usually exhaustive –

there are gaps in our knowledge, so that completely unexpected events may occur. We may possess no knowledge about the specific likelihood of an uncertain event. For many environmental catastrophes, such a concept may, in fact, have no meaning. The purpose of the distinction is to separate choices over outcomes that could unknowingly lead to disaster, from those that will not.

To cope with making difficult decisions, humans organize and order the information they possess. We have to make estimates of the magnitude of potential problems and of the probability of their occurrence. There is an inevitable human tendency, when doing so, to suppress the problem of the complete absence of knowledge about the possibility of unknown future events. It is not possible to anticipate all eventualities, but neither is it realistic to assume that all possibilities that are not apparent are irrelevant or benign.

A standard example of risk, as opposed to uncertainty, would be that of a public authority making a decision to undertake some road improvement scheme, which would have some implication for safety on the road. At the individual level, there is risk involved in travelling along the stretch of road. The individual driver can, at least in theory, evaluate that risk, when making decisions about whether and how frequently to use the road. (Note that as discussed later in this essay, it is likely that individuals both misperceive the degree of risk, and fail to evaluate the loss of well-being associated with an accident.) However, at the aggregate level of society, the picture is quite different. While no one knows *who* in particular may have an accident on the road, there is little uncertainty about the number of accidents that will occur. Similarly, the existence of excessive amounts of identified toxic substances in air or drinking water will cause health deterioration in some, even if we cannot *ab-initio* identify who will suffer. While ethical considerations should, in these circumstances, be important in evaluating alternative safety programs, the problem is concise, in that the scope of the issues facing the decision maker is known.

By contrast, the construction of a road through a previously unspoilt area would create environmental effects about which there would be uncertainty. Disruption to the ecosystem could result in irreversible changes to the hydrology of the area, and thereby to plant and animal life. Careful studies can reduce the likelihood of major problems, but can by no means eliminate them. Meticulous engineering of the road could generate entirely predictable risks to drivers, but uncertainty about the environmental effects could not be removed. Here, then, the scope of the problem is indeterminate. Some possible outcomes can be identified, but their probabilities can only be "guestimated" – there is no body of statistical data on which to base reasonable probabilities. There may be other outcomes that cannot *a priori* be identified at all, because there is no basis on which to be aware of their existence.

The competitive economic system fails to provide appropriate incentives for producers to reveal all pertinent safety information about their products, or for consumers to seek out such information for themselves. In the context of environmental issues, the competitive system results in a variety of market failures, which generate inefficient levels of the affected "goods and bads" in the market. We therefore appoint government to act as a clearing house for such information, to decide appropriate levels of environmental safety and somehow to enforce those levels. As government agencies make their evaluations, they face the crucial problem of balancing the risks and uncertainties involved in each alternative program.

Current approach to the analysis of risk and uncertainty

The method most commonly used to incorporate uncertainty into CBA is the expected-utility framework originated by von Neumann and Morgenstern (1944).[7] While that approach provides useful insights for simple individual static decisions, it is appropriate only for situations in which all possible outcomes are well defined and their probabilities are known (or can reasonably be estimated). Many of the assumptions utilized to incorporate uncertainty into CBA are also inappropriate for intertemporal analysis, particularly when projects have irreversible environmental impacts. Machina (1989) gives a good summary of the ways in which the assumptions of the von Neumann–Morgenstern analysis are violated in practice. The next sections summarize the problems listed by Machina, and others considered here to be relevant.

Analytical problems with the current approach

This section considers five issues.

1   The difference in valuation of gains and losses
2   The perception of probabilities
3   The inconsistencies between attitudes to private and social risk
4   Bias in estimating probabilities and in valuing outcome
5   State-dependent preferences

Difference in valuation of gains and losses

Research over the last decade has uncovered significant divergence from the traditional economic theory of value. Recent work on attitudes towards willingness-to-pay (WTP) and willingness-to-accept (WTA) has shown that typical attitudes towards gains and losses are not symmetrical.[8] Knetsch and Sinden (1984) show that people's valuation of a change in their economic circumstances depends on whether the change is an improvement or a deterioration from their initial condition. As Willinger notes in this volume, the systematic differences observed between WTP and WTA stem from the failure of the assumption that preferences are invariant to circumstances. These differences are influenced by many factors.

The strength and consistency of these results reflect not just individual preferences over immediate consumption goods, but a common underlying deontological system of ethical values. People's attitudes towards losses are fundamentally different to attitudes to gains. If we already possess something, we consider that its loss would, in some way, violate our rights. Particularly, in the context of the environment, we appear to feel that people have a basic right to some "acceptable" (minimum) quality. We try to adjust our circumstances so that they suit our preferences. To the extent that this is feasible, and we are successful, our circumstances become optimal given the constraints we face. Having achieved this balance, we resent any threat to it, and would therefore require greater compensation for its loss than we would pay to achieve it in the first place.

Perception of probabilities

Another issue in the approach to risk and uncertainty is the non-linearity of attitudes towards risk. Recent empirical work has shown that perceptions of risk, and attitudes towards probabilities frequently differ from true statistical probabilities. Our perception of risk seems to be non-linear, in that we apparently give undue weight to events that have a low probability of occurrence, particularly events that would result in large amounts of damage.[9] These effects invalidate the use of simple expected-utility analysis, which ignores such asymmetry and assumes linearity in probability; see, for example, Puppe (1991, pp. 20ff).

Fischoff, Watson and Hope (1990) distinguish "objective" risk, the projected statistical outcome, derived from the product of research, survey, analysis, from "subjective" risk, the non-expert perception of the intuitive likelihood of the occurrence of some event. These, they note, can diverge widely even for apparently simple events. As Fischoff et al. suggest, the creation of concern about some possible event can, by itself, change our subjective perception of its probability of occurrence. Wilson and Crouch (1987) note also that it would appear that we "do not always compare the risk averaged over time, but worry more about the risks that are sharply peaked in time" (p. 417). One commercial air crash, for example, generates far more widespread concern than road accidents that kill the same number of people.

Some writers have suggested that this shows a misperception of the true underlying probability of the event occurring. An alternative view is that it is really a true reflection of the attitude to risk. People dislike even small amounts of risk, and there is a level below which the low probability of a possible event does not diminish its psychological importance. The existence of the concern results in a statistically disproportionate weight being attached to the possibility. Other possibilities are the lack of information or the inability to comprehend or process it.

Some of the non-linearity in attitude to risk appears also to be due to a difference in attitude to risks that we take voluntarily, as opposed to those imposed on us. Most people accept the non-trivial risks associated with car driving – many on the presumption that they possess superior driving skills that reduce the probability that will lead to an accident. They feel safer behind the wheel of a car than in an aeroplane over which they have no control.[10]

Inconsistencies between attitudes to private and social risk

A similar phenomenon is that of differing social attitudes towards different types of risk, for example, the risks created by technology. As a society, we often accept far greater risks for people who work using a technology than for those who use the products of the technology.[11] This may stem from the attitude that workers accept the additional risk "voluntarily," and are therefore less concerned, even less entitled to be concerned, about the problems. Social belief in the efficiency of a free-enterprise system misguides us to believe that anyone who undertakes risky work consents freely to the exposure. This belief is engendered by the notion that all individuals possess equal economic power in the market. If one accepts that, in the real world, individuals have unequal influence, the efficiency results that justify a competitive system disappear.

Bias in estimating probabilities and in valuing outcomes

For environmental issues for which there is little or no precedent, even experts may underestimate the probability of the occurrence of problems (Shrader-Frechette and McCoy, 1993, p. 154). The typical approach of the risk assessor, when evaluating an unknown technology, is to analyze each component of the risky technology separately. The assessor then builds up the total risk from the probability of failure of each part. This approach can never overestimate the total risk, since no one can imagine all possible new combinations of factors that may lead to problems. Experts in a technical area tend to favour their technology, and to be over-optimistic about the risks and uncertainties associated with its use. The US Nuclear Regulatory Commission (1975) (hereafter WASH 1400) analysis of nuclear power plant construction in the USA, which led to the construction of many plants that were later discontinued, was an archetypal example of this (USNRC, 1975).

Shrader-Frechette and McCoy (1993, p. 188) cite a later analysis of the WASH 1400 study by Dutch researchers. The writers of WASH 1400 had to estimate failure frequencies for each component of the reactors, intended to represent a 10 percent probability of failure. The later study examined seven major sub-system of the reactors, and found that, in practice, all failure-frequency values fell outside a 90 percent confidence band, as opposed to the 10 percent that an unbiased study should have generated.

There are inherent biases in the process of analysis. The net monetary values created by a project are frequently readily apparent, but the costs of potential damage to the environmental may not all be as easy to predict. The "winner's curse" of game theory illustrates how the likelihood of a project being implemented increases as cost components are accidentally omitted.[12] This phenomenon is particularly acute when the benefits of a project are concentrated in a few hands, while the costs are dispersed across a wider populace.

Several different types of error can be made when deciding environmental policy issues. A decision maker can approve a project that will cause more harm than is justified, (type-II error) or can prevent a project whose benefits do justify its being carried out (type-I error). Shrader-Frechette and McCoy (1993) suggest that environmental impact assessors currently tend to prefer to make type-II errors. There is a tendency for impact assessments to be carried out by those associated with the development, and the natural bias of such assessors is to assume that the risk of unidentified hazards is negligible.[13]

State-dependent preferences

Standard mechanisms used to analyze risky issues reflect trade-offs that individuals say that they will make, given their perceptions of the degree of risk and their evaluation of the various outcomes. However, the preferences used to formulate such valuations are individuals' attitudes at the time of surveying. Research in the area of behaviour towards risk and uncertainty suggests that this is not an appropriate method of valuation.

It is highly likely that our preferences are state-dependent. A change in the quality of life due to health problems will cause a reduced ability to enjoy not only aspects of living associated with the facet of the environment at issue, but also with many other aspects of life. The potential for enjoyment diminishes in the presence of a dominating problem, and both total and marginal well-being suffer. An implication of this is that for those who are unfortunate enough to suffer damage, the loss of well-being *ex-post* may be quite different to their *ex-ante* expectation, with the discrepancy being entirely predictable. Policy decisions based on inaccurate *ex-ante* perceptions of the loss of well-being are likely therefore to err on the side of permitting too much damage.

Consider, for example, the evaluation of health problems caused by smoking. A survey will elicit responses from a variety of people, only a few of whom will have any detailed understanding of the suffering involved in lung disease. Many of those surveyed will not smoke and will not have experienced any of the problems smoking causes. Even those who do smoke tend to hope that they will not develop health problems, and believe that if problems do arise, they will not lead to a slow painful death. The most careful survey cannot extract knowledge a respondent does not possess.

A survey taken from people already suffering from emphysema or lung cancer will obtain quite different responses. The respondents will know how unpleasant the problems are, and the extent to which their lives have been changed by the illness. Serious disease or impending death affects the ability to enjoy all aspects of life. A lung cancer victim will value his or her health quite differently from someone in a good physical state. This is a form of non-convexity, in that the occurrence of the problem induces a change in the evaluation of the issue itself, as well as many other facets of life.[14]

As Willinger notes in this volume, preferences are state-dependent. Thus, when policy makers compare *ex-ante* evaluations of expected damage with expected benefits, costs are underestimated while benefits are more fully captured. A more appropriate method would be to compare *ex-post* damage with *ex-ante* costs. Without this, decisions will not be consistent.

Prospect theory

One recent approach to decision making under uncertainty is "prospect theory," developed initially by Kahneman and Tversky (1979). In outline, this postulates that individuals, facing a complex and uncertain problem, transform each option into a set of uncomplicated prospects. We use a process of simplification, assigning decision weights to the probabilities of occurrence of each possible event. Most probabilities are underweighted, with the important exception that events with very low probabilities are overemphasized. People designate values to gains and losses from a starting position, rather than evaluate just the final outcome of a decision.

Tversky and Kahneman (1992) have developed their earlier prospect theory to incorporate a distinction between risk and uncertainty, and to allow for different weighting functions for gains and losses. If it can be translated into practice, the Tversky and Kahneman approach may resolve some of the criticisms of current practice of incorporating risk and uncertainty in CBA within a utilitarian framework. The inappropriate ethical precepts underlying the use of CBA, however, are not amenable to revisions of the technique.

Moral issues

This section considers collective rights and individual rights.

Collective rights

The underlying thrust of most work in the area of environmental policy is that of sustainability. While there are many definitions of this concept, the basic notion is fairly clear. Any approach to environmental policy design needs to reflect the idea of organizing development so that standards of well-being in the future can be at least as good as today. Defining and operating a sustainable development strategy inevitably involves the choice of ethical principles, which cannot be derived from a utilities-based analytical framework. Environmental analysis, therefore, inherently involves normative assessment – society has to cope with problems that are by their nature not purely quantitative, but involve comparisons of the well-being of others. Ethical criteria then should be specified clearly, rather than be applied *ex post* in an *ad hoc* manner. The incorporation of the well-being of future generations into CBA should be specified and evaluated explicitly.

Since one can reduce or eliminate risk with insurance or other financial instruments, there is no moral problem with the Tversky and Kahneman (1992) approach that in effect minimizes our concern about risky outcomes. For uncertainty that cannot be reduced or eliminated, their method is not appropriate. Important environmental resources do not have close substitutes. Consequently, there is no way that we can insure future generations against profound irreversible environmental damage.

There are strong similarities with the issue of discounting. Negative outcomes of uncertain events occur in the future, and the two factors of time and uncertainty combine to reduce the psychological immediacy of the consequences. For irreversible environmental effects, there is no moral justification for scaling down the valuation of permanent damage, whether for its remoteness in time or because we are not sure whether it will occur and how extensive its consequences may be.

Consider, for example, a decision that carries the small probability of a major environmental disaster many years in the future. Under standard von Neumann–Morgenstern analysis, the impact of the disaster would be treated as a non-infinite value, discounted both for its remoteness in time and also for its non-certainty. Its final weighting in the comparison will not reflect the feelings or rights of the victims who may suffer its effects. This approach violates the rights of those who may have to face the problem when it eventually occurs.

Here, the example of ozone depletion is relevant. Any decision that results in the release of potentially ozone-destroying substances into the atmosphere now carries a small possibility of inducing a catastrophic increase in ultraviolet radiation at some time in the future. There is no way for the current generation to provide insurance for future generations for the damages that loss of the ozone layer would cause. Neither is there any conceivable physical capital that we could produce and leave to future generations as a substitute.

Policy formulation in such areas is very difficult. Policy makers understandably tend to hide behind the distinction between a statistical life and an actual life, but this is a psychological "security blanket" rather than an appropriate moral distinction. The implication of that approach is that the question of safety should be tackled differently if one knew the identity of the individual(s) whose lives would be lost or damaged. While such artifice may make policy formulation less stressful, it violates any moral framework that respects individual rights. Not knowing the identity of the individual affected does alter the moral aspects of a decision to exchange a life for some monetary value.[15]

Individual rights

Any policy decision over risky or uncertain outcomes involves the imposition of uncertainty at the individual level. Gilroy (1992, p. 217) regards each individual as an "imprisoned agent," with given levels of goods, such as public goods and externalities, being "forcibly" imposed through a process that involves the imperfect aggregation of misperceived preferences. No policy decision can accommodate the preferences of all individuals. This is due to the diversity of attitudes – in particular, the degree of aversion to risk – which determine the trade-offs between certain current commodities and uncertain future health problems or environmental deterioration.

Shrader-Frechette and McCoy (1993) discuss the important distinction between "negative" rights and "positive" rights. They suggest that negative rights, for example that to protection from serious harm, should logically precede positive rights such as the right to medical care.[16]

Negative rights generally need to be upheld at the social level – for example, public goods such as clean air and unpolluted lakes and rivers. Positive rights such as health care, however, can at least in principle be provided privately, and that is the mode in many societies. A primary responsibility of any government or social decision maker should therefore be the preservation or enhancement of these negative rights. The existence of the negative right to a safe environment requires that others do not interfere with that right by misusing the environment. Not only that, but in addition to preventing the mistreatment of the environment, the existence of a positive right to a safe environment requires that society repair previous damage that has reduced that safety. The existence of negative rights is a far easier position to support than that of a positive right.

Given the potential effects of many environmental problems on life expectancy and health, project evaluation should begin with a procedure to ensure that these overriding rights are respected. If a project violates negative rights then CBA is not an appropriate method of evaluation, and should not be undertaken. Expenditure to enhance the negative right to a safe environment should take precedence over expenditure on income-enhancing projects.

Rawls' (1971) ideas of the principles of justice are those that "free and rational persons concerned to further their own interests would accept in an initial position of equality as defining the fundamental terms of their association ... those who engage in social co-operation choose together, in one joint act, the principles that are to assign basic rights and duties and to determine the division of social benefits" (p. 11). On the concept of liberty, Rawls suggests: "A rather intricate complex of rights and duties characterises any particular liberty. Not only must it be permissible for individuals to do or not to do something, but government and other persons must have a legal duty not to obstruct" (p. 203). Rawls makes it clear that he is not suggesting that we can all enjoy full liberty over all choices, since this would result in the chaos of conflicting rights. Liberty can come only within a framework of mutually acceptable constraints. Acceptable, that is, from Rawls' "original position."

It is not possible then for every individual to retain complete freedom of choice over all possibilities. The acceptance of restrictions that limit our individual choice set is inevitable, so that, collectively, we can enjoy wider scope than would otherwise be the case. That does not mean, however, that all individual rights have to be subsumed into a collective ethic. Any society comprises distinct, diverse individuals, who have the right individually to formulated wants and choices, within a socially feasible framework.

The essential difference between individual and collective decisions over risky and uncertain situations can be illustrated by comparison to a lottery. The individual can choose whether and how many lottery tickets to buy, although, for many environmental goods, the degree of choice may be quite limited. Government, on the other hand, designs the whole lottery, deciding within constrained alternatives on the rules and the payoffs. While each individual wants to win the lottery, it is not socially desirable that we should design the lottery to serve only the interests of any one person. The problem facing Government, therefore, is of a different nature from that of the individual. It is not desirable then that Government should just mimic the risk-taking behaviour of individuals. Policy formulation by aggregation of observed WTP or WTA compensation for marginal changes in low probability risks is inappropriate.

People have the right to the absence of pervasive harm. This implies that policies should at least *offer* the option of alternatives that would cause least damage, even though generally people may not choose the lowest risk unless it is costless. Thus, government decisions that constrain people into situations in which there are serious and unavoidable risks to their health fail to observe the basic right to life and health.

The standard Paretian liberal approach to CBA embodies only efficiency goals. When the primary objective was increasing output, this was appropriate. The evolution of society's aspirations from this limited concept of efficiency to the sustainability goals of inter- and intra-generational equity requires explicit revision to these underpinnings. It is essential now to incorporate explicitly individual rights into our calculus, if we are to achieve sustainability.

Conclusion

Traditional micro-theory, developed for simple analysis of consumption goods, yields realistic answers to simple comparative static questions. It serves us less well when extended to the analysis of environmental issues. The issues are uncertain rather than risky, so the ethical and analytical foundations of micro-theory make its use inappropriate. Some improvement can be achieved by incorporating recent theoretical advances such as those outlined by Tversky and Kahneman (1992), but this is still appropriate only for risky situations, rather than those that are uncertain. True uncertainty cannot be incorporated into the traditional CBA framework, when attempting to achieve the objective of sustainable development.

Current approaches to the incorporation of uncertainty into CBA are inappropriate from both empirical and ethical standpoints. The essential problems are that the expected-utility approach and its derivatives contain many flaws, and that the ethical underpinnings are inappropriate. There is an acceptance among economists that their analyses should be subject, after completion, to the *ad-hoc* imposition of "political adjustment" to correct for political or ethical factors. This substantially reduces the validity of such economic analysis, and for long-term environmental impacts, can make it misleading. It is important to change the treatment given to risk and uncertainty in CBA, if economic analysis is to provide appropriate policy prescriptions on environmental issues.

In the context of uncertainty, the most important change has to be to separate the treatment of uncertainty from that of risk. Uncertainty creates entirely different problems to risk, and the failure to recognize and allow for the difference can lead to highly inappropriate policy prescriptions. The only common factor between these two is that the outcome of a policy decision is not known in advance. The important dichotomy is between risk that can at least conceptually be quantified, and uncertainty which cannot. These correspond closely but not completely to the soft/hard definitions in Vercelli (1994). For risk, the "softer" category, Vercelli's definition, close to Knight's risk, is appropriate. Vercelli's "hard uncertainty" needs the addition of an empirical dimension, to allow for problems of measurability.

Ecosystems are complex and highly interrelated, so that successful sustainable environmental management of stressed ecological systems requires continuing control, rather than a single inaugural action. For complex dynamic systems, the ability to monitor accurately and to implement timely control measures is unlikely. If we can neither know nor control the state of the system and its response to intervention, then risk-taking is not an acceptable management option.

There are both theoretical and empirical differences between risk and uncertainty. For an issue to create risk rather than uncertainty, it must be possible to identify all possible outcomes *ab-initio*, and to estimate their probabilities, which, as Vercelli notes, must be unique, additive and stable. It is essential also that it is possible to observe and control the changing states of the environmental variables in question. There is little point in launching into a CBA when we cannot measure or control the potential outcomes we are evaluating.

Environmental goods are by nature not susceptible to market exchange, and the use of an analytical framework constructed for a different context inevitable results in entirely inappropriate decisions. New approaches with explicit moral foundations are necessary if we want to establish realistic sustainable development policies.

This paper proposes that the process of sustainable development requires a system of negative rights as its ethical foundation. All persons from all times and places have the right to a safe environment, though the interpretation of safety will inevitably evolve over time as scientific knowledge improves. Acknowledgement of these basic rights would result in the automatic exclusion of projects that reduce safety. The HK compensation principle becomes invalidated in the context of environmental uncertainty.

No system can eliminate uncertainty. However, by precluding decisions that knowingly degrade any component of the environment below safe levels, society can avoid many of the worst potential problems. At the individual level, risk cannot be eradicated. However, the recognition and support of negative rights will prevent decisions that unnecessarily threaten basic safety.

Few disciplines other than economics insist on summarizing all information in a single scalar variable. Even straightforward commercial investment decisions are usually multi-dimensional, although an explicit "bottom line" is essential in that context. For decisions involving human life and health, the condensation of multidimensional information into a single monetary scalar is inappropriate. The idea of sustainable development is sufficiently complex that the reduction of all relevant factors to a single measure has too high a cost in terms of lost information. Economic prescriptions would have far greater credibility if they displayed more than one aspect of the issue. Such multiple dimensions might include human health, monetary and ecological factors. Political policy makers are quite familiar with the idea of considering several different measures at once.

Decisions on projects that will have significant environmental effects should be dealt with on the basis of a hierarchy of criteria, before being evaluated using CBA. Any project should have to pass fundamental tests, before being considered in detail. There are some basic principles that can be derived both from preferences and from deontological ethics. Examples of absolute criteria might start with the survival of the human race, the survival of a particular race, or of a particular segment of the population, of a component of a culture, of an ecosystem, etc.

Each of these requirements should be applied in sequence before the next is considered. Few projects would fail such obvious criteria, but as one moved through the list, it is likely that, at some point, acceptability would become less obvious. This should be highlighted before human lives are reduced to their economic equivalents in CBA. An important outcome of such an approach is that it would remove the evaluation of human health and natural environments from the discounting effects of time and uncertainty.

Given the diversity of belief systems, the search for a unique, absolute moral system is inappropriate at the current stage of human development. Nonetheless, there are many criteria that are acceptable and indeed required by many of the belief systems of the world, and could readily form the basis of an organized structure for project appraisal.

Notes

1 I am most grateful for the help of Alessandro Vercelli, Mohammed Dore, Marc Willinger, and other participants at the "Limits To Markets" Conference, Cornell University, April 1994. The support of the SSHRC is also gratefully acknowledged.
2 Haveman and Weisbrod (1975, p. 44) note: "To determine allocative efficiency one must ignore considerations of which particular people are made better off or worse off as resource allocation alternatives are considered. The issues of how alternative resource allocations affect the well-being of a particular people are captured by the distributional – or equity – goals"; cited in Hanley and Spash (1993, p. 47).
3 See for example the discussion of the risk-engineering approach used in the development of North Sea oil and gas projects, in Chapman (1992) and also Ballard (1992, pp. 15–40 and 95–104).
4 In some instances, forward markets exist, which enable these uncertainties to be reduced. This does not eliminate the uncertainty at the social level, but moves it to other markets that specialize in gambling type insurance.
5 "Risks are probabilities, whether this connection is obvious . . . or indirect. . . ." (Finkel 1990, pp. 3ff).
6 A panel at the 1994 Annual Meeting of the Canadian Economics Association noted that a major problem with the management of Canada's Atlantic cod fishery was the inaccurate estimation of fish stocks, and the failure to deal appropriately with uncertainty in those stock levels.
7 See, for example, the treatment of risk in LaGrega et al. (1994, Chapter 14, pp. 837ff).

8 Several alternative explanations have been offered for the existence of these effects. For example, see the work of Kahneman and Tversky (1979) and Knetsch and Sinden (1984).

9 For example, Viscusi (1992), pp. 124ff, shows willingness to pay for statistically identical incremental risk reductions. Marginal valuations of risk reduction initially fall, but then increase for very low probability risks.

10 See, for example, Juas and Mattsson (1987, pp. 131–50).

11 Moore and Viscusi (1990) give an excellent survey of wage compensation for job risk, and many surrounding issues.

12 In a common-value auction, in which the value must be estimated, the obvious strategy is for a player to bid up his estimate of the value. This, however, makes the payoff negative, because the winner is the bidder who has made the largest positive error in his calculation (Rasmusen, 1989, p. 252).

13 The classic example of this phenomenon is again the WASH 1400 study of the safety of nuclear reactors as generators of electricity.

14 See Kleindorfer, P. and H. Kunreuther (1988, pp. 80ff) for an analysis of the similar issue of wearing seatbelts.

15 I am not suggesting that we can avoid these difficult issues, but that it is essential to take into account not solely monetary factors but also the rights of those who will be affected.

16 This concept originates with Isiah Berlin's (1966) approach to positive and negative liberty.

References

Ansell, J. and Wharton, F. (eds) (1992) *Risk: Analysis, Assessment and Management*. Chichester: John Wiley.

Berlin, I. (1966) Two concepts of liberty. In I. Berlin, *Four Concepts of Liberty*. Oxford.

Ballad, G. M. (1992) Industrial risk: Safety by design. In Ansell and Wharton (1992).

Chapman, C. B. (1992) A risk engineering approach to risk management. In Ansell and Wharton (1992).

Finkel, A. (1990) *Confronting Uncertainty in Risk Management*. Washington, Centre for Risk Management, Resources for the Future.

Fisher, I. (1906) *The Nature of Capital and Income*. New York and London: Macmillan.

Fisher, I. (1930) *The Theory of Interest*. New York and London: Macmillan.

Fischoff, B., Watson, S. and Hope, C. (1990) Defining risk. In T. Glickman and M. Gough, (eds) Readings in Risk, Resources for the Future, Washington.

Gilroy J. M. (1992) Public policy and environmental risk: Political theory, human agency and the imprisoned rider. *Environmental Ethics*, 14, 217–37.

Hanley, N. and Spash, C. L. (1993) *Cost-benefit Analysis and the Environment*. Aldershot: Edward Elgar.

Haveman, R. H. and Weisbrod, B. A. (1975) The concept of benefits in cost-benefit aualysis: with emphasis on water pollution control activities. In H. M. Peskin and E. P. Seskin (eds) *Cost Benefit Analysis and Water Pollution Policy*. Washington DC: the Urban Institute. Hirshleifer, J. (1992) *The Analytics of Uncertainty and Information*. Cambridge: Cambridge University Press.

Hirshleifer, J. (1992) *The Analytics of Uncertainty and Information*. Cambridge: Cambridge University Press.

Juas, B. and Mattsson, B. (1987) Valuation of personal injuries: The problem. In Sjoberg (1987).

Kahneman, D. and Tversky, A. (1979) Prospect theory: An analysis of decision under risk. *Econometrica*, 47 (March), 263–91.

Kleindorfer, P. and Kunreuther, H. (1988) Ex ante and ex post valuation problems: Economic and psychological considerations. In G. Peterson, and R. Gregory (eds) *Amenity Resource Valuation: Integrating Economics with Other Diciplines*. State College PA: Venture Publishing, 77–86.

Knetsch, J. L. and Sinden, J. A. (1984) Willingness to pay and compensation demanded: Experimental evidence of an unexpected disparity in measure of value. *Quarterly Journal of Economics*, XCIX (August), 507–21.

Knight, F. (1921) *Risk, Uncertainty and Profit*. New York: Houghton Mifflin.

LaGrega, M., Buckingham, P. and Evans, J. (1994) *Hazardous Waste Management*. New York: McGraw-Hill.

Machina, M. (1989) Dynamic consistency and non-expected utility models of choice under uncertainty. *Journal of Economic Literature*, 27, 1622–68.

Moore, M. J. and Viscusi, W. K. (1990) *Compensation Mechanisms for Job Risks: Wages, Workers' Compensation and Product Liability*. Princeton: Princeton University Press.

Puppe, C. (1991) *Distorted Probabilities and Choice under Risk*. Berlin: Springer-Verlag.

Rasmusen, E. (1989) *Games and Information*. Oxford: Basil Blackwell.

Rawls, J. (1971) *A Theory of Justice*. Oxford: Oxford University Press.

Ruckelhaus, W. D. (1990) Risk, science and democracy. In T. Glickman and M. Gough (eds) *Readings in Risk*. Resources for the Future, Washington, 105–18.

Shackle, G. L. S. (1949–50) A non-additive measure of uncertainty. *Review of Economic Studies*, 17 (1), 70–74.

Shrader-Frechette, K. S. and McCoy, E. D. (1993) *Method in Ecology: Strategies for Conservation*. Cambridge: Cambridge University Press.

Sjoberg, L. (ed.) (1987) *Risk and Society: Studies of Risk Generation and Reactions to Risk*. London: Allen and Unwin.

Tversky, A. and Kahneman, D. (1992) Advances in prospect theory: Cumulative representation of uncertainty. *Journal of Risk and Uncertainty*, 5 (4), 297–323.

Vercelli A. (1994) *Hard uncertainty and environment*. Manuscript, Università di Siena.

Viscusi, K. (1992) *Fatal Tradeoffs*. New York: Oxford University Press.

von Neumann, J. and Morgenstern, O. (1944) *The Theory of Games and Economic Behaviour*. New York: Wiley.

Wilson, R. and Crouch, E. A. C. (1987) Risk assessments and comparisons: an introduction. In *Science*, 236, 267–70.

USNRC (1975) *Reactor Safety Study: An Assessment of Accident Risks in US Commercial Nuclear Power Plants* (WASH 1400). Washington DC: USNRC.

III
Population and the Environment

7

The Dynamics of Socio-environmental Change and the Limits of Neo-Malthusian Environmentalism[1]

Peter Taylor and Raúl García-Barrios

Sustainable development, steady state economics, and zero population growth are serious proposals. The economic and environmental problems motivating these goals are severe, and the social and economic changes their implementation seems to require are sweeping. Yet, the proponents of such steady state and sustainable goals often picture the dynamics of unsustainability, economic growth, and population increase very simplistically. Aggregated categories and abstract analyses of statistical trends predominate over investigations of concrete and *differentiating* social, economic and environmental dynamics. Policies and other social or technical practices are more likely to succeed without unintended and undesirable effects if they are based on a sufficient description of the causes underlying such dynamics; any sustainable social order will have to be constructed through interventions within these dynamics (Max-Neef, 1986). Serious conceptual and empirical work to understand those dynamics are needed.[2]

At the same time, we recognize that simplistic or poorly framed analyses do not just happen spontaneously. The sociology of scientific knowledge indicates that certain courses of action are facilitated over others in the very formulation of science, and not just in its "downstream" applications. If our analysis is to shift the direction of policy making, and other action, we also need some interpretation that exposes the practical bases of the science behind any steady state proposals. Ideally, this would then help us to contribute to building conditions favourable to alternative science and politics; that last project, however, requires much more work than one written intervention can accomplish.

To make concrete the directions we think such analysis and interpretation should take, this paper focuses on one form of steady state environmental discourse, what we call neo-Malthusian environmentalism, and, in particular, on its account of the interrelations between the poor in rural societies and their environments.[3]

Positioning this critique

Upon entering this terrain one is quickly faced with contested definitions of who and what constitute neo-Malthusianism, with popular slogans concerning the global and local, self-evident truths about the finiteness of the Earth, and the well-guarded disciplinary turf of demography. Let us, therefore, clear some ground for ourselves by defining some terms and making several distinctions, and provide a basic map of the surrounding area.

For us, neo-Malthusianism means more than a focus on overpopulation[4] and population control; we shall refer to that focus as population discourse or the population problem. We use the term neo-Malthusianism when ultimate bio-physical limits, often global, are being invoked to strengthen claims that population growth presents a serious problem, one that should be kept at the centre of our attention. When degradation of environment and exhaustion of resources is directly related to such population growth, we call this neo-Malthusian environmentalism (Ehrlich and Holdren, 1971; Ehrlich and Ehrlich, 1990; Bongaarts, 1992; Meffe et al., 1993; Hall et al., 1994; Pimentel et al., 1994).

Demography, the scientific discipline spawned by and now dominating – population discourse, can be divided into three orientations (Preston, 1989):

1 macro-economic, concerned with the effects of population growth on a nation's production and economic growth
2 micro-economic, concerned with allocating the true social and economic costs of having children to those who bear them, and
3 reproductive health and choice, concerned with enabling mothers (sometimes fathers also) to have the number of children they desire and raise them healthily.[5]

Each of these orientations may be developed with a neo-Malthusian tone. It is macro-economic considerations, however, that are most commonly associated with neo-Malthusian environmentalism and so our discussion will speak most directly to that orientation.[6]

Global change is a very popular term these days, but, with a view both to identifying causes and to designing policy responses, we consider global formulations to be weak and unhelpful.[7] Global statistics and trends, or, more generally, aggregate regional or national figures, are abstractions which give very little insight into the concrete social, economic and environmental processes (Palloni, 1994).[8] Whatever the scale of observation, differentiation among social groups is at the centre, not just an addition to, all such processes.[9] Let us tease out this assessment of undifferentiated thinking (including global formulations) with a simple scenario.

Consider two hypothetical countries having the same amount and quality of arable land, the same population size, the same level of technical capacity, and the same population growth rate, say 3 percent per year. Country A, however, has a relatively equal land distribution, while country B has a typical 1970s Central American land distribution: 2 percent of the people own 60 percent of the land; 70 percent own just 2 percent. Both countries double their populations very rapidly but, five generations (120 years) before anyone is malnourished in country A, all of the poorest 70 percent in country B already are. This is not just an issue of relative timing of the crisis in the two countries. The likely level at which

B's poor would first experience what others call population pressure would be food shortages linked to inequity in land distribution (Durham, 1979; Vandermeer, 1977). Inevitably, given that no real country is like country *A*, the crises to which actual people have to respond come well before and in different forms from the crisis predicted on the basis of the aggregate population growth rates and calculations of ultimate biophysical limits. Anyone focusing on population control policies could justifiably be viewed by the poor in a country like *B* as taking sides with those who benefit from the inequitable access to productive resources. The point here is not just that in any district, country, or ecosphere there are richer and poorer people, but that groups with different wealth and power exist, change, and become involved in crises because of their dynamic interrelations.

From this scenario, we can identify three analytical and policy orientations, differing in the units of analysis and the implied limits:

1   uniform units, which can be simply aggregated, with biophysical limits
2   stratified units – the economic squeeze on the poor leads them to face biophysical limits but the rich, while buffered for some time from such limits, can take anticipatory action or help the poor in facing their limits
3   differentiating units, linked in their economic, social and political dynamics – the limits are thus social.

We will concentrate on the contrast between uniform and differentiated analyses, because stratified accounts, while acknowledging the existence of rich and poor, often do not provide an account of the dynamics of formation and maintenance of inequality. Without such dynamics, they occupy an uncertain middle ground.[10] Are the policies and other social or technical practices proposed for the poor any different from those from a uniform analysis? If so, we need to know more – how and why are the proposals supposed to work? If not, then this essay's critique applies.[11]

In criticizing uniform, aggregate analyses we must also make clear that, for us, the contrast to global is not local. The local can easily be viewed as a place to become marginalized with respect to more fundamental global trends, or, at best, as a mere instance of those trends. Instead, we advocate differentiated analyses that are "locally centered" and "trans-local." That is, one should begin from local situations to keep always in sight the concrete (always differentiating), interconnected social, economic, and environmental dynamics, knowing, however, that understanding these dynamics will require tracing of their trans-local, -regional and -national linkages (Arizpe et al., 1994). After all, to continue the scenario above, the land distribution of country *B* had a history, and probably resulted from land being taken to produce for export, often by foreign or transnational corporations. Understanding locally centered situations and appreciating how they are concretely interlinked is a task of much greater complexity than global analysis, or any account of processes using aggregate and undifferentiated categories. Moreover, the most appropriate point(s) of intervention or engagement are

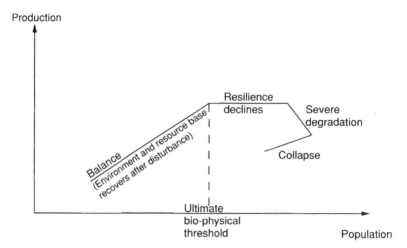

Figure 7.1 Population, production, and environment: The sequence of stages implied from global or undifferentiated, aggregate trends

not at all clear in advance of examining the particularities of the situation and the resources one would bring into it. Nevertheless, the work needs to be done; "think globally, act locally" does not do that job.

The contrast between global and locally centered and trans-local is not an issue of simplification for the sake of generality versus accumulation of detail, synthesis versus focusing on particular cases, first approximations versus more qualified accounts, or choice of temporal and spatial scale. Locally centered and trans-local analysis entails a qualitative change in perspective. Let us illustrate this using some schematic diagrams of the relation between population growth, production and environmental degradation.

Figure 7.1 corresponds to the global formulation of the population problem. It shows production increasing as population increases until some ultimate bio-physical threshold is reached. Above this, the resource base and the environment begin to become stressed and production cannot keep up with population growth. Eventually environmental and resource degradation reduces the absolute production capacity, and a population collapse may occur. Although technological progress may shift the biophysical threshold to the right, it cannot do this indefinitely; it is natural to reach a production plateau – according to Vitousek et al. (1986) humans in 1986 consumed 40 percent of the earth's primary production; the 100 percent threshold cannot be too far off at present population growth rates.

Figure 7.2 shows the sequence of stages observable in any locally centered situation. (Any aggregate trend is actually an integration of diverse locally centered situations.) In figure 7.2, biophysical thresholds have already been reached in various places at various times and the local peoples have initiated processes of reorganising social institutions (in the broad sense of the term) and technology so that production could keep pace. (In fact, the world's population would never

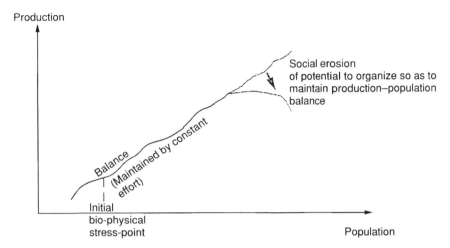

Figure 7.2   The sequence of stages observable in any locally centered situation. (Any aggregate trend is actually an integration of diverse locally centered situations.)

have been able to reach the level of 40 percent consumption of primary production without such processes). At any population size, the balance could be upset if the bases for these institutions and for use of technology were undermined. When this process falters and environmental and resource stress or degradation occurs, there are always social forces (analyzed on pages 145–52) to account for the erosion. (The forces integrate both local and external changes, i.e., are locally centered and trans-local.) Conversely, given that people work with and modify institutions and technology to respond to crises, they will have the most chance of recovering some balance if they appreciate the social origins of the crises they have been and will be confronting.[12]

Two different notions of balance are represented in the contrasting formulations (figures 7.1 and 7.2). The conventional view of the population–resource use system is that the different forces stimulating the population to exploit its resources push the system out of its basic condition of balance to which it will return if the forces diminish. We might picture this as being like a ball in a basin (which becomes shallower as one moves through the stages in figure 7.1). If, however, the forces push the system over a threshold, one considers the resource to be overexploited. Once outside the basin, the system rolls down the hill to a new stability condition, usually the resource's degradation or extinction. A contrasting picture is that in many places the environment (e.g. topsoils, rainforests, and water bodies) has already been deeply transformed and thus a local threshold has long been reached and surpassed, but various social conservative forces are sustaining the resource from rolling down the hill (which may become steeper as one moves through the stages in figure 7.2), into a situation of degradation. Therefore, it is the failure of these forces to work efficiently which may precipitate the resource system falling into degradation and extinction.

The second view has six further implications for a critique of the population problem, which we state here and support in the sections to follow:

1   Population size and growth are not at the centre of the dynamics of social erosion, and the abstract dynamics of population growth do not provide a sufficient description of the causes of environmental and resource degradation.[13]

2   Given that the local population figures aggregated into any global or regional population figure measure only one facet of the locally centered social, economic and environmental dynamics producing such growths, demography (i.e. the study of population as a system) is not a natural, sufficient or powerful framework in which to explain population growth.[14]

3   Regulation of population growth cannot be achieved independently from the poor and less powerful regaining some capacity to reorganize their local social institutions and technology, and through this some greater control over production and consumption (Ostrom, 1990).

    Our introductory mapping is nearly complete; the general coordinates of our position and the vector of our orientation should be becoming clear. But, before moving into detailed arguments, we want to establish our distance from three formulations that are probably well-known to environmentalist readers, formulations that also point to the potential for reorganizing social institutions and technology so that production and population keep pace with each other.[15]

4   The anti-Malthusian, Julian Simon, celebrates the power of creative individuals who, when unfettered by government restriction and uninhibited by neo-Malthusian pessimism, are able to generate the knowledge, inventions and other responses needed to forestall resource scarcity (Simon, 1990). The implied account of how institutions and technologies enhancing production are generated (and undermined) is simplistic, based primarily on his pro-free enterprize and anti-government ideology. Like those he seeks to debunk, Simon's analyses are abstract and statistical; not surprisingly, his hyper-optimism discounts the extent to which locally centered and trans-local crises are already widespread and require attention.

5   Large-scale international aid efforts, in contrast, begin from the position that most local and national institutions in poor societies are inadequate to keep production and population in line. This "institutional insufficiency" is used to justify the focus of aid being placed on modernizing the technology, institutions, or otherwize adjusting the structure of the economy (Southgate and Basterrechea, 1992). Such a focus, by discounting the potential for endogeneously generated reorganization, undermines one of the bases we hold to be essential for generating sustainable institutions of production, reproduction and consumption.

6   Finally, we are sympathetic politically and ethically with those who call for empowerment of the poor, of local communities, or of women, and who insist that this empowerment must be part of efforts to alleviate poverty or improve reproductive health and choice (Cohen, 1993; Dixon-Mueller,

1993; Population Reference Bureau, 1993; Institute for Philosophy & Public Policy, 1993; Stein, 1995). Nevertheless, our emphasis differs. We do not want the justification of any of these efforts to include their effectiveness in reducing population growth.[16] Population does not need to be the focal (independent or dependent) variable in any analysis of causes or formulation of responses to economic hardship and environmental degradation. Instead, it is important to understand the processes by which the capacity of women and the poor have become unable to respond effectively to economic, environmental and other social changes, and make this understanding central in designing interventions to reverse these processes. We develop this argument in the next section.

Labor surplus and institutional insufficiency: Contrasting analyses of the social dynamics of poor populations and environmental degradation

Neo-Malthusian environmentalism has an implied view of the relationships among population, labor supply, the social organization of production, technology, and environmental degradation. Let us examine this by contrasting it with other views of the origins and nature of institutional insufficiency common in poor societies.

Boserup and Lewis

As a starting point for our discussion of the social, economic and environmental dynamics of human populations let us consider Esther Boserup's still influential argument (Boserup, 1965). She challenged the conventional neo-Malthusian position that population growth must outstrip resources, arguing that population, resources and technology are linked in a progressive manner, in which population pressure provides a useful economic stimulus to technical and institutional innovation. In particular, population pressure on land stimulates agricultural progress and institutional adaptation, which then allow unprecedented levels of population concentration. In the light of the large-scale historical evidence on the evolution of the world's agriculture, Boserup's argument seemed quite reasonable. However, Boserup's mechanism cannot be operating universally, since technological and institutional adaptation is not now occurring in most poor societies. Why has the Boserupian stimulus stopped functioning, allowing overpopulation or, for that matter, allowing resource depletion of any kind?

We approach this question by exploring how market mechanisms fail to provide an efficient and flexible monitoring system of natural resource scarcity, and thus any lag in the transmission of information of resource depletion due to population increase (or any other cause) results in insufficient technological and institutional responses. (We say something about this approach later.) A second approach derives from the idea that the major part of the poor human populations of the world constitute an unproductive, capital-scarce and otherwize institutionally insufficient "labor surplus."

The concept of labor surplus was originally introduced by Arthur Lewis (1954) to characterize what he considered the primitive productive condition of "traditional" societies in underdeveloped countries. According to Lewis, in those societies, the physical relationship between a large population and scarce resources led to zero marginal productivity of labor. It was assumed that the existence of a large portion of non-productive labor, or surplus labor, in the pre-modern sector provided developing countries with a mechanism of growth that was economically (and hence institutionally) neutral to rural productivity. As Lewis (1954) pointed out, in such conditions "the holding . . . is so small that if some members . . . obtained other employment, the remaining members could cultivate the holding just as well" (p. 141). Such labor surplus may also be conceived, more fundamentally in our view, as labor that does not endogeneously reorganize its institutions and use of technology to improve its efficiency in production. When poor overpopulated human societies constitute a labor surplus with such a restricted ability to reorganize locally, their own increasing numbers and demand do not stimulate agricultural progress and institutional adaptation. With this insight, one can begin to see why Boserup's mechanism is by no means universal.

The origins and dynamics of the poor's inability to reorganize collectively in response to new challenges, and thus of this "reorganizing-restricted" labor surplus, may be subject to different explanations. In his theory of development, Lewis implicitly assumes it is due to intrinsic characteristics of large traditional populations (their social and economic institutions being primitive, weak and inefficient) and is determined by physical resource restrictions, i.e. scarcity of physical capital and land relative to population size. Given the reorganizing and restricted character of this rural labor surplus, the only way to transform it into productive labor is through its absorption by another sector, namely, a modern industrialized sector. The surplus, in short, must be upgraded as human capital.

Neo-malthusian institutional insufficiency

Lewis' interpretation of rural labor surplus underlies most analyses of the relation between poor rural societies and ecological change, including neo-Malthusian ones. Unlike Lewis, however, neo-Malthusians have little confidence in industrialized sectors to absorb the labor surplus, which leads them to maintain an emphasis on the situation of the poor. In particular, poor human populations are held to be, as a consequence of their institutional insufficiency, deeply involved in three vicious circles.

1   The poor mismanage or deplete their resources, which, in turn, reduces land productivity, increasing environmental degradation, and limiting future income options.

2 Because of their lack of physical and human capital and the distortions in the markets, prices, and credit systems in which they operate, the poor are inefficient and uncompetitive producers, which further restricts their capacity to acquire necessary new capital and overcome their economic disadvantages. (The first circle is emphasized more by environmentalists; the second by international financial institutions such as the World Bank.)

3 A central feature of the resource mismanagement by the poor (in circle 1), enhanced by their lack of economic security (in circle 2), is that they are not able or are unwilling to regulate their numbers, which, on average, leads to further impoverishment.

Given these vicious circles connecting impoverishment, environmental and resource degradation, and population growth, neo-Malthusians can conceptualize the dynamics of poor populations in terms of their increasing rate of consumption, and hence resource depletion and rapid approach to biophysical limits. The policy prescriptions that follow are directly related to stopping the population and labor surplus from increasing and depleting the natural resources. This view is moderated by a small concession to Lewis' idea of upgrading human capital, namely that reproductive education, health programs and direct welfare assistance may help break the vicious circles between poverty, population, and environmental degradation and gradually transform the rural poor into a sustainable sector. (The power of such programs has not, however, been demonstrated in any practical way; see Pritchett (1994).)

In spite of its great popularity, Lewis' assumption on the origins and nature of labor surplus is weakly supported by historical and contemporary studies. Moreover, anthropological, sociological and historical studies on the transformation of pre-capitalist poor societies under the impact of new capitalist social relations seem to point towards explanations quite different from intrinsic weakness and inefficiency of their social and economic institutions. In the next two sections, we present an explicit and more plausible interpretation of the causes and dynamics of any labor surplus that is restricted in its ability to reorganize locally. Through this framework one can understand better the socially conditioned biophysical limits experienced by the poor.

A structural and social psychological account of institutional insufficiency

Poor populations of the capitalist world are not economically autonomous, but participate in a complex arrangement of institutional and economic relations with other social groups and the state, which involve market and non-market transactions at the local and regional levels. In this context, several structural factors and policies contribute to the ongoing production of generalized poverty and disruption of social organization. Various authors[17] have documented:

- policies and public investment priorities (especially with the onset of the debt crisis in the 1980s)

- structural and institutional contexts that are unfavorable to rural development, including inegalitarian land tenure systems and institutional biases against smallholders in the provision of public goods and services and in their access to them
- economic policies and technological biases that reduce employment creation in both the non-agricultural sector and in commercial agriculture
- household-specific market failure, economic discrimination and adverse selection in the labor, product and credit markets
- monopolistic power in local formal and informal markets
- compulsory transactions which, like usury, lead to the expropriation of their resources
- direct private and state coercive violence.

These factors amount to many societies having a disarticulated economy, that is, one in which, because investment is directed towards producing for export, these economies depend very little on the growth of their own internal consumption and can prosper despite, in fact, because of, wages being kept low (De Janvry, 1980). Moreover, many of the transactions entered into by the poor who face this unfavorable economic context constitute part of their survival strategies. Once established, however, most of these transactions become involuntary and compulsory, and many reproduce at the same or greater scale their poverty and dependency conditions.

These structural conditions constitute a systematic discrimination against the rural poor evidenced in their low productive capacity, an increased instability and uncertainty of their market transactions (i.e. usually in the labor and product markets), and a reduction of opportunities to establish and maintain viable and stable non-market transactions that could circumvent market failures. In short, the structural conditions generate institutional insufficiency and continuing impoverishment. The structural conditions also reduce systemically the capacity of the poor to reorganize endogenously in the face of new challenges, that is, to build up or alter contracts and associations to sustain desirable efficient production, resource management and technological change. Their institutional insufficiency is reorganizing and restricted.

As a consequence of this reorganizing and restricted institutional insufficiency, there is a labor surplus. Most rural population must become semiproletarian, that is, survive through off-farm activities involving market transactions which increasingly demanding a high mobility and detachment from the land and social community. This peasant brain and labor drain is not just a matter of external, structural conditions disrupting a community, but interacts with the prevailing social psychology in many serious ways. The individual's decision to incorporate into the market and mobilize the household labor force may be rational from his or her point of view because it increases and stabilizes monetary income. Nevertheless, it acts against the community's institutional arrangements by eroding the bases of local cooperation and social norms.

For example, high population mobility reduces face-to-face interaction and the probability of future and repeated relationship between rural agents. More profoundly, high mobility changes the moral and social normative references in local communities (e.g. the prestige system and moral economy) that had previously maintained the goodwill and trust between the economic agents, even when hierarchical relationships or highly exploitative economic transactions were dominant. Integration into developed markets thus undermines the basis for reciprocity and partial gift exchanges and increases the presence of moral hazard and local conflict among individual and social groups. As a consequence of the social psychological disruption, rural production becomes more individualized and controls over collective resources, infrastructure and labor are eroded. Recalling our introductory comments, such processes clearly involve differentiating populations and trans-local dynamics. Let us give an example.

We have traced severe soil erosion in a mountainous agricultural region of Oaxaca, Mexico to the undermining of traditional political authority after the Mexican revolution. Collective institutions had maintained terraces and stabilized the soil dynamics, reducing erosion and maybe even stimulating soil accumulation. This type of landscape transformation also needed continuous and proper maintenance, since it introduced the potential for severe slope instability. The collective institutions revolved around the rich caciques being able to mobilize peasant labor for key activities. The caciques benefited from what was produced, but were expected to look after the peasants in hard times (a moral economy). Given that the peasants felt security in proportion to the wealth and prestige of their cacique and given the prestige attached directly to one's role in the collective labor, the labor tended to be very efficient. The revolution, however, ruptured this moral economy; transactions and prestige became monetarized following migration to industrial areas and semiproletarianization of the rural population; and the collective institutions collapsed (García-Barrios and García-Barrios, 1990; García-Barrios et al., 1991).

Implications for resource management, institutional insufficiency, and population

The social psychological disruption, together with the effective decrease of the household size due to the migration of the youngest and sometimes most productive members of the family and the continuing poverty of peasant households, reduces the labor and other resources available for land and resource management. That is, the bases not only of economic production, but of environmental and resource conservation and restoration are eroded with reorganizing and restricted institutional insufficiency. Recall the second picture from the introduction of how a balance between population and production is maintained or eroded. Rural populations have traditionally stimulated the regeneration of their natural resources, but this depended on collective practices, whose organizational basis is being undermined. Without this basis, externalities can accumulate, such as the production of waste, the environmental carrying capacity decreases and the "biophysical" limits to resource management and economic development are rapidly reached.[18]

The breakdown of local cooperative institutions concerned with terracing of mountainous areas, evident in Oaxaca, has been more widespread. After the conquest and colonization by European people of many mountainous areas in Latin America, Africa and the Middle and Far East, the local societies proved unable to maintain such cooperative institutions and agricultural infrastructure rapidly degraded. The history was somewhat repeated after World War II, when, due to massive emigration and semiproletarianization of their inhabitants, societies all around the world, including South Europe, failed to provide the necessary labor force and cooperation to sustain landscape infrastructure. As a consequence, many terrace systems and agricultural infrastructure are now rapidly degrading, promoting severe soil removal in some areas, downstream siltation, and increasing agricultural poverty.

The degradation of pasturelands in recently colonized tropical areas, in contrast, seems to reflect the inability even to develop (as against sustain) local cooperative institutions of resource management. Weed proliferation is the main cause of the short lifespan of pasture lands (five years or less) and arrested rainforest regeneration in the Amazon (Hecht, 1988). In Brazil, an important purpose of both small and large ranches is speculation. Little emphasis is paid to their appropriate management for optimal long lasting production. Such ill-managed pasture lands become sources of weeds propagules. This increases the probability that neighbouring lands become infested, even when these are adequately managed (De Janvry and García-Barrios, 1988).

Let us now insert this (re)organizing and restricted institutional insufficiency into our picture of population and environmental degradation. First note that, in the breakdown of terracing and subsequent soil erosion in Oaxaca (and other places), the environmental and resource degradation is linked to an absolute population reduction in rural areas where peasants are subject to out migration due to extensive semiproletarianization or market integration. As populations are greatly reduced, institutional insufficiency may worsen and land abandonment becomes more widespread, producing, in the long run, the collapse of the carrying capacity of the environment. Therefore, one might turn Boserup's claim about population increase and technological innovation completely upside down to analyze the dynamics of many "modernized" rural societies: communities with a rapidly decreasing population due to semiproletarianization may suffer from institutional, technological and resource degradation because of their inability rapidly to adjust their economic and social institutions to the new circumstances.

Clearly, poverty induction and institutional insufficiency may also occur where rural populations are increasing, as occurs in recently colonized tropical frontier regions where institutions regulating open access are systematically opposed by local interests. The size and/or growth of the population, however, may not tell us much; instead, to explain the escalation of consumption pressures on land, one needs to examine the structural conditions of land tenure and resource distribution, and larger socioeconomic forces that restrict employment creation and enhance social and geographical mobility. These pressures may be occurring even where ultimate carrying capacity is far from being reached – the situation in, for example, most rural and forested areas of Latin America (Collins, 1987) and Africa (Little, 1987); see also Arizpe et al. (1994).

Similarly, environmental problems associated with expansion and intensification of agriculture, such as over-drawn aquifers and polluted runoff, occur in countries with high population densities, such as India. Yet the problems also occur in countries with no absolute or large consumption pressures, showing that a neo-Malthusian emphasis in responding to environmental and agricultural crizes is misplaced. In fact, we are now in a position to comment on the limitations of most population policies.

The limitations of population policies

The discussion of the structural and social psychological basis of institutional insufficiency shows that a change in the poor's capacity to reorganize their own means of existence is a necessary, but overlooked condition for attaining sustainability in resource use (Ostrom, 1990). The links between poverty and resource degradation may only be broken by improving the endogenous capacity of poor societies to reorganize and improve their institutional means for collective action and technological change, that is, by improving their capacity to reduce reorganization-restricted labor surplus.

In several ways, neo-Malthusian programs centered on education, development or welfare assistance are limited by their irrelevance to, and sometimes their erosion of, the capacity of poor societies to reorganize and improve their institutions. For a start, the invocation of ultimate biophysical limits does not illuminate the current situation that the poor experience. Rather, the causes are to be found in structural poverty, which determine the moral and social context in which poor households define their rational responses and survival strategies. Knowledge of these causes enables us to understand why, at times, the poor increase the number of their expected offspring and "mine" natural resources.

Even when education focuses on technological and organizational development, it may be misdirected if the problem is not the absence of local education or culture but the impossibility for the people to use their sometimes profound local environmental knowledge to solve the problems of production and of the environment. In recent years, the overuse or careless use of mechanical technology and agro-chemicals has created major ecological threats for the rural and urban populations, spreading doubts about whether modern technologies are really better than traditional ones in the long run and spawning extensive research which has shown the conservation potential of the very sophisticated land management practices embodied in traditional knowledge systems and in modern agroecology (Faucheux, 1996; Richards, 1983; Hernández-Xolocotzi, 1985; Altieri and Anderson, 1986; Wilken, 1987). This same research, however, also shows the lack of effective use and rapid deterioration of this knowledge basis.

Among rural societies diffusion of any type of labor or organization-intensive technology, even when this has been developed according to the patterns of local culture is difficult. Making use of externally supplied education, knowledge and culture has an opportunity cost to poor populations and, in the absence of a proper institutional framework, may be difficult to transform into useful resources for survival. Rejection of, or resistance to, programs is thus likely. (The same is true with many programs of health and reproductive education.)

Economic, social and political organizing by the poor is, unlike simple externally supplied education, often threatening for national governments. National governments and international funds usually avoid providing resources (including organizational education) to stimulate such reorganizing. As a consequence, the potential benefits of cultural development are not realized.

There is an emerging consensus that welfare assistance to combat poverty should be clearly separated from production subsidies, since subsidies produce distortions in the market prices and hence generate welfare "basket cases." Since such schemes do not address reorganizing and restricted institutional insufficiency, they can only partly alleviate the poverty and the vicious circle of resource degradation.

Finally, given that continuous external assistance degrades the cultural, moral and psychological basis of individuals and societies, resource degeneration may even be exacerbated.

Moralistic and technocratic environmental discourse

The examples and interpretations in the previous sections indicate that there are many conceptually and empirically challenging issues that need further investigation if we are to develop a sophisticated understanding of the relationships among population, social organization, technology and environment in different situations. We are well aware, however, that we are not the first to offer a critique of the population problem.[19] Despite strong criticism, the belief persists that environmental concerns necessitate first and foremost (numerical and demographic, and sociological) population control measures.[20] Given that this reductive formulation of socioenvironmental change holds a strong attraction for many environmentalists, we need to explore the sources of its popularity if we are going to move neo-Malthusians; from experience, the conceptual and empirical challenges are unlikely to be sufficient to achieve that end.

To develop this line of discussion, we shift to a different style of analysis. Whereas, earlier, we pointed to the conceptual and empirical weaknesses of neo-Malthusian environmentalism, now we interpret this area sociologically. The sociology of science has, over the last fifteen years, observed the shaping of what counts as scientific knowledge, especially during controversies, and come to the conclusion that the truth of any contested result is rarely sufficient to account for its acceptance, and conversely, falsity for its rejection; see, for examples, Collins and Restivo (1983), Star (1988) and Woolgar (1988). The previous sections have indicated that other analyses of the dynamics of population and resources exist. Therefore, the fact of exponential growth of the global population and of many regional populations is *not* sufficient to account for why people believe in the population problem. Instead, we suggest, one can gain critical perspective on adherence to the idea of overpopulation by way of four propositions (adapted from Taylor's (1997) discussion of global environmental discourse), which we state and then develop:

1   It is fairly obvious that most environmental analyses are performed for some sponsor or client, or at least with some agency that would implement policy in mind. What is not so obvious is that certain courses of action are facilitated over others in the very formulation of scientific knowledge – in the problems chosen, categories adopted, relationships investigated, and degree of confirming evidence required (Taylor, 1989, 1992, 1995). Politics – in the sense of courses of social action pursued or favored – are not merely stimulated by scientific findings; politics are woven into the fabric of scientific knowledge.[21]

2   In the population discourse and, more generally, in steady-state discourse, two allied views of politics – the moralistic[22] and the technocratic – have been privileged. Both views of social action emphasize people's common interests in controlling growth while, at the same time, steering attention away from the difficult politics that result from differentiating social groups and nations having different interests in causing and alleviating environmental degradation. People know that there is a population problem, in part because they act as if they are unitary and not many differentiated groups.[23]

3   Inattention to the localized social and economic dynamics involving population change will ensure that scientists, environmentalists, and policy makers are continually surprized by unintended outcomes, unpredicted conflicts, and undesired coalitions.

4   To the extent that people attempt to focus on over population, to stand above such coalitions and the conduct of such conflicts, and to discount their responsibility for the unintended outcomes, they are more likely to facilitate increasingly coercive responses to environmental degradation.

Let us begin our elaboration of these four propositions by identifying a contradiction or, at least, a tension in our argument. Acceptance of the first proposition, when combined with the emphasis in the previons section on differentiated analysis, should lead one to seek multifaceted analyses of the politics woven into environmental knowledge, in preference to or before making any generalizations. Clearly, the other three propositions are generalizations. Moreover, the second proposition might, by analogy, lead one to interpret any such generalizations as an attempt to avoid dealing with the particularities, and other difficulties of achieving change (here, the change to be achieved would be in environmental analysis and policy). We acknowledge the contradiction. However, we have chosen not to attempt any differentiated, locally centered, translocal analyses of the politics of environmental knowledge making (Taylor, 1992, 1995). We think the generalizations in this section are provocative and useful heuristics to bring about some much needed reflection on the politics of knowledge. At the same time, we recognize that our raised level of polemic will not bring every-one around to our side. With this admission of this essay's limitations, let us forge ahead.

Recall the scenario of countries A and B (page 140–1). Clearly the story is too simple to constitute a sufficient description of the social dynamics in which people contribute differentially to environmental problems; see page 145. The conclusion can, however, be drawn that any demographic analysis separated from the differentiating social dynamics is taking a definite political stand. Everyone, of course, acknowledges that there are rich and poor, that the rich consume more per capita, and that it may be poverty that compels the poor when they "mine" their resources. Acknowledging the statistics of inequality does not, however, constitute an analysis of the *dynamics* of inequality. In the absence of serious intellectual work – conceptual and empirical – heartfelt caveats about the rich and the poor do not substantially alter the politics woven into the neo-Malthusian framework.

The politics of neo-Malthusian discourse can be characterized by allied moralistic and technocratic tendencies. Moralistic politics emphasizes that everyone must change (reduce their family size) to avert catastrophe. Coercion is rejected; each individual must make the change needed to preserve the environment. Technocratic, on the other hand, signifies that objective analyses (of population growth) identify the severity of the crisis and technical measures such as contraception and sterilization are developed and provided (with the appropriate policy stimuli) for individuals and countries to adopt. There is little tension, however, between voluntary individual responses and the managerial and technical ones. They are alike in attempting to bypass the political terrain in which different groups experience problems differently and act accordingly.[24] They appeal to common, undifferentiated interests as a corrective to corrupt, self-serving, naive and/or scientifically ignorant governance. Moreover, like all appeals to universal interests, special places are implicitly built into the proposed social transformations – the scientist as analyst and policy advisor; the moralist as guide, educator and enlightened leader (Taylor, 1988, 1997). In fact, in the absence of any analysis of differentiated interests, population discourse offers logically no other standpoints for an environmentalist to take.

So far, this is an interpretation based on the conceptual structure of neo-Malthusianism population discourse. That is, the privileging of moralistic and technocratic responses is entailed by the aggregate categories of demography and the invocation of ultimate limits (as against analyses of dynamics of differentiation) and by the focus on technical problems, such as contraceptive delivery (as against social-political reorganizing). One can, however, observe similar conceptual structures and privileging of the moralistic and technocratic more generally in environmental discourse (Taylor, 1988, 1992, 1997). We need to look, therefore, for pragmatic and practical reasons why a scientist might be susceptible to these moralistic and technocratic tendencies.

One reason might be that moralistic recruitment to a cause, and appeals to universal interests, can be effective as political tactics – human rights campaigns in times of severe political repression demonstrate that. More generally, political mobilization usually depends on stressing commonality of interests and playing down differences. Similarly, a technocratic outlook is an understandable orientation for scientists who would rather apply their special skills as best as they can to benefit society, than to expend energy in political organizing for which they have little experience or aptitude. However, perhaps the most important reason why a scientist might be susceptible to the moralistic and technocratic tendencies is the language that predominates in global environmental discourse (of which neo-Malthusian environmentalism is just one strand). It seems very difficult for anyone to engage in that discourse, and enlist others to their point of view, without slipping into the languages of moralistic recruitment and education or management. This was brought home to us in reviewing the discussion papers and notes circulated in preparation for a recent volume on equity and sustainability (Smith et al., 1994) and in reading an editorial for the journal *Conservation Biology* (Meffe et al., 1993). We will quote from these sources to illustrate how language that is familiar and well-meaning partakes of these two tendencies; many other texts would, however, have made our point equally well.[25]

In the papers, we read of a call for "a total picture of the world" and "*rechannel*ing activity into sustainable forms," phrases that reflect the hubris of a technocrat. Moralistic language was, however, more pervasive. Recruitment to the cause of responding to "our" common prospect was implied in the recurrent use of "we," "our culture," "our existence," "humanity," and in phrases such as "*our* builtin limitations of perception," "time available for *us* to change *our* ways." One paper discussed whether "society could be changed quickly enough," basing its claims around behavioral characteristics supposedly given to humans by their evolutionary history; that is, we are all fundamentally alike, being members of the same species. Individual behaviour and social dynamics were often expressed in the same undifferentiated terms, with individual metaphors used for social ideas and without mention of any structure between the individual and society: "Will humankind take the fork leading to disaster or . . . to survival?" Does society have the "*will* to alleviate poverty?" "Affluent societies can choose," despite the "perennial foot-dragging of the establishment." "Individuals vary [therefore] societies vary."

The editorial (Meffe et al., 1993) speaks of conservation biologists "possessing the professional responsibility to teach humankind about the perils" (p. 2) of continued population growth, "having the obligation to provide leadership in addressing the human population problem and developing solutions" (p. 2), and being able to "help promote policies to curb rapid population growth" (p. 3). "The population problem is stunningly clear and ought to be beyond denial" (p. 2). "The human species ignores or denies" the impending calamity (p. 2) – presumably those who draw attention to the population problem are excused from this collectivity. A brief mention of the "critical importance . . . of educating and empowering women" (p. 3) in the next to last paragraph hints that all people might not be equally responsible, but the conclusion returns to the dominant undifferentiated formulation: "Action is needed from everyone, at every turn . . . [in the cause of] human population control. Life itself is at stake" (p. 3).

Once we start to notice undifferentiated language, it seems to be everywhere, used by many who would prefer not to be labelled technocrat or moralist. So how can we make this interpretation work for us? It is obvious that we oppose neo-Malthusian environmentalism; we consider its science to be conceptually inadequate and often empirically superficial, and we want to assert the need for a differentiated politics in all environmental discourse. How can we move discussion of population and environmental degradation in this direction? Notice that we have pointed to the *practical* facilitations of the moralistic and technocratic tendencies, so we cannot expect these tendencies to be undermined by a mere counter-interpretation, that is, something working mostly on an intellectual and textual level. One approach, as we mentioned earlier, would be to go beyond the generalizations above, investigate particular cases of environmental knowledge making, and based on the diverse facilitations observed (Taylor, 1992, 1995), contribute to building conditions favourable to an alternative science. The step we take here, however, is to raise our polemical level and push our generalized critique further.

By arguing that certain politics (here, the moralistic and technocratic tendencies) and the science that facilitates them are not dictated by the nature of reality, we have intended to establish that scientists and other social agents choose to contribute to such science-politics. They are thus partly and jointly responsible for their consequences. Then, to urge neo-Malthusians (both self-professed and by disposition) to acknowledge that responsibility, we want to stress that their science-politics does have consequences. Policies based on abstract aggregated analyses make unintended effects and undesirable surprises inevitable, and, especially when these policies are promoted through crisis rhetoric that feeds on fears about the future, coercion and violence become more likely.

For example, in the early 1980s in Chiapas in southern Mexico, villagers became angry when they discovered that internationally funded health workers were sterilizing women after childbirth without their consent. The villagers killed two of these workers, only to have the government call in the military to raze the village in retaliation. This may be an extreme case, but it is not "unfortunate;" implicated in its causes is the underlying conceptualization of population control policies: The population problem translates readily into medical and clinical measures to reduce birth rates, which do not seem to require analysis of particular social and economic dynamics. Lacking such analysis, there is a much reduced chance that resistance would be anticipated, understood or tolerated by the international agency and the government. Also, the outlook that institutions in poor societies are generally weak and corrupt excuses the heavy handed action by some states, without shedding light on why some poor states are not so heavy handed. Moreover, the Chiapas event is not an isolated case. In India, during the 1960s and 1970s, especially during the Emergency of 1975–76, population programs resulted in injuries and deaths (Blaikie, 1985, pp. 98ff). In the resistance and revolt that occurred, democratic aspirations were linked with opposition to family control programs, surely an unfortunate coalition in the eyes of most Western environmentalists.

Over the last generation population growth has declined in many countries, and, in some cases, statistically significant effects of population control programs have been discovered, but see Pritchett (1994). Yet, the successful programs have piggy-backed upon other social changes favoring reductions in birthrates, such as employment of women in the formal work force, reductions in infant and child mortality, increased value of educating children at the same time as this education incurring a cost to the family, and so on (Blaikie, 1985). Analysis of the differentiating social and economic dynamics of particular situations would not only help to explain the occasional successes, but also to plan the broader family welfare programs needed to accompany birth control programs. Conversely, such analysis would help in anticipating the ways that the broader measures, such as adult literacy campaigns or the development of appropriate technology, can be undermined by the dynamics of labor scarcity or by those whose interests are threatened in some way. For these reasons alone, one might abandon the population problem as a framework for analysis and action, but let us push the critique yet one step further: the violent and coercive dimensions of the Chiapas program and programs in India of the 1960s and 1970s suggest the need to examine the population framework for inherent tendencies to coercion or violence.

The moral posture of most environmentalists – lifeboat ethicists (Hardin, 1972) and certain biocentric deep ecologists (Bradford, 1987) aside – is to support sustainable, liveable and equitable futures for all, free from economic and political coercion. In fact, many neo-Malthusian environmentalists reinforce their appeal for population control on the grounds that, without it, coercive measures will surely be taken when the crisis becomes more severe; see Ehrlich and Holdren (1971). The population framework, however, works against this professed commitment in many ways. Undifferentiated categories, such as population, affluent societies, and human nature, facilitate, as we have described, moralistic and technocratic discourse which provide little purchase, either in explaining the outcome of population control programs or in generating successful ones. The lack of analysis of the interrelations among population, social organization, technological change and the environment makes any analysis of the interrelation between the affluent and poor difficult, and, at best, holistic and simplistic. This, in turn, facilitates the abstraction of considering the poor and the affluent separately, in fact, as essentially different types in their institutions, consciousness and social possibilities (Ehrlich and Holdren, 1971; Cohen, 1995). The essential conception (McLaughlin, 1993) of affluent and poor people permits a simplistic analysis of the possibilities of productive and creative institutional response in societies that may be classified as, on average, affluent or poor. Furthermore, it reinforces the moral authority to educate or otherwise intervene that accrues to the affluent by virtue of their potential, through education and capable political and technical institutions, to respond to environmental problems.

Several factors then combine to make the discourse and practice of neo-

Malthusian environmentalism and population control susceptible to shifting into a coercive posture:

- frustration in the face of failed population control programs
- the urgency of the environmentalists' crisis rhetoric (Ehrlich and Ehrlich, 1990; Meffe et al., 1993)
- the lack of any differentiated categories and intermediate standpoint between the individual and society
- the contrast between capable and fair institutions in affluent societies and weak and corrupt in poor societies, and
- the moral authority to intervene.

In fact, what options other than inaction or coercion are available to a consistent neo-Malthusian environmentalist? Coercion is not just an abstract possibility, but one environmentalists more generally must pay attention to, as Nancy Peluso's (1993) analysis of the coercive dimensions of internationally endorsed conservation schemes, such as wildlife reserves in Kenya and forest conservation in Indonesia, indicates. Many conservation schemes require or assume state control over natural resources, whereas this is often resisted by local peoples who have been gaining some of their livelihood from the resources in question – elephant tusks, game, products from the forests, and so on. Conservation schemes have thus given the state and militarized institutions opportunities to gain more control of territory and peoples under a seemingly benevolent banner.

A different path to coercion derives, ironically, from the endorsement by various population theorists and steady state advocates of the market as a means to protect and promote individual freedom. Contrary to the ideology that market relations are a natural form of interaction among individuals, real markets always have to be constructed and the motivation to construct them generally depends on institutional arrangements that ensure the possibility of accumulation (Rees, 1992).[26] Deregulation and dismantling of the centralized state enhance the power of corporations to dictate more freely the terms of their exchanges. As Marginson (1988) observed, only capital is set free by the free market; people are not. More than a decade of deregulation has enhanced the freedom of corporations to decide the form and location of their investments (Leyshon, 1992). Given this, many environmentalists critical of the results of current economic development have made tactical alliances with corporate-led economic policy making to achieve any of their aims (Donahue, 1990). That is, they have acceded to the power of corporations to control labor and other resources, preferably not in the environmentalists' backyard, but, nevertheless, somewhere; see Daly and Goodland (1994).

Conclusion

We have argued that there are many reasons to break open neo-Malthusian environmentalist discourse into a social analysis of environmental change (Taylor and García-Barrios, 1995), to examine the complex ways social organization intervenes between population change and resource use. Arguing that there are favored courses of social action woven into all science, we have tried to challenge concerned population scientists and neo-Malthusian environmentalists to examine the standpoint they take in research and action. We have prodded them to see that a commitment to non-coercion and anti-violence should lead one to avoid moralistic and technocratic discourse, to dig deeper than the conventional analyses, which – in their structure, if not always explicitly – hold poor populations to be the most important drag for the construction of a sustainable world. Neither strongly expressed sympathies for the poor nor reduced personal consumption and fecundity exempt a neo-Malthusian environmentalist from our critique. The complex politics of differentiating, local and transnational resource management and environmental protection mean that being prepared to resist any repressive measures undertaken in the name of sustainability requires both serious conceptual and empirical work and difficult political engagement.

These challenges are, we think, worthy of the attention of all environmentalists and economists wanting to build a framework for sustainability and equity.

Notes

1   We thank Chris Finlayson and Reem Saffouri for research assistance, Phil Smith (Smith et al., 1994) for prodding us to lighten our argument, and Elena Alvarez-Buylla, Ron Herring, Henry Shue and David Mayer for their helpful comments. Travel funds from the Cornell International Institute for Food Agriculture and Development facilitated our collaboration.

2   There is a substantial body of research in social analysis of environmental change upon which the construction of sustainability should be building, but scarcely has been to date. For reviews, see Faucheux (1996), Norgaard (1984), Watts and Peet (1993), Neumann and Schroeder (1995), and Taylor and García-Barrios (1995). For analyses sympathetic to that in this essay, see Stonich (1989) and Arizpe et al. (1994).

3   The focus on the poor is justified by our observation that actually existing population discourse, especially around formulation of policy, is well developed only where it focuses on the poor (UN Population Fund, 1991). Notwithstanding this specific focus, we hope that readers, even those who distance themselves from neo-Malthusianism, will think about how our points can be translated and extended to other areas. In particular, the social, economic and environmental dynamics of the urban poor and of affluent consumers invite similar treatments. At various points in the paper and notes, we also indicate some extensions of our critical interpretations to market-based responses to environmental degradation, attempts to bring equity considerations into the heart of economics and global environmental discourse in general. In these areas, discussion is limited to the extent that it steers attention away from the concrete and *differentiating* social, economic and environmental dynamics governing the maintenance of inequality, and environmental degradation in actual markets.

4   It is important to recognize that the term "population" is used in the numerical and demographic sense, as well as the sociological, sense.

5   Demeny (this volume) combines the three orientations, but with the macro-economic being dominant. He acknowledges that reproductive choice and health are more and more being used to justify family planning and population [control] programs, but

believes that, if the collective, macro-economic benefits are stressed, such programs will be better supported by donors and governments of lesser developed countries (LDCs). Moreover, the programs need to be of higher quality for people to use them more than they do in most LDCs. Similarly, while he makes reference to the ways parents have made child-bearing decisions on (micro-)economic grounds ("market-based outcomes"), Demeny justifies government policies aimed at modifying these decisions by invoking the positive effects on any LDC's economic growth. Caveats about complexity and local pecularities notwithstanding, his discussion centres on a direct causal relation between (numerical and demographic) population and economic growth (the environment is not his focus). When governments have scarce resources, population programs deserve to be singled out for support. In contrast, our essay posits a qualitatively different form of explanation, in which population is not analytically central, and social action is not conceptualized as either individual decisions or government interventions. We would view the poor performance of population control programs as an invitation to examine how local institutions and practices, including those supporting market transactions, are organized, maintained, or eroded. One point in common between the essays is that neither argues against the reproductive health and choice justification for making contraception more widely accessible.

6 Jolly (1994) distinguishes four macro-economic theories relating population and the environment and the UN Population Fund (1991) provides a clear example. The reproductive health and choice orientation became prominent in the policy arena during the buildup to the UN Conference on Population and Development held in Cairo, September 1994 (International Women's Health Coalition, 1993), and was emphasized in the "Program of Action" endorsed by the conference. Neo-Malthusian environmentalists have been acknowledging this theme in their recent statements about population control (Ehrlich and Ehrlich, 1990, p. 216; Meffe et al., 1993).

7 We are tempted to declare that there are very few global problems – present, past, or future – but, to be more subtle, we need to ask who sees problems as global (Taylor, 1997). In this spirit, on pages 152–8, we interpret globalized discourse in terms of the particular social actions and politics privileged by it.

8 We recognize that aggregate figures can draw attention to problems requiring attention or explanation: changing sex ratios of infants in China with the imposition of the one child per couple policy pointed to increasing female infanticide; Taiwan and South Korea, but not the Philippines, achieving demographic transitions after World War II, pointed to the importance of successful land and educational reform (Hartmann, 1987). Nevertheless, the explanation or the successful policy response requires going well beyond the aggregate figures.

9 Ehrlich and Holdren formulated their neo-Malthusian position in 1971 explicitly in terms of a mathematical equation, $I = PF$, where I is the negative impact of population, P is the population size and F is a function denoting the per capita impact. Population biology, Ehrlich's field, has, in recent years, begun to pay attention to the qualitative differences in predictions based on models that distinguish individuals within a population (in terms of their spatial location or other characteristics) when compared with the older style of using aggregate variables to describe a population (Huston et al., 1988). Nevertheless, the aggregate equation, with F spelled out as AT (affluence × impact of technology used) remains central to the analyzes of Ehrlich and his collaborator (Ehrlich and Ehrlich, 1990; Meffe et al., 1993).

10 For an example of such ambiguity, see UN Population Fund (1991), in which a diagram of "links between demographic and natural resource issues" (p. 13) is consis-

tent with a complex account of interconnected social, economic, and environmental dynamics, but the discussion centres on the population growth and natural resource degradation of poor countries.

11   Discussions or even condemnations of the disproportionate resource use of the rich do not negate our criticisms. The key question for this essay is what responses are logically consistent with the causes being identified (Harvey, 1974), not whether an environmentalist shows awareness of inequality among and within nations.

12   A society's demands on resources and the speed of growth in those demands will condition the possibilities and processes of sociotechnical reorganizing and erosion, but the sheer size of the population or its resource demands do not, either by themselves or as some "root causes," determine the timing and nature of the environmental degradation.

13   By extension, if the population problem for affluent societies is cast in terms of overconsumption and its consequences, the same is true for the abstract dynamics of consumption growth. Instead, we should examine the inability of the affluent to reorganize social institutions and technology so as to ensure satisfaction without compulsive consumption (Roberts, 1979; Max-Neef, 1986).

14   Folbre (1994) makes an analogous and much more thoroughly developed case in her analysis of the social, economic and technological dynamics involved in the reproduction of labor. Mainstream demographers are also now recognizing that, even to explain such established ideas as the demographic transition, they need to invoke mediating variables and undertake find grained analyses; see Handwerker (1986), Simmons (1988, p. 91ff) and Preston (1989, pp. 15–16). The field's rationale remains, however, to explain population changes and the reproduction and migration patterns associated with those changes. Although our critique is focused on neo-Malthusian environmentalism, the shifts of perspective promoted in this paper can be extended to demography. Some younger demographers are preparing the way. For example, Elliott (1994), aiming to bridge aggregate statistical analysis and case studies, proposes a "Boolean based comparative method" for analyzing the relationship between population and deforestation. Riley (1995) reviews the challenges feminist perspectives raises for demographic questions, methods, and theory, and for policy based upon demography. Folbre (1994) should become an important guide or model for such work. See also references cited in Riley (1995) and in Ginsburg and Rapp (1991).

15   In this chapter, we invert the priority of justification from some moral or microeconomic foundations to analysis of social context and social constructedness of situations and of discourse about them. People wanting to develop a moral-economics need to depart from foundationalist thinking, because neo-liberal economists will probably win on those terms. They can readily construe moral arguments as reinforcing their basic tenet that people are egoistic utility maximizers; it is because this drives behavior that we need morals to check the undesired consequences. See also note 21.

16   See note 6.

17   See Bartra (1979); Bhaduri (1983); Bardhan (1984); Binswager and Rosenzweig (1986); Cornia and Stewart (1987); De Janvry and García Barrios (1988); García-Barrios and García-Barrios (1990); Watts and Peet (1993).

18   Moreover, this has usually occurred in local and national societies where the local and national state has not been able or willing to induce the innovation and diffusion of technologies for sustainable agriculture adapted to the new labor conditions, nor to generate institutions able to provide adequate public goods and the means of internalizing the externalities which have arisen.

19   For critiques of neo-Malthusian environmentalism, see Commoner (1971), Harvey (1974), Schnaiberg (1981) and Arizpe et al. (1994). For critiques of neo-Malthusianism more generally and population discourse, see Finkle and Crane (1975), Bondestam (1980), Hartmann (1987), Mehler (1989), Duden (1992), Nair (1992), Population Reference Bureau (1993), Greenhalgh (1994) and Stein (1995).

20   We have observed that this is especially true among Americans who came of age in the 1960s, a fact inviting social-historical analysis and interpretation.

21   This emphasis on knowledge as politics is consistent with an interpretive style of analysis that pays attention to the language and rhetoric of any discourse, and refuses to take literally what is said. Claims about reality become vulnerable to deconstruction and reinterpretation (see note 26) and it becomes more difficult to make generalizations or to enlist support for policy recommendations. In contrast, the premise of many papers in this volume is that basic principles are needed to govern actions and institutions.

22   Moralistic is not an ideal term, because for some readers it connotes the moralist accusing noncompliers of being bad. In contrast, we want to emphasize the connotation of the moralist recruiting to a cause, proselytizing or evangelizing.

23   One could analyze the constructions of population control that are more purely technocratic, but we have chosen to concentrate on the combined moralistic and technocratic dimensions of neo-Mathusianism, considering this interpretation to have more relevance to environmentalists.

24   We might also describe this as "consensus-seeking," noting that among steady-state proposals the population problem is the only formulation likely to generate much consensus. The resistance of those with an interest in capital accumulation means that other policies with a general and clear impact on development and sustainability cannot generate political consensus at the national and international levels.

25   In the resulting volume (Smith et al., 1994), quotations such as those given in the text were accompanied by much more attention to stratification within and among nations, and the technocratic currents were less apparent. (Copies of the precirculated documents are available from the authors.) Taylor (1997) indicates how the languages of moralistic recruitment and management are equally mixed in Meadows et al. (1972), Clark and Holling (1985), and Clark (1989); see also Brandt (1983) and Ehrlich and Ehrlich (1990). Language does not, however, stand on its own and the reader should not forget the conceptual argument about the aggregate categories and undifferentiated dynamics entailing moralistic or technocratic responses.

26   A generation ago, the social historian E. P. Thompson described 18th century struggles over the constitution of the modern market against traditional face-to-face markets, struggles which were underwritten by appeals to a moral economy; see Thompson (1991). In other words, the abstract ideal of a market was being generated at the same time, ironically, as its concrete counterpart was being eclipsed by transactions based on unequal information about and unequal control over supplies, demand, and prices. Acknowledgment of the constructedness, rather than naturalness, of market transactions would add complexity and depth to economic and moral-economic theory. If the perspectives of our essay were extended to environmental economics, analysis would begin with models of an already and always politicized economy. History of science may also provide some guidance in making such a conceptual inversion. In recent years, it has been providing social histories for key notions, such as risk, rationality, factuality, objectivity, truth and individuality. A great deal of social negotiation over conflicting and changing conventions precedes the establishment of any of these "foundational" concepts; in fact, the apparent stability of such concepts requires ongoing maintenance; see Shapin (1994).

References

Altieri, M. and Anderson, M. (1986) An ecological basis for the development of alternative agricultural systems for small farmers in the Third World. *American Journal of Alternative Agriculture*, 1, 30–8.

Arizpe, L., Stone, M. P. and Major, D. C. (eds) (1994) *Population and Environment: Rethinking the Debate*. Boulder, CO: Westview Press.

Bardhan, P. K. (1984) *Land, Labor and Rural Poverty: Essays in Development Economics*. New York: Columbia University Press.

Bartra, A. (1979) *La Explotación del Trabajo Campesino por el Capital*. Mexico: Ed. Macehual.

Bhaduri, A. (1983) *The Economic Structure of Backward Agriculture*. New York: Academic Press.

Binswanger, H. and Rosenzweig, M. (1986) Behavioral and material determinants of production relations in agriculture. *Journal of Development Studies*, 22, 503–39.

Blaikie, P. (1985) *The Political Economy of Soil Erosion in Developing Countries*. London: Longman.

Bondestam, L. (1980) The political ideology of population control. In L. Bondestam and S. Bergström (eds) *Poverty and Population Control*. New York: Academic Press, pp. 1–38.

Bongaarts, J. (1992) Population growth and global warming. *Population and Development Review*, 18, 299–319.

Boserup, E. (1965) *The Conditions of Agricultural Growth: the Economics of Agrarian Change Under Population Pressure*. London: Allen and Unwin.

Bradford, G. (1987) How deep is deep ecology: A challenge to radical environmentalism. *Fifth Estate*, 22 (3), 3–64.

Brandt, W. (ed.) (1983) *North-South: a Program for Survival*. London: Pan Books.

Clark, W. (1989) Managing planet earth. *Scientific American*, 261, 46–54.

Clark, W. and Holling, C. (1985) Sustainable development of the biosphere: Human activities and global change. In T. Malone and J. Roederer (eds) *Global change*. Cambridge: Cambridge University Press, pp. 474–90.

Cohen, J. (1995) *How Many People Can the Earth Support?* New York: Norton.

Cohen, S. (1993) The road from Rio to Cairo: Towards a common agenda. *International Family Planning Perspectives*, 19, 61–6.

Collins, J. (1987) Labor scarcity and ecological change. In P. Little, M. Horowitz and A. Nyerges (eds) *Lands at Risk in the Third World: Local Level Perspectives*. Boulder: Westview, pp. 19–37.

Collins, R. and Restivo, S. (1983) Development, diversity, and conflict in the sociology of science. *Sociological Quarterly*, 24, 185–200.

Commoner, B. (1971) *The closing circle*. New York: Knopf.

Cornia, G., Jolly, R. and Stewart, F. (eds) (1987) *Adjustment with a Human Face: Protecting the Vulnerable and Promoting Growth*. Oxford: Clarendon Press.

Daly, H. and Goodland, R. (1994) An ecological-economic assessment of deregulation of international commerce under GATT. *Population and Environment*, 15, 395–427, 477–503.

De Janvry, A. (1980) *The Agrarian Question and Reformism in Latin America*. Baltimore: The Johns Hopkins University Press.

De Janvry, A. and García-Barrios, R. (1988) Rural poverty and environmental degradation in Latin America: causes, effects, and alternative solutions. Unpublished paper presented at the International Consultation on Environment, Sustainable Development, and the

Role of Small Farmers, International Fund for Agricultural Development, Rome, October 11–13.

Dixon-Mueller, R. (1993) *Population Policy and Women's Rights: Transforming Reproductive Choice.* Westport, CT: Praeger.

Donahue, J. (1990) Environmental board games. *Multinational Monitor*, (March), 10–12.

Duden, B. (1992) Population. In W. Sachs (ed.) *The Development Dictionary: A Guide to Knowledge as Power.* New Jersey: Zed Books, pp. 146–57.

Durham, W. (1979) *Scarcity and Survival in Central America: Ecological Origins of the Soccer War.* Stanford, CA: Stanford University Press.

Ehrlich, P. and Ehrlich, A. (1990) *The Population Explosion.* New York: Simon & Schuster.

Ehrlich, P. and Holdren, J. (1971) Impact of population growth. *Science*, 117, 1212–17.

Elliott, J. R. (1994) Population and deforestation in central America: An alternative approach. Unpublished paper delivered to the American Sociological Association, Los Angeles, August 5–9.

Faucheux, S. (1996) *Models of Sustainable Development.* Aldershot: Edward Elgar.

Finkle, J. L. and Crane, B. B. (1975) The politics of Bucharest: Population, development and the New International Economic Order. *Population Development Review*, 1, 87–114.

Folbre, N. (1994) *Who Pays for the Kids? Gender and the Structures of Constraint.* New York: Routledge.

García-Barrios, R. and García-Barrios, L. (1990) Environmental and technological degradation in peasant agriculture: A consequence of development in Mexico. *World Development*, 18, 1569–85.

García-Barrios, R., García-Barrios, L. and Alvarez-Buylla, E. (1991) *Lagunas: Deterioro Ambiental y Tecnológico en el Campo Semiproletarizado.* Mexico: El Colegio de México.

Ginsburg, F. and Rapp, R. (1991) The politics of reproduction. *Annual Review of Anthropology*, 20, 311–43.

Greenhalgh, S. (1994) Controlling births and bodies in village China. *American Ethnologist*, 21, 3–30.

Hall, C. A. S., Pontius, R. G., Coleman, L. and Ko, J-Y. (1994) The environmental consequences of having a baby in the United States. *Population and environment*, 15, 505–24.

Handwerker, W. P. (1986) Culture and reproduction: Exploring micro/macro linkages. In W. P. Handwerker (ed.) *Culture and Reproduction: An Anthropological Critique of Demographic Transition Theory.* Boulder, CO: Westview, pp. 1–28.

Hardin, G. (1972) *Exploring New Ethics for Survival.* New York: Viking Press.

Hartmann, B. (1987) *Reproductive Rights and Wrongs: The Global Politics of Population Control and Contraceptive Choice.* New York: Harper & Row.

Harvey, D. (1974) Population, resources and the ideology of science. *Economic Geography*, 50, 256–77.

Hecht, S. (1988) Conversion of forest to pasture in Amazonia: Some environmental and social effects. Unpublished working paper, Department of Urban and Regional Planning, University of California, Los Angeles.

Hernández-Xolocotzi, E. (1985) *Xolocotzia, Tomo I: Revsita de Geografía Agrícola* (Xolocotzia, 1: Review of Agravian Geography) México: Universidad Autónoma de Chapingo.

Huston, M., DeAngelis, D. and Post, W. (1988) From individuals to ecosystems: A new approach to ecological theory. *Bioscience*, 38, 682–91.

Institute for Philosophy & Public Policy (1993) Ethics and global population. *Philosophy & Public Policy*, 13 (4), 1–32.

International Women's Health Coalition (1993) Women's declaration on population policies. *Race, poverty and the environment*, 4 (2), 37–8.

Jolly, C. L. (1994) Four theories of population change and the environment. *Population and Environment*, 16, 61–90.

Lewis, A. (1954) Development with unlimited supply of Labor. *The Manchester School*, 22, 139–92.

Leyshon, A. (1992) The transformation of regulatory order: Regulating the global economy and environment. *Geoforum*, 23, 249–68.

Little, P. (1987) Land use conflicts in the agricultural/pastoral borderlands: The case of Kenya. In P. Little, M. Horowitz and A. Nyerges (eds) *Lands at Risk in the Third World: Local Level Perspectives*. Boulder: Westview, pp. 195–212.

Marginson, S. (1988) The economically rational individual. *Arena*, 84, 105–14.

Max-Neef, M. (1986) *Desarrollo a Escala Humana: Una Opción Para el Futuro*. Motala, Sweden: CEPAUR-Fundación Dag Hammarskjold.

McLaughlin, P. (1993) Essentialism, generative entrenchment and the Agrarian question. Unpublished working paper, Sociology Department, Rutgers University, Newark, NJ.

Meadows, D., Meadows, D., Randers, J. and Behrens, W. (1972) *The Limits to Growth*. New York: Universe Books.

Meffe, G. K., Ehrlich, A. H. and Ehrenfeld, D. (1993) Human population control: The missing agenda. *Conservation Biology*, 7, 1–3.

Mehler, B. (1989) History of the American Eugenics Society. Ph.D. Thesis. Champaign-Urbana: University of Illinois.

Nair, S. (1992) Population policies and the ideology of population control in India. *Issues in Reproduction and Genetic Engineering*, 5 (3), 237–52.

Neumann, R. and Schroeder, R. (eds) (1995) Manifest ecological destinies: Local rights and global environmental agendas, Special issue. *Antipode*, 27 (4), 321–448.

Norgaard, R. N. (1984) Coevolutionary development potential. *Land Economics*, 60 (2), 160–73.

Ostrom, E. (1990) *Governing the Commons: The Evolution of Institutions for Collective Action*. New York: Cambridge University Press.

Palloni, A. (1994) The relation between population and deforestation: Methods for drawing causal inferences from macro and micro studies. In Arizpe et al., pp. 125–65.

Peluso, N. (1993) Coercing conservation: The politics of state resource control. In R. Lipschutz and K. Conca (eds) *The State and Social Power in Global Environmental Politics*. New York: Columbia University Press, pp. 46–70.

Pimental, D., Harman, R., Pasenza, M., Pecarsky, J. and Pimentel, M. (1994) Natural resources and an optimum human population. *Population and Environment*, 5, 347–69.

Population Reference Bureau (1993) What women want: Women's concerns about global population issues. Report to the Pew Charitable Trust Global Stewardship Initiative, June 1993.

Preston, S. (1989) The social sciences and the population problem. In J. Stycos (ed.) *Demography as an Interdiscipline*. New Brunswick, NJ: Transaction Publishers, pp. 1–26.

Pritchett, L. (1994) Desired fertility and the impact of population policies. *Population and Development Review*, 20 (1), 1–55.

Rees, J. (1992) Markets – The panacea for environmental regulation? *Geoforum*, 23, 383–94.

Richards, P. (1983) Ecological change and the politics of land use. *African Studies Review*, 26, 1–72.

Riley, N. (1995) Challenging demography: Contributions from feminist theory. Unpublished working paper, Sociology Department. Brunswick, Maine: Bowdoin College.

Roberts, A. (1979) *The Self-Managing Environment*. London: Allison & Busby.

Schnaiberg, A. (1981) Will population slowdowns yield resource conservation? Some social demurrers. *Qualitative Sociology*, 4 (1), 21–33.

Shapin, S. (1994) *A Social History of Truth: Civility and Science in Seventeenth-Century England*. Chicago: University of Chicago Press.

Simmons, O. (1988) *Perspectives on Development and Population Growth in the Third World*. New York: Plenum.

Simon, J. (1990) *Population Matters: People, Resources, Environment, and Immigration*. New Brunswick, NJ: Transaction Publishers.

Smith, P. B., Okoye, S. E., Wilde, J. D. and Deshingkar, P. (eds) (1994) *The World at the Crossroads: Towards a Sustainable, Equitable and Liveable World*. London: Earthscan.

Southgate, D. and Basterrechea, M. (1992) Population growth, public policy and resource degradation: The case of Guatemala. *Ambio*, 21 (7), 460–4.

Star, S. (1988) Introduction: The sociology of science and technology. *Social Problems*, 35, 197–205.

Stein, D. (1995) *People Who Count: Population and Politics, Women and Children*. London: Earthscan.

Stonich, S. (1989) The dynamics of social processes and environmental destruction: A Central American case study. *Population and Development Review*, 15, 269–96.

Taylor, P. (1988) Technocratic optimism, H. T. Odum and the partial transformation of ecological metaphor after World War 2. *Journal of the History of Biology*, 21, 213–44.

Taylor, P. (1989) Revising models and generating theory. *Oikos*, 54, 121–6.

Taylor, P. (1992) Reconstructing socioecologies: System dynamics modeling of nomadic pastoralists in sub-Saharan Africa. In A. Clarke and J. Fujimura (eds) *The Right Tools for the Job: At Work in the Twentieth Century Life Sciences*. Princeton: Princeton University Press, pp. 115–48.

Taylor, P. (1995) Building on construction: An exploration of heterogeneous constructionism, using an analogy from psychology and a sketch from socioeconomic modeling. *Perspectives on Science*, 3, 66–98.

Taylor, P. (1997) How do we know we have global environmental problems: Undifferentiated science-politics and its potential reconstruction. In P. Taylor, S. Halfan and P. Edwards (eds) *Changing Life: Genomes, Ecologies, Bodres, Commodities*. Minneapolis: University of Minnesota Press, pp. 149–74.

Taylor, P. and García-Barrios, R. (1995) The social analysis of environmental change: From systems to intersecting processes. *Social Science Information*, 34, 5–30.

Thompson, E. P. (1991) *Customs in Common*. London: Merlin Press.

UN Population Fund (1991) *Population and Environment: The Challenges Ahead*. New York: United Nations Population Fund.

Vandermeer, J. (1977) Ecological determinism. In Ann Arbor Science for the People (ed.), *Biology as a Social Weapon*. Minneapolis: Burgess Publishing Co. pp. 108–22.

Vitousek, P., Ehrlich, P., Ehrlich, A. and Matson, P. (1986) Human appropriation of the products of photosynthesis. *Bioscience*, 36, 368–73.

Watts, M. and Peet, R. (eds) (1993) Environment and development, special double issue. *Economic Geography*, 69 (3), 229–311 and 69 (4), 329–448.

Wilken, G. (1987) *Good Farmers: Traditional Agricultural Resource Management in Mexico and Central America*. Berkeley: University of California Press.

Woolgar, S. (1988) *Science: The Very Idea*. London: Tavistock.

8

Population Growth and the State: Reconciling Private Wants and the Public Interest

Paul Demeny

Once an esoteric concept, the size of the global population is now a statistic of common currency. The UN tells us, for example, that the figure for 1995 is 5.7 billion and that it was 2.5 billion at mid-century. The estimates are often quoted at a level of precision down to the nearest thousand – such as 2,519,742,000 in 1950 and 5,716,407,000 in 1995.[1] Of course, even the rounded numbers are to be taken with a degree of caution, but the true global figure may be reasonably expected to lie within an interval not wider than perhaps 100 million on either side of these estimates.

Calling attention to the possible numerical inaccuracy of the global estimate is less important, however, than noting its statistical provenance. There is no such thing as a world census; the global population is a composite of population sizes separately enumerated or estimated for the key constituting elements of the contemporary world system, the nearly 200 independent states.[2] Not surprisingly, in many contexts the substantive significance of the global total is elusive – often it is not much more than a demonstration of the statistician's capacity to add. The same proposition applies to other demographic characteristics calculated for the world as a whole, such as birth and death rates, or characteristics of the composition of the population. In other contexts – such as the human impact on the global environment, the political, economic, and military significance of shifts in relative population size, inequalities generated by differential rates of material development as affected by differences in demographic dynamics, the regulation of cross-border migratory flows – global (or else broad continental or regional) population figures and other demographic attributes *are* meaningful as well as of increasing importance. However, understanding such over-arching issues is best approached by seeing them in their primary manifestation: as matters of concern to the separate actors in the international arena. In interaction with each other, individual players in that arena extend their domestic functions by seeking to advance their separate national interests. They do so through engaging in bargaining and cooperation with other nations, and, in that process, applying persuasion and intellectual argument, or deploying economic, political, and military power in the service of their particular ends.

Indeed, in the absence of supranational authority – an absence that, save for modest developments, can be confidently extrapolated into the indefinite future – it is the national state that represents the preeminently important large frame for political and economic organization in the modern era. Within their defined geographic boundaries, states endeavor to establish and maintain a legal order that guarantees peace and security, to set and enforce the formal rules that condition the modes of social interaction, and to provide, directly or indirectly, a range of services to the citizenry – to the nation – or various subgroups. Population size, composition, and population dynamics are important attributes that can influence the degree of success with which states perform these functions, hence the level of welfare enjoyed by the citizenry. The state cannot be indifferent as to the demographic characteristics of the population it represents.

Demographic characteristics, therefore, are potential policy variables: candidates for purposeful intervention by the state. The putative rationale for such intervention would be the claim that demographic behavior exhibits a special form of market failure – namely, that private decisions in the demographic domain, shaped only by spontaneous interaction among lower-level social groupings, result in outcomes that, in terms of some relevant measure of welfare, are inferior to what could be achieved through modifications of those demographic outcomes by means of policy measures instituted and carried out by the state.

In one formulation, welfare can be thought of as a measurable, or at least directly assessable, attribute of society as a whole. Potentially attainable demographic outcomes can be ranked by their relative desirability as to their effect on social welfare, a ranking that admittedly involves difficult issues of interpersonal, intergroup, and intergenerational comparisons. To the extent that some of these potential demographic outcomes are available only through application of deliberate policy measures, judgment about their desirability must of course also take into account the cost of the policies necessary to attain them. Lacking an all-knowing and impartial observer whose judgment is accepted by the citizenry, decision making about the role of the state in shaping demographic behavior is the task of the political process. The nature and characteristics of the rules governing that process – the degree of participation by the potentially affected individuals, their relative positions of power and influence, the range and nature of acceptable modes of state intervention set by prior agreement, the validity of the knowledge base brought into the deliberations – will be crucial determinants of the population policy choices that may be adopted. Similar factors will also condition the success – the costs and the effectiveness – of the execution of the policies themselves, hence their ultimate effect on social welfare.

An alternative approach to policy making in the domain of population as in other matters – no less difficult in application but more congruent with the ethos of modern constitutional democracy – focuses not on the outcomes of any given policy but on the policy process itself. In this formulation, a state is understood as an instrument in the service of the individuals constituting that state, with its powers deriving from, and constrained by, explicit agreement by the citizens. Conceptually, such agreement is embodied in a constitutional contract, ideally adopted under a veil of ignorance,[3] spelling out the fundamental rights of the contracting parties, the basic rules that circumscribe the power and functions of the state and protect those rights, and the institutional mechanisms through which the polity is to confront and tackle specific, including yet unforeseen, issues. Modification of the constitutional agreement itself is typically subject to stringent constraints of near-unanimity. In the post-constitutional stage, agreed-upon decision making rules are permitted to be more flexible – such as requiring simple majority support for the adoption of specific policy measures, as long as those measures are consistent with the provisions of the basic constitutional contract.

Given such arrangements, the need to pass judgment over the welfare significance of alternative social configurations, including the relative desirability of demographic outcomes, does not arise: any outcome that results from observing the codified rules of the political decision making process is *ipso facto* accepted as optimal. Dissatisfaction with any given state of affairs on the part of the citizens – including dissatisfaction with demographic matters – may arise. Such discontent is expected to generate proposals that, in the opinion of those making them, would lead to an improvement – not only enhance their own welfare but also be accepted as an improvement by their fellow citizens. In strict terms, improvement in the democratic polity is to be interpreted in the sense of Pareto: increasing the welfare of at least some without hurting others, or causing an improvement in the welfare of some that is sufficiently high so that those who gain could compensate those who lose. Plausible proposals for improvement are then submitted to the agreed-upon political process: those passing the test are adopted; those failing are rejected. The constitutional agreement on less stringent decision making rules in most policy matters, and the common interest in observing such rules, can permit adoption of proposals (on matters not encroaching on constitutionally protected rights) that do not meet the strict Pareto criteria. By the rules of the democratic polity, changes so generated will still represent an improvement.

The aim of this chapter is to discuss the stance of the state in modern history in intervening in demographic matters – manifestations of the aggregated choices of private decision makers – seeking to represent the public interest or at least some approximation thereof. The focus of the discussion is on the variables that have traditionally attracted the greatest attention in public policy considerations concerning population: the rate of population growth, and its main proximate demographic determinants and consequences, notably fertility and mortality. A common, if heroically stylized summary of the last two hundred years' population history depicts individual countries as traveling on a path of "demographic transition." The transition starts from an initial situation characterized by high mortality and more or less matching high fertility, hence little or no population growth. It ends in a situation characterized by low mortality and more or less matching low fertility, hence, once again, little or no population growth. This familiar construct provides a convenient roadmap for the narrative that follows. It proceeds roughly along chronological lines, tracing the influences that generated the transition, especially the decline in fertility, and the role of the state in that historical process, with particular emphasis on the paradigmatic Western experience. In the concluding section, I discuss the role of the state in third-world transitions and consider the emergence of the issue of population growth as an important topic on the international agenda.

The state and early demographic transition

When the average level of mortality in a population is high, survival necessitates maintenance of a high average level of fertility. If, for example, the expectation of life at birth (a summary measure of mortality in a population) is 35 years, the total fertility rate (the average number of children born to women who survive until the end of their childbearing years) must be approximately four in order to keep the rate of aggregate population growth from falling below zero. With an expectation of life at birth of 20 years, the fertility rate that assures a zero rate must be approximately six children per woman; see Coale and Demeny (1966).

Mortality levels of such orders of magnitude were typical in preindustrial populations – the higher survival figure just cited characterizing Western Europe, the lower figure commonly found in the populations of south and east Asia, and in Africa. Apart from variation of average levels between populations, mortality also fluctuated over time, reflecting the impact of periodic epidemics or setbacks in food production caused by climatic adversity or by war or other social turmoil. Under such circumstances, collective survival required effective mechanisms to keep fertility high.

High fertility in preindustrial populations, however, did not mean uncontrolled fertility. In all known populations, fertility was always much below the levels that would be permitted by human biological potential; indeed, such control was undoubtedly a key to the evolutionary success of the human species. In traditional societies, the behavioral patterns limiting biological fertility – such as late marriage, lengthy breastfeeding periods, or postpartum abstinence – reflected primarily generalized social, rather than purposeful individual, control. Social controls, conditioned as they were by cultural contingencies and by local history, yielded fertility levels that showed significant variations from society to society; to call such fertility "natural" – as demographers often do – represents a high degree of linguistic license in labeling. Social controls operated through internalized norms, shared expectations on proper personal conduct, and religious injunctions but these cannot be regarded as arbitrarily selected or random; they undoubtedly reflected historically evolved and tested group interest. Through such social mechanisms conformity of individual behavior to the collective interest was informally but effectively enforced.

However, the customary interpretation which in pre-industrial (or "pre-transition") societies denies the role of individual agency in fertility behavior by pointing to the force of such social control mechanisms in shaping levels of fertility is tenuous. Conformity to social expectations and rules by individuals must have reflected general congruence of individual and collective interests. If substantial rewards existed in a society that would have made lower or higher fertility appealing for many of its individual members (or member-families), there is little doubt that the appropriate behavioral responses would have been forth-coming, either through systematic deviation of individual behavior from the patterns prescribed by social norms, or by appropriately accommodating shifts in the social norms themselves.

It is true, however, that with the traditional fertility regulating mechanisms, responses to unforeseen opportunities, such as opened up by changing demo-graphic circumstances (for example, a fortuitous fall in mortality) or to techno-logical advances or environmental challenges, were generally sluggish, as well as varying from society to society. Thus the demographic dynamics of pre-industrial populations present examples of patterns of behavior that appear dysfunctional in the short or medium run, if evaluated by the material interests of the popula-tions that experienced those patterns. Success in avoiding such "market failures" – failures of spontaneous social interaction and individual-level responses to yield results that would best serve the collective interest – varied from population to population. When, for example, opportunities for accommodating substantial population increases were limited, the dominant demographic configuration in early modern Western Europe succeeded in maintaining a relatively low average level of mortality by means of a lowering of birth rates (notably through changes in the average age at marriage) thus keeping population growth low.[4] A contrast-ing adjustment pattern, such as found in China and India, was probably less conducive to human happiness: it combined a high level of fertility with slow population growth by virtue of allowing death rates to rise near to the level of the prevailing birth rate.

Whatever the general level of harmony (or lack of it) between individual (or family-level) fertility preferences and the collective interest in traditional societies, detailed historical examination of this issue in particular societies tends to reveal differences in the benefits of demographic behavior by social class. Relatively advanced and populous pre-industrial societies, whether in Europe or in Asia, exhibited strongly stratified social structures. Attitudes of the upper strata of these societies were invariably "populationist:" demographic size and demo-graphic growth were correctly perceived as a key source of economic surplus and military strength, and an instrument of territorial expansion. The nascent urban bourgeoisie had a strong interest in an abundant supply of free labor and in a sizable market for its goods; neither consideration was a likely source of senti-ments aimed at discouraging population growth. The emerging administrative machinery of the national states in Europe was, in turn, increasingly effective in creating conditions that catered to populationist preferences, if only as a byproduct of its expanding economic and political functions.

The factors that were especially important in this regard include maintenance of internal order, encouragement – direct or indirect – of industry, development of transport facilities and urban infrastructures, protection of the internal market, and establishment of overseas colonies serving as sources of raw materials and food as well as providing opportunities for outmigration. Success in these domains and concomitant technological progress helped to reduce fluctuations in mortality and fostered the maintenance of fairly high levels of fertility. Thus population growth markedly accelerated in much of Europe and North America. Around 1700, the population of Europe (excluding the Russian Empire) was still appreciably below 100 million; by the end of the eighteenth century that number rose to 145 million, supplemented by a population of some five million in North America, by that time predominantly European in origin. Demographic expansion during the century was equally rapid – indeed, in the second half of the eighteenth century even more rapid – in Russia and in China.[5] In the former, this was in part a demographic response to the opening of the land frontier; in the latter, it reflected rapid growth of agricultural productivity.

Laissez faire's policy prescriptions

Anxieties about the precariousness of not only individual but collective survival, commonly felt in former times, tend to diminish or even disappear in societies experiencing robust demographic growth. The average annual rate of population increase in Europe (as defined above) was 0.3 percent in the first half of the eighteenth century; the rate doubled in the second half. Time became ripe for a shift in sentiment and thought concerning demographic dynamics. Malthus's theory about the implications of population growth, about its sustainability and likely consequences, came to be highly influential. A salient element in his 1798 *Essay* and in subsequent writings was disapproval of aspects of British, and by extension continental, statecraft – such as schemes for poor relief – that were likely to encourage irresponsible reproduction among the lower classes of society. Malthus held efforts of the paternalistic state to reduce poverty to be misguided: by stimulating fertility, hence rapid population growth, such efforts would generate only more misery. The state's correct stance in demographic matters, as in the economy at large, was *laissez faire*, which would foster prudential habits among the poor – habits that already existed among the propertied classes. It would do so by assuring that the costs of childbearing were not shared by society at large but were fully born by the individual couples having children.

Heeding such a prescription did not imply that the state was to play a passive role in demographic matters. Malthus's 1820 tract *Principles of Political Economy* spells out a broader agenda which, if often poorly articulated and imperfectly and halfheartedly executed, nevertheless expresses the dominant philosophy that underlay Western political economy in the nineteenth century. Malthus, in his usual pessimistic mode, considered it likely that material improvements – such as high wages for labor – would be "chiefly spent in the maintenance of large and frequent families", but he could also envisage a different, altogether happier outcome: "a decided improvement in the modes of subsistence, and the conveniences and comforts enjoyed, without a proportionate acceleration in the rate of [population] increase" (Demeny, 1986a).

The possibility of such diametrically different responses to what are posited to be identical economic stimuli – higher wages – suggests the large element of indeterminacy in fertility behavior that to this day befuddles demographers. What are the causes of these different responses? Malthus identified them as "the different habits existing among the people of different countries and at different times." This is an answer that would be appreciated by historians or anthropologists; although not very helpful for demographers seeking to translate it to the language of multiple regression equations, it does identify the only frame – contingent on location, culture, and history – in which human fertility behavior can be understood. Malthus further linked the first result – "large and frequent families" – to "all the circumstances which contribute to depress the lower classes of people, which make them unable and unwilling to reason from the past to the future and ready to acquiesce for the sake of present gratification in a very low standard of comfort and respectability." The second, felicitous, demographic result, in contrast, was linked to "all the circumstances which tend to elevate the lower classes of society, which make them approach the nearest to beings who 'look before and after,' and who, consequently, cannot acquiesce patiently in the thought of depriving themselves and their children of the means of being respectable, virtuous and happy."

But what were those circumstances and how could they be achieved? Could such description be translated into what would be a prescription for a population policy seeking the felicitous demographic outcome? Malthus provided a recipe:

> Among the circumstances which contribute to the character first described [dissipation of economic gains through high fertility], the most efficient will be found to be despotism, oppression and ignorance: among those which contribute to the latter character, civil and political liberty, and education.
>
> Of all the causes which tend to generate prudential habits among the lower classes of society, the most essential is unquestionably civil liberty. No people can be much accustomed to form plans for the future, who do not feel assured that their industrious exertions, while fair and honourable, will be allowed to have free scope; and that the property which they either possess, or may acquire, will be secured to them by a known code of just laws impartially administered. But it has been found by experience, that civil liberty cannot be secured without political liberty. Consequently, political liberty becomes almost equally essential. (Malthus, 1989, p. 250–1)

In nineteenth-century Europe and North America, the interplay of economic, political, and cultural changes shaped by the industrial revolution created a milieu that fostered the prudential habits of parents to "look before and after," rendering the micro-level calculus of the costs and benefits of children increasingly salient. For most of the population, those costs, even in earlier times, were always primarily born by the family; capitalism and the minimalist state made sure that children's costs remained so internalized. Local level social safety nets that formerly provided a degree of protection for the poorest segments of the population were weakened, and most formal entitlements to relief from economic distress were abolished. In the harsh market order of emerging industrialization, the effect of the prudential calculus on fertility decisions remained, however, ambiguous for a more or less extended period, contingent on the particular balance of fertility-enhancing and fertility-depressing forces that varied greatly according to local circumstances. Rising demand for labor, including greater use of child labor, and rising income levels, in and by themselves helped to sustain high fertility and even stimulated it. Rising material expectations, broadening opportunities for social mobility, and the patterns and circumstances of urban living pulled in the opposite direction. Increasing spatial mobility tended to loosen family ties, and the development of financial markets offered alternatives to relying on children as supports for old age, thus eroding the relative value of a large family as old-age insurance. Eventually, new arrangements concerning education and child labor, instituted and enforced by the state, powerfully accelerated this process: education was made compulsory and employment of children in industry was severely restricted. Furthermore, the ideology of responsible parenthood, long practiced by the propertied classes and embraced by the emerging urban bourgeoisie, filtered down and eventually came to be imposed on all layers of society with the active encouragement of the state.[6] This cultural change, inseparable from the market's requirement for a better trained, better educated, and healthier supply of labor and from the corresponding interests of the state, imposed higher expectations and higher responsibilities on the family, greatly increasing the level of material and emotional investment that proper upbringing of children required from parents. These expectations emphasized the father's obligation to provide for the family's economic sustenance – obligations that came to be buttressed through explicit legal sanctions by the state – and imposed exacting and time-consuming responsibilities on the mother in the domestic sphere. In turn, the relative returns to investment in children – as measured by higher wages and improved chances for upward social mobility – increased, providing a powerful market incentive for substituting what economists call "higher quality" – more costly – children for higher numbers of children. As these fertility-depressing forces came to dominate the parental calculus underlying fertility decisions, interest in family limitation through birth control increased, and the force of cultural, notably religious, injunctions against contraception and sometimes abortion became ineffectual. Improved communication of relevant information on these matters – including parental responsibilities, children's education, information on local and distant job markets, options for saving, investment, and old age annuity contracts, contraceptive practice, family hygiene, and so on – was facilitated by an open political process, transparency and stability of the legal order, urban living, the printed word, exposure to propaganda emanating from and participation in voluntary organizations, and access to the expanding private health market.

Why fertility fell: Contending explanations

The result was a decline of marital fertility. Birth control within marriage came to be a prime proximate determinant of overall fertility, its effect being added to, and sometimes partly replacing, fertility control through late marriage or permanent celibacy. Lowered infant and child mortality in the West was in part a consequence of falling birth rates, which permitted greater attention to the needs of each child. When the fall of child mortality preceded the decline of marital fertility, it provided an additional stimulus to the adoption of birth control.

Demographic transition theory in its early formulations[7] provided a persuasive description of the complex interaction of socioeconomic factors that led to a decisive decline of fertility in the Western world but it was shy of quantitative detail. Attempts to find a close correspondence between the forces identified by transition theory as the main determinants of fertility have foundered on the seeming irregularities of the timing and pace with which the transition occurred.[8] Comparing in any given country "premodern" fertility with fertility in that country's advanced stage of urban-industrial development unfailingly yields the expected contrast between "high" and "low" fertility, but the process of transition itself – its onset and speed – are poorly predicted by the customary quantitative indicators of "development."

Even the most cursory glance at the opaque aggregate measures of development and fertility reveals a lack of close correspondence between these two kinds of variables, thereby demonstrating that the process of fertility decline is conditioned by circumstances peculiar to the particular societies experiencing such change. A steady decline of fertility, noticeable even in aggregate birth rates, started in France and the USA at the beginning of the nineteenth century. In Holland, a country more advanced by any plausible index of economic development than either of these "pioneer" countries, and also far more densely populated, such a decline began only a century later. Britain, in the vanguard of urban-industrial development throughout the nineteenth century, saw its fertility dropping rapidly only beginning about 1880 – at the same time as this happened in economically far more backward Hungary and Sweden. Similar examples of "irregularity" could be cited from Western demographic history almost at will.

Observing the geographic patterns of fertility change, demographers sometimes seek to explain these irregularities by a process of diffusion, in particular diffusion of contraceptive practice. In this view, adoption – indeed, discovery – of contraceptive practice occurs in some traditional societies as a radical innovation – a sharp break with former patterns of demographic behavior. From the original locus of discovery, contraceptive knowledge and practice then spreads, facilitated by spatial, cultural, and linguistic contiguity and contact, somewhat in the manner of an infectious disease, an epidemic. An alternative reading of the historical record rejects this interpretation. Emphasizing the well-documented presence of fertility regulating behavior throughout human history, it sees the process of "transition" to low fertility as a continuity with the past: an adjustment to changed material and cultural circumstances and to the related changes in institutional arrangements affecting the patterns of social interaction.[9]

Whatever the relative merits of these contending interpretations, the diffusionist argument has resulted in an unwarranted neglect of the role of the state, and more broadly, of the role of institutions, in explanations of Western fertility change. Virtually at all times in the past – indeed up to the early decades following World War II – the state in Western countries was at best indifferent, but typically strongly opposed, often with the force of legal sanctions, to the spread of contraception. Abortion was criminalized during most of the modern period. Accordingly, demographers who concluded that the practice of birth control was not simply a means couples elected to adopt in the service of overriding personal objectives – objectives which were sanctioned by society or even actively imposed by the state – but was the central explanatory factor in the fertility transition, also came to conclude that the role of the state in the transition was strongly negative. It became commonplace to claim that Western fertility decline occurred in spite of the stubborn pronatalist stance of the state.

However, as the preceding arguments suggest, this is a misinterpretation. The agency of the state in the West as a framer and guarantor of an institutional structure had effects, even if largely unplanned and unintended, that were far more important than its ineffective interference with the market for birth control information and devices, and its desultory intrusions into the bedroom. States in the West were largely successful in adopting and maintaining policies that assured, to paraphrase Malthus as cited above, that the industrious exertions of the citizenry were allowed to have free scope, by guaranteeing security of property, either possessed or to be acquired, under a code of laws, impartially administered. The resulting entrepreneurial activity, technological progress, and the accumulation of physical and human capital sparked a theretofore unprecedented expansion of the economy. The consequent transformation of the social structure and the concomitant cultural changes, in turn, had far-reaching consequences for demographic dynamics. During the nineteenth century, Europe's population roughly doubled, from 145 million to 294 million, and that of North America multiplied eighteenfold, from 5 to 90 million. However, by 1900, birth rates were retreating in most places in these two continents, and estimates for certain subnational populations clearly suggested the likelihood of a continuing headlong rush toward very low levels of fertility. In the USA, for example, by the late nineteenth century, fertility of white women of native parentage living in urban areas was below replacement level (Sanderson, 1987).

Not coincidentally, Western governments became increasingly involved in establishing institutions aimed at lessening the exposure of individuals to risks of economic insecurity and ill health – forerunners of the coming welfare state. An especially important early sign of this was the Bismarckian scheme of state-sponsored compulsory old-age insurance, later widely copied in Europe and eventually also in America. There was no intent to interfere with family decisions with childbearing, but the demographic byproducts of such measures, guaranteed by the power of the state, were on balance clearly and strongly antinatalist. In most countries of Western and Northern Europe, by around 1930, fertility was below the level necessary for the long-term maintenance of population size, given contemporary levels of mortality. Thus, by demographers' usual reckoning, in these countries (with the exception of France where replacement fertility was reached several decades earlier), the slide of fertility from its pretransition plateau to replacement took about fifty years. Fertility declined further in the 1930s. Country-level total fertility rates prior to World War II reached a record low in England and Wales at 1.72 per woman in 1933; the rate in Germany was only slightly higher. Among relative latecomers in Europe, the rate of fertility decline tended to be especially rapid. In 1922, the birth rate in economically backward and still predominantly agricultural Bulgaria was 41 per 1,000 population; seventeen years later, the rate dropped to 21 per 1,000; see the Appendix tables in Chesnais (1992).

Post-transition dilemmas of population policy

Even when fertility sank below replacement level, the rate of natural increase (the difference between the birth rate and the death rate) remained positive during the interwar years in all Western countries. This reflected the still prevailing relatively youthful age structures, inherited from earlier decades when birth rates were high. Also, death rates were still declining, thus contributing to population increase, but, short of a rise in fertility, this was predictably a temporary phenomenon. During the 1920s and 1930s, and sporadically even earlier, a growing number of demographers, politicians, and various other observers expressed worry about Europe's demographic situation, foreseeing a "twilight of parenthood" and incipient population decline. In a number of countries, governments introduced social policies – such as family allowances and subsidized care for preschool children – with an explicit pronatalist aim. Not surprisingly, in the face of strong countervailing pressures, these efforts had only a minor, and generally only temporary, effect on fertility.[10]

Calmer voices could have suggested that the completion of fertility transition in the West was a signal success of its social and economic system. In the long run, cessation of population growth was an undisputable economic and environmental necessity. In Europe and its overseas offshoots, this was achieved before population pressures became acute, and it was achieved as a result of voluntary action of individuals and individual couples. Reinforcement and guidance by the state of the spontaneous micro-level coordination of fertility behavior was merely a byproduct of policies that served goals commanding wide social support. Slow and eventually zero population growth, or even a period of moderate population decline had numerous potential benefits, including the prospect of lessened environmental pressures and looser resource constraints, a more even income distribution, greater investments in human capital per person, and more rapid income growth if measured on a per capita basis. The drawbacks – primarily originating from an age structure heavily weighted with the older age groups – appeared eminently manageable at tolerable costs.[11]

However, settling down to the pleasures and headaches of a stationary or declining population turned out not to be on the immediate Western agenda. To the surprise of all informed observers, very much including demographers, the end of World War II brought not parenthood's twilight but the baby boom. This was more than a temporary upturn of the birth rate marking the soldiers' return, as happened to a degree after World War I, but a sustained rise of fertility to a level well above that of the interwar years, and lasting roughly for a quarter century. It affected all countries in which fertility had reached very low levels in the 1930s. In the USA, postwar fertility peaked in 1957; in that year, the total fertility rate was 3.77 – higher than at any time during the preceding fifty years. In Western Europe, the peak occurred in or around 1964. The immediate postwar decades were also a period of growing economic prosperity. Thus the facile generalization – current at least in popular versions of transition theory – that rising incomes necessarily produce low birth rates, was shown to be false.

With the baby boom, worries about rapid population growth returned and, at least in the USA, taming unduly high domestic fertility through deliberate antinatalist policies was placed, for the first time, on the public policy agenda. During the first year of the Nixon administration, a presidential commission on population growth and the American future was appointed; its report, submitted in 1972, endorsed the goal of a stationary population. Ironically, 1972 was also the first postwar year when US fertility once again fell below replacement level; it did so without any explicit prodding by antinatalist policy. It has remained there, albeit only by a narrow margin, ever since. In Europe, beginning with the mid-1960s, birth rates receded more spectacularly. By the early 1990s, total fertility rates were below replacement everywhere, often by a wide margin. In Germany, Italy, and Spain, the rate in recent years has been 1.3 children or less per woman. While such cross-sectional measures cannot reliably predict the ultimate number of children reckoned cohort by cohort at the end of the reproductive life span, it is virtually certain that completed generational fertility of cohorts born after the war's end will be well short of replacement in the majority of European countries. With population aging, crude death rates are also likely to rise. Thus, apart from the temporary momentum of population growth imparted by the large baby boom cohorts, and apart from possible counterbalancing effects of net immigration, fertility levels presage negative rates of population growth in most European countries in the not too remote future. As of 1995, deaths already outnumber births in a dozen European countries. These include Germany and Italy; the others are countries of the former Soviet bloc, where the phenomenon is in part due to relatively high death rates, reflecting deteriorating health conditions.

Even though current levels of fertility in Europe are now generally below the levels attained in the 1930s, and the prospects of population decline are now more imminent, public attitudes concerning these matters are more mature and more relaxed than was the case in the interwar period. Government policies in the West reflect these attitudes. Although no government contemplates with equanimity the rapid decline in population size and the consequent rapid shift to a much older age structure that continuation of current fertility levels would imply, explicitly pronatalist policies are nowadays conspicuous by their rarity. Many facets of the modern welfare state do replicate measures once introduced with the intent of stimulating fertility, but today, political support for such programs is sought and obtained by governments on the ground of the programs' merits as directly welfare-producing activities, rather than on the ground of their aggregate demographic pay-off. This reflects a general social consensus in Western societies that grants individual couples full formal rights to make decisions about reproduction according to their private preferences. It is safe to suggest, however, that a tacit assumption that underlies this stance – namely, that the aggregate result of those private decisions adds up to a figure that falls within an upper and lower bound demarcating what would be considered socially acceptable. Western societies are in the politically comfortable situation that this assumption is now more or less satisfied, at least as far as the total number of births is concerned. Should the nexus of the social and economic constraints that condition the exercise of individual rights in deciding about fertility fail to yield this happy result, those rights would be no doubt reinterpreted by invoking the individual's social responsibility in reproductive matters.

Such a hypothetical reaction would be especially likely in case of a substantial rise of aggregate fertility. To pose an admittedly extreme counterfactual, if US fertility returned to a level matching that attained in the late 1950s, commissions would once again address the question of how to return to demographic stability, and proposals to adopt antinatalist policies, qualifying individuals' reproductive freedom, would promptly reappear on the public policy agenda. Concern with high fertility (which, in the example just given, if sustained, would double the size of the US population in roughly thirty years and would increase it more than eightfold in a century) once centered on the classic Malthusian worry about food supplies and related resource constraints. Today, it would very likely crystallize around issues of environmental quality and ecological balance.

Speculation about public policy reaction to a more likely future demographic scenario – fertility settling seemingly permanently below replacement – must be more cautious. Here, despite past and current brushes with low fertility, Western governments would be entering new territory. In an advanced industrial society, crafting policy measures that through various incentives would constrain individual rights to reproduce, while maintaining the stance – or, rather, the fiction – that those rights are inalienable and fundamental, is a relatively simple matter. Designing and providing politically acceptable incentives that would induce individual couples to have children they do not want is bound to be far more difficult and costly. Adequate political support for such incentives would be unlikely to be forthcoming under conditions of moderate population decline; most low fertility societies would probably be willing to tolerate, or indeed learn to welcome, mildly negative rates of population change even over an extended period. Such an attitude would be supported by the not unreasonable but hardly guaranteed expectation that, as a result of natural feedbacks, fertility would eventually return to replacement level without special intervention by the state.

How societies would react if fertility sank to, and remained at, a level far below replacement, is even more difficult to guess. Such a fertility pattern is by no means implausible. A concomitant of fertility decline in the West has been the virtual disappearance of large families; indeed, that process continued even during the baby boom period. In much of Europe, families with a completed fertility of four children or more have became a rarity. Thus, to a close approximation, average fertility's deviation from the replacement level now depends on the degree to which women with three children balance the number of women who remain childless or have one child only. There are strong indications that, in industrial societies, individual reproductive choices are leading to a situation in which the former greatly outnumber the latter. However, long-term total fertility rates, close to the now prevailing German or Italian levels, would eventually lead to precipitous decline of population size and to an extreme degree of population aging. The challenge posed to a state seeking to reconcile individual desires and the collective interest in such a situation would be unprecedented and extremely difficult.

Third world transitions and the state

In the last chapter of his autobiography, written in 1944 while under British internment, Jawaharlal Nehru contemplated the demographic aftermath of World War II, then soon to come to its end. Repatriation and rehabilitation of populations displaced by hostilities will be a task, he thought, "of prodigious complexity," but he went on:

> Of far deeper and more far-reaching significance are the changes . . . that are rapidly changing the population of the world. The Industrial Revolution and the spread of modern technology resulted in a rapid growth of population in Europe, and more especially in northwestern and central Europe. As this technology has spread eastward to the Soviet Union, aided by a new economic structure and other factors, there has been an even more spectacular increase in population in these regions. The eastward sweep of technology, accompanied by education, sanitation, and better public health, is continuing and will cover many of the countries of Asia. Some of these countries, like India, far from needing a bigger population, would be better off with fewer people. (Nehru, 1946)

A bigger population was indeed forthcoming. Post-Partition India's population was 358 million in 1950, just after Independence and the bloodshed that followed it; by 1995, it had grown to 936 million. During the same forty-five years, China's population went from slightly below 550 million to 1.2 billion; Indonesia's grew from 80 million to 198 million. In other parts of pre-Partition India, population growth was even more rapid. Bangladesh grew from 42 million to 120 million; Pakistan from 40 million to 140 million. Thus, the combined population of these five Asian countries grew from less than 1.1 billion in 1950 to 2.6 billion in 1995. The latter figure exceeds the entire population of the world in 1950.

The rest of what came to be called the "third world" – now a label of antiquarian flavor – had lesser demographic weight but even more rapid rates of population growth. There, population between 1950 and 1995 more than tripled: from 644 million to 1,956 million[12], representing an average annual rate of increase of 2.5 percent.

This spectacular demographic expansion was the direct consequence of a historically unprecedented rapid decline of mortality. In India, for example, the average expectation of life at birth in the early 1950s was still below 40 years. By the early 1990s, life expectancy exceeded 60 years. The corresponding figures for China are 41 and 67 years. In and by itself, this change – pervasive throughout the less developed world, if at varying degrees – is a signal success story; the increased length of life undoubtedly was a major contribution to greater human welfare. The change in mortality that made it possible was both wanted and technologically feasible. Fulfillment of Nehru's implicit wish for India, and by extension for Asia's populous countries – "would be better off with fewer people" – was not in history's cards.

Nehru's comment, however, did identify a potential conflict between what people individually wanted for themselves – a healthier and longer life – and their interest in the aggregate demographic characteristics – size and rate of growth – of the society of which they were part. That conflict was not without precedent, but at mid-century, and in the decades that followed, it presented a more urgent problem than ever before in human history, or so it seemed to most observers who analyzed the situation of the developing countries, and made forecasts about the expected evolution of the demographic and economic characteristics of these countries, and to policy makers who consulted the experts. Their conclusion was a straightforward and eminently reasonable modification of Nehru's dictum: countries facing rapid population growth – virtually all less developed lands, but particularly those densely populated – would be better off, if not with smaller populations then with slower growth, and the rate of population growth *was* a potential policy variable. Given mortality trends, and given the predictable quantitative insignificance of international migration in affecting demographic trends, reducing the rate of population growth required reduction of fertility.

In the early postwar decades, those concerned with such matters, experts and policy makers alike, were predominantly from the "first world," and mostly American. As was noted above, in the USA, the 1950s and 1960s generated heightened and explicit policy interest about the implications of that country's own baby boom; these concerns now came to be extended to the much higher and seemingly immobile fertility levels in the third world. The subsequent appearance of population growth and, specifically, fertility levels, as an item on the international agenda, first on the analytic plane then as a policy issue, was wholly novel; such matters in past times were the exclusive domain of domestic policy. The classic Malthusian anxiety about excessive fertility came to be projected on to the international scene: socially improvident fertility behavior, once seen as the scourge of the working classes by the worried rich, now became the perceived bane of the developing world at large, and a source of distress for the developed world.

It has been often suggested that Western, and in particular, US concern with the reduction of third-world population growth reflected a fear by the West of the anticipated major shifts in the demographic balance between the developed and the developing countries in favor of the latter. The policy advice that flowed from that concern, in this view, was prompted by the wish to mitigate the magnitude of this inevitable shift. There is little evidence to support such a charge. "In favor," in any case, would have been considered a gross misnomer: rapid population growth was seen as jeopardizing the chances for development – a sign of malfunction in the body politic, not a source of strength. Thus, Western concern was, in the first place, humanitarian; it reflected a facet in the analytic understanding of the causes of underdevelopment, and the policy advice that it generated – "fertility ought to be reduced" – was part of a package of prescriptions intended to help countries to escape that condition in their own best interest.

However, Western advice on demographic policy also had a geopolitical motive, embedded in the cold-war competition between the first and second worlds for influence in the third. To the extent that rapid population growth was undermining economic progress and, with it, political stability, it was seen as creating conditions favorable for communist ideological and, eventually, economic and political, penetration in the developing world. Policies to speed the demographic transition would promote economic development, hence help to create conditions favorable to maintaining Western economic and political influence.

The need for deliberate policies aimed at reducing fertility rested on two main propositions: that early spontaneous decline was unlikely, and that rapid population growth exerted a drag on development. The prospects for a spontaneous fertility adjustment in the developing countries were judged remote because the factors that helped to explain fertility transition in European populations were held to be missing. The large majority of the populations in question were agrarian, levels of literacy were low, poverty was widespread, and traditional cultural norms that strongly favored high fertility remained largely intact. Most of the high-fertility societies were also strongly patriarchal, allowing little or no voice in fertility decisions to women. Modern methods of birth control – such as they were in that pre-pill age – were virtually unknown or were unavailable.

To the extent that these factors precluded individual interest in fertility lower than prevailing in any given situation, the expectation of stable birth rates was indeed warranted, but evidence to counter this expectation was ready to hand. Even in these high fertility societies, fertility was far below biological capacity. This observation suggested the presence of social adjustment mechanisms that under the right circumstances – circumstances that created individual desires for fewer children – would come into play. The notion that various indexes of "modernization" have to reach a fairly high level before interest in lower fertility can become manifest in economically backward societies was also contradicted by a large amount of evidence that accumulated during the process of the fertility transition in European populations. Fertility *was* reduced in a number of societies that were agrarian and largely illiterate, had low incomes, were culturally traditional and strongly patriarchal, and lacked knowledge and access to "modern" methods of birth control. Such features in and by themselves are certainly favorable for keeping fertility high, but not a necessary barrier to birth control if, for whatever reasons, a lower number of children becomes advantageous for families, or, at any rate, for the person who makes the relevant decisions in the family.

Also, the record of countries that were "outliers" in previous fertility transitions strongly suggested that emergence of desires for lower fertility is not closely tied with specific "thresholds" of development. For example, a relatively low level of infant mortality – such as less than 100 infant deaths for 1,000 births – was commonly held to be a prerequisite for the onset of fertility decline in the developing countries. In the German-speaking provinces of the Habsburg Empire, however, infant mortality never fell below 250 per 1,000 births until the end of the 1880s, by which time fertility was also declining, and infant mortality was still around 175 per 1,000 when the fertility transition was already well advanced. Legal and political emancipation of women often lagged well behind the onset of, and substantial progress in, fertility transition. Also, the entire record of Western fertility transition demonstrated that access to modern methods of birth control is not a necessary precondition for achieving low fertility.

Prospects for fertility change in the developing world were also enhanced by the latecomer status of the countries in question. The accelerating speed of later European fertility transitions was predictive of a similar pattern in the subsequent transitions. Improved methods of communication and increasing exposure to the outside world, and, given no interference by the state, the prospects for increasing access to modern methods of birth control supplied by private markets were additional encouraging elements in the postwar world. Demonstration effects – creating new aspirations for material improvement, or stimulating efforts to avoid downward social mobility and deterioration of relative economic status – were important in inducing behavioral shifts in the past; they could have been expected to become potent also in the developing world. All these considerations could have underscored the conclusion that the crucial element in setting the speed of third-world fertility transitions would be the same as it was in earlier transitions: individual-level desires to limit family size.

The second proposition calling for policy intervention aimed at reducing fertility had to do with the economic consequences of rapid population growth. In circumstances typical of the economies of third world countries in the postwar period, the consequences were held to be highly deleterious for development. In the grimmer versions of the relevant analyses, set forth mainly by biologists and popularized by the mass media, developing country populations were pictured as rapidly approaching limits of "carrying capacity," foreshadowing near- or medium-term declines in living standards, large-scale famines, and rising mortality. Most social scientists rejected the relevance of such catastrophic population growth scenarios, except, perhaps, in the very long run. Could the Earth (or some particular country) support more people? If so, how many more? Such questions were considered pointless: it was taken for granted that the answer to the first question is invariably in the affirmative, and to the second the typically correct answer is "many times more." However, their analyses led to the conclusion that rapid population growth was a serious hindrance to development; that while rapid population growth and development were not inconsistent, slower population growth, *ceteris paribus*, would permit greater improvement in material welfare, and it would offer the prospect of narrowing the vast gap that separated the low income countries from the affluent regions of the world significantly faster than would be feasible if fertility remained high.[13]

These assessments of the expected economic effects of rapid population growth (of the two types, the second version became dominant), in combination with the commonly accepted discounting of the prospects for a spontaneously generated fertility decline, led to the conclusion that, in the developing countries, vigorous direct intervention by the state aimed at lowering fertility was a crucial condition for economic development. International policy advice on development increasingly emphasized the need for reconciling individual fertility behavior reflecting individual interests, and the putative interest of the same individuals in an aggregate demographic outcome that was obtainable only if individual-level fertility behaviors were substantially modified. By the mid 1960s, this emphatic advice became a formal part of development policy discussions between the USA and recipients of its foreign aid program. A few years later, international organizations, notably the World Bank, followed suit, and a special component of the UN was created to provide multilateral population assistance, directed especially to the reduction of fertility. In turn, increasing numbers of third-world governments came to the conclusion that deliberate state intervention to alter population growth was a necessity and sought assistance for formulating appropriate policies.

It might have been expected that the advice and assistance that was forthcoming would draw on the accumulated record of the West's own successful experience in navigating the demographic transition – experience that was part of a broader and highly successful development strategy. Salient aspects of that strategy are illustrated in Malthus's 1820 tract cited above. They center around the role of the state as a limited but crucial player in development: a guarantor of a stable institutional framework – a known code of just laws, impartially administered – that, in population matters, identifies the family as the fundamental unit of society and recognizes the right of parents to make reproductive choices without coercion and according to their best lights. The rules of the game set by the state impose on the family the costs of bringing up children by narrowly limiting the extent to which such costs are permitted to be socialized, and at the same time set legal standards and convey moral expectations on the quality of care and education to which children are entitled. Asserting the principle that couples can have as many children as they wish, as long as they bring them up properly, as defined by the broader community, constituted, by the testimony of history, a potent fertility policy; and the broader institutional stance of which that principle forms part is also a demonstrably sound foundation for economic and social development writ large.

This was not, however, the approach Western advice and assistance to third-world countries followed. Collectivist economic and social planning was in the ascendancy in most of the world, and the same impulse also permeated state-to-state assistance from developed to developing countries. The "new economic structure" – to use Nehru's words – of the Soviet Union was a major influence in this development; a greatly extended role of the state was widely seen as providing a short-cut to modernization for developing countries. The rapid postwar expansion of the Western welfare state, with its appealing smorgasbord of social and economic entitlements and rights was a second important influence in setting the agenda of third-world governments.

Population policy aimed at reducing fertility was shaped to fit into the emerging general scheme of comprehensive state planning. First, the structure of the underlying population problem, or at least the component of the problem that was deemed correctable, was redefined. Instead of recognizing a conflict between private want and public interest concerning fertility, an underlying harmony between the two was posited; a harmony that was frustrated only by the inability of individual couples to realize their fertility desires. That inability, it was held, reflected not deficient motivation but lack of knowledge about or access to efficient methods of birth control. The second step logically followed from the premises of that reformulation: the task of the state was to supply the appropriate birth control information and services to a population presumed to lack both. This called for organizing a special sectoral program – a family planning program – delivering modern contraceptive technology to those who want it. Such a program embodied the importance assigned by the state to reducing the rate of population growth; it was also a ready recipient of population-targeted international assistance, reflecting the interest of the outside world in seeing the aid-recipient state succeed in "population control."

There are at least three main problems inherent in such a programmatic conceptualization of state intervention to alter fertility. First, the assumption that the heart of the problem is that couples desire fewer children but do not know how to go about it without help, is questionable. It is inconsistent with historical experience in this matter; and the implication that couples are unable to act rationally in their own interest in making fertility decisions contrasts with such ability demonstrated in other domains of life. Also by denying the likely existence of a genuine conflict between individual wants and public interest, and locating the problem as one of technology, policy attention is diverted from the potentially more difficult problems of motivation and incentives that shape individuals' fertility decisions.

Second, by the logic of comprehensive state planning, a government program for delivering family planning services is typically just one among many similarly ambitious government programs delivering many kinds of services. The state running such service programs often also directly manages and administers large segments of the entire economy. Thus population programs tend to exist within a general context characterized by a chronically overextended state, leaving them short of the endowment in human talent and financial resources which, by the programs' design, are necessary for success. Foreign assistance, as *deus ex machina*, often fills some of the gaps, but at the price of making the programs hostage to unpredictable contingencies and introducing organizational features not closely attuned to the local institutional and human environment.

Third, by in effect monopolizing the supply of birth control technology, the programs discourage the emergence of a market-based supply system; one that by much evidence elsewhere and in other fields could be more flexible and more efficient in catering to clients' diversified needs in this domain than the typically underfinanced and overbureaucratized system run by the state. This displacement effect also discourages emergence of innovative institutional arrangements for service delivery, and fosters an attitude of passivity and a sense of dependency in the client population.

Actual population programs, as they evolved during the past three decades or so in the third world, often were at variance with the characterizations just offered. In particular, in several Asian countries, the crux of the population problem was identified as individual-level preferences for a larger family size than was deemed socially desirable. In these countries, the state explicitly sought to lower those preferences through persuasion, propaganda, and a system of incentives and disincentives calibrated to discourage high fertility. Such measures were sometimes complemented by explicit laws defining permissible fertility behavior, supported by appropriate penalties. The extreme instance of such an approach is the one-child population policy adopted in China – a home-grown system that has generated wide international disapproval as an infringement on a basic human right. However, as the Chinese government would argue, all rights cannot always be simultaneously satisfied; temporary curtailment of the right to reproduce was effected to protect other rights – such as the right of future generations to adequate food supplies and to an agreeable physical environment. The principle is defensible in the abstract; the validity of its application depends on the representativeness and legitimacy of the political process that took the decision, on the soundness of the factual analysis mustered in its deliberations, and on comparisons with alternative policies that might have also lowered fertility but at a lesser human cost. The principle of voluntarism, consistently endorsed in international forums, was also interpreted loosely in Indonesia, and, intermittently, in India. In these countries, the service delivery program itself played double duty: delivering strong messages on the need for limiting family size. The effectiveness of that function was assured, however, by also enlisting the support of various levels of the administrative apparatus of the state.

As was noted above, when family planning programs were first organized, the perceived drag exerted by rapid population growth on development was a crucial rationale offered to justify such programs. That such a drag existed and was, in quantitative terms, important in third-world development was long taken for granted by the agencies that ran or financed population programs, and little research was undertaken to make sure that rationale could withstand objective scrutiny. By the 1980s, however, the economic case for deliberate population policies was in a parlous state.[14] The reaction of policy makers, especially as manifest in international discussions of population policy issues, was evasive. The economic justification for state intervention was largely abandoned, as was indeed the explicit claim that the goal of such intervention is to lower aggregate fertility. To be sure, programs were expected to affect birth rates by serving the individual needs of their clients, but the ultimate aim of the programs was articulated as providing a public good: a service to the community at large. What was formally a means, came to be reinterpreted as first and last a service to the program's clients: satisfying the demand for contraception or, as the now accepted interpretation has it, for reproductive health.

The 1994 International Conference on Population and Development represented a strong formal endorsement of this shift in policy rationale.[15] Yet the case for downscaling the macroeconomic advantages numerous developing countries could derive from lower aggregate levels of population growth is far from proven; indeed, it is more likely to reflect the limitations of neoclassical economic modeling than the intrinsic importance of the population-development nexus.[16] Abandoning the stance that lower population growth under the circumstances of most developing countries represents a public good relegates population programs to the status of merely one contender among many possible welfare-enhancing service programs for scarce government resources. It is far from certain that, in such a competition, government-financed provision of contraceptive technology would or, for that matter, should rank very high.

Third-world fertility, with the notable exception of East Asia's newly industrializing countries which closely followed the rapid postwar drop of fertility in Japan, remained largely stable until the second part of the 1960s. China's total fertility rate was at that time approximately six per woman, the same as the average level of fertility in developing countries at large. India's fertility was lower by a slight margin. By the early 1990s, China's fertility was about two; apparently below replacement level and not too far above the average level in all developed countries. India's fertility was estimated at 3.7, and developing countries as a whole had an average total fertility rate of 3.5.

Thus, fertility transition progressed rapidly during the last quarter century. The process was the combined result of the spontaneous self-regulating mechanisms present in all human societies, the deliberate efforts of most, although by no means all, third-world states to foster fertility decline through family planning programs, and the economic and social policies pursued by states in the service of non population-related objectives. Scholarly opinion is divided about the relative importance of these factors. Better understanding of the limits and potentials of collective action aimed at demographic adjustment could make a significant contribution to human welfare.

Notes

1   The source of these estimates, and population estimates and projections for 1950 and later years is (UN, 1995).
2   There are also a number of territories and dependencies, typically of small population size. Their combined population is well below one percent of the global total.
3   That is, without the contracting parties having knowledge about their particular position in the society in question, hence having an interest in agreement that they consider best whatever their actual position would turn out to be in the society governed by the constitutional agreement; see Rawls (1971).
4   The best existing documentation of such a pre-industrial pattern is for Britain; see Wrigley and Schofield (1981).
5   For these and other pre-1950 population estimates, see the compilations in Demeny (1990), based on Durand (1967) and Biraben (1979).
6   For a discussion of this process, with a special focus on the case of Britain, see Johansson (1991).
7   For a classical statement, see especially Notestein (1945).
8   For a thorough examination of the European record of fertility transition, demonstrating its lack of close correlation with the standard indexes of "modernization," see Coale and Watkins (1986).
9   A discussion of fertility transition as a discontinuity in history, and a description of its spread through diffusion is offered in Coale and Watkins (1986). For arguments

supporting the continuity hypothesis, see Carlsson (1966) and Blake (1985). Institutional determinants of fertility behavior are analyzed in McNicoll (1980, 1994), and Greenhalgh (1990).

10 For a discussion of these policies, see Demeny (1986b).

11 In a 1930 essay, "Economic possibilities for our grandchildren," J. M. Keynes painted a rosy picture of the long-term future, suggesting that "the economic problem may be solved, or at least within sight of solution, within a hundred years." The economic problem, he suggested, "is not – if we look into the future – the permanent problem of the human race." He specified two conditions for the validity of his forecast, restricted essentially to the developed world. The two conditions were that, first, there be "no important wars" and, second, there be "no important increase in population" (Keynes, 1963, pp. 365–6).

12 These figures relate to the less developed world as currently defined by the UN, i.e. including the Asiatic republics of the former USSR. All Asian countries outside Japan and Asiatic Russia are still defined as less developed, regardless of actual levels of industrialization or income.

13 For comprehensive discussions of the relationship between population growth and economic development, see McNicoll (1984), World Bank (1984), Birdsall (1988), Kelley (1988), and Cassen et al. (1994).

14 The most noted attack on the economic rationale was mounted in Simon (1981). The influential report of the US National Research Council (1986) concluded that slower population growth could be helpful for economic development, but considered the relationship at best marginal.

15 See the Programme of Action adopted by the ICPD (UN, 1994).

16 For relevant commentary, see Demeny (1986a), Dasgupta (1993), and McNicoll (1995).

References

Biraben, J.-N. (1979) Essai sur l'évolution du nombre des hommes, *Population*, 34 (1), 13–25.

Birdsall, N. (1988) Economic approaches to population growth. In H. Chenery and T. N. Srinivasan (eds) *Handbook of Development Economics*, vol. I. Amsterdam: North Holland, pp. 477–542.

Blake, J. (1985) The fertility transition: Continuity or discontinuity with the past? In *International Population Conference*, Florence, vol. 4. Liège: IUSSP.

Carlsson, G. (1966) The decline of fertility: Innovation or adjustment process. *Population Studies*, 24, 413–22.

Cassen, R. and contributors (1994) *Population and Development: Old Debates, New Conclusions*. New Brunswick: Transaction Publishers.

Chesnais, J.-C. (1992) *The Demographic Transition: Stages, Patterns, and Economic Implications* (translated by E. and P. Kraeger). Oxford: Clarendon Press.

Coale, A. J. and Watkins, S. C. (eds) (1986) *The Decline of Fertility in Europe*. Princeton: Princeton University Press.

Coale, A. J. and Demeny, P. (1966) *Regional Model Life Tables and Stable Populations*. Princeton: Princeton University Press.

Dasgupta, P. (1993) *An Inquiry into Well-being and Destitution*. Oxford: Clarendon Press.

Demeny, P. (1986a) Population and the invisible hand. *Demography*, 23 (4), 473–87.

Demeny, P. (1986b) Pronatalist policies in low-fertility countries: Patterns, performance, and prospects. In K. Davis, M. S. Bernstam and R. Ricardo-Campbell (eds) *Below-replacement Fertility in Industrial Societies: Causes, Consequences, Policies*. New York: Oxford University Press, pp. 335–58.

Demeny, P. (1990) Population. In B. L. Turner, II et al. (eds) *The Earth as Transformed by Human Action*, New York: Cambridge University Press, pp. 41–54.

Demeny, P. (1994) *Population and Development*. Distinguished Lecture Series. Liège: IUSSP (International Union for the Scientific Study of Population).

Durand, J. D. (1967) The modern expansion of world population. *Proceedings of the American Philosophical Society*, 111, 136–59.

Greenhalgh, S. (1990) Toward a political economy of fertility: Anthropological contributions. *Population and Development Review*, 16 (1), 85–106.

Johansson, S. R. (1991) "Implicit" policy and fertility during development. *Population and Development Review*, 17 (3), 377–414.

Kelley, A. C. (1988) Economic consequences of population change in the Third World. *Journal of Economic Literature*, 26 (4), 1685–728.

Keynes, J. M. (1963) *Essays in Persuasion*. New York: W. W. Norton and Co.

McNicoll, G. (1980) Institutional determinants of fertility change. *Population and Development Review*, 6 (3), 441–62.

McNicoll, G. (1984) Consequences of rapid population growth: An overview and assessment. *Population and Development Review*, 10 (2), 177–240.

McNicoll, G. (1994) Institutional endowments and fertility. In K. Lindahl-Kiessling and H. Landberg (eds) *Population, Economic Development, and the Environment*. New York: Oxford University Press, pp. 199–230.

McNicoll, G. (1995) On population growth and revisionism: Further questions. *Population and Development Review*, 21 (2), 307–40.

Malthus, T. R. (1989) *Principles of Political Economy*. Vol. I. Cambridge: Cambridge University Press.

National Research Council (1986) *Population Growth and Economic Development: Policy Questions*. Washington, DC: National Academy of Sciences Press.

Nehru, J. (1946) *The Discovery of India*. New York: Harper and Row.

Notestein, F. W. (1945) Population – the long view. In T. W. Schultz (ed.) *Food for the world*. Chicago: University of Chicago Press, pp. 36–57.

Rawls, J. (1971) *A Theory of Justice*. Cambridge, MA: Harvard University Press.

Sanderson, W. C. (1987) Below replacement fertility in nineteenth century America. *Population and Development Review*, 13 (2), 305–13.

Simon, J. L. (1981) *The Ultimate Resource*. Princeton: Princeton University Press.

UN (1994) *Report of the International Conference on Population and Development*. A/CONF. 171/13, 18 October. New York: United Nations.

UN (1995) *World Population Prospects: The 1994 Revision*. New York: United Nations.

World Bank (1984) *World Development Report 1984*. New York: Oxford University Press.

Wrigley, E. A. and Schofield, R. S. (1981) *The Population History of England, 1541–1871*. Cambridge, MA: Harvard University Press.

IV

After Rio: Global Action on Equity and the Environment

9

Greenhouse Negotiations and the Mirage of Partial Justice[1]

Erik Schokkaert and Johan Eyckmans

In recent years, global warming as a consequence of the growing concentration of greenhouse gases (GHGs) in the atmosphere has become a top priority among all international environmental issues. Global warming is a typical example of a global commons problem. A multitude of economic agents emit GHGs, which are mixed uniformly in the atmosphere of the Earth. The most important of these gases, carbon dioxide (CO_2), is produced mainly by burning fossil fuels. The (possibly) ensuing climate changes affect all individuals in all countries of the world. If one wants to reduce the risk of such climate change, emissions of GHGs must be curbed significantly.

Economists tend to emphasize that the coordination of efforts with respect to global commons problems raises huge questions of efficiency. These problems are especially acute in the international context, because there is no government that can impose these efforts. However, it is obvious from observing the reality of international negotiations that arguments related to international distributive justice also play an important role. Leaders of developing countries emphasize that their economic situation justifies a lower abatement effort, the more so since the industrial world has been responsible for the large bulk of CO_2 emissions in the past. The problem is further complicated by the asymmetries related to costs and benefits of greenhouse policies. Although there is still much uncertainty about the economic effects of global warming, it can be predicted that they will be spread unevenly over the various parts of the globe. There also exist huge international differences in the cost of abating emissions. An efficient worldwide abatement effort will require abatement levels which differ between countries and, in most cases, such cost-efficient allocation will require greater efforts from the poorer countries. We give somewhat more details about these different aspects on pages 194–203.

One can approach international environmental negotiations from two different angles. First, one can try to gain a better insight into the actual mechanisms of the negotiation process. This positive explanatory approach belongs to the realm of noncooperative game theory. Second, there is the normative perspective; from this perspective, one wants to evaluate the existing situation and the different solutions which are proposed, not with respect to their feasibility or their degree of realism but with respect to their ethical desirability. Justice considerations are playing a central role in this evaluation. This paper follows the second line. We will use the global warming case as a starting point (on page 203) for a more general discussion concerning the relationship between environmental policies and international distributive justice. We will emphasize that it is not acceptable to strive for "partial justice," i.e. to isolate environmental problems such as the greenhouse effect from their broader social context.

Of course, the positive and the normative approaches are interrelated. Once we have defined an ethically attractive solution, it will have to be implemented through the actual process of international negotiations. Since there is no international authority which could impose the ethically desirable solutions, one has to take into account the fact that nations will only be willing to participate in an international agreement if they feel that this is in their own interest. These aspects are discussed on pages 209–14. In that same section, we also discuss how efficiency considerations can be integrated into our ethical framework.

The greenhouse effect: A description of the problem

In this section, we describe briefly some important characteristics of the problem of global warming. We first concentrate on the scientific discussion. We then sketch the building blocks of the distributive problem: international differences in the benefits from greenhouse policies, in abatement costs and in starting positions. We finally summarize the present state of the international negotiations.

Natural and enhanced greenhouse warming[2]

According to the influential 1990 and 1996 Reports of the Intergovernmental Panel on Climate Change (IPCC), it is important to distinguish natural from enhanced or anthropogenic greenhouse warming. The natural greenhouse hypothesis is a generally accepted fact among atmospheric scientists. Atmospheric GHGs like water vapour, carbon dioxide (CO_2), methane (CH_4), or nitrous oxide (N_2O) are relatively transparent to incoming solar radiation but absorb much of the outgoing infrared energy. They therefore act as a blanket trapping heat at the surface of the Earth. It is believed that this natural greenhouse effect raises the global mean temperature on Earth by about 30°C. This warming is vital to the survival of all currently living species.

During the last decades, however, scientists discovered in data from different sample points a continuously rising trend in the atmospheric concentration of the main GHGs. IPCC (1996) mentions that the concentration of atmospheric CO_2 rose from 280 ppm (parts per million) in 1850 to 358 ppm in 1994 and is projected to reach 700 ppm by 2100. It is believed that increased human activity since the industrial revolution is responsible for substantial annual emissions, mainly of carbon dioxide, methane, and nitrous oxide adding to the natural atmospheric stock of these gases. This anthropogenic increase in atmospheric

concentrations of GHGs causes concern among scientists because it might enhance the natural greenhouse effect and disturb the Earth's climate equilibrium.

However, many scientific uncertainties remain concerning this enhanced
greenhouse effect. First, the link between a rising atmospheric concentration of
GHGs and an increase in global mean temperature is still questionable. Since the
1880s, mean temperature in the Northern hemisphere rose by between 0.3°C and
0.6°C, but this increase is not uniform over the observation period and it is too
early to conclude that it is correlated with increasing atmospheric concentrations
of GHGs. Second, the relation between human activities and rising concentrations of GHGs is not established with certainty because of the multiple interactions and feedback effects between the atmosphere, the oceans, clouds and
vegetation. It is not clear whether high atmospheric concentrations of GHGs are
the cause or the result of global warming. Analysis of air bubbles trapped in the
Antarctic ice showed that high GHG concentration levels coinciding with increasing global mean temperature occurred earlier in the Earth's climate history
without humanity being responsible for it. Third, several feedback effects are
known to exist, but their importance cannot be estimated accurately. For example, trees and oceans sequester carbon dioxide from the atmosphere but their
buffer capacity and the time lags involved are unknown. Global warming would
stimulate evaporation of the oceans resulting in higher concentrations of the
GHG water vapour in the atmosphere, but, on the other hand, clouds reflect
sunlight and can temper greenhouse warming.

Despite the remaining uncertainties, most scientists agree on the natural greenhouse effect and on the possibility of an enhanced greenhouse effect resulting
from anthropogenic emissions of GHGs. The IPCC states in its authoritative
1990 Report that there exists a natural greenhouse effect, and that emissions
resulting from human activities significantly enhance this natural warming. The
real controversy starts when one tries to quantify the future temperature rise and
to determine its regional impacts. We will return to this question later.

A comprehensive approach to global warming should include all the important
GHGs: carbon dioxide (CO_2), methane (CH_4), nitrous oxide (N_2O), chlorofluorocarbons (CFCs)[3] and ozone (O_3). In this short paper, we will focus on what is
generally perceived as the most important contributor to greenhouse warming:
carbon dioxide (CO_2). IPCC estimates that CO_2 is responsible for more than half
of the increase in radiative forcing during the 1980s and that it would require a
60 percent to 80 percent decrease in CO_2 emissions relative to 1990 to stabilize
atmospheric CO_2 concentration levels by the beginning of the next century. The
main anthropogenic emission source of carbon dioxide is fossil fuel combustion,
with 5.0 to 6.0 billion tons of carbon per year.[4] Coal is the most carbon-intensive
fuel with 1.07 tons of carbon per ton of oil equivalent whereas, for natural gas,
one ton of oil equivalent contains only 0.61 tons of carbon. Oil takes an intermediate position with 0.81 tons of carbon per ton. Carbon emissions resulting from
land clearing and deforestation are uncertain. According to Grubb (1989), estimates for deforestation range between 0.5 and 2.6 billion tons of carbon per year.
Attempts to reduce, or slow down, global warming will have to focus on fossil
fuel combustion and deforestation.

Building blocks for the distributive analysis

Here, we will first consider the questions of who is responsible for the bulk of CO_2 emissions in the past, who is emitting carbon dioxide today, and what are the trends for the future. We will then turn to the benefits and costs of greenhouse policies. Since, for a normative analysis, we cannot be satisfied with the global effect, we will also consider the interregional variation in these benefits and costs.

Starting positions and cumulative carbon emissions

Figure 9.1 shows carbon emission data for the OECD and non-OECD countries between 1925 and 1990. Trends are extrapolated until the year 2000. OECD emissions rose steadily until the beginning of the 1970s, but then the oil crises of 1974 and 1979 were followed by sharp decreases in oil consumption and lower carbon emissions. During the 1980s, OECD emissions started rising again, but at a lower rate than before. On the other hand, non-OECD carbon emissions rose continuously, and, by the beginning of the 1980s, had caught up with OECD emissions. Toward the end of the century, non-OECD carbon emissions are expected to continue their rapid rise because of further industrialization of large countries like India, China, and Brazil. These countries are endowed with massive reserves of coal, the most carbon-intensive fossil fuel, and have repeatedly expressed their intention to use this natural resource for meeting their future energy needs.

In figure 9.2, historic emission data have been translated into cumulative carbon emissions. By 1990, the OECD countries accounted for approximately 61 percent of cumulative carbon emissions, but around the year 2000 the OECD share would have declined to some 57 percent. As we will indicate later, developing countries often stress the responsibility of the industrialized world for the current stock of GHGs.

Figure 9.3 gives a more detailed disaggregation of current carbon emissions resulting from fossil fuel consumption. North America (including the US and Canada), although it only represents 5.3 percent of world population, accounted for more than a quarter of all carbon emissions in 1991; the second largest emitter is OECD-Europe with 16.4 percent. In figure 9.4, we show the emissions per capita for different regions. Per capita carbon emissions for North America are almost ten times higher than for China and more than 27 times higher than developing Asia.

Effects of climate change: Benefits of greenhouse policies

Knowing that atmospheric CO_2 concentrations are bound to rise far into next century, the main question is by how much global mean temperature will rise and how regional climate conditions will be affected. Most scientists today agree upon the IPCC (1990) central estimate that a doubling of CO_2 concentrations would lead to a 2°C (±1.5°C) increase in global mean temperature. If current carbon dioxide emission trends persist into the future, this doubling would occur before

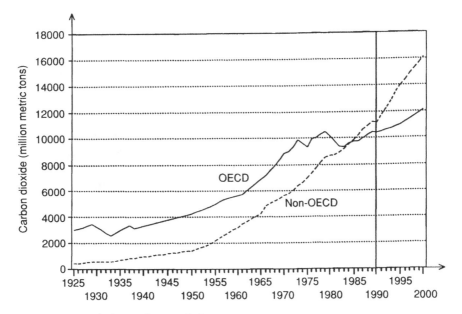

Figure 9.1 Cumulative carbon emissions

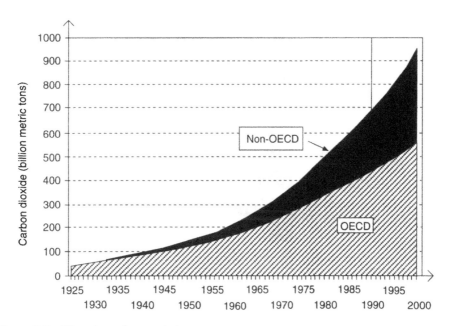

Figure 9.2 Historic carbon emissions

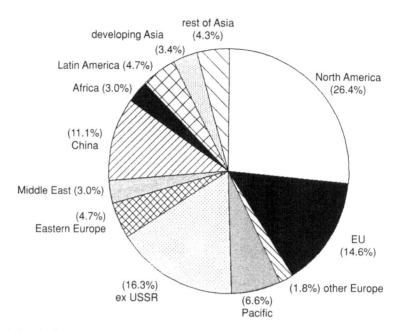

Figure 9.3   Carbon emissions 1991

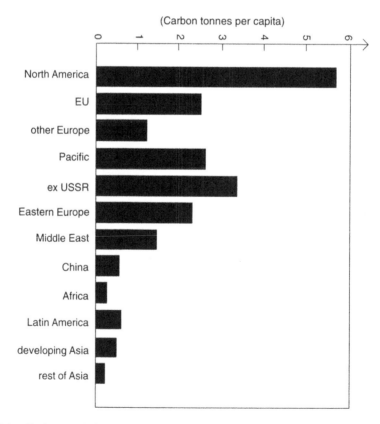

Figure 9.4   Carbon emissions per capita 1991

the year 2050. There exists also a consensus that current global climate simulation models are not capable of predicting regional climate changes in a reliable way. Nevertheless, many specialists predict that the land surface will warm more rapidly than the oceans, and that high Northern latitudes will warm more, and semiarid tropical regions less, than the global mean.

Scientists agree that a 1°C to 3.5°C increase in global mean temperature will cause substantial regional disturbances in temperature, rainfall, evaporation, cloud cover, wind pattern, and potential of drought affecting agriculture, water supplies and human health. However, given the unreliability of the regionally differentiated estimates of crucial climate variables, it remains a difficult task to predict the precise repercussions of global warming for a particular region. We are only able to make some general statements. We will focus upon two major effects of global warming:

- the effects on agriculture, and
- the rise of the sea-level.

Jodha (1989) argues that agricultural production in developing countries is likely to be affected more negatively by changes in climate conditions than is agricultural production in the industrialized world. Moreover, the agricultural sector is a relatively more important contributor to the GNP of developing countries than to the GNP of industrialized economies. Agriculture in developing countries often consists of a large subsistence sector and a small surplus-generating modern export sector. The subsistence sector especially is vulnerable to changes in climatic conditions because it encompasses marginal areas which depend more directly on natural factors like precipitation. In addition, the subsistence sector employs poor people who are not able to insure themselves against risks. The modern export sector, on the other hand, is less vulnerable given its high capital intensity and the policy bias of developing countries' governments.

Not all physical effects of enhanced greenhouse warming are expected to be negative. One expects, for example, that the thawing of tundra areas in Siberia and Canada would open up possibilities for expanding agricultural cropland. Another widely cited positive effect of high CO_2 concentration levels on agriculture is carbon fertilization. Laboratory experiments indicate that higher concentrations of atmospheric CO_2 stimulate photosynthesis and plant growth, but the importance of this effect in real world conditions is not yet known.

Probably the most spectacular and dangerous consequence of global warming is the projected rise in the sea level due to the thermal expansion of the oceans and, to a lesser extent, the partial melting of polar glaciers. Before the end of next century, IPCC predicts a 50 cm increase in the average sea level and even more if the West Antarctic ice sheet should disintegrate and melt.

Again, it should be noted that this increase will not be uniform across the Earth but that it can differ regionally as a function of local geological characteristics. Hekstra (1989) claims that a 1-m sea level rise might directly or indirectly affect 3 percent of the Earth's land area and more than one third of all agricultural cropland. Much of the area is densely populated, and as many as one billion people might be affected. Among the areas most likely to be affected are the Netherlands and Flanders in Western Europe, many river basins like the Po in Italy, the Nile in Egypt, the Ganges in Bangladesh, the Yangtse and Hwang Ho in China, the Indus in Pakistan, the Mekong in Vietnam, the Orinoco and Amazon in South America, and the Mississippi in the USA. Very seriously threatened are island states like the Maldives, Kiribati and the Seychelles.

The physical effects must be related to the economic means of the various countries. Developing countries are likely to experience greater damage than industrialized nations because the latter have a far greater financial and techno-logical adaptation potential to build additional coastal defenses. Hekstra (1989), for example, quotes a study by the Dutch public authority, Rijkswaterstaat, which estimates that adapting to a 1-m sea-level rise would cost the Netherlands some 5 to 6 billion $US spread over 50 to 100 years. When we compare this figure to the costs of the Delta works (7.5 billion $US over 30 years) it becomes clear that adapting to a 1-m sea-level rise does not appear an infeasible project for the Netherlands. The situation in Bangladesh, however, is completely different, and one can expect large migration flows originating in some of the severely affected developing countries.

Should anything be done to slow down GHG emissions or should we simply "wait and see" until more scientific evidence becomes available? The benefits of greenhouse policies are still doubtful. Moreover, since it can be predicted that global warming will have more pronounced negative effects in developing coun-tries than in the richer OECD-countries, it is important to remember Schelling's (1992) remark that "the best defense of the developing countries against climate change may be their own continued development." Then, surely, emission abate-ment is not the adequate policy for these countries.

However, Schelling also points to an important reason for starting immedi-ately with emission abatement: the possibility of catastrophes. The rather mild consequences predicted now for the rich countries hold for a moderate climate change, but if we continue emitting CO_2 at an increasing pace, we commit ourselves to warming for centuries ahead, and the longer we wait to take action, the higher the risk that we will have to cope with very large warming effects. Even if the probability of an accident is small but the expected losses are very high, risk averse agents are willing to pay a risk premium to insure themselves against that risk. This insurance principle is perhaps the best argument to implement preven-tive strategies like investment in energy efficiency or switching to less carbon intensive fuels (Proost, 1992).

Carbon dioxide emission abatement costs

The last important factor is the difference between nations' emission abatement costs. The ratio of emissions to GDP, given in figure 9.5, can be interpreted as a measure of energy efficiency. Eastern Europe and China perform badly in this respect. The IEA (1992) figures also indicate that the Scandinavian countries and Japan are extremely efficient fossil energy users. Figure 9.6 presents another picture of the same reality: it shows some marginal cost curves for emission abatement, as calibrated by Eyckmans et al. (1993, 1994) on the basis of simula-

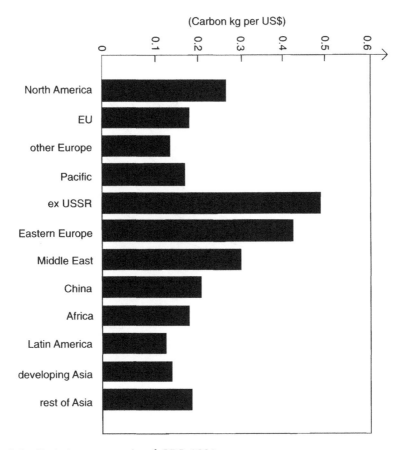

Figure 9.5   Emissions as a ratio of GDP 1991

tion results obtained with the OECD-GREEN-model (Burniaux et al., 1991; Nordhaus, 1991).

Cost efficiency calls for a distribution of emission abatement efforts resulting in equal marginal abatement costs for all participants in the agreement. For efficient energy users like Japan or Scandinavia, it would be extremely costly to improve their fossil energy efficiency because they already made important efforts in the past. Cheap emission abatement on the other hand can be obtained from inefficient fossil fuel users like ex-USSR or China. These findings have been used frequently to argue that, from an economic point of view, the richer countries should contribute relatively less to global carbon emission reduction. We will return to this argument later.

The present state of the negotiations

Unlike our success with the ozone depletion problem, there does not yet exist an effective international agreement to coordinate greenhouse policies. In

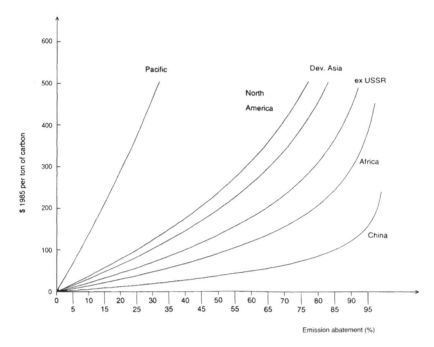

Figure 9.6 Estimated marginal costs of emission abatement

1992, several countries, however, announced unilateral emission reduction targets:

- Unconditional commitments with plans for action and supported by a carbon tax – Denmark and the Netherlands
- Unconditional commitments without specific plans – Austria, Canada, Iceland, Luxembourg, Switzerland
- Non-binding and/or conditional commitments with carbon tax – Finland, Norway
- Non-binding and/or conditional commitments – Australia, Germany, Italy, New Zealand, UK
- Target in function of need for economic growth – Spain
- Conditional target in function of per capita emissions – France, Japan
- Commitment to set of policies stabilizing emissions – USA
- Regional target: EU, EFTA

The Climate Change Conference held at Kyoto, Japan in December 1997 did produce a Protocol for industrialized nations to reduce emissions of GHGs from 1990 levels by 2008–12. The EU agreed to an 8 percent reduction and Japan to a 6 percent reduction. The USA initially opposed making any reductions, but, by the end of the conference, agreed to a 7 percent reduction. It is not at all clear whether this agreement will be ratified by the US Congress because no binding targets for GHGs were made by developing nations. It remains to be seen whether developing nations will establish effective "voluntary" targets.

Summing all the commitments made by industrialized nations corresponds to emissions that are 70 percent of the "business as usual" scenario for industrialized nations by the year 2010 (*New York Times*, 12/12/97). Since most of the growth of emissions of GHGs will be in developing nations, however, it is clear that much remains to be done.

First things first: A framework to evaluate international distributive justice

Many authors have been aware of the distributional implications of global warming and have discussed "fair" solutions for greenhouse negotiations; see Rose (1990, 1992), Rose and Stevens (1993), and Barrett (1992) for overviews. We feel, however, that concentrating on the greenhouse problem in isolation is an unattractive approach. Therefore, we will start in this section with the formulation of an "ideal" and global framework to evaluate the international welfare distribution. We return to the more concrete arguments on page 209.

The general practice in economics is to refrain from discussing distributive justice, and to concentrate instead on economic efficiency. For non-economists, this must seem like putting the cart before the horse. Indeed, for them, it is obvious that before we can talk about efficiency in a meaningful way, it is necessary to define the objectives with respect to which we measure efficiency; the interpretation given to distributive justice certainly is part of this definition of social objectives.

There is a large economic literature on how to give concrete content to the definition of distributive justice, but it is impossible to formulate in this short paper a general theory of justice; see Schokkaert (1992) for an overview of the literature. We will therefore confine ourselves to our intuitive paradigm which might be acceptable to many readers and which will prove to be sufficient for structuring our analysis of the greenhouse problem. Perhaps the first and foremost challenge in our contemporary world is the fact that millions of people do not reach a minimal living standard. In our opinion, the top ethical priority is to raise these millions of human beings above this minimum threshold. Our concept of living standard is intended to reflect the possibilities for human beings to live valuable lives and therefore refers to both economic and political rights. Of course, there is a huge problem of constructing an index that captures all these considerations, but, for our purposes, it is not necessary to be specific about this formal problem.

The basic idea of concentrating on the poorest people in the world is quite incomplete as a conception of justice and is rooted in many different ethical systems. This preferential option for the poor also plays an important role in most religious traditions, including the Judeo-Christian and Islamic ones. Therefore, although our starting point is certainly incomplete, it is not vague. In fact, it allows us a clearer view of some of the approaches and arguments that are quite popular in the current discussions on the greenhouse effect. The first is the treatment of "nations" as the most important entities in the ethical debate. The second is the emphasis on cumulative past emissions. The third is the ecocentric critique on economics. The fourth is the sum-ranking of traditional utilitarianism and the ensuing interpretation of efficiency. The reader should keep in mind that we are sketching an ideal approach and that it will be necessary to use practical approximations for any real-life application. However, it is instructive to have an ideal (although in the present situation, not operational) model in mind, to avoid taking the pragmatic approximations as a true image of reality.

The ethical status of states: Avoiding fantasy

In the current debate on the greenhouse effect, there is a tendency to talk about nations as if they were human beings. One then uses arguments such as: "Bangladesh should be helped because its income per capita is so small", or: "The USA has a huge responsibility because it is responsible for a large part of past CO_2 emissions." Worse still are references to the "poor South" and the "rich but irresponsible North." Sen (1981) describes this approach of anthropomorphizing nations as "fantasy," "fiction of all nations throbbing as symbolic individuals in existence."

There are at least two problems with this "fantasy." From an explanatory point of view, it reflects an oversimplified vision of the world neglecting the complex interplay of different political and economic forces within each country. This may lead to an excessively optimistic or pessimistic view on the position of individual nations in the international negotiations. Note, for example, how important a change of the ruling political majority can be in this respect. From a normative point of view (and therefore more important in this context), the practice of "fantasy" leads to a neglect of the inter-individual or inter-regional variation within one country with respect to, among other things, income levels and consequences of global warming. Our basic concern for the poorest people might be rejected by the ruling elites of the poorest countries. Moreover, it would be quite inaccurate to impose on powerless (and possibly also poor) people in the rich countries, a part of the responsibility for the misery in other parts of the world.

Our normative approach proposes to take into account the internal distribution of well-being and power within the different countries. Of course, this is an ambitious project and, at the present stage, we do not possess the information (nor do we have sufficient theoretical insights) to make it fully operational. For practical purposes, we will therefore have to fall back on aggregate information to approximate the complexity of the real world. This does not mean that we are playing "fantasy," if we only remain aware of the fact that this is a short-cut, and that internal differences must be taken into account in a second step.

Responsibility for past emissions and consequentialism

Normative economics has been strongly influenced by utilitarianism, which defines social welfare as the simple sum of individual utilities. When using utilitarianism as a starting point for his writings on economics and ethics, Sen factorizes it into its constituent parts: consequentialism, welfarism and sum-ranking; see, for example, Sen and Williams (1982). We now take up these different aspects.

A special concern for the poor can easily be introduced in consequentialist approaches. In fact, our basic idea is a weaker version of the Rawlsian difference principle (Rawls, 1971) which has been so influential in contemporary political philosophy, and our idea of living standard is closely related to Sen's concept of basic capabilities; – see, for example, Sen (1987) – and many recent similar proposals. Consequentialism evaluates social states on the basis of the characteristics of these states and, hence, actions on the basis of the consequences of these actions. In the extreme version of consequentialism, information about consequences is the only information we need to evaluate actions and other information (i.e. on the historical background or the motivation of the action) is irrelevant. In a less extreme interpretation, one could say that these other considerations may play a role, but that, in any case, consequences do matter, i.e. that the ethical evaluation must be consequence-sensitive (to use Sen's terminology).[5] In our context, the extreme poor have the right to be helped and the rich, therefore, have the ethical duty to help the poor, because a social state with many poor is ethically inferior to a social state with only a few poor people.

It is interesting to confront this starting point with the actual greenhouse debate, where the position of the third-world countries has been aptly summarized in the 1991 Beijing Ministerial Declaration of Environment and Development: "the developed countries bear responsibility for the degradation of the global environment. Ever since the Industrial Revolution, the developed countries have over-exploited the world's natural resources through unsustainable patterns of production and consumption, causing damage to the global environment, to the detriment of the developing countries. Responsibility for the emissions of greenhouse gases should be viewed both in historical and cumulative terms, and in terms of current emissions. On the basis of the principle of equity, those developed countries who have contaminated most must contribute more". This argument of responsibility for the past keeps cropping up in the debate.

Yet, in an extreme consequentialist approach, the argument is totally irrelevant. The rightness of actions now must be evaluated on the basis of the future consequences of these actions and not on the past. Of course, this does not change the conclusion that the developed countries have to contribute more. Even if the rich countries were not responsible for the bulk of emissions in the past, they still would have a duty to stimulate the development of the poor countries. In a weaker version of consequentialism, one could say that past emissions create a specific obligation for the rich countries to compensate the victims of these emissions, but here also, the duty of the developed countries to bear the largest burden of emission abatement now is not exclusively dependent on the pattern of past emissions, as long as we judge that the fight against poverty is the main social objective.

Until now, we have reasoned within a consequentialist setting. The alternative extreme would be the pure procedural libertarian position that the consequences of actions do not matter for the ethical evaluation of these actions. Within this approach, the action of a person is just if that person had the right to take that action, whatever the consequences. If I own a good, I can do whatever I want with my possession. This approach is incomplete, unless one settles in a satisfactory way the problem of the initial allocation of property rights. Moreover, at first sight, the libertarian conclusions go strongly against our intuition that the extreme poor have a right to be helped and should not be dependent on the charity of the rich.

However, we should be careful with the latter conclusion. In fact, even in a libertarian setting, one could derive the conclusion that the rich countries have to bear the largest part of the cost of emission abatement. In Kolm's (1985) theory of the liberal social contract, the importance of the poor can follow from the ideas of implicit and fundamental insurance (closely related to consequentialism), or, more important in this context, from the duty to compensate for past illegitimacies. With more caveats, the compensation argument could also follow from Nozick's (1974) analysis. A "leftist-libertarian" position would start from the idea that all human beings have an equal right to nature and that these equal rights have been violated to arrive in the present situation. In all these cases, the argument that the richer countries should bear the largest burden follows from past behavior: their duty is a duty to compensate for their past actions. Somewhat paradoxically, the argument from the Beijing declaration, which was largely irrelevant in a consequentialist approach, is the cornerstone to justify the responsibility of the rich countries in this procedural-libertarian framework.

What should we think about this argument? Formulated in a direct way we ask: do the developed countries have the ethical duty to pay more, just because they are rich, or do they have the duty because they have emitted more carbon dioxide in the past? We do not feel that the second answer is the most convincing one. A few decades ago nobody was aware of the negative environmental consequences for the environment of emitting CO_2, and it seems difficult to blame economic agents in the developed countries for the decisions they have taken in this situation of ignorance. To see the point more clearly, consider the following thought experiment. Assume we would discover that a huge global environmental problem (X) is caused by the consumption of a commodity which is heavily concentrated in a poor area of the world, e.g. cassava, a tropical plant with starchy roots from which tapioca is obtained. At the time of the consumption, nobody knew that cassava consumption could be the cause of such a problem. Are we going to use the responsibility argument to claim that Africa should bear the burden of the policies aimed at reducing X? Or, would we feel that even if Africa has been (unconsciously) responsible for X, the rich countries should still bear the larger burden? We favor the second answer, but this immediately implies that the burden of the past-argument is dominated by the unequal starting positions-argument. Moreover, even if one would consider it to be relevant, we do not really need it in our consequence-sensitive approach to distributive justice.

Living standards and the ecocentric critique

Although our framework is consequence-sensitive, we are not welfarist. Since we have defined "poverty" in terms of an index of individual (economic and political) rights, we have implicitly taken a position against the welfarist position embodied in utilitarianism. Nor did we take the other extreme position of concentrating exclusively on monetary income (another popular approach in economics). In our framework, non-income factors are crucial but they are not channeled exclusively via individual utility, whether interpreted as subjective well-being or as the representation of consumer preferences. A full justification for this non-welfarist position is beyond the scope of our paper. Suffice it to refer to the many contributions by Sen or the more empirically oriented paper by Dasgupta (1990).[6] In this section, we only want to suggest how the non-welfarist framework relates to the ecocentric critique on economics.

We have given special attention to the satisfaction of the needs of the poor (although we have interpreted these needs in a broad sense). This makes our framework vulnerable to the ecocentric critique that the emphasis on human needs without due respect for the needs (some would even say, rights) of the natural environment leads to the abuse of Nature. Ecocentrists claim that Nature has an intrinsic value, independent of its potential for satisfaction of human needs. Man exists within a wider ecological or cosmic whole, that is valuable in and of itself.

The extreme ecocentric position does not guide us very efficiently in the context of the greenhouse problem. It certainly implies that we should use energy in an economical way, but how far do we have to go? We should remind ourselves that the costs of global warming (and, hence, the benefits of emission abatement) are very uncertain at this moment and, to a large extent, can be expressed in terms of human suffering. The cost of emission abatement can easily be expressed in terms of GDP and will probably be very large. An adequate ethical framework must help us to structure the trade-off between material welfare now and in the future, and must also suggest a procedure to weigh the position of different individuals at different welfare levels. The extreme ecocentric position does not help with such careful weighing of costs and benefits of specific actions. Rose (1992) and Rose and Stevens (1993) translate ecocentrism into the "general operational rule" that "emissions should be cut back to maximize environmental values." They make this concrete in the context of CO_2 in saying that it is necessary to "limit permits associated with vulnerable ecosystems." These rules are extremely vague, too vague in fact to guide us in defining social priorities.

There is a less extreme position, however, which admits that trade-offs have to be made, but emphasizes that the intrinsic value of nature must be accorded an important position in the value system guiding these choices. The basic inspiration for this stance is extremely valuable and it offers a powerful antidote to the exploitation of nature inspired by crude materialism. Such crude materialism indeed may be reflected in a singular focus on GNP-growth or a shallow interpretation of utilitarianism. However, the non-welfarist framework offers room to integrate a real concern for Nature even if this would not be reflected in short-sighted individual consumer preferences. Our concept of the living standard is a normative concept and can therefore include the harmonious integration of human beings in Nature as one important component. Yet, for reasons explained earlier, one may doubt whether this element will play a dominant role in the evaluation of policies with respect to global warming.

Sum-ranking and efficiency

Utilitarianism takes the simple sum of individual utilities and is therefore not concerned about the distribution of utilities. In the non-welfarist setting, an analogous procedure would compute the "overall" living standard by summing the different individual living standard indices.[7] However, these two philosophies leave us in want of income redistribution if the marginal effect of income on the living standard would be decreasing over income level; thus, we do not pretend to defend the approach of either utilitarianism or non-welfarism.

Our basic intuition that the first ethical priority of economic policy must be to raise the poorest people above a minimum threshold implies that they should be given a larger weight in the calculation of the aggregate than people with a high living standard. Or, formulated differently: an increase in the living standard of an individual below the poverty threshold accompanied by an equivalent decrease in the living standard of a person above the threshold will be evaluated as a social improvement.

This intuition excludes simple sum-ranking but is still compatible with many other approaches. One possible position would be to claim that distribution no longer matters once all people are lifted above the threshold. Alternatively, one could make the social welfare function a strictly concave and symmetric function of the individual living standards, perhaps with a marginal weight equal to infinity for the individuals below the poverty threshold. The Rawlsian maximin idea would be the extreme case where only the poorest people are given a positive weight in the social welfare function, even if everybody is lifted above the threshold (and this is the reason why we claimed earlier that our approach is a weak version of the Rawlsian difference principle). For the present analysis, we do not have to choose between these different options, but it is obvious that they will lead to sharply opposed policy prescriptions in other concrete settings.

Our framework can be used to evaluate the popular economic approach of maximizing overall GNP (or, in the context of global warming, the simple sum of the monetary benefits for all countries). This is sometimes justified as a "value-free" choice for economic efficiency, because it would allow avoiding value-loaded judgments on distributive justice. This simple justification is obviously not valid. Taking the simple sum of the monetary benefits for all countries implies a specific, and, in our view, extremely unattractive choice of value judgments. It reflects the use of a social welfare function where the concept of living standard is reduced to material income (from marketed sources) and where the income levels of all individuals in all countries are simply added, i.e. where giving one additional unit of income to the richest person in the world has the same ethical value as giving one additional unit of income to the poorest person.[8]

We therefore conclude that the practice of looking for the maximum of world GNP implies the acceptance of unattractive distributional values and should therefore be avoided. The statement that concentrating on efficiency (interpreted in this sense) is value-free is completely mistaken. Note, however, that this does not imply that productive efficiency is not a crucial objective in the social calculus of costs and benefits. We will return to that point on page 210.

Economic and political constraints: Efficiency and participation

In the previous section, we have given an abstract and idealized framework to structure the discussion on international distributive justice. Let us now return to the more concrete setting of international greenhouse policies. This will require us first to come down to earth and to formulate a more operational interpretation of our lofty ideals. We will then show how considerations of productive efficiency can be integrated in our framework and what the implications are of the absence of an international government.

A pragmatic shortcut

Let us sketch once again our "ideal" ethical framework. Social states should be evaluated on the basis of the distribution of living standards of individuals all over the world. The concept of living standard is non-welfaristic: it is to be seen as an index of economic and social rights. Two main problems then come to the fore. First, how should this index be computed, or, how should we trade off different rights? In this respect, we mentioned the possibility that the value of nature could influence the index (as a separate dimension or as influencing the ethical trade-offs). Second, how should we evaluate different distributions of individual living standards, or, should we trade off the living standards of different individuals? Without giving a complete answer to this question, we suggested that, in the present world situation, there can be no doubt that the first priority is to combat the extreme poverty in some parts of the world.

This framework defines a very ambitious research program, and, in the present state of information and insight, it is necessary to make some provisional approximations. We suggest concentrating on the distribution of GNP per capita over the world, with the first priority being to the GNP of poor countries. It should be obvious that the burden of greenhouse policies to be borne by the different countries should then be inversely related to their GNP per capita. In a formal analysis, one could work with a strictly concave social welfare function. Within the context of huge international income differences, we see a rather moderate value for the degree of inequality aversion in an additive iso-elastic specification of the social welfare function, e.g. 1.5, as advocated by Stern (1976). This leads to extreme differences in the marginal social valuation of one unit of income in the rich and the poor countries; see Eyckmans et al. (1993).

This approximation brings us close to the traditional economic approach and may seem perhaps even somewhat ridiculous after the (lengthy and now apparently superfluous) exposition of the previous section. It is therefore useful to summarize what we have learnt from that exposition.

First, we have learnt to be aware that this approximation is only an approximation and in which direction it should be expanded. For starters, the analysis could be refined by introducing measures of income inequality within the different countries and more information concerning the relationship between GNP per capita and satisfaction of basic needs. In a later stage, the more basic questions concerning the construction of an index of living standards should be settled.

Second, it must be stressed that, despite similarities, our operational approach is very different from the model often used for the economic analysis of greenhouse negotiations. We emphatically reject the procedure of maximizing overall world GNP or the simple sum of the monetary benefits of greenhouse policies for different countries. In our opinion, these amount to an ethically unacceptable procedure of equally weighing the income changes of rich and poor people. We derived our conclusions without relying on the argument of responsibility for past emissions. Of course, distributional weights based on past emissions are highly correlated with distributional weights based on present GNP per capita, because there is a high correlation between GNP per capita and past emissions. This does not in the least diminish the relevancy of trying to define the best theoretical basis for these weights; in fact, it becomes even more so because the relationship between cumulative emissions and GNP per capita will change in the future.

Allocative and productive efficiency

We have argued before that one can only talk sensibly about efficiency if one has first defined clearly the objectives with respect to which it will be measured. Since, in the previous section, we have described an operational version of a social welfare function, we can now treat the efficiency problem in an adequate way. We will address two questions. The first is the question of productive efficiency: given that a target for the global level of emission abatement has been fixed, how should the efforts be distributed among the different countries? The second is the question of what could be called allocational efficiency: at what level should that global target itself be fixed?

The question of productive efficiency is the easiest one. Given the differences in marginal costs sketched earlier (see pages 194–203), a huge efficiency gain can be realized by concentrating emission abatement efforts in countries where these costs are relatively low. Since these countries tend to be poor, it might seem that there is a sharp conflict between this efficiency prescription and our justice criteria. Fortunately, there are instruments to overcome the conflict. The first is the use of tradable carbon emission entitlements (UNCTAD, 1992). Trade in these entitlements will lead to an efficient allocation of the abatement efforts over the different countries, whatever the initial distribution of these entitlements. This implies that the initial distribution can be based on justice considerations. The second instrument is the imposition of an international carbon tax with redistribution of the proceeds (Hoel, 1992). The uniform tax would lead to cost-efficiency; the receipts can be redistributed so as to realize a desired distribution. Given the existence of these instruments, there is no reason why an international

agreement should not strive for productive efficiency.[9] If the gains from cooperation are larger, there is more to redistribute and this will be advantageous for the
poor nations too.

The problem of allocational efficiency is much more difficult. As we are in a
second-best situation with a far from optimal income distribution, we know that
the Samuelson rule is no longer valid. Distributional weights must be taken into
account when adding the WTP (willingness-to-pay) of the different countries; see,
for example Atkinson and Stiglitz (1980). As mentioned before, the international
setting is characterized by huge differences in the distributional weights, and it is
therefore to be expected that the optimal level of emission abatement should to a
large extent be determined by the WTP of the poor countries. From a formal
point of view, this statement could only be given a more concrete structure after
a careful and elaborate empirical analysis. Keeping in mind the uncertainty which
still surrounds estimating the benefits of greenhouse policies, such analytical
derivation of "the" optimal level of emission abatement remains an extremely
awkward problem. However, one can also interpret our basic insight in a less
formal way. In reality, the global level of emission abatement will be decided
upon through a complicated process of international negotiations. One could
loosely interpret distributional weights as the weights to be given to the different
partners in these negotiations. Our reasoning then suggests (in line with our
basic starting point) that the poorest countries should have an important say in
the matter.[10]

Participation constraints and the mirage of "partial" justice

It is obvious that the fulfillment of our basic ethical requirement of lifting all
human beings at least above a minimal standard of living will require a huge
transfer of means from the rich to the poor countries. At the national level,
regional development schemes and interpersonal redistribution are taken care of
by the political system. At the international level, however, there is no political
body with the authority to impose a large-scale redistribution scheme. Redistribution can only take place if it is voluntarily accepted by the rich. Apparently, the
rich in the world are not sufficiently altruistic or sufficiently sensitive to the justice
argumentation developed in the previous sections to accept such redistribution.
How do we incorporate these facts into our normative analysis?

Figure 9.7 conveys the basic insights. The vertical and horizontal axes give the
level of living standard for the (presently) poor South and rich North respectively.
These living standards have to be interpreted in a dynamic sense: they capture
both actual and future levels. The inner curve SS' gives the production possibilities in the case where no greenhouse policies are implemented, the outer curve
TT' gives the production possibilities after the optimal level of emission abatement has been reached. The figure may be somewhat surprising at first sight,
because, interpreted in a narrow sense, greenhouse policies may be expected to
lead to a smaller level of material welfare. Remember, however, that "living
standard" is interpreted here in a broad sense, and includes social and economic

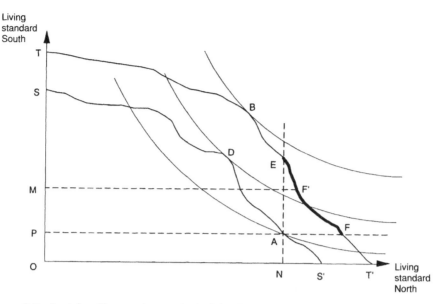

Figure 9.7 Social welfare optima and participation constraints

rights and possibly even ecocentric-like considerations. The exact position and curvature of SS′ and TT′ depend on all the uncertainties described earlies (see pages 194–203).

Point A is the starting point on the inner curve with an extremely unequal distribution. The indifference curves drawn represent a concave social welfare function (in the spirit of the previous sections). The true ethical optimum would be at point B. To go from A to B, two steps have to be taken: first, greenhouse policies have to be implemented, taking us from SS′ to TT′; second, an international redistribution has to take place (and, in fact, the rich will have to give up part of their high living standard). The consequences of the absence of an international government can easily be shown in this figure. If we are at point A and if the North is driven by self-interest, it will never accept a policy which would bring the economy to the left of NE, because this would imply a lower living standard. An analogous reasoning holds for the South and limits us to agreements above PF.

The figure is a tremendous simplification of complex reality, but it allows us to illustrate clearly some basic points. First, in a situation without world government and where nations are driven by self-interest, the best we can hope for are Pareto-improving agreements bringing us somewhere on the segment EF. Neglecting this fact would be an indication of extreme naïveté. It is understandable therefore that an author like Barrett (1992) in his analysis of "just" distribution of carbon emission entitlements concludes that "a virtue of the OECD modeling exercise is that tradable carbon emission entitlements are initially allocated in such a way that the transfers are not too large" (p. 124). However, it is important to realize that this restriction has nothing to do with justice; rather, it follows from the power and the pursuit of self-interest by a large part of the world. It is better, therefore, to speak about participation constraints that restrict us to reaching ethically preferable situations.

Second, the ethically "best" and feasible agreement is easily defined: it is found at point E. Given the extremely unequal starting positions, the gains from co-operation should go completely to the presently poor South. Note that this does not imply that the North gives up part of its living standard: this remains at level ON, both in the status-quo position A and in the preferred (feasible) situation E. We can relax the specification with a strictly concave social welfare function and keep to the more basic intuition that the poor should be lifted above a certain minimum. If we assume that this minimum would be OM (smaller than NE), then we would only discard the allocations on F'F and the choice of a specific policy bringing us somewhere on the segment EF' could follow from other justice considerations. This point, however, should not distract us from the basic insight that regardless of the case, the needs of the poor South should come first in the greenhouse negotiations.

Third, we must think about how all the specific proposals for just "solutions" of the distribution problem fit within the context of greenhouse negotiations. These negotiations are often represented as a "positive sum game," in which all participants would gain if an agreement could be reached. The problem then becomes one of dividing the gains from cooperation. One wants to find the "just" point on EF. Alternatively, given the difficulty of measuring the benefits, one concentrates on the distribution of the abatement efforts and asks what would be a just distribution of these efforts. Seen from this perspective, our "solution" may seem a very extreme one, in which all the gains go to the poorest partner (point E), or alternatively, all efforts are borne by the richest partner. However, the perspective is misleading, because it tends to neglect the grossly unjust starting positions of the different partners in the negotiations. One cannot reasonably speak of a "just" distribution of efforts or gains from greenhouse negotiations if one does not situate these negotiations within the broader context of unequal international income distribution. "Partial" justice is a mirage, if the broader context is extremely unjust.

Let us illustrate this basic point with some of the equity criteria proposed by Rose (1990, 1992) and Rose and Stevens (1993) within the partial context of the greenhouse problem. Consider their "egalitarian" criterion leading to the opera-tional rule of "cutting back emissions in proportion to population;" this interpre-tation of egalitarianism is far removed from the usual one which would aim at an equal distribution of *ex-post* levels of living standard, and seen from that angle, their "egalitarian" criterion is extremely unjust. Consider "market justice" (make greater use of markets) and "consensus" (seek a political solution promoting stability criteria); these criteria are closely related to the philosophical literature on the justice of market and political outcomes respectively, but this literature is

214 SCHOKKAERT AND EYCKMANS

very careful in making explicit the conditions on starting positions under which these market or political outcomes can be just. The initial distribution of property rights and political power is essential in these contexts. In a situation (such as the present negotiations on greenhouse policies) where these conditions of economic and political starting positions are not fulfilled, the ethical power of the "market justice" and "consensus" criteria is very limited.

This is not to say that these specific criteria are useless. They may be quite important as focal points in the international negotiations (and this is in fact the interpretation given to them by Rose). The same is even true for the set of extremely *ad hoc* proposals from the literature that base the distribution of gains or abatement efforts on easily quantifiable criteria such as emissions per capita or population, or even land area. What we want to emphasize is that, whatever the value of these criteria as focal points, their ultimate ethical justification requires a more elaborated reasoning and that such a complete reasoning cannot separate the greenhouse problem from the broader economic context. As a final example, let us return to the argument that richer countries should abate more because they are responsible for the bulk of past emissions. We argued that this argument is not fully convincing and that it is preferable to base the duty of the richer countries simply on the fact that they are richer. It is somewhat paradoxical that the past-emissions argument is playing such a central role in the argumentation by the third world. We suggest that this is due to the fact that discussion remains centered on the global warming problem itself: in such a partial context, the past emissions argument may act as a roundabout means to introduce into the debate the issue of unequal global income distribution. In our broader setting, there is no need for this roundabout argument.

Conclusion

With this paper, we tried to sketch a normative perspective on international greenhouse negotiations. Until now, this perspective has been rather neglected in the economic literature, where more attention has been devoted to the concrete analysis of the process of international negotiations. We think that the approaches are complementary. The normative analysis should not be naïve and should take into account the economic and political feasibility of its proposals. On the other hand, a consistent ethical framework may help us to understand better the actual negotiation process, but the emphasis is different. What we can expect from the negotiations is not necessarily fair, and the ethical analysis must keep a critical distance. This has been the main focus of this paper.

From an ethical perspective, the extreme poverty in large parts of the world remains the main challenge for the economic system. We tried to situate this position within a broader framework, but our basic intuition has its roots in many different ethical systems. Nevertheless, we have clearly opted against the narrow utilitarian and libertarian positions and have explicitly rejected the tradition of concentrating only on economic efficiency. It is true, however, that our approach remains firmly rooted in the Western cultural tradition and we are aware that this is an important limitation for a treatment of problems of international distributive justice.

Seen from our perspective, it is not sensible to isolate the greenhouse problem and look for solutions which would be "partially just." International distributive justice requires directly addressing the development problem. Of course, this is not what we can expect as a result of real-world negotiations (and this is where critical distance is absolutely necessary). The defense of the status-quo position by richer nations should not be justified with pseudo-ethical arguments, but can better be seen as a constraint restricting the set of feasible states.

Our analysis has remained abstract and perhaps gives the impression of being far removed from reality. However, this may be only an impression. Consider the practical scenario sketched by Schelling (1992). He argues that it may be unrealistic to expect soon a broad universal agreement, because "it is altogether improbable that the developing world, at least for the next several decades, will incur any significant sacrifice in the interest of reduced carbon." He adds: "Nor would I advise developing countries to do so." This implies that any international regime for carbon abatement can seriously include only the developed countries. If these countries want to involve the third world, they will have to persuade it. Schelling continues: "While the developed countries are feeling their way into some common attack on their own carbon emissions, a tangible expression of their interest and an effective first step would be to establish a permanent means of funding technical aid and technology transfer for developing countries, as well as research, development and demonstration in carbon-saving technologies to those countries." Developing countries might be interested, he adds, because "cleaner fuels and more efficient fuel technologies bring a number of benefits other than reduced carbon." This is a practical proposal, apparently more realistic than the ambitious schemes based on a universal international agreement. It is, of course, far removed from our ethical ideal, but, within the feasible set, it is undoubtedly a step in the right direction. Our normative framework suggests that it is not only more realistic but perhaps even more attractive than some of the universal schemes proposed.

Notes

1   This paper has been prepared for a conference on "Limits to Markets: Equity and the Global Environment" (Cornell University, April 1994). Comments by participants at the conference, especially Mohammed Dore and Marc Willinger, are gratefully acknowledged.

2   Cline (1991, 1992) provide interesting introductions to the scientific background of the effects of GHGs. This section draws heavily upon Eyckmans (1993).

3   Alarming reports on the hole in the ozone layer above Antarctica turned public opinion toward the detrimental effects of CFCs, but, apart from their ozone-destructive capacity, CFCs are also strong contributors to greenhouse warming. The 1987 Montreal Protocol on "Substances that Deplete the Ozone Layer" and the 1990 Adjustments and Amendments to the Protocol require the production of CFCs to be phased out by the beginning of the next century. Hence, for the climate change problem, one can expect that CFCs will not pose much of a problem in the next century.

4   All emissions are expressed in terms of carbon. One tonne of carbon is equivalent with 3.66 tonnes of CO_2.

5   The difference between these options is not so clear if one uses the economic apparatus of "social states." As Dasgupta (1990) writes: "The distinction between acts and consequences in this broader framework (of social states) is formally so tenuous that it is difficult to see how so central a classification as is provided by the labels 'deontological' and 'consequentialist' can be sustained on its basis. If actions matter intrinsically, they can be made part of a description of consequences, and then the distinction collapses."

6   However, note that a non-welfarist interpretation of living standards makes it much easier to solve the awkward problems related to interpersonal comparisons.

7   Assume, for the moment, that we can measure these living standards at a level which makes adding meaningful.

8   There exists a more sophisticated economic justification for concentrating on efficiency. If the conditions of the second welfare theorem hold, i.e. if we are in a first-best world with a government disposing of a lump sum-redistributive instrument and using it to reach an optimal welfare distribution, efficiency and justice considerations can be separated. However, since it is obvious that such an international government disposing of lump sum-instruments does not exist, the second welfare theorem does not rescue the one-sided economist studying the greenhouse effect.

9   There are some nuances, however. In the tradeable entitlements case, dynamic considerations with respect to the distribution of future entitlements may interfere with the pursuit of efficiency. In the international tax case, there is an analogous problem: countries know they will share the proceeds and this will have consequences for their emission abatement decisions. Eyckmans et al. (1994) show that this latter effect remains relatively small.

10   Closely related in spirit to this approach is the computation of a so-called inverse optimum solution: given an international agreement on emission abatement, one then determines the implicit set of weights justifying that agreement; see Eyckmans et al. (1993) for some empirical results.

References

Atkinson, A. B. and Stiglitz, J. (1980) *Lectures on Public Economics.* Maidenhead: McGraw-Hill.

Barrett, S. (1992) Acceptable allocations of tradable carbon emission entitlements in a global warming treaty. In UNCTAD (1992, pp. 85–113).

Burniaux, J. M., Marrtin, J. P., Nicoletti, G. and Oliviera-Martins, J. (1991) GREEN – A multi-regional dynamic general equilibrium model for quantifying the costs of reducing CO_2 emissions. OECD Working-Paper No. 115. Paris: OECD.

Cline, W. R. (1991) Scientific basis for the greenhouse effect. *Economic Journal*, 101, 904–19.

Cline, W. R. (1992) *Global Warming: the Economic Stakes.* Washington DC: Institute for International Economics.

Dasgupta, P. (1990) Well-being and the extent of its realization in poor countries, *Economic Journal*, 100 (Conference 1990), 1–32.

Eyckmans, J. (1993) On the nature and economics of the greenhouse effect. *Tijdschrift voor Economie en Management*, 38, 175–204.

Eyckmans, J., Proost, S. and Schokkaert, E. (1993) Efficiency and distribution in greenhouse negotiations. *Kyklos*, 46, 363–97.

Eyckmans, J., Proost, S. and Schokkaert, E. (1994) A comparison of three international agreements on carbon emission abatement. In E. Van Ierland (ed.) *International Environmental Economics*. Amsterdam: Elsevier, pp. 13–43.

Grubb, M. (1989) *The Greenhouse Effect: Negotiation Targets*. London: Royal Institute for International Affairs.

Hekstra, G. P. (1989) Sea-level rise: Regional consequences and responses. In Rosenberg et al. (1989, pp. 53–67).

Hoel, M. (1992) Carbon taxes: An international tax or harmonized domestic taxes. *European Economic Review*, 36, 400–6.

IEA (International Energy Agency) (1992) *Climate Change Policy Initiatives*. Paris: IEA/OECD.

IPCC (Intergovernmental Panel on Climate Change) (1990) *Climate Change: the IPCC Scientific Assessment*. Cambridge: Cambridge University Press.

IPCC (1996) *Climate Change 1995 – The Science of Climate Change*. Contribution of Working Group 1 to the Second Assessment Report of the Intergovernmental Panel on Climate Change. Cambridge, MA: Cambridge University Press.

Jodha, N. S. (1989) Potential strategies for adapting to greenhouse warming: Perspectives from the developing world. In Rosenberg et al. (1989, pp. 147–58).

Kolm, S.-Chr. (1985) *Le Contrat Social Liberal: Philosophie et Pratique du Liberalisme*. Paris: Presses Universitaires de France.

Nordhaus, W. D. (1991) The cost of slowing climate change: A survey. *The Energy Journal*, 12, 37–65.

Nozick, R. (1974) *Anarchy, State and Utopia*. New York: Basic Books.

Proost, S. (1992) Beleidsvoorstellen voor de broeikasproblematiek. *Leuvense Economische Standpunten No. 62*. Leuven: Centrum voor Economische Studin, KU.

Rawls, J. (1971) *A Theory of Justice*. Cambridge, MA: Harvard University Press.

Rose, A. (1990) Reducing conflict in global warming policy: The potential of equity as a unifying principle. *Energy Policy*, 18, 927–35.

Rose, A. (1992) Equity considerations of tradeable carbon emission entitlements. In UNCTAD (1992, pp. 55–83).

Rose, A. and Stevens, B. (1993) The efficiency and equity of marketable permits for CO_2 emissions. *Resource and Energy Economics*, 15, 117–46.

Rosenberg, N. J., Easterling III, W. E., Crosson, P. R. and Darmstadter, J. (eds) (1989) *Greenhouse Warming: Abatement and Adaptation*. Washington DC: Resources for the Future.

Schelling, T. C. (1992) Some economics of global warming. *American Economic Review*, 82, 1–14.

Schokkaert, E. (1992) The economics of distributive justice, welfare and freedom. In K. Scherer (ed.) *Justice: Interdisciplinary Perspectives*. Cambridge: Cambridge University Press, pp. 65–113.

Sen, A. (1981) Ethical issues in income distribution: National and international. In S. Grassman and E. Lundberg (eds) *The World Economic Order: Past and Prospects*. London: Macmillan, pp. 464–94.

Sen, A. (1987) *The Standard of Living*. Cambridge: Cambridge University Press.

Sen, A. and Williams, B. (eds) (1982) *Utilitarianism and Beyond*. Cambridge: Cambridge University Press.

Stern, N. (1976) The marginal valuation of income. In M. J. Artis and A. R. Nobay (eds) *Essays in Economic Analysis*. Cambridge: Cambridge University Press, pp. 209–54.

UNCTAD (1992) *Combating Global Warming*. New York: UNCTAD.

10

Market-structuring Regulation and the Ozone Regime: Politics of the Montreal Protocol

Ronald Herring

Externalities, commons dilemmas and environmental regimes

Market failure is typically addressed with some appeal to a larger set of rules and authority, typically the state. In international environmental issues of the tragedy-of-the-commons type, appeals must be to some form of supra-national regime with state-like properties but no coercive power. Market failures cannot be met with authority unproblematically, particularly at the global level. There are political failures just as there are market failures, and for the same reasons: preferences do not necessarily aggregate to produce the common good and initial endowments are unevenly distributed. Moreover, collective action problems abound, as is commonly recognized.

Less commonly recognized is that collective agreements among nations acting as agents for societal principals represent a small part of international public good provision. Much of the signing of international accords is symbolic politics of and between state elites, acting at a distance from constraints of domestic politics because their public is not engaged. Failures come, as Anthony Downs (1972) correctly argued in his work on "issue-attention cycles," when the accords are implemented, through real legislation, and compliance is achieved, through real administration. Nevertheless, the ozone regime faces relatively good prospects for compliance in comparison to international environmental accords which entail restrictions on subsistence routines and natural resource use, e.g. biodiversity and climate change; see Herring and Bharucha (1999). These prospects have more to do with the nature of the threat, side payments and market-structuring than with resolution of competing interests and notions of justice which delayed collective action.

The Montreal Protocol on Substances that Deplete the Ozone Layer (1987) establishes international regulations for phasing out substances that deplete the stratospheric ozone layer. It is widely cited as evidence that the global-commons type problems are tractable through international collective action (albeit with side-payments). A global public good identified by an international scientific community is well on its way to being provided despite differences in national interests. The process which produced the ozone regime, however, was conflictual

– issues of both interest and justice, predominantly assuming a North–South conflict, blocked collective action until alterations in the regime answered concerns from the South. How was a regime created in the face of deep North–South differences on issues of developmental interests and notions of justice? What does the Montreal experience tell us about prospects for global public goods in the environmental sphere?

The plan of this chapter is to utilize the experience of one large industrializing nation to explore these issues. India was a leading nation in the opposition of the Group of 77 to the Montreal Protocol and a major force behind the London amendments of 1990 which altered the accord in ways that permitted major players in the South to sign on. Amendments to Montreal in London in 1990 solved only part of the justice problem with side-payments; its real force came through rigging markets.

However, successful bargaining for a regime at the international level – where state elites problematically represent themselves as agents of societies – is only a necessary condition for the regime to work. It is not a sufficient condition, not only because that agency is contested when information trickles down, but because state capacity and will are variable over time and over issues considered.

Nations in the "underdeveloped" world are often assumed to be less likely to implement international environmental accords – both for reasons of capacity and because of unresolved issues of justice which compromise political will. India's decision to comply with the Montreal Protocol is both normatively and practically contingent on elements of justice amended into the treaty – technology and financial transfer mechanisms. India acknowledges this contingency officially. Compliance of other poor nations is *de facto* contingent as well. Nevertheless, the Montreal Protocol is likely to be effective in the South – where its underpinnings in justice remain shaky – because of the powerful market-structuring effect of the treaty on emergent industrial nations.

Bargaining and the ozone regime: North–South framing

The Montreal Protocol has often been hailed as a landmark of international cooperation: science produced evidence of imminent collective threat; the scientific community verified the threat and proposed solutions. Nations acted quickly and collectively – despite differing interests – resulting in a fairly effective international regime.[1] Moreover, the regime was not another empty promise, quickly relegated to benign neglect. It was strengthened over time: phaseouts were accelerated, new substances controlled, and compensation mechanisms established to cover incremental conversion costs in poorer nations. Limits to markets were explicitly recognized and seemingly overcome. Yet the response to a "global-commons" problem was not smooth; divergent interests and conceptualizations of international justice structured the political process.

India was one of the early prominent opponents of the Protocol – along with Brazil and China – primarily on grounds challenging the underpinnings of justice in the original treaties. India initially refused to sign the framework Vienna

Convention of 1985 and the Montreal Protocol of 1987; she was the last holdout among large industrializing countries.[2] India's reluctance to sign the Montreal Protocol, particularly when compounded by that of China, threatened to scuttle the accord.[3] India's eventual agreement was attained through a process which framed ozone protection as a North–South conflict, not a commons dilemma, and left India's compliance contingent.

Unlike India's other international environmental treaty obligations, the Montreal Protocol imposed significant problems of implementation[4] for India. International accords protecting nature and natural resources made no significant new demands on India's already stringent (*de jure*) regime of internal environmental regulation and protection, which is, on paper, among the strictest in the world. In Montreal, perception of the problem, mechanisms to address the problem and means to do so were almost entirely external to the national political and scientific environment. Signing accords protecting nature and natural resources in a sense ratified India's own internal legislation; Montreal raised real issues of sacrificing the objectives of development in service of a global collective good.

India began international discussions on ozone in earnest in 1988, under international pressure. The nation was not a major producer or consumer of ozone-depleting substances (ODSs). Moreover, domestic scientific research on the stratosphere was not concerned with ODSs; there was no indigenous science to spur concern. Reinforcing these two factors was the clear position of the policy elite in India that ozone was a western problem, which neither affected India nor was a consequence of India's past actions. Nor was the "Western" perception of the global public good in question uniformly acknowledged in poor countries.[5]

India's initial response was understandably rooted in developmental concerns. In 1988, a tri-partite study team was established: Development Alternatives from the NGO sector; Navin Flourine and Sri Ram Compressors from the industrial (ODS-producing and consuming) sector; and the Ministry of Environment and Forests as the government representative. This quasi-corporativist structure continued throughout the planning process. Industrialists paid their own way to the meetings; they had a deep interest in ensuring that India engage Montreal on terms acceptable to industry.[6]

The terms of reference for this first study group structured considerations almost exclusively along economic lines. Their report, *The Economic Implications for the Developing Countries of the Montreal Protocol*, did not specifically calculate India's burden in compliance, recognizing the technology-dependent nature of any estimates, but rather established a conceptual framework. The most important contribution was a broad conceptualization of transition costs, including costs of "retardation" of growth of user industries, consequent losses to the national economy, and costs related to loss of export markets (Development Alternatives, 1990, p. 13). The growth retardation was calculated as the "hiccup cost" and was expected to continue for ten years (of lowered growth rates in CFC-dependent activities) (p. 26). More significantly, given India's critical electric power situation, an estimate of added power consumption was made: up to an additional 500 MW of installed capacity (p. 27). India entered serious discussion with the Montreal process with a model which projected serious costs in terms of economic progress to poor countries.

International pressure mounted on India when it became clear that the Protocol without India, Brazil and China would be meaningless. China, at the time, had announced plans to increase domestic production and export capacity of CFCs to meet the third-world demand if the OECD countries blocked international trade in CFCs. From India's perspective, China and India were in something like a prisoner's dilemma game; in cooperation, they could either force concessions from industrialized nations, or meet demand of other industrializing countries for CFCs, but either could defect and reap the benefits of defection.[7] Both were lumped together as "the two rotten apples in this basket of global goodwill – India and China, who had not agreed to sign the protocol." Reflecting opinion in the industrialized countries at the time, an article in the *Christian Science Monitor* essentially accused the two giants of "international blackmail" and "implied threat." As a report from the influential environmental Indian thinktank, the Centre for Science and Environment, stated: "As these countries could not conceivably be blamed for what had happened in the past – using just 2 percent of the world's CFCs – they were being blamed for what could happen in the future" (Agarwal and Narain, 1992, p. 7).

The USA, in particular, pushed India's accession to the treaty; India's position was essentially that ozone was not its problem. If sacrifices had to be made to solve a problem that the West had created, then the West would have to pay for them. The UK then offered to fund a study to see what the costs of transition in various poor countries would be.[8] The resulting Touche Ross (TR) report then came to be India's guide to negotiation, since the tripartite team set up internally came to no definitive conclusions but rather presented a methodology for estimating costs, once technical parameters were known.

India argued officially that there must be compensation to three kinds of losers in Protocol implementation: producers, industrial users, and consumers. Using these categories, the TR report produced a figure for transition costs of US $1.2 billion. In terms of political process, both the absolute figure of the TR report and the conceptual matter of what is to be included proved to be critical. In the UNEP-sponsored meetings with industrial countries, the Indian Secretary of the Environment stated "we are willing to cooperate but we will not take your burden on our shoulders." Compensation for transition costs became a *sine qua non* for considering signing.

Compensation, technology and conditionality in principle

Among rich nations, the USA was most adamantly opposed to additional compensation as well as to new institutional arrangements to provide compensation. Although the UK joined the USA in proposing that compensation under the protocol not be additional to development aid and should be administered through an existing multilateral institution such as the World Bank, the USA was the last holdout among OECD countries on the compensation issue, agreeing to go along only days before the London conference. The USA insisted that there be no precedent involved in the decision (Porter and Brown, 1991, p. 32). As a practical matter, though early estimates of the global cost of Montreal were low, Washington worried about a precedent for any global warming convention, where compensation to the South would be far too large to be politically practicable in the North. It was only the assurance of the Low Countries and the Scandinavian nations, and later Germany, that convinced India to stay in the negotiations. Had these European nations not promised to pressure the USA on the issue of a separate fund for compensation, India might have dropped out altogether.

The critical juncture in negotiations was the second meeting of the parties to the Protocol in London in June of 1990. New urgency was generated when the increasingly institutionalized international community of scientists discovered new evidence of significant thinning of the ozone layer. European nations which had earlier favored a slow phase-out switched sides at the first meeting of the parties in Helsinki in May 1989 (Porter and Brown, 1991, p. 77). This new urgency – spurred in part by evidence that the thinning was affecting not just Antarctica but also the Northern hemisphere – was instrumental in producing amendments to the Protocol in London to satisfy nations such as India and China.

India became the spokesperson for the Group of 77 on the issue of compensation, yet India was a divided agent at this point; a rift developed between the political and administrative wings of the Indian delegation. The Minister of State for Environment, Maneka Gandhi, felt that the monetary concessions for the developing world made in London were sufficient: "We got $40 million for us and $40 million for the Chinese."[9] The paucity of the compensation (in relation to the estimate of $1.2 billion) was aggravated, in the view of her permanent Secretary in the ministry, Mahesh Prasad, by the fact that not all the promised $40 million was new money, nor was it all for phase out of ODSs: rather, much of the promised money was for reforestation and other projects, and had been moved out of other aid pockets.[10]

Technology – and technological dependence – figured as prominently as compensation in India's concerns. Z. R. Ansari, the Indian Minister of Environment, had in 1989 grounded India's refusal to sign the Protocol in existing and future global asymmetries of technology and finance: "the technology of substitutes, conservation, recycling and equipment modification will be the monopoly of a few countries in the developed world . . . the question that haunts us is the extent of resources required to get the technology as well as the products from the companies in the developed world."

The Protocol would create a rigged and captive market to India's national disadvantage. Ansari noted that the language calling on industrial countries to "facilitate" access and make provisions for subsidies was "delightfully vague." There was a notable asymmetry: vagueness on issues of concern to India but clear and very specific provisions for restrictions on India (Agarwal and Narain, 1992, p. 9; *Times of India*, April 6, 1991).

Maneka Gandhi argued in London for mandatory technology transfer to poor

"Article 5" nations. When Western governments argued that technology was privately owned, and thus not controlled by governments, Gandhi retorted that the entire Montreal process was about government restrictions on technology use by private firms, and that intervention by governments in matters of this kind was universal. Her conclusion was: "Either you [sell us] the technology or you change your laws or you change your patent rights . . . Start working on it."[11]

Her permanent Secretary in the Ministry, Mahesh Prasad, had a more radical solution, going to the roots of the nature of property: if the ozone problem truly constituted a global commons dilemma, the technology to solve the problem should be available as common property. The USA reacted vehemently: these are private firms which *own* the technology. Prasad understandably answered: so are the firms we must tell to change their production technology, and coerce to do so if we sign. Are we then to tell them that they may have to buy from monopolists with scarce hard currency, when the shift is mandated in the presumed interests of the global "community"? The Secretary thus felt that India should not be satisfied with the London amendments: another round of negotiations was necessary to iron out difficult issues of technology ownership, control and transfer. Prasad argued that ownership of substitute technology should vest in the parties collectively, through the multilateral fund, not in private companies.[12] This solution would have solved the concerns not only of India, but those expressed by the delegations of Brazil, China, Malaysia and others that the concentrated ownership of replacement technology would permit oligopolistic price gouging – what Malaysia's Minister of Science, Technology and Environment termed "environmental colonialism" (Benedick, 1991, p. 189).

Opponents of the original Protocol from the South attempted in London to use their bargaining power to establish linkage between compliance and the availability and affordability of substitute technologies. In their proposed draft amendment, "the obligation to comply" would have been made subject to adequate financial compensation *and* "preferential and non-commercial" transfer of technology (Benedick, 1991, p. 189). (In the final draft, "preferential and non-commercial" was reduced to "on fair and most favorable terms.") Industrial nations opposed making compliance formally contingent on the size of the compensation fund. Their concern was that cost calculations could be a subject of dispute, permitting poor countries a way out of their obligations under the treaty.

The final amendment on compensation was a compromise between these positions. Annex II, Article 5 states that "developing the capacity to fulfill the obligations . . . will depend upon the effective implementation" of the transfer of technology and the financing thereof. One way to read this language is that the compromise formulation merely recognizes reality: the capacity of poor nations to comply is literally dependent on transfers of technology and finance. In the Northern view, this statement of dependency does "not go so far as to release parties from their treaty obligations."[13] In the view of the Government of India, Article 10 makes national compliance conditional on international transfers of money and technology in an ethical and legal, not merely practical, sense. Both interpretations of the amendment have generated problems for compliance.

Compensation in practice: Calculating costs

Given the conflict in London, and the ambiguous language of the resulting compensation amendment, figuring the costs of compliance became a potential flashpoint between rich and poor nations. To figure those costs, India constituted the "Task Force on National Strategy of Phasing Out Ozone Depleting Substances" on May 29, 1991, almost a year after the London amendments but a year before India became a party to the Montreal Protocol (on June 16, 1992). The task force was modeled on the tri-partite committee which initially addressed economic effects of compliance: business, government and the NGO sectors were represented.

India's current per capita consumption of controlled substances is 8.8 grams and unlikely to exceed 20 grams – a very small number relative to the global problem and to the level of 300 grams allowed under the protocol.[14] Nevertheless, minimizing the costs of conversion, and thus disruptive economic impact, presents a real dilemma. To jump into intermediate technologies (e.g. HCFCs) is potentially costly as technology outstrips the intermediates and HCFCs themselves become obsolete under the Protocol. On the other horn of the dilemma, waiting for the technology air to clear creates two negative effects: dependency on whoever develops the new technology and the "hiccup" effect of suppressing investment during the waiting period.

Some costs of conversion are straightforward and easy to calculate, but others raise difficult conceptual and moral issues. For a time, the dominant understanding in India, as expressed by Indian delegations abroad, was that a major cost would have to be borne by consumers; refrigerators in particular came to symbolize the dilemma. Minister of State for Environment, Maneka Gandhi had said publicly "if I sign this treaty, even my father will throw me out of the house." The assumption was that, in the West, people are so rich that they throw away refrigerators every few years, but in India, refrigerators are kept forever. Thus Montreal was a special threat to India because it would render refrigerators (and other consumer durables) obsolete (Interview, February 8, 1993). For this reason, the three-tier compensation system insisted on by India in Nairobi in 1989 included costs to consumers.

Consumers figured heavily in the *National Programme* produced for approval of the Multilateral Fund for compensation.[15] That report documents the rising consumer tide that is a critical political issue in Montreal. Sales of consumer goods that involve use of ODSs (air conditioners, refrigeration, consumer electronics, aerosol sprays, etc.) had been increasing at a rate of about 15 percent per annum, whereas real per capita expenditures had been increasing at 2.4 percent per year. The disproportionate increase was attributed to liberalization, higher incomes, and to increasing availability of consumer credit (Government of India, NP 1993, p. 16).

The political importance of Montreal initially focused on relatively wealthy consumers: "the prime market for consumer goods and services will be largely confined to the top 20–25% of the population who account for 50% of the national income . . . [T]his population class . . . will number over 45 million households in 2000 and about 60 million households in 2010 (equal to the current number of households in Germany, France and Britain combined . . ." (Government of India, NP, 1993, p. 16). India here projects the image, so often used in the attempt to lure foreign investment, of a small Europe embedded in a dualistic consumer society. The projection of growth rates for what were once considered luxury items resonates with projection of a middle class of 200 million, but conceals the ways in which ODSs are expanding into fields of non-luxury consumption (health delivery, fire-fighting, food preservation and shipping, etc).

Neither refrigerators, nor even CFCs generically, turn out to be the critical issues in India's compliance with Montreal (see below), but the political metonymy of refrigerators has been important. Refrigerators were symbolically important in two ways. First, they served as a symbol of international inequality: even moderate middle-class aspirations in the poor world were threatened by solutions for a problem created in countries where refrigerators were taken for granted (even thrown away periodically). Perhaps more importantly, refrigerators were the connection to export markets that India was just beginning, making CFC regulation not simply a matter of privileged national consumers, but also of India's place in the international political economy.

Halons presented a more difficult issue than CFCs because of their strategic importance. Halons are not produced domestically and must be imported at a (perceived) high price (Government of India RTF, 1993, p. 6). Recently, halons have been commercially deployed in small fire extinguishers which seem to be increasingly present in urban India. However, the main issue was strategic. Halons are used for fire fighting in enclosed spaces where CO_2 applications are inappropriate because they would adversely affect human beings. Critical applications include tanks and military vessels. The military was involved in the formulation of the *National Programme*. A domestic program for halon production has been initiated by the Defense Institute of Fire Research. Subsequently, two firms have developed capacity to produce Halon-1211. Because India believes that halons constitute essential use items and is uncertain about world supplies as Montreal comes on line, the Task Force recommended continued efforts to reach self-sufficiency in halon production. Research on halon substitutes "will be faster if we master the Halon production process" (Government of India, RTF, 1993, pp. 6, 8). Likewise, problems with substitution for solvents (especially carbon tetrachloride) and foam fillers, propellants and other chemicals are proving difficult to monitor or predict.

India is a special case for compliance and compensation issues among poorer countries because of its extensive industrial and technical base. It is now self-sufficient in production of CFCs and their applications and a minor exporter to Southeast Asia. There are five industrial units that manufacture CFCs; many are quite new and will not reach their break-even point for some time. "The country has invested heavily in this industry and has paid out large sums for importing the technologies" (Government of India, RTF, 1993, p. 5). Air conditioning and refrigeration are less clearly "luxuries" in India than in the North. Energy is a major bottleneck in India's industrial development, and any penalty attached to conversion (as now seems inevitable in thermal insulation applications of ODSs) will be difficult to justify. Conversion thus entails considerable risk and is difficult to quantify.

Given the uncertainties inherent in cost calculations, a fluid and dynamic estimate within a range is to be expected. The task force estimated the cost to be between US$ 1.4 and 2.45 billion (Government of India, RTF, 1993, p. 20). These calculations include costs to producers and intermediate users as well as R&D programs and costs to consumers (the latter now disallowed under Montreal). As importantly, the estimate does *not* include costs of recovery and recycling, costs of destroying substances and equipment which cannot be recycled or converted, costs of substitutes for cleaning applications of ODSs, any halon substitution costs and, most ambiguously, the social costs of plant closings and the "economic drag" of the hiccup effect.

India's *National Programme* (Government of India, NP, 1993) for phaseout estimates the total cost of phasing out to be $1.639 billion up to the year 2010. Administrative costs are 15 million dollars. Refrigerators may not be the most difficult issue in India's compliance (at an estimated cost of $620 million), despite their symbolic importance in framing politics. Large costs for technology development, transfer and adaptation to "local production and circumstances" are included. The cost per kilo phased out is $9.85 (Government of India, CP, 1993, p. 64, table 13). But transition costs are so technology-dependent that no estimate is reliable. For example, the *Times of India* of May 12, 1993 reported new estimates far below those of the task force which had reported only two months earlier. One reason is that the costs of substitutes then contemplated were falling fast. HCFC 22 fell from Rs 1,000/kg just two years previously to Rs 100 in 1993. The ineligible cost to India, both to the state and to consumers and producers, is held to be considerable, but is not calculated (Government of India, NP, 1993, p. 58).

India took on the obligations of the ozone regime with a clear understanding that the problem was not of its making and that compensation for dislocations of compliance was a necessary condition for participation. As a number of both politicians and officials have said: we can always pull out if technology and financing are not available. The multilateral fund has yet to collect as much money as any of India's estimates, and there are other large claimants. Given India's position that its compliance is contingent under the linkages established by the London amendments, this issue becomes a major concern for global compliance.[16]

Planning compliance, dismantling planning

Compliance with Montreal, even for a country at an early stage in development of ODS applications, is a complex planning task. A major problem is determining a plan of substitution which does not endanger the environment locally or globally. Some of the currently available substitutes have high levels of global warming potential, flammability, toxicity or other undesirable externalities (particularly the class of volatile organic compounds). There are serious economic and environmental trade-offs, complicated by uncertainty and lack of control of the technical change path. Once some mix of substitutes for ODSs is specified, compliance presupposes a network of public policy instruments to change behavior: regulation, taxation, subsidies for R&D, low interest loans for switchovers, etc. Specific projects must be identified for forwarding to the multilateral fund for transfer of resources. The state will inevitably be central in this process.

Representation in the planning process has remained consistent since the first initiative in 1988: a tripartite quasi-corporatist structure of technical NGO, private capital, and officials (representing the crucial sectors of industry, environment and defense). Decisions will ultimately have to be communicated to a myriad of unorganized sector operators, producers, repair and maintenance people. There are plans for a media blitz on the switchovers, but no representatives of the "unorganized sector" have been major players in planning. In part this is inevitable, since the unorganized sector is, after all, unorganized. Yet much of the discussion of recycling, recapture and storage of ODSs will be fruitless unless it accords with realities on the ground as experienced by the actual contact point between ODSs and their real applications. Consultation is in part only an efficiency desideratum; the power is in the hands of the organized sector. Once the supplies are shut off or switched over, the unorganized sector will have no alternative but to comply.

Planning has produced surprises. The final task force was divided into six cells to reflect problems of ODS use in India. Carbon tetrachloride (CTC), for example, was hardly mentioned in the 1993 task force report, but is emerging as the largest source of ODSs in India, at nearly 50 percent of use. It is used in electronics, rubber manufacturing, pharmaceuticals, pesticides, and other applications. Little is known about the distribution of CTC uses, nor of adequate substitutes. The energy penalty of switchover, which is not part of the compensation guidelines of the Protocol, remains uncertain as technologies for foam insulation and chemical production continue to change.

The planning for this massive changeover is in its infancy. To give some idea of the complexity, we can sketch the actors involved. Central planning and the now-disgraced license-permit-quota *raj* (regime), along with the infancy of ODS industries in India, produced a concentrated production structure amenable to regulation. There are only five CFC-producing firms, four CTC firms, one MCF firm.

Though production is concentrated, about 65 percent of the *use* of ODSs is in the small-scale sector, the accounting of which is just beginning: foams, aerosols, solvents, halons, refrigeration and air-conditioning, ice-candy machines and the like. Halons are produced through two Government-initiated enterprises. Aerosols are slightly more complicated administratively; there are 200 medium-scale firms, but numerous, literally uncounted, small-scale fillers in the unorganized sector. Foams are concentrated in 300 medium-scale firms. Many uses are, however, in identifiable economic units which are relatively concentrated: domestic refrigerators, refrigerated cabinets, water coolers, car air conditioners (since

1984), road transport refrigeration and air conditioning, train air conditioning, central air conditioning, cold stores, room air conditioners, process chillers, and walk-in coolers. For all the political rhetoric about refrigerators, the largest use of ODSs in India is CTC at 4,000 metric tonnes, virtually all domestically produced.

These matters cannot be wholly left to the market if compliance is to be comprehensive, but planning presupposes a very effective state. The 1993 task force took as central to its action plan the notion that there should be "no economic drag" due to substitution till 1997. Beginning in 1998, quotas on production and consumption would have to be enforced. Their report envisions a combination of "market-based measures" with "command and control" measures to phase out controlled substances.

There is a certain irony in this process. The international system is simultaneously asking, even compelling, India to move in two contradictory directions of economic policy at the same time. Liberalization envisions a lesser role for the state in economic processes. Global environmental engineering presupposes an activist, interventionist state, not simply monitoring allocations, technologies and production processes, but actively intervening to guide them. Integral to this contradictory process is risk, in conjunction with lingering justice concerns, both slow compliance: "India need not take any hasty decisions on the switch-over as they may prove to be costly. In any case our contribution to ozone depletion is negligible" (Government of India, RTF, 1993, p. 17).

The Montreal Protocol symbolizes the emergence of a global environmental control regime with state-like properties. At both the international and national levels, this regime necessitates planning, monitoring and intervention in economic processes and property relations. Simultaneously, a more coherent global neo-liberal economic regime encourages the demise of planning. Hence, these are the two contradictory directions.

Emergence of contradictory tendencies in regime properties creates tension in implementation of global environmental accords, but is inevitable. Karl Polanyi's (1957) notion of a "double movement" in the transition to market society argues that constraints on markets are the inevitable consequence of market growth.[17] There is political strain in the global demand that the international system become more of a "free" market, without state meddling, and the simultaneous global demand that market failures and externalities (of which ecological integrity is perhaps the most egregious) be addressed at a global level.

India was one of the holdouts in the global movement toward state-displacing, market-oriented development strategies which began in the late 1970s (Walton and Seddon 1994). India's transition was not driven by electoral mandate, but by a centrally directed opening under severe balance of payments pressure. Before its recent conversion, a dominant view in India had been that both liberalization and environmentalism are tainted by hypocrisy: the North is asking that the South do as they say, not as they did. There is suspicion that international environmental regulatory regimes will make the South's process of industrialization slower and more costly than that of the North precisely because of the uncounted, non-internalized externalities of the North's process of industrialization. Montreal is one of the clearest manifestations of this position.

Residues of negotiation: Contingent compliance

Despite the London amendments and the Multilateral Fund, issues of international justice in the Protocol are still not resolved in India. The 1993 task force, for example, stated that "the amended Montreal Protocol treats all developing countries as a homogeneous block and prescribes the same treatment for all of them . . ." Just as developed countries fine-tuned their phase-out schedules to their domestic needs, the report argued that flexibility within the prescribed limits was essential. The limits themselves are subject to question: "The allocation of per capita consumption limits is disproportionate at the moment and appears to be arbitrary and the reasons therefore are not explained anywhere" (Government of India, RTF, 1993, p. 27). "The USA after implementing control measures . . . would consume about 2.2 million tonnes of CFC-11 and 12 up to the year 2000 [compared to India's limit of about 0.1 million tonnes]. On a per capita basis [this] works out to be 97 grams and 8461 grams for India and USA respectively."

As a result, unlike some developing countries, India is planning to increase production and consumption right up to the allowed limits and is giving serious attention to building up halon banks.[18] Though the net effect may not be as eco-friendly as a more rapid phase-out, there are issues of economic growth and international justice which drive this result.

India's conditionality in observing the provisions of the MP is quite clear from all official publications and public statements on the matter. The *National Programme* (Government of India, NP, 1993, p. 31) states: "In view of the shortage of funds at the disposal of the GOI and the non-availability of appropriate technology, ODS phaseout progress in India will be determined by the availability of assistance from the Multilateral Fund. This assistance is expected to include cost of conversion of existing facilities, costs arising for premature retirement or enforced idleness, and costs of patent and designs for establishing new production facilities." The national program established for compliance "seeks to ensure that the small and tiny enterprises are in no way affected and are fully compensated for phaseout, including appropriate retraining and provision for worker severance."

The Executive Committee which implements the Multilateral Fund for compensation has challenged India's *Country Programme* for "double counting" and inclusion of non-fundable categories (Dasgupta, 1994). More seriously, the Fund seems to be rationing resources, which will almost certainly be less than India's claims. A Negative List for compensation has been established, expanded and altered, often after a proposal has begun its journey toward funding. Internal delays in choosing proposals to forward, as well as uncertainty about criteria of the Executive Committee and Implementing Agencies have discouraged firms from formulating projects, slowing compliance. Technicians at the World Bank and UNDP as implementing agencies are assuming *de facto* control of the allocation process rather than the parties to the Protocol; administrative costs are very high.

Deterioration of trust in this process caused Minister of State for Environment Kamal Nath, previously Chairman of the Executive Committee, to suggest at the Sixth Meeting of the Parties that Article 5 countries stop the switch-over until developed countries gave full assurances of timely and predictable replenishment of the Multilateral Fund. Noting the large arrears in contributions, he argued that the Protocol was being "whittled away at the implementation level," creating a mood of "distrust and discontent."[19]

Compliance at this stage is inevitably slow because private firms and the nation face difficult choices. To adopt intermediate technologies (HCFCs) is risky as HCFCs themselves become proscribed under the protocol. Industry worries "if we go through two cycles, they will not compensate the second time – maybe not the first."[20] Waiting for resolution of the technology flux creates two negative effects: dependency on whoever develops new technology and the "hiccup" effect of suppressing investment during the waiting period. Both dangers, long feared by Indian officials, are now real. The energy penalty of switchover is not part of the amended compensation guidelines, nor is R&D for adaptation to local conditions; both are critical industrial issues. For example, industry has delayed conversion to HCFCl34a in refrigeration since the substance will become illegal and has other negative environmental effects, pressed on Indian firms by European NGOs. Alternative hydrocarbon-based systems being developed in Europe present safety problems under Indian conditions (TERI, 1994); amelioration of these problems is on the "negative list" for compensation.

Compensation from the Multilateral Fund has been slow and meager – about $11.5 million, roughly 0.5 percent of the roughly $2 billion estimated in the *Country Programme*. India's current Environment Minister has complained of disproportionate payouts. By his figures, of the $200 million sanctioned by late 1994, China had received more than $37 million, or 19 percent of total, and India only 6 percent. Even the Philippines, which joined after India, received more funds, as did Egypt and Thailand. The Ministry has three major concerns: first, phaseout resources lag behind what the West promised; second, after the ozone hole is mended, there is no incentive for the fund to be replenished; finally, the South will be left behind in the global economy: after the North eliminates controlled substances, it will ban products made with them, stranding those at the bottom of the product cycle.[21]

To counter these developments, the Minister agreed at a meeting in October, 1994, with representatives of industry, to pursue the following objectives at the international level:

- avoiding enforcement of the negative list and frequent changes in funding mechanism;
- facilitating transfer of technology for ODS phaseout and ODS production in India without any preconditions (technology bundling, demands for equity position, etc.);
- avoiding efforts to accelerate phaseout schedule of CFCs, halons, and HCFCs;

- retraction of the 15 percent production capacity allowed to developed countries (to allow India to meet that residual market demand).[22]

Success in these negotiations will determine the Government's commitment to accelerating compliance.

Developments at the international level make opponents of the Montreal Protocol now seem prophetic, and the assurances of London problematic. After seemingly successful international bargaining, India agreed to help to solve a problem it did not create. Nevertheless, negotiations were restricted almost entirely to a thin stratum of officials, elite NGOs and private capital; costs were putative, and compensation assumed. The real costs of Montreal have not been – arguably could not have been – debated in anything like a plebiscite. Neither consumers nor small enterprises – the bulk of ODS users – were engaged. The government's stated contingency of compliance leaves room for retreat if anyone with power notices the costs. Frequent celebration of Montreal as a success in resolving global commons dilemmas obscures both the problematic sense in which state actors represent their societies and the persistent feelings of injustice emanating from lower tiers of the international political economy.

Side-payments, justice and structural power

There are two indigenous political views on India's response to international politics around Montreal. In one view, Indian negotiators sold out, settling for a petty side-payment in an unequal and unfair treaty; see, for example Bidwai (1991). In this view, Montreal was the pivotal point of third-world power in the postwar period and India got very little for its trump card (not even the principle that consumers should not have to pay). The alternative view is that India's compliance is conditional and the nation had no choice. From a weapons-of-the-weak perspective, India won, since the power imbalance is such that it could have done worse.

A good case from the framework of structural political economy can be made that signing was the right decision. As India became an exporter and a player in industrial sectors implicated in ODSs, it became clear that going along with Montreal was inevitable if the North were insistent on the Protocol. The alternative was losing a new market niche created by regulation while emergent comparative advantage was regulated away. Non-parties to the Protocol were subject to trade sanctions on ODSs, as well as products containing ODSs or even manufactured with processes employing ODSs. Moreover, on the eve of the London meeting, India was moving into international markets sensitive to Montreal. Exports of refrigerators had reached the level of 4,000 annually and were climbing (largely to the USSR and West Asia). Navin Fluorine won a contract to supply a turnkey CFC plant worth $28 million to Iraq, an event which caused considerable friction between India and the USA.[23]

As India redirected its development strategy towards attracting foreign investment and technology after severe balance of payments pressures in 1991, cooperation from holders of international economic power became increasingly crucial.[24] As Indian capital achieved the maturity to play on the international stage, a potential internal blockage was transformed into a force for international engagement; industry recognized that the international market was being irrevocably restructured by Montreal. Global firms with deep pockets, strong R&D budgets and economies of scale cannot be matched in India – or in the poor world generally. Joint, often asymmetric, ventures – or deepened import dependence – are necessitated by the ozone regime. Montreal reinforces global integration of Indian firms to allow technical tie-ins that are Protocol-compliant but indigenously unavailable; see, for example Seshan (1995, p. 180).

The Protocol's dependency effects had been of concern to all of India's negotiators. Mahesh Prasad, once India's Secretary of the Environment, reflected a common sentiment in the South when he said in 1993: "The West had known about this ozone hole since 1974. They waited to do anything until they had developed substitutes they could sell as monopolists (Interview April 8, 1993)." Industrial producers of ODSs were indeed prominent on the national teams – particularly those of European nations – during negotiations of the protocol. Dupont first broke ranks with producers – arguing first for a global cap on production and later (on March 23, 1988) for phaseout by 1991. Just before, and increasingly after, the Protocol, Dupont progressively increased its investments in research on substitutes, from $5 million in 1986 to $30 million in 1988. The previous position of the CFC giant had been to oppose regulation, then to announce that alternatives might be developed if market conditions warranted. This shift took place as the scientific evidence of CFC damage to the stratosphere mounted (Parson, 1992, pp. 18, 24). The Montreal Protocol ensured that there would be a global market for substitutes to banned chemicals.

Transfers of technology for substitutes are proving Indian opponents of Montreal to have been prophetic: multinational corporations (MNCs) do not want to sell or license new technology – partly for fear that Indian industry would then become low-cost competition for those MNCs – but instead hold out for majority equity participation in joint-ventures.[25] The global market-structuring effects of Montreal are more important for the ozone layer than either will or capacity to comply with the Protocol in the poor world.

Reactions of the South to the Montreal Protocol, as reflected through the Group of 77, reflect most of the issues of international justice confronted in formation of new international environmental regimes. Their demands were first of all that the "polluter-pays" principle should be implemented through mandatory contributions from the rich nations; that these contributions be *additional* to existing development programs; that decision-making institutions should consist of parties to the convention, not be routed through institutions such as the World Bank which disproportionately represent rich nations; and that all incremental costs of compliance by poor countries be compensated from a fund financed by the wealthy (Porter and Brown, 1991, p. 132; Benedick, 1991). The notion of justice here is not ability to pay but rather compensation owed for damage done (or sinks used). Distributive justice is complemented by a notion of procedural justice: international democracy demands that Bretton Woods institutions not dominate compensation.

Being less dependent than neighbors and most poor countries, India has been able to pursue an independent course in global negotiations, but unable to ignore its structural dependence in the long run. India has a sophisticated R&D apparatus and considerable scientific talent. Its comparatively varied industrial base provides adaptability on ODSs compared to other poor nations. Yet real technological independence is illusive. This structural position enabled India to act as a spokesperson for the Group of 77 and press for changes in Montreal on grounds of justice, but simultaneously precluded opting out of Montreal. With the London amendments, India won on its insistence on the "polluter-pays" principle; it remains unclear how much the polluter can or will pay. Full implementation of Montreal requires continuing international flows of technology, expertise and cash. The best-case scenario for full compliance is one in which the Multilateral Fund is large enough and the definitions of costs flexible enough for India to remain a full participant.

Does justice matter? Prospects for global environmental goods

Agreement on an ozone treaty required at least partial resolution of deeply disputed claims about international justice and developmental priorities. Before the London amendments, then Minister of Environment of India, Z. R. Ansari said:

> The developing countries muster the resources to meet the minimum needs of their citizens at great sacrifice. These countries will be unable to spare further resources for the substitutes to CFCs. The poor of the developing countries will look askance at a government that spends resources on substitutes to CFCs to prevent depletion of the ozone layer . . . while they continue to wallow in poverty, hunger, disease and ignorance (Rosencranz and Milligan, 1990, p. 313).

This claim, along with the "polluter-pays" principle, eventually won out over more skeptical interpretations of Southern interests. In Montreal, as in all North–South framed questions, there is a dramaturgy of selective presentation of state-self. There should be no question that much of the appeal to social justice is instrumental, part of a dramaturgy staged by relatively wealthy elites who claim to speak for the poor. It is also true that real benefits from the global environmental crisis – consultancies, travel, appointments, market niches, employment – are captured not by the global poor, but the relatively well-off in both North and South. Nevertheless, at the normative level, Ansari is right; issues of international justice cannot be ignored if global commons issues are to be resolved. Unresolved issues of justice place some limits to the effectiveness of Montreal, but these limits are minimized by the market structuring effects of the accord.

Environmental regulation as solution to global commons dilemmas suffers from lack of political authority. In turn, willingness of nation-states to cede authority hinges on agreement on the public good in question and the justice of solutions. Agreement on the public good, and the science that undergirded it, was not automatic in Montreal, but the real sticking point in negotiations was justice. Former Minister of State for Environment and Forests, Maneka Gandhi, who negotiated the London Amendments, recalled in 1993: "they tried to scare us with skin cancer . . . this is really all about money."[26]

Reaching agreement is obviously a necessary but not sufficient condition for success. As Anthony Downs (1972) noted, when costs become a matter of political process, obstacles to compliance that were invisible under the restricted and less public ratification process become apparent. Precisely this dynamic has undermined compliance with other accords.

States as unitary actors sign treaties, representing themselves as agents of complex societies, and as capable of controlling behavior. Both claim and capacity vary across arenas and issues. Decisions on ODS use are made at literally thousands of points of production. State capacity to monitor and enforce is limited. The Montreal process was restricted almost entirely to the governing class – a thin stratum of politicians and officials and concerned elite NGOs and private capital. The obligations and costs of Montreal have not been debated or ratified in anything like a representative fashion. Neither consumers nor small-scale industry (the bulk of ODS users) in India were meaningfully engaged in the planning process. This is where adjustment pain will fall. There will be lapses in compliance, in India and globally.

Nevertheless, Montreal should prove more effective than other international environmental treaties, where direct issues of livelihood are at stake, and norma-tive and political claims against state interference are strong (Herring and Bharucha, 1999). In important respects, ozone differs from more politically contested and economically costly global environmental problems. Concentration of production – at least of CFCs – in relatively large firms globally and nationally facilitates regulation. Alterations in the global market direct rational businesses to invest in alternatives, especially to CFCs. Most importantly, because of its esoteric and indirect ramifications in the economy, and the compensation fund for direct producers, it is not clear that publics will ever know the costs of Montreal, nor who is paying them, despite the dramaturgy of North–South conflict which surrounded negotiation of the regime.

Successful rigging of global markets was possible because new market niches advantaged nations and their firms, which already dominated the global produc-tion of ODSs. For nations which lack indigenous manufacturing capacity, Montreal's effects in the North dramatically reduce ODS use; imports are increas-ingly Montreal-compliant. In more industrialized nations of the South, market rigging provided successful structural pressure on both internationalists in the business class and states concerned with their place in the global economy. Necessity substitutes for agreement on justice.

Relative success in the ozone regime then derives in part from its ability to rig markets, to which beneficiaries understandably agreed. The experience with planning, monitoring, control and compensation under Montreal lays a basis for the biodiversity and climate change treaties which are more environmentally important. However, market-rigging creates an inconsistency between international normative regimes of economics which is not missed in the South. The magic of the market (liberalization) and market failure (environmental externalities) are used simultaneously to exhort poor nations to incur economic and political pain. At a normative level, pressure to let the market rule despite national "adjustment pain" while reining in the market when a *global* interest is at stake is politically corrosive.

Unfortunately for global environmental protection, the major lesson from the Montreal process may be: that the North–South structure is still important normatively and politically; that simultaneous global pressure for market rule and ruling the market contradictory; that economically hurtful change in poor nations will require large flows from the North; and that there is not enough money to buy off all claimants with legitimate concerns about international justice. Maneka Gandhi said during the negotiation of the London amendments: "The resolution of these issues in respect of the Montreal Protocol to enable the developing countries to be partners in saving the ozone layer is an acid test of the willingness of the developed countries to promote a true partnership among all the countries of the world for managing global change."[27] Without the market-structuring effects of Montreal, more comprehensive environmental treaties will depend more on justice and political will to solve global commons dilemmas.

Notes

1   Porter and Brown (1991, p. 78) consider the time to completion of the ozone regime "long" (from 1977 to 1990), but for serious concerted action on an issue without precedent, the time span seems remarkably short. UNEP introduced the issue in 1975, funded a conference with 32 nations in 1977, which adopted a Plan of Action on the Ozone Layer, followed by a framework convention (Vienna Convention) in 1985 and the Montreal Protocol in 1987. The concert of action was largely among developed nations with CFC-producing capacity; poor nations were not involved at the early stages; see Porter and Brown (1991, pp. 75–6). World use of CFCs is declining rapidly; virtually all industrializing nations of any size have now signed. See Parson (1992) on the international institutions now available for sharing technical information and the importance of scientific communities.

2   Brazil signed before the London Amendments of 1990 were finalized; China signed after London, but before the amendments were accepted by enough parties to be binding. India did not sign until the amended protocol had been ratified by enough nations to take effect. For explication of the justice argument, see Makhijani et al. (1990).

3   Richard Benedick (1991, pp. 183–6) was involved in ozone negotiations at a very high level on behalf of various US delegations from 1985 onwards. On the sequencing of agreement by reluctant states to sign on, see Parson (1992).

4   Implementation in the special case of international law means to enact policy instruments domestically (laws, regulations, administrative rules, etc.) which carry out the obligations of the treaty. Compliance, in contrast, means the effective administration of such policies such that the nation is in conformity with legal obligations entailed in the treaty. This study is part of the National Implementation project of the SSRC, with funding from the NSF, Ford and MacArthur Foundations. My collaborator in this

project is Dr Erach Bharucha, who bears no responsibility for this essay. Sections of the
text follow our contribution to the larger project.

5   For a time, ozone depletion was dismissed as a problem for people with light skins; I've
heard it termed "the California problem" in India, reducing complex effects of increased
ultraviolet radiation to skin cancer alone. Consumption of CFCs, which was the center
of attention in early negotiations, was concentrated in industrial countries; "developing
nations" accounted for only 15 percent of global consumption, but use was growing
rapidly; see Agarwal and Narain (1992: 7 et passim), Sims (1994), Porter and Brown
(1991, p. 131). Production was concentrated almost entirely in the North. Accumulation
of CFCs in the stratosphere, which persists for decades, was even more clearly a product
of long-term use in rich countries.

6   This information was obtained from a member of this group. The Minister (Environment and Forests), Mr Ansari, played little role, reflecting the low priority of the issue
for India.

7   Minister of State for Environment, Maneka Gandhi, told me that India feared that the
$80 million being discussed as addition to the proposed multilateral fund was to be
evenly divided between India and China; it was believed that if only one signed, the
entire amount would go to that country. Since the fund was to cover only additional
conversion costs, this reading is almost certainly wrong.

8   It was, of course, a UK consultant that did the study. This historical account of India's
positions is based on interviews with the principals in New Delhi in July–August 1993.
All quotations, unless otherwise cited, are from these interviews.

9   When asked whether this might have been too little, given the then-known cost
estimates of changing over, Ms Gandhi said, "no, we got one-third (of the $1.2 billion)."
At the Cabinet meeting to discuss the London amendments, the Prime Minister simply
asked if the treaty was good for India. "Yes," Ms Gandhi replied, "we got forty million
dollars." The Prime Minister said "OK" and the matter was finished. For so important
and controversial a treaty, engaging long-standing national positions on international
justice, ratification was remarkably little discussed. The account in the text is primarily
from Maneka Gandhi and her permanent Secretary, Mr Mahesh Prasad.

10   The London agreement is misleading in this regard. In Benedick's (1991, p. 188)
words: "It was also agreed in London that a donor country could count bilateral aid of
up to 20 percent against its putative contribution to the multilateral fund, provided that
this aid was additional and specifically in accord with the fund's criteria." Mahesh
Prasad was correct in worrying about fungibility of aid.

11   This is Ms Gandhi's personal account, supplemented by newspaper coverage and
Benedick's account; quotation from Benedick (1991, p. 189).

12   Interview, February 2, 1993 in New Delhi. The Minister disagreed, explaining that
the Secretary, like all bureaucrats, wanted to continue meetings endlessly only for the per
diems and foreign travel. Disagreements between the Minister and her Secretary eventually found their way into the press.

13   Benedick (1991, p. 196). The matter is open to interpretation. Parson (1992, p. 30)
notes that "one delegate described the intent of this as 'to acknowledge that they are not
required to do the impossible, without permitting a unilateral assessment that they
haven't been given enough.'"

14   Government of India, RTF (1993, p. 15). All references to the text are to the revised
report of March 31, 1993. Though a new task force was constituted to report in
November 1993, the process suggested by the first task force, and the models of analysis
therein, have been followed in subsequent policy development.

15 Government of India, NP (1993). The National Programme was produced by the ozone cell of the Ministry and the NGO Tata Energy Research Institute with technical support from the UNDP, vetted by a wide-ranging body of officials (from several ministries, including Defense), industrialists and technical NGOs in Delhi in September.

16 The government officially understands the modified Article 10 to make national compliance contingent on implementation of mechanisms for financial assistance and transfer of technology; see for example Government of India, CP, 1993, pp. 2, 35).

17 Polanyi's (1957) classic text is *The Great Transformation*; for an application to environmental issues, see Herring (1991).

18 Brazil and Mexico have announced that they would keep to the schedule of the industrialized countries. Even as non-parties to the protocol, South Korea and Taiwan "are implementing controls to avoid trade sanctions (Parson, 1992, p. 38)."

19 As a result, India was awarded a sum of $4 million in anticipation of projects to be approved later. *Pioneer* (New Delhi), October 3, 1994; October 8, 1994; *Hindustan Times* October 8, 1994; *Times of India* October 9, 1994 and interviews in Delhi, February 1995.

20 Interview with Confederation of Indian Industry specialists on Montreal compliance, February 3, 1995, New Delhi. HCFCs contain less ozone-depleting potential than CFCs, but are nevertheless destructive and have been scheduled for phaseout after a longer lag.

21 The Minister's comments were reported in *Pioneer* October 3, 1994. This section also draws on interviews in the Ministry and with technical NGOs and business representatives in India in 1995.

22 Confederation of Indian Industry WS4/SKJ/ACTION no date New Delhi [Oct 94]: unpublished memorandum; see also, the Minister's comments *Hindustan Times* October 9, 1994; also *Times Of India* October 8, 1994.

23 The US ambassador sent a nasty note to the GOI about the plant. India responded that neither Iraq nor India had signed the Montreal Protocol and the deal was perfectly legal. The US position later appeared hypocritical when documents from Iraq (obtained by us from the former Secretary, MOEF) surfaced. It turns out that a US firm had bid on the same contract and lost out to India on cost grounds, turning the US position to one of sour grapes.

24 Vanita Shastri (1994) illustrates the dynamics of growing power of the liberalization "change team" within India's highest policy circles even before 1991, but adherence to the "Washington consensus" followed the balance of payments crisis. In this shift, the Confederation of Indian Industries (CII), with a more international outlook than traditional business lobbying groups, became far more influential. CII in turn has taken a lead role in international environmental affairs, including planning for compliance with Montreal.

25 Interviews, New Delhi, January–February 1995; also, Sumita Dasgupta (1994).

26 Interview, New Delhi, August 2, 1993. The Minister's position was explained in Parliament on April 23, 1990 (Lok Sabha Questions 6061). In India, as in much of the third world, the ozone-hole scare was often dismissed as a problem for people with light skin. The *Maharashtra Herald* of July 7, 1992 quoted A. P. Mishra, an Indian atmospheric scientist, to the effect that there will be no ozone holes over the subcontinent. Anil Agarwal and Sunita Narain (1991), of the influential Centre for Science and Environment, published their telling article: "MNC cons the third world with ozone hole scare," in *Economic Times* November 17, 1991.

27 *Hindustan Times* April 19, 1990. India's current Minister has made precisely the same linkage in international fora.

238HERRING

References

Agarwal, A. and Narain, S. (1991) MNC cons the Third World with ozone hole Scare. *Economic Times*, November 17.

Agarwal, A. and Narain, S. (1992) *Toward a Green World*. New Delhi: Centre for Science and Environment.

Benedick, R. E. (1991) *Ozone Diplomacy*. Cambridge: Harvard University Press.

Bidwai, P. (1991) Montreal protocol: Has India capitulated? *Economic Times*, June 8.

Dasgupta, S. (1994) Ozone Fund. *Down to Earth*, May 31, 17–19.

Development Alternatives (1990) *The Economic Implications for Developing Countries of the Montreal Protocol (A Study for UNEP)*. New Delhi: UNEP.

Downs, A. (1972) Up and down with ecology: The issue-attention cycle. *The Public Interest*, 28, Summer, 38–50.

Government of India (1992) Ministry of Environment and Forests, National Conservation Strategy and Policy Statement on Environment and Development. New Delhi: June.

Government of India, CP (1993) Ministry of Environment and Forests, Country Programme: Phaseout of Ozone Depleting Substances under the Montreal Protocol (New Delhi: Sept 1993).

Government of India, EIP (1993) Ministry of Commerce Export-Import Policy 1 April–31 March 1992 [With Amendments up to 31 March 1993] (New Delhi).

Government of India, RTF (1993) Report of the Task Force on National Strategy of Phasing Out Ozone Depleting Substances (New Delhi March).

Government of India, NP (1993) Ministry of Environment and Forests, India: National Programme: Phaseout of Ozone Depleting Substances Under the Montreal Protocol (New Delhi 1993).

Herring, R. (1991) Politics of Nature: Commons Interests, Dilemmas and the State. Cambridge: Harvard University Center for Population and Development Studies Monograph Series.

Herring, R. and Bharucha, E. Capacity, will and governance: India's compliance with international environmental accords. In E. Brown Weiss and H. Jacobson (eds) *Engaging Nations: Implementation and Compliance with Global Environmental Accords*. Cambridge: MIT. (In press)

Makhijani, A., Bickel, A. and Makhijani, A. (1990) Ozone depletion: Cause and effect. *EPW*, xxv, March 10, 493–6.

Parson, E. A. (1992) *Protecting the Ozone Layer: The Evolution and Impact of International Institutions*. Cambridge: Center for International Studies, Harvard University.

Polanyi, K. (1957) *The Great Transformation*. Boston: Beacon.

Porter, G. and Brown, J. W. (1991) *Global Environmental Politics*. Boulder: Westview.

Rosencranz, A. and Milligan, R. (1990) CFC abatement: The needs of developing countries. *Ambio*, xix:6–7, October, 312–16.

Seshan, S. (1995) Plugging the hole in the sky. *Business India*, February 13–26, 180.

Shastri, V. (1994) "The political economy of policy formation in India: The case of industrial policy." Draft PhD dissertation, defended September 21, 1994. Ithaca, NY: Cornell University.

Sims, H. (1994) The stratosphere's the limit. *Asian Survey*, XXXV:3, March, 268–79.

TERI (Tata Energy Research Institute) (1994) CFC Phaseout – Hydrocarbon Based Refrigeration. In *Proceedings of the Planning Workshop ECOFRIG Phase – IV*. New Delhi: TERI mimeo.

Weiss, E. B. (1989) *In Fairness to Future Generations: International Law, Common Patrimony and Intergenerational Justice*. Dobbs Ferry: Transnational Publishers Inc.

Walton, J. and Seddon, D. (eds) (1994) *Free Markets and Food Riots: The Politics of Global Adjustment*. Oxford: Blackwell.

11
Lessons from the Earth Summit: Protecting and Managing Biodiversity in the Tropics

P. S. Ramakrishnan

Conservation of biodiversity is not merely *ex situ* conservation through collection and storage, nor is it just centered around creation and protection of nature reserves for *in situ* conservation, but has ecological, economic, social, cultural and indeed developmental dimensions. The 1992 UN Conference on Environment and Development (UNCED) in Rio de Janeiro has endorsed environmentally sustainable development as the only option available to us for conserving biodiversity for future use and, at the same time, ensuring ecological integrity of the biosphere. However, there were no major international agreements reached at the conference. In particular, little progress was made on protecting biodiversity.

The basic reasons for biodiversity depletion arise out of two type of pressures that are exerted on natural resources:

1 pressures that are extrinsic to the system, for example, multinationals going in to a country like Brazil for the sake of exploiting natural resources, and
2 pressures intrinsic to the system, as is often the case in a country like India, where population pressure leads to degradation of resources.

In the former, the humans work from outside the ecosystem boundary, where in the latter situation, the humans could be viewed as part of the ecosystem function. The end result is the same.

This paper addresses the reasons for the difficulties faced by the world community in resolving the complex issues:

* determining biodiversity depletion in the developing world
* using this information in addressing the problem of biodiversity conservation, and
* creating a new economic order that would ensure some semblance of compatibility between the interests of the developing and the developed world.

Biodiversity depletion: The issues

In this section, we will consider a number of issues:

- Population growth and biomass resource depletion
- Agriculture and food security
- Deforestation

Population growth and biomass resource depletion

The rate at which natural resources are used up for the growth of the world economy outstrips the rapid growth of population. While developed countries of the world use up a large chunk of the world's natural resources for supporting a much smaller population, population pressure is the bane of the developing world, through the highly restricted per capita demand on resources that arises. Also, as a result of rising expectations, people in developing nations expect to have greater resources available per capita.

It is also important to recognize that generally larger family size in developing countries is often seen as a risk minimization measure that arises out of extreme poverty. Ensuring better quality of life with improved educational levels would contribute to population control. Although individual family level decisions are important, policy level decisions with appropriate emphasis on the determinants that affect population growth are equally important. Therefore, a holistic approach, encompassing sustainable livelihood/development, education and empowerment and family planning measures, is crucial to tackle the problem. The problem of coping with the twin problems of population and resource depletion has to be viewed in this context.

Increases in world population are projected to continue to occur overwhelmingly in the developing world. A very large fraction of the 3.2 billion increase in world population through 2025 is expected to be in the developing world. About half of the population growth during this period is expected to be in Asia, with the two most populous countries being China and India.

As in other developing countries, the twin problems for India center around rapid population growth and urbanization (Kayastha, 1989). India's present population of more than 850 million people is projected to reach 1043 million by the year 2000. The urban population of India in 1981 was 156.18 million, with an increase by about 49 million during the decade 1971–81. With Calcutta, Bombay and Delhi predicted to have more than 10 million each in 2001, the total population of million-plus cities would cross the 100 million mark by the turn of the century. The intense pressure on civic amenities has already contributed to the development of urban slums, with a fifth of India's urban population living in slums.

The population migratory patterns, common to many developing countries – rural to urban, rural to rural, and circulatory (Lambert, 1962; Ishwaran, 1966; Kayastha, 1989), may have serious social consequences, depending upon the given situation. The concentration of population in urban centers has already choked the natural ability of urban environments to absorb the wastes and emissions from human activities. This, in turn, has led to a variety of environmental health hazards. Rural to rural and circulatory migration, when they are from resource-depleted regions to richer areas, can accelerate the process of environmental degradation. A classic example of this occurs in the North-eastern region in India, where shifting (*jhum*) agriculture has recently become unsustainable. The agricultural cycle, which until recently has been twenty years or more, has fallen drastically to less than five years, partly because of large-scale industrial exploitation of forest resources and the consequent land degradation.[1] The increase in population pressure from within and through migration is only one of the factors contributing to this breakdown of the shifting agriculture system. Indeed, large areas in this high rainfall region have been decertified because of pressure originating from outside the region. In the tribal areas of the North-east, the adverse consequences were not only ecological, but social and economic (Ramakrishnan, 1992a).

The impact of humans on natural resource depletion has often been discussed as directly related to increased numbers. This argument arises from the biological concept of the carrying capacity of resources such as soil and water. However, this concept cannot be applied in a simple way to humans since a variety of other factors such as trade, technology and consumption patterns alter the carrying capacity in drastic ways. The notion that carrying capacity could be enhanced through technology and wealth is a short-sighted view, since the external energy subsidies that may be required for enhancement may not make it sustainable in the long run, and may often have adverse environmental consequences. Finer patterns of adaptation at a local level may better mitigate stress on the resource base.

One could also see the implications of the differences in consumption levels between the developing and the developed world. The per capita lifetime consumption level is at least twenty times greater in the developed world than in the developing countries. In the light of this, today's *de facto* population of Europe, in terms of resource dependency, is not 400 million, but 8,000 million (Suryakumaran, 1992). This might be contrasted to the population of India, which is only 800 million. In our anxiety to curb population growth, we conveniently set aside this uncomfortable reality. Population control in the developing world is critical, but is only a partial remedy and not a total remedy to conserving our natural resource base. No doubt, there are strong connections between the twin issue of poverty and population. However, equally important is resource use control in the developed world.

Agriculture and food security

Agriculture is an important economic activity for a large population of the developing world. In India, for instance, the "green revolution" has had positive repercussions in terms of general self-sufficiency in food production. However, it is largely confined to a small section of India's rural society and has had its negative impacts as well. First, it is an energy intensive activity and is still confined to a small sector of our predominantly agricultural society. Vast sections of rural communities are left out, leading to wide disparities in (a) access to resources, and (b) income generation, for want of effective and affordable appropriate technology. In spite of overall self-sufficiency in food production, more and more farmers (over 40 percent) have been marginalized. The worst affected are the entire tribal/ traditional population residing in different parts of the country; much of India's biodiversity also occurs in these zones, e.g., the hill people in the entire Himalayan region, the North-eastern hills, the Western Ghats, the Andaman and Nicobar islands, etc. Not only have these communities been adversely impacted by the activities of industrial man in over-exploiting the natural resources, their problems have also been accentuated because of increasing population pressure and the consequent fragmentation of the land holdings, now impoverished by environmental degradation. This is apart from the difficulties faced at a national level by many developing countries to have access to non-renewable resources like petro-based chemical fertilizers and pesticides to sustain the "green revolution" itself in the face of increasing population pressure and to cope with the larger problems of environmental degradation caused by excessive and uncontrolled use of water and chemical subsidies.

A special mention of gender and poverty would be appropriate at this stage. Traditionally, women have played a key role in agricultural activities, in one form or the other. Even as agriculture employs 70 percent of the total working population, it employs 84 percent of all economically active women. However, the green revolution has had an adverse impact on this vulnerable section of our society (Shiva, 1988; Venkateswaran, 1992). From a position of being a key player in the food production system, the woman has been marginalized more and more. Sometimes this change has been as extreme as that from a cultivator to a laborer. Furthermore, within a given household, there is overwhelming evidence to suggest that women as a group are more vulnerable than men to extremes of poverty and its consequences (World Bank, 1991). In the light of this marginalization, we must ask ourselves whether agricultural intensification can take place without social disruption.

A common perception about agroecosystems is that their composition is deficient in biodiversity and their structure and function impaired under human management. This is a limited view, based upon perceptions arising generally from agricultural management of the Northern hemisphere (Swift et al., 1994). Such a perception of agriculture is becoming more and more obvious in the developing world as well under the impact of the green revolution. The rich diversity in agroecosystem types that existed not too long ago is being lost rapidly, along with crop diversity at the specific and subspecific levels.

The problem of deforestation

Tropical forests cover about 7 percent of the land surface and constitute one of the Earth's most important natural resources. These forests have historically been used by the local communities on a sustainable basis, providing shelter, food fodder, fuelwood and a variety of other services. With a high biological diversity, these forests are thought to harbor about two thirds of all living species, numbering at least 30 million. Tropical forests affect the local environment through conservation of soil and water, and they possibly also influence regional and global climate. Whereas local impacts of tropical forests in the environment are well documented, global impacts are a matter of concern that have started to receive attention only recently.

A close relationship between population growth and agricultural land extension, with the latter tied directly to deforestation, has been suggested in a number of cross-country and country studies. While reducing population growth could reduce local pressures on the forest and other natural resources, this relationship is by no means a simple and straightforward one. For example, at the local level, the worst affected are the more vulnerable sections of the society, including women who have to work harder to collect their daily requirement of fodder and fuelwood. These and other impacts of deforestation exist in addition to the oft-quoted global consequences of climate change arising out of deforestation.

Being largely restricted to the developing countries of the world, tropical forest exploitation is closely linked with their concern for economic development. Increasing demand from both within the region itself and from the developed world are important factors for tropical forest conversion (Myers, 1980). Desperate to earn foreign exchange so as to ease international debt, countries find low-price timber from these forests to be an easy option too difficult to resist.

The consequences of deforestation are very complex. Deforestation for economic growth starts a vicious cycle that leads to a widening gap between the richer few and the poorer majority in the tropics. This disparity, in turn, leads to faster rates of deforestation. The vast majority of the people in these forested areas live in poverty, and are subject to malnutrition and chronic deprivation. It is ironic that the very process of deforestation carried out in the name of "development" is responsible to a large extent for the steady erosion of the natural resource base and the very life-support system of these forest dwellers.

Out of about 30 million species thought to exist (some estimates being as high as 90 million), about two-thirds are estimated to be from the tropics. Only about 500,000 tropical species are so far catalogued. Thus, the rate at which species are being lost even before they are catalogued is only in the realms of guesswork. With tropical forests disappearing at the rate of 76–90 thousand sq. km per year and, according to one estimate, at least as much of the forest being degraded, the implications for biological diversity are alarming. A significant impact of forest conversion would be on the extinction rates. Predicted extinction rates are complicated at local and regional levels by the type of ecosystem and disturbance regimes caused through human interactions. Indeed, in any discussion of biodiversity and tropical forest management, human dimensions cannot be ignored (Ramakrishnan, 1992b).

"Decertification" is a term used to explain a process of decline in the biological productivity of an ecosystem. While this phenomenon is linked to the arid, semiarid and subhumid ecosystems, even in the humid tropics the impact could be most dramatic. Impoverishment of human-impacted terrestrial ecosystems may exhibit itself in a variety of ways: accelerated erosion, salinization and site-quality decline. A major consequence of deforestation is related to adverse alterations in the hydrology, and related soil and nutrient losses. This is illustrated in the study done by us on shifting agriculture systems in North-east India[1]. The study revealed highly complex interactions due to the obvious linkages between ecological aspects with social, economic, and cultural dimensions of the tribal communities living in the humid tropical forests.

Agriculture and animal husbandry are two important economic activities of rural communities. Ill-conceived agricultural activities are often responsible for social disruption. An elegant example of this is the creation of agricultural settlements on a 50-km belt along a network of roads in the forested Amazonia in Brazil. In its eagerness to resettle the increasing population of Brazil and for economic development of the sparsely populated wilderness areas, the Brazilian government offered to each settler brought from the famine-stricken north-east 100 ha of land with incentives. Many settlers tried to grow crops often unsuitable to the clear-cut areas, and the soil was soon impoverished. Soon a large number of the 50,000 or so colonists were afflicted by disease and ill-health. More deforestation and land degradation led to further deprivation of the settlers, and social tensions developed among them and with the local tribes. The government agencies eventually abandoned the project. However, over 65,000 km^2 of forest with the associated biodiversity had been lost in less than ten years. In the ultimate analysis, what is important is the need for careful land-use planning before transmigration occurs into forested areas.

The forest farmers of the humid tropics have traditionally lived in harmony with their environment, and have maintained shifting agricultural cycles (the length of the fallow period between two successive croppings on the same site) of ten years or more (Ramakrishnan, 1992a). However, in more recent times, rapid shortening of the agricultural cycle has led to large-scale forest conversions. According to mid-1970 estimates, forest farmers number at least 140 million and cover 2,000,000 km^2 of tropical biome. It is believed that they eliminate an estimated 100,000 km^2 of forest each year, of which a substantial part is closed forest. Indeed, this land use with a variety of other complementary sedentary systems such as the valleyland rice system and home gardens strikes at the previous harmony with the environment of the forest farmer.

Fuelwood extraction is another important cause of deforestation. This, in turn, has led to an extreme shortage of this commodity. In the Asian tropics, about 600 million people are estimated to experience acute shortage of fuelwood. Apart from its direct effect, the economy is also indirectly affected by the diversion of cow dung for burning, which otherwise could be a valuable fertilizer for crop production. In excess of 400 million metric tons per year of cow dung is so diverted in the Asian and African region. In economic terms, this would mean a 50-kg decline in grain output for each ton of cowdung so diverted.

Poverty and deprivation of the rural poor arising from deforestation would eventually result in higher rates of conversion of land for agriculture, related animal husbandry, and domestic sectoral activities. At least one group of futurologists predicts that future forest clearing for agriculture-related activities would significantly influence levels of tropical hardwood removal and export. Viewed in this context, the future scenario for the developing world is grim unless urgent measures are taken for the reversal of the present trends.

Coping with the problems

In this section, we consider:

- sustainable agriculture
- forest conservation and management
- population, resource depletion and rural development
- rehabilitation of the rural landscape.

Sustainable agriculture

A growing inapplicability of modern agriculture has led to a renewed interest in traditional systems of agriculture. These systems presumably offer a basis for ecological efficiency and sustainability, together with social justice. Sustainable agriculture not only demands efficient use of water and nutrients based on locally available resources, but also regulated cropping done in a manner that would contribute towards sustaining soil fertility. Application of incorrect technology and/or over-exploitation of natural resources may give short-term gains but could often lead to ecological degradation and unsustainability. It is in this context that we looked at the whole question of sustainable development of the tribal communities of the north-eastern hill region in a holistic way[2] by building upon traditional technology as the starting point (Ramakrishnan, 1992a).

There exists in the tropics a wide range of complex agroecosystem types with biodiversity comparable to that of natural ecosystems and indeed, occasionally, exceeding it. This biodiversity contributes in a variety of ways towards ecosystem function such as production, decomposition, nutrient cycling dynamics and thus towards stability and resilience. Specific examples of these agroecosystem types (Ramakrishnan, 1992a) are shown in figure 11.1. The figure presents varied levels of management ranging from the casual to high intensity, eventually leading to modern monocropping systems (Swift et al., 1994).

It is generally acknowledged that biodiversity decreases as habitats change over the range of different intensities of management: from forest to traditional agriculture, and then on to modern agriculture (Gliessman, 1990). Biodiversity concerns, so far, have largely been confined to natural ecosystem management and the consequences of conversion of a forest to agriculture, while different agricultural systems themselves are not adequately emphasized. While a variety of models for loss in biodiversity under varied intensities of management regimes for agriculture are proposed, it is suggested that biodiversity decline is sharp somewhere in the area close to the middle intensity of management. If so, it is crucial to have a level of management that is close to this critical area for sustaining biodiversity in agriculture (Swift et al., 1994).

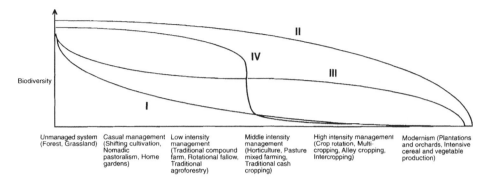

| Unmanaged system (Forest, Grassland) | Casual management (Shifting cultivation, Nomadic pastoralism, Home gardens) | Low intensity management (Traditional compound farm, Rotational fallow, Traditional agroforestry) | Middle intensity management (Horticulture, Pasture mixed farming, Traditional cash cropping) | High intensity management (Crop rotation, Multi-cropping, Alley cropping, Intercropping) | Modernism (Plantations and orchards, Intensive cereal and vegetable production) |

Figure 11.1 Biodiversity changes (four patterns) as related to agroecosystem types and intensity of management
Curve I and Curve II represent two extreme possibilities that seem to be unlikely. Curve III is a softer version of the ecologist's expectation, while Curve IV seems to be more likely and is the most interesting from the point of view of biodoversity conservation (Swift et al., 1994)

There could be three different pathways for sustainable agriculture[3] (Swift et al., 1994):

1 evolution by incremental change
2 restoration through the contour pathway, and
3 development through the auto-route.

Realizing that biodiversity does contribute in a variety of ways to ecosystem functions (Gliessman, 1990; Ramakrishnan, 1992a) and that agroecosystems do harbor a great deal of biodiversity valuable for human welfare (Pimental et al., 1992), it is reasonable that we utilize a combination of several of these options. This "mosaic" would consist of natural ecosystems coexisting with a wide variety of agroecosystem models derived through all the three pathways. Such a highly diversified landscape unit is likely to have a wide range of ecological niches conducive to enhancing biodiversity and, at the same time, ensuring sustainability of the managed landscape.

Forest conservation and management

The management of tropical forests may be undertaken for a variety of purposes: timber for industrial needs, forest products for rural communities, watershed protection for multipurpose use, and land-use alterations based on land capability and/or conservation. Depending upon the objectives, the approach to management could differ considerably. Timber extraction could be based on conversion into plantation forests of selected tree species, or it could be based on management of natural forests through selective extraction and natural/induced regeneration for sustained yield. Watershed/forest management for multipurpose use by rural communities could be even more complex.

Plantation forestry is the most common practice in the tropics today. This conversion essentially implies replacing a species-rich natural ecosystem by the species-poor monoculture of trees. Such a conversion can be done quickly and efficiently, with the emphasis being on highly focused commercialization for short-term economic gains. Often, fast growing tropical pines or eucalyptus are preferred. The long-term sustainability of such conversions is typically not evaluated (Ramakrishnan, 1992b). Mixed programs of plantation forestry using native species need to be integrated into any tropical forest management plan. This is particularly important since reforestation in the tropics has not kept pace with logging, with only about 600,000 ha of plantation being established, compared to an annual logging rate of 5,000,000 ha and deforestation more than double that.

Attempts to manage tropical forests and to harvest valuable species have not always been successful. In particular, the forests in the Indian subcontinent and 2–3 percent of the cut-over forest elsewhere are under some cutting regime followed by silvicultural treatment and protection. The chief obstacles to natural forest management are the low rate of return on investment, lack of knowledge, and human population pressure. These obstacles are so great that production in the managed forests in India, for example, does not exceed $1 m^3$ yield per hectare.

Ecological inputs are important for determining management decisions. Knowledge from areas such as tree biology and architecture, patch dynamics, ecophysiology of developing forest communities, reproductive biology and nutrient cycling processes could be integrated into the current management processes and future management options (Ramakrishnan, 1992a). In such an integrated approach to management, the socio-economic and socio-cultural issues and traditional knowledge coming from the local communities need to be reconciled. This is seen from our North-east Indian case study, where the sustainability criterion was the touchstone for designing management strategies;[4] see also Note 2.

Sustainable land-use management in the North-east Indian context has to be based on a series of compromises. A short-term strategy is required, and must be acceptable to the community. It should be based on a redeveloped management system using traditional knowledge as the starting point, and must take into consideration local perceptions about development. Working towards a more ideal long-term strategy is an issue that demands considerations related to appropriate technology development, transfer mechanisms and institutional arrangements.

The concept of sustainability implies the use of natural resources in a manner that satisfies current needs or options of future generations. Therefore, one could have only a set of guidelines (as given in Note 4), rather than a unified definition, adaptable to specific situations. In arriving at compromises, one needs to reconcile ecological sustainability with economic concerns.

Biosphere reserve management, because it demands people's participation, cannot be governed by a standardized set of strategies. While ecological, silvicul-

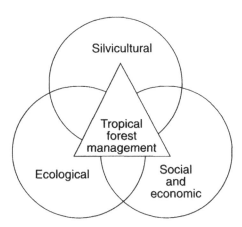

Figure 11.2 Interdisciplinary interactions called for in tropical forest management and conservation (Ramakrishnan, 1992b)

tural, developmental and educational issues can be broadly defined, the specifics have to be tailored to the needs of a given situation. This is because of the possible social, economic and cultural differences among the local populations and the ecological settings in which they may be based. This, again, is demonstrated in the north-eastern India example; see again Note 1. This means building upon the traditional knowledge and wisdom of the people. If eco-development is based on a value system that the people concerned cherish and with which they can identify, then their participation in management and conservation of natural resources may be ensured.

Because population pressure is very intense in the developing world, and large sections of the society are dependent upon forests for their livelihood, deforestation in the tropics is essentially a human problem, and a narrow-based forestry initiative alone cannot tackle it. A broader-based interdisciplinary approach would facilitate the sharing of knowledge that arises from the three major components of the management strategy (figure 11.2). Linking forestry with sustainable development in rural communities by making adequate provision for food, fodder, fuelwood, and timber to meet daily needs is critical. Through this effort, and by providing cash income for a better quality of life, multipurpose species for agroforestry, social forestry, and mixed plantations programs can play a useful role. These programs could also markedly reduce pressure on natural forests.

Conservation and management of tropical forests are two sides of the same coin. What is applicable to forest management is also important for conservation of biodiversity. Apart from local initiatives, regional and global efforts are called for to conserve the remaining hot spots of biological diversity, through initiatives based on environmental holism. The relationship between poverty, deforestation and conservation is clear, but the case studies suggest that it is not inevitable.

Population, resource depletion and rural development

The whole question of coping with the twin problems of population growth and natural resource depletion is centered around sustainable development with people's participation. We have to ensure sustainability of our rural ecosystems so as to reduce urban migration and thus improve the quality of life in our urban environment. Overly rapid urbanization could be checked through balanced developmental strategies for the rural areas. Rural development with emphasis on regeneration and sustainable management of natural resources alone can ensure conservation of natural ecosystems, both terrestrial and aquatic.

Long before India had launched into planned development in the traditional economic sense, Mahatma Gandhi had perceived the concept of development in a much broader sense. Gandhi conceived ideas for the total development of society as a whole through self-sustaining "village republics." His emphasis was on villages as self-sustainable systems. Though this may seem utopian in the modern context of a globalized economy, his emphasis was clearly on priorities – particularly rural development. For an economy that is "biomass driven," which describes the vast majority of the rural Indian population, sustaining the natural resource base through appropriate conservation measures has always been critical. Yet, during the last few decades, partly because of a blind faith in the Western models of development, the application of often inappropriate technologies, a closed-door policy for development, and rapidly increasing population pressure, rural development in the Indian context can, at best, be described as patchy. A very large segment of the population has been marginalized at the expense of the much smaller segment which has over-exploited the natural resources to its advantage. It is in this context that the whole concept of sustainable development assumes significance and leads us toward reviving the wisely conceived Gandhian concepts as an additional major pathway for development. This pathway is seen as additional because the developing world needs to have more than one model for development, and to apply these models, as dictated by the specific situation, to arrive at sustainability of the biosphere. In this effort, it is critical to reconcile sustainable livelihood concerns with the market economy through appropriate support mechanisms and policy initiatives.

Rehabilitation of the rural landscape

Agriculture, forestry and fisheries are traditional activities in the rural environment of the Asian tropics. Forest conversion has been accelerated by activities associated with rapid industrialization, such as mining and energy generation through large hydro-electric projects. Nevertheless, much conversion is still due to the extraction of timber for industrial uses and to meet the needs of the rural poor in terms of food, fodder and firewood. In the Asian tropics, degraded systems essentially make up over a third of the irrigated agricultural land, about half of the rainfed agricultural land, and almost three-quarters of the pasture land. It is in the context of reconciling the needs of the vast majority of the human population with sustainable utilization of natural resources that the rehabilitation of degraded ecosystems must be viewed.

Ecosystem rehabilitation and sustainable development, or more specifically, sustainable management of natural resources, are closely interlinked, one leading to the other. The disciplines of ecology, sociology, economics, anthropology and culture must be tied together to constitute a meaningful rehabilitation strategy.

This implies again that we have to make a series of compromises in such a way that we do not lose track of the ultimate objective, namely, rehabilitation and management of natural resources in a manner that satisfies current needs, at the same time allowing for a variety of options for the future.

Though an ecosystem type (man-made ecosystems such as agriculture or a fish pond in a village or the village itself and/or natural ecosystems such as grazing land, forest or river) may be the appropriate unit for convenient handling of rehabilitation, a cluster of interacting ecosystem types (a "landscape") may be the most effective (figure 11.3). A watershed is one such landscape unit. While one may bear in mind a long-term ideal objective to be achieved, ecological, socio-economic or cultural constraints may necessitate designing short-term strategies for rehabilitation. To quote one example, while forest-based economic activities and plantation programs may be the most appropriate long-term alternatives to shifting agriculture in North-east India, there is no option except to have a redeveloped agroecosystem package for the region using traditional knowledge and technology as the starting point (Ramakrishnan, 1992a).

Indicators of sustainable development are varied; therefore, compromises are called for. Monitoring and evaluation of rehabilitation has to be done using a number of diverse currencies including:

1   ecological – land-use changes, biomass quality and quantity, water quality and quantity, soil fertility, and energy efficiency
2   economic – monetary input/output analysis, capital savings or asset accumulation, and dependency ratio, and
3   social – quality of life using more easily measurable indicators such as health and hygiene, nutrition, food security, morbidity symptoms, more difficult to quantify measures such as societal empowerment, and the less tangible ones in the area of social and cultural values.

Furthermore, institutional arrangements have to ensure people's participation, through a bottom-up approach to their organization. It should be ensured that each household takes part in the decision-making process at the lowest level of the hierarchy, and special dispensation should be made for the weaker and more vulnerable sections of the society.

Resources in a rural ecosystem are of three types (private, common, and public) and the prevalence of each type depends largely on the situation. The chief difference between common and public resources lies in that the former are

- Landscape as a unit
- Site specific
- Time frame (short/long-term strategy)
- Strengthen internal controls and
    reduce subsidies
- Soil and water conservation/management
- Traditional/appropriate technology
- Enhance biodiversity
- Resource optimization

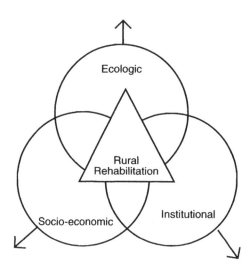

- History and causes
    of degradation
- Sustainable livelihood
- Cost/benefit sharing
  Community participation
- Role of women
- Empowerment
- Tenurial rights
- Value system

- Village level organizations
- Flexibility
- Monitoring
- Credit/marketing
- Linkages with gos/NGOs/
                scientists
- Incentives

Figure 11.3   Components of a rural landscape, based on access to resources
Integrative diagram linking the three major issues and many sub-issues crucial for rural
rehabilitation

owned by the community as a whole, whereas the latter could be either exclusively under the control of the government, or could be characterized by poorly
defined ownership rights. While a landscape may be an appropriate spatial unit
for rehabilitation, the nature of access to the resources by different sections of the
community may be crucial for designing strategies for rehabilitation. In a landscape, they form interacting components, each demanding a set of specific strategies under a generalized framework (figure 11.3) complete with assumptions[5]
and hypotheses[6] (Ramakrishnan et al., 1994).

In a detailed analysis of the issues centered around rehabilitation of rural landscapes in the Asian tropics, (Ramakrishnan et al., 1994) have raised a set of general hypotheses based on certain assumptions derived from a number of detailed case studies considered by them. From these assumptions[5] and general hypotheses,[6] more detailed hypotheses have been developed for private, common, and public resources, and ecological and social issues are considered separately.[7]

Ecosystem rehabilitation in the rural landscape of the Asian tropics is a complex exercise involving three interacting major issues: ecological, socio-economic and institutional with a number of sub-issues under each one these three (figure 11.3). In Notes 4–6, details about these sub-issues in the form of assumptions and hypotheses are outlined. Ecosystem rehabilitation has to be site-specific, emphasizing the strengthening of internal controls of ecosystem function rather than based on external energy subsidies. Understanding socio-economic concerns and developing appropriate institutional mechanisms between village communities and other actors in the developmental scene is crucial.

Rehabilitation of degraded rural landscapes/enhancing biodiversity through *in situ* conservation in the Asian tropics and sustainable livelihood represent two sides of the same coin. Many large-scale efforts initiated by governmental agencies often have missed the opportunity to integrate the social, economic and cultural dimensions of the problem. The traditional institutional frameworks presently available in the regions are often not geared to integrate the varied dimensions and take a holistic approach to natural resource enhancement and management. Therefore, either we need to create new organizational mechanisms or we should modify the existing mechanisms. In this effort, various actors – the people, non-governmental grass root level workers, governmental agencies and the scientific community including social scientists have to come together. It is a difficult challenge.

Environmental decision making has to be based on participatory research that recognizes the traditional value system. Environmental education, based on two-way interaction, is a key element for the participation of individuals in sustainable development. At a local, national, and most importantly, at a global scale, we need to reconcile ecology, economics, and ethics. This was crisply summed up by Mahatma Gandhi: "The Earth provides enough to satisfy every man's need but not every man's greed." This implies that both the developed and the developing world have to contribute towards coping with the twin problem of population growth and resource depletion.

Where do we go from Rio?

In this final section, we look at the way forward.

- Towards managing biodiversity at the ecosystem level
- Managing biodiversity through *ex-situ* conservation
- A policy framework for biodiversity use

Towards managing biodiversity at the ecosystem level

Ecologists still do not have adequate knowledge about natural ecosystem function and the way many interacting components operate, let alone the highly complex interactions at the landscape level. In other words, it is difficult to make management decisions for biodiversity conservation based on predictions of the effects of perturbations on ecosystem and landscape level function. What we do know is that heterogeneity in ecosystem types at the landscape level is likely to be of value for conserving and indeed enhancing biodiversity.

Pristine ecosystem types are often found within the broad landscape of highly modified and distorted man-made ecosystem types that are sustained by heavy energy subsidy. As a result, conserving large patches of those pristine ecosystems does not seem to be a solution for conserving biodiversity. Ehrenfeld (1991) talks of a management plan that is decentralized, flexible, capable of small-scale operations, information sensitive, and contains elements that are integrated yet independent. Contrasted with the present management plans that are large, prioritized, single protocol, single-theory, generalized schemes, patch dynamics is a powerful ecological tool for designing management strategies.

This new style of management plan has to be coupled with appropriate linkages between biological issues and social, economic and cultural dimensions, as shown by us in the North-east Indian case study (Ramakrishnan, 1992a). Otherwise the information flow to decision makers will be hampered and the involvement of local communities whose livelihood is dependent upon the effective management of biodiversity will be curtailed.

At a local level, keystone species such as the Nepalese alder or bamboo (see Note 3) could trigger biodiversity generation and enhancement within a given ecosystem. These ecologically important keystone species contribute towards managing biodiversity through their influence on ecosystem level processes. Thereby, we avoid the need to worry about conserving each and every species present. Since many of these ecologically important keystone species are also socially valued (Ramakrishnan, 1992a), local community participation in biodiversity conservation is assured. However, at a regional or global level, a key symbolic organism such as the panda or the Bengal tiger could have popular appeal and thus help in the conservation effort.

The key to environmental decision making for sustainable management of biodiversity and the natural resource base is participatory research in ecology integrated with education as a two-way interactive process between the local communities and scientists. Bringing ecologists together with social scientists and economists is crucial for sustainable development.

Organizational restructuring is necessary for this, because the present structures which emphasize over-centralization in planning and development hamper local initiatives that are so important for sustainability. An example of desirable institutional organization is that of the Village Development Boards (VDBs) in the Indian state of Nagaland. These boards include representation for each family in the village and ensure women's involvement in making village level decisions. Thus, the village organizational structure in Nagaland is bottom-up.[8]

National and international organizations concerned with conservation and sustainable management of biodiversity have to combine local initiatives with national and even regional planning. An integrated and holistic approach is called for, so that over-consumption of resources by some is effectively combated and reconciled with sustainable livelihood for the vast majority in biodiversity rich regions of the world.

Managing biodiversity through ex-situ conservation

Ex-situ conservation, which involves collecting genetic resources of most field crops, has long been recognized as a means to support the needs of the plant breeder involved with developing improved crop varieties. A comprehensive collection should have common alleles and adapted genotypes from as many different populations as can be identified – usually 4,000 seeds is recommended, from 50 to 100 plants per population and with about the same number of seeds per plant (Holden et al., 1993). For some species, seeds are not satisfactory for storage; *in vitro* culture methods are required to preserve plant parts or embryos through tissue culture techniques. For safeguarding genetic diversity, seeds have to be stored at 0°C for current use and at −10°C to −18°C for long-term storage. The latter could be expensive for tropical countries. This may have to be further supplemented through field genebanks in garden conditions. Collection and storage in genebanks could be very expensive, often beyond the means of many developing countries. It is for this reason that genetic resources, so far considered to be freely available to those who use them for the benefit of mankind, are of great value for developing countries. While research exemption is suggested to be available under the new scheme proposed for patenting biodiversity, this by itself is of little value to developing countries unless commercial use within national jurisdiction is assured. Gene banks held as international germplasm collections should be freely available for all users.

Policy framework for biodiversity use

Agenda 21 speaks of cooperation between the contracting parties (nations) for conserving biodiversity and its sustainable use. This has to be supported by designing national strategies for both *in-situ* and *ex-situ* conservation. However, with a sharp divide in perceptions between the developed and developing countries, which in any case is unfortunate, reconciling national interests with international obligations is daunting.

Already, one could foresee difficulties arising out of varied perceptions of intellectual property rights for life forms. Problems may arise between "product patents" as distinct from "process patents" for genetically engineered products of biotechnology. Furthermore, less developed countries may experience difficulties stemming from the imposition of the same rules for intellectual property rights (e.g. strict product patent regulations) as are imposed on their more technologically competitive developed counterparts.

An appropriate legal framework is crucial for developing nations to conserve and manage biodiversity. The Queensland government in Australia is one of the few to enact laws upholding intellectual property rights for the genetic resources and chemistries of the state's flora and fauna and allowing for collection of royalties on the sale of commercial products using these materials. This offers a framework for many developing countries to enact laws that recognize the proprietary rights of nations. However, what is equally important is to create a mechanism for:

1 rewarding individual members of the farming community for their conservation efforts, possibly through a separate fund to be created
2 protecting the right of the farmer to save seeds from his crop
3 protecting breeders' rights for "process patents" rather than only for "product patents," and
4 determining rights in space (national jurisdiction) and in time (period of protection).

In brief, one could visualize ways in which biodiversity becomes incorporated into the market economy, through ecosystem rehabilitation and sustainable livelihood/development, with benefits accruing to the local communities who have been the custodians of biodiversity. The sharing of benefits between the developing and the developed world is important for the sustainable management of biodiversity.

General considerations

Environmental awareness at all levels is crucial to be able to empower local communities, to develop appropriate strategies for environmental management, and to design policy options. However, progress in environmental education at different levels has been somewhat uneven in developing countries. At the university level, although distinct environmental courses have emerged in many developing countries, they often lack focus. However, in countries such as India, the environmental component of the school curricula and short-term professional and in-service specialized courses are becoming popular and gaining ground.

Although environmental awareness and informal education programs for local communities are being developed, they suffer from several serious deficiencies:

1 Often, they are not related to local situations.
2 Emphasis is on one-way delivery rather than two-way interactive education.
3 Vulnerable and key sectors of the society, such as women, are not effectively targeted.

There is much scope for improvement in the area of environmental education at all levels.

In the Asian tropics, there has been a recent and continuous upgrading of governmental environmental institutions, growth and maturation of NGOs, and proliferation of environmental legislation (ESCAP, 1992). However, further upgrading of institutions calls for improved integration between different governmental agencies, better coordination with the non-governmental sector, and decentralization of functions with empowerment of local communities. Some localized efforts, such as the development of joint Forest Management Committees for effective community participation in forestry management in countries like India and Nepal (Ramakrishnan et al., 1994) indicate that such a change may be forthcoming.

Efforts to integrate ecology and economics on a broader scale are urgently needed. Lack of funding and problems of trained personnel are major constraints in implementing environmental regulations. The World Resources Institute (1985) arrived at a total of 5.3 billion US dollars of support needed to implement the tropical forestry action plan over the next five years. FAO's tropical forestry action plan also arrives at a figure close to this for implementing forestry development with emphasis on food security for rural poor in developing countries (FAO, 1985). Suggesting a broader approach to manage the rural and urban environment in an integrated manner, the World Bank (1992) has predicted a whopping 75 billion US dollars a year by the end of the decade, or about 1.4 percent of the combined GDPs of developing countries. Forest protection, rehabilitation of degraded sites and clean-up operations do not figure into their calculations (table 11.1). These estimates could at best be considered indicative. It is presumed that these financial resources have to be generated locally and collectively through regional cooperative efforts. However, cost-sharing between developed and developing countries is essential, since benefits accrue to both.

Policy formulations at the national or regional level should be developed with an understanding of the local problems as those affected perceive them. For this, a bottom-up approach is required that would one hopes, avoid misconstrued policies that could lead to unexpected and undesired results.

Institutional mechanisms have to be developed; where they already exist they should be further refined and strengthened. Integrating biodiversity concerns into international economic policies and effectively linking them with developmental assistance is a challenge for the future. Although biodiversity is undoubtedly a global concern, it is inextricably tied to sustainable livelihood for a vast majority of the population living in developing regions. The North-east Indian case study has shown how this integration might be achieved. The poor need not worry about biodiversity, and yet biodiversity concerns still might become well-integrated into sustainable developmental considerations (Ramakrishnan, 1992a).

International institution building and legislation for regional cooperation in the Asian tropics have been progressing at a rapid pace (ESCAP, 1992). The establishment of the ASEAN Agreement on the Conservation of Nature and National Resources in 1985, for example, was a step in the right direction. However, progress has been slow, and implementation in the Asian region and elsewhere has been tardy and ill-coordinated. Better regional coordination and

Table 11.1 Estimated costs and long-term benefits of selected environmental programs in developing countries

Program	Additional investment in 2000		
	Billions of dollars a year	As a percentage of GDP in 2000[a]	As a percentage of GDP growth 1990–2000
Increased investment in water and sanitation	10.0	0.2	0.5
Controlling particulate matter (PM) emissions from coal-fired power stations	2.0	0.04	0.1
Reducing acid deposition from new coal-fired stations[b]	5.0	0.1	0.25
Changing to unleaded fuels; controls on the main pollutions from vehicles[b]	10.0	0.2	0.5
Reducing emissions, effluents, and wastes from industry	10.0–15.0	0.2–0.3	0.5–0.7
Soil conservation and afforestation, including extension and training	15.0–20.0	0.3–0.4	0.7–1.0
Additional resources for agricultural and forestry research, in relation to projected levels, and for resource surveys	5.0	0.1	0.2
Family planning (incremental costs of an expanded program)[c]	7.0	0.1	0.3
Increasing primary and secondary education for girls[c]	2.5	0.05	0.1

[a] The GDP of developing countries in 1990 was $3.4 trillion, and it is projected to rise to $5.4 trillion by 2000 (in 1990 prices). The projected GDP growth rate is 4.7 percent a year.
[b] Costs may eventually be lowered by the use of new combustion technologies and other measures.
[c] Recurrent expenditures on these items are counted as investments in human resources.
Source: World Bank (1992)

cooperation is crucial, not only for dealing with the complex and interactive issues of the region, but also for effectively negotiating in the world forums for the collective interests of the developing countries. Only then could transfers of technology and resources from developed to developing countries occur without the usual strings attached, and thus contribute toward international equity.

Notes

1   See Ramakrishnan (1992a). North-eastern India has over 100 different tribes, linguistically and culturally distinct from one another; the tribal designations often change over very short distances, a few kilometers in some cases. Shifting agriculture, or *jhum*, as the tribals call it, is their major economic activity. This highly organized agroecosystem is based on empirical knowledge accumulated through centuries and was in harmony with the environment as long as the *jhum* cycle (the fallow length intervening between two successive croppings) was long enough to allow the forest and the soil fertility lost during the cropping phase to recover.

   Supplementing the *jhum* system is the valley system of wet rice cultivation and home gardens. The valley system is sustainable on a regular basis, year after year, because the wash-out from the hill slopes provides the needed soil fertility for rice cropping without any external inputs. Another supplement to *jhum* is home gardens, which are found extensively in the region and have economically valuable trees, shrubs, herbs and vines. These small gardens form a compact multi-storied system of fruit crops, vegetables, medicinal plants and many cash crops; thus the system imitates a natural forest ecosystem in its structure and function. The number of species in this small area of less than a hectare may be 30 or 40; it therefore represents a highly intensive system of farming in harmony with the environment.

   Linked with this land-use are the animal husbandry systems which are traditionally centered around pigs and poultry. The primary advantage of these systems is that they are detritus-based or based on the recycling of food from the agroecosystem unfit for human consumption, and thus require little external input.

   The increased human population pressure and decline in land area resulting from extensive deforestation and *jhum* has brought the *jhum* cycle down to four years or less. Where population densities are high, as around urban centers, the burning of slash is dispensed with, leading to rotational/sedentary systems of agriculture. These are often below subsistence level, although they are attempting to maximize output subject to rapidly depleting soil fertility. Inappropriate animal husbandry practices, such as goat or cattle husbandry, introduced into the area could lead to rapid site deterioration through indiscriminate grazing/browsing and fodder removal, as has already happened in the Himalayas. The serious social disruption has caused demands for an integrated approach to managing the forest–human interface.

2   For improving the system of landuse and resource management in North-eastern India, the following strategies suggested by Ramakrishnan (1992a) and his coworkers are based on a multidisciplinary analysis. Many of these proposals have already been put into practice.

   •   There exist wide variations in cropping and yield patterns under *jhum* practiced by over 100 tribes under diverse ecological situations. However, the transfer of technology from one tribe/area to another could improve the *jhum*, valleyland, and home garden ecosystems. Thus, for example, an emphasis on potatoes at higher elevations and on rice at lower elevations has led to a manifold increase in economic yield despite low fertility of the more acid soils at higher elevations.

   •   Maintain a *jhum* cycle of at least ten years (this cycle length was found critical for sustainability when *jhum* was evaluated using money, energy, soil fertility biomass productivity, biodiversity, and water quality as currencies), by means of greater emphasis on other landuse systems such as the traditional valley cultivation or home gardens.

- Where the *jhum* cycle length cannot be increased beyond the five-year period that is prevalent in the region, redesign and strengthen this agroforestry system by incorporating ecological insights on tree architecture, e.g. the canopy form of tree should be compatible with crop species at ground level so as to permit sufficient light penetration and to provide fast recycling of nutrients through fast leaf turnover rates.
- Improve the nitrogen economy of *jhum* at the cropping and fallow phases by introducing nitrogen-fixing legumes and non-legumes. A species such as the Nepalese alder (*Alnus nepalensis*) is readily accepted by villagers because it is based on the principle of adaptation of traditional knowledge to meet modern needs. Another such example is the lesser known food crop legume *Flemingia vestita*.
- Some of the important bamboo species, valued highly by the tribals, can concentrate and conserve important nutrient elements such as nitrogen, phosphorus, and potassium. They could also be used as windbreaks to check the wind-blow loss of ash and nutrient losses in water.
- Speed up fallow regeneration after *jhum* by introducing fast-growing native shrubs and trees.
- As a long-term strategy, move to a cash crop-based plantation economy that builds upon the traditional home garden concept (where trees, shrubs, herbs and vines form part of a tightly packed production system of an individual village family). The objective here is to avoid alienating tribals from their land and to avoid social disruptions.
- Shorten the time span of forest succession and accelerate the restoration of degraded lands. This should be based on an understanding of tree growth strategies and tree architecture, and should be accomplished by adjusting the species mix in time and space.
- Improve animal husbandry through improved breeds of swine and poultry.
- Redevelop village ecosystems through the introduction of appropriate technology to relieve drudgery and improve energy efficiency (cooking stoves, agricultural implements, biogas generation, small hydroelectric projects, etc.). Promote crafts such as smithcraft and products based on leather, bamboo and other woods.
- Strengthen conservation measures that are based upon traditional knowledge and value systems with which tribal communities identify, e.g. the revival of the sacred grove concept. (This cultural tradition once enabled each village to have a protected forest. Few now remain.)

3 The "autoroute" to maximal productivity: Modern agriculture as a production system is based upon heavy external energy subsidies, and in that sense, is different from natural ecosystems that are regulated by internal controls. An appropriate metaphor would be the engineer who plans an autoroute (highway) by drawing a straight line from place to place on a map and then proceeds to build a straight and level road regardless of the physical impediments. Such an agroeco-system type developed following this pathway would stand apart as an artificial entity. It would constitute an attempt to convert the natural ecosystem into one that contains only those biological and chemical elements that the planner desires, almost irrespective of the background ecological conditions. e.g., the "Green Revolution" model.

Restoration through the "contour pathway": The contour pathway seeks to acknowledge and work with the ecological forces that provide the base on which the system must be built, while also acknowledging the social, economic and cultural requirements of the farming communities. This approach works with nature, rather than dominating it, and would involve active planning with the state of the existing ecosystem fully in mind.

The Sloping Agricultural Land Technology (SALT) developed in the Philippines is one such system that approaches this pathway. Unfortunately, the initial reaction to the application of SALT has not been very encouraging for reasons related to: (a) land tenure difficulties and (b) heavy labor investment. Many agroecosystem types in the "low" and "middle" intensity management categories (see figure. 1.1) will come under this pathway.

Evolution by "incremental change": Many traditional agricultural systems need to be redeveloped through incremental, rather than quantum, change; anything drastic may not find acceptance by the local communities. To follow incremental change towards sustainable development, one may have to consider a short-term strategy that may be constrained because of ecological, economic, social or cultural reasons. A more ideal and perhaps more desirable long-term strategy may come at a later time. A forest farmer who practices shifting agriculture and other land uses, and then picks up an appropriate variant of the local types that may be available, is illustrative of this pathway for sustainable development. Another example of incremental change might be a farmer strengthening the agroforestry component of a distorted short-cycle shifting agriculture system through the introduction of the Nepalese alder (*Alnus nepalensis*)

Landscape mosaic: Compared with the landscape model that is often seen now, i.e., pristine unmanaged ecosystems set in a sea of intensive large-scale agroecosystems, it may be desirable to have a mosaic of agroecosystem types, derived through all the three pathways, coexisting with natural ecosystem types, either managed or unmanaged. Maintenance of the overall sustainability of the system requires the patchwork mosaic that would, albeit inadvertently, be the best plan for biodiversity conservation in general.

4   The guiding principles of ecologically sustainable resource management, adapted from (Hare et al., 1990) are:

- inter-generational equity – providing for today while retaining resources and options for tomorrow
- conservation of cultural and biological diversity and ecological integrity
- constant natural capital and "sustainable income"
- anticipatory and precautionary policy approaches to resource use, erring on the side of caution
- resource use in a manner that contributes to equity and social justice while avoiding social disruptions
- limits on natural resource use within the capacity of the environment to supply renewable resources and assimilate wastes
- qualitative rather than quantitative development of human well-being
- pricing of environmental values and natural resources to cover full environmental and social costs
- global rather than regional or national perspective on environmental issues
- efficiency of resource use by all societies
- strong community participation in the transition to an ecologically sustainable society.

5   The north-east Indian case study illustrates the linkages between ecologic, economic, social, cultural and political dimensions and the value of appropriate institutional mechanisms in ensuring sustainable land use redevelopment (Ramakrishnan, 1992a). The twelve assumptions forming the basis for rehabilitation of rural landscape in the Asian tropics (from Ramakrishnan et al., 1994) are listed here.

A1   Rehabilitation ecology has effectively to integrate the ecological, economic, social, cultural, and political dimensions of the setting in which it is attempted. As such, ecological concepts and processes should be linked with social processes and perceptions.

A2   To integrate these components, it is essential to have effective linkages between the people and their institutions, governmental agencies, NGOs, scientists, and technologists.

A3   Since there are many interconnections between ecosystem types in a landscape, and since tinkering with one type may affect another, it becomes imperative for the process of rehabilitation to consider the landscape as a networking unit. The approaches for a given ecosystem type may differ, but still exist within a given framework.

A4   An understanding of the ownership and use patterns of natural resources (private, common, public, or any combination) is critical for strategies and will require different rehabilitation tactics.

A5   Rehabilitation may have to operate under varied ecological, economic, social, legal, political and/or cultural constraints. Furthermore, the objectives of rehabilitation may differ, and one may have to consider different time frames: short term (up to ten years) or long term (up to 100 years).

A6   Although rehabilitation work should provide a wide range of benefits to stake holders, the socio-economic needs of the local communities and user groups should be a major consideration.

A7   Ecological and socio-cultural concerns should determine technological interventions so as to ensure that the outcome agrees with local perceptions and value systems.

A8   Appropriate policy decisions are important for effective implementation of rehabilitation programs. While doing so, such decisions should take into consideration all the ramifications (ecological, social, cultural and economic) that may act as an incentive or disincentive for rehabilitation.

A9   Soil and water conservation and management are crucial for ecosystem rehabilitation.

A10   Understanding the history and the causes of the present status of ecosystem degradation is crucial for designing strategies for rehabilitation and management.

A11   Ecosystem rehabilitation and management are dynamic processes and, therefore, should be monitored continuously, and should be flexible and responsive to modifications.

A12   Ecosystem rehabilitation and management are site specific.

6   The eleven general hypotheses forming the basis for rehabilitation of the rural landscape in the Asian tropics (from Ramakrishnan et al., 1994) are listed here.

G1   Rehabilitation and management will only succeed if short-term economic benefits are assured to local communities, separate from the long-term benefits envisaged.

G2   If rehabilitation and management strategies are to be effective and successful, the participation of women is necessary.

G3   Without a broad understanding of the complexities of the system (through rapid appraisal methodology), rehabilitation strategies may not succeed.

G4   Unless ecosystem rehabilitation and management leads to a general improvement and maintenance of soil fertility and water quality, it is not sustainable.

G5   Ecosystem rehabilitation will be sustainable only if: (a) internal control of processes (e.g. resource recycling) within the ecosystem is strengthened; (b) dependence on external subsidies (e.g., fertilizers) is minimized; and (c) self-regenerating capacities are enhanced, to the extent feasible.

G6 To succeed, ecosystem rehabilitation should have strong community participation in the planning, management, implementation, and continuous monitoring of all these parameters.

G7 Unless rights and responsibilities of ownership are clearly defined and understood by all the participants, ecosystem rehabilitation is not likely to succeed.

G8 If community participation is to be effective, community/user group institutions will have to be built into the rehabilitation strategy.

G9 Unless land capability analysis and classification are integrated, taking into consideration scientific/traditional knowledge, rehabilitation work will not be effective and sustainable.

G10 Empowerment (training, institutions, access to facilities and resources, etc.) of local communities, particularly vulnerable sections (landless and women), is crucial for the success of any rehabilitation program.

G11 To ensure that rehabilitation work is sustainable, surface and ground water resources and their exploitation should be monitored and appropriately regulated through institutional mechanisms.

7   The seven hypotheses related to institutional and policy matters for rehabilitation of the rural landscape in the Asian tropics (Ramakrishnan et al., 1994) are listed here.

IP1 Without appropriate legal and legislative frameworks which clearly define the rights and responsibilities (tenure, access, etc.) of all the stake-holders, ecosystem rehabilitation efforts will not succeed.

IP2 Without clear operational guidelines and explicit and transparent contractual agreements between stakeholders, rehabilitation efforts will not succeed.

IP3 Ecosystem rehabilitation will be viable only if pricing reflects the true value (ecological and economic) of the regenerated resource.

IP4 The effective coordination of different village level leasing agencies/departments is crucial for the success of rehabilitation.

IP5 To institutionalize ecosystem rehabilitation, it is necessary to build the knowledge base/skills/management capabilities of the stake-holders.

IP6 Unless credit facilities, markets, and appropriate marketing channels are available and incorporated into rehabilitation and management, it will not be sustainable.

IP7 Appropriate institutional mechanisms should be available at the local level for conflict resolution between different stake-holders, so that conflicts arising during and as a consequence of ecosystem rehabilitation can be quickly settled.

8   Anonymous (1980). *Village Development Boards – Model Rules, 1980 (Revised)*. New Delhi: Dept. of Rural Development, Govt. of Nagaland.

References

Ehrenfeld, D. (1991) The management of biodiversity: A conservation paradox. In F. H. Bormann and Kellert, S. R. (eds). *Ecology, Economics, Ethics: The Broken Circle*. New Haven, Conn: Yale Univ. Press, pp. 26–39.

ESCAP (1992) *State of the Environment in Asia and the Pacific*. Thailand: United Nations Economic and Social Commission for Asia and the Pacific.

66

FAO (1985) *Tropical Forestry Action Plan.* Committee on Forest Development in the Tropics. Food and Agric. Research Organiz., United Nations.

Gliessman, S. R. (ed.) (1990) *Agroecology: Researching the Ecological Basis for Sustainable Agriculture.* Ecological Studies 78. New York: Springer-Verlag.

Hare, W. L., Marlowe, J. P., Rae, M. L., Gray, F., Humphries, R. and Ledgar, R. (1990) *Ecologically Sustainable Development.* Fitzroy, Victoria: Australian Conservation Foundation.

Holden, J., Peacock, J. and Williams, T. (1993) *Genes, Crops and the Environment.* Cambridge: Cambridge University Press.

Ishwaran, K. (1966) *Tradition and Economy in Village India.* London: Routledge and Kegan Paul.

Kayastha, S. L. (1989) Sustainability of metropolitan centres in third World Countries. In S. N. Singh, M. K. Premi, P. S. Bhatia, Ashish Bose (eds) *Population Transition in India.* Vol. 2. Delhi: B. R. Publ. Corp, pp. 327–34.

Lambert, R. D. (1962) The impact of urban society upon village life. In Turner, R. (ed) *India's Urban Future*, Berkeley and Los Angeles: University of California Press, pp. 117–40.

Myers, N. (1980) *Conversion of Moist Tropical Forests.* Washington D.C.: National Academy of Science.

Pimental, D. A., Stachow, V., Takacs, D. A., Brubaker, H. W., Dumas, A. R., Meaney, J. J., O'Neil, J. A. S., Onsi, D. E. and Corzilius, D. B. (1992) Conserving biological diversity in agricultural and forestry systems. *Bioscience*, 42, 354–64.

Ramakrishnan, P. S. (1992a) *Shifting agriculture and sustainable development.* In *Interdisciplinary Study from North-Eastern India.* MAB Book Series. Carnforth, Lancs., UK. Parthenon Publishing; Paris: UNESCO.

Ramakrishnan, P. S. (1992b) Tropical forests. Exploitation, conservation and management. *Impact of Science on Society*, 42 (166), 149–62.

Ramakrishnan, P. S., Campbell, J., Demierre, L., Gyi, A., Malhotra, K. C., Mehndiratta, S., Rai, S. N. and Sashidharan, E. M. (1994) *Ecosystem Rehabilitation of the Rural Landscape in South and Central Asia: An Analysis of Issues.* New Delhi: Special Publication, UNESCO (ROSTCA).

Shiva, V. (1988) *Staying Alive: Women, Ecology and Survival in India.* New Delhi: Kali for Women.

Suryakumaran, C. (1992) *Environmental Planning for Development.* Colombo, Sri Lanka: Centre for Regional Development Studies.

Swift, M. J., Vandermeer, J., Ramakrishnan, P. S., Anderson, J. M., Ong, C. K. and Hawkins, B. (1994) Biodiversity and agroecosystem function. In Mooney, H. A., et al. (eds) *Biodiversity and Ecosystem Properties: A Global Perspective.* SCOPE Series. Chichester, UK: John Wiley.

Venkateswaran, S. (1992) *Living on the Edge: Women, Environment and Development.* New Delhi: Friedrich Ebert Stiftung (FES).

World Bank (1991) *Gender and Poverty in India.* Washington, DC: The World Bank.

World Bank (1992) *Development and the Environment: World Development Indicators.* Oxford: Oxford University Press.

World Resources Institute (1985). *Tropical Forests: A Call for Action. Part I. The Plan.* Washington, DC: World Resources Institute.

V
Sectoral Studies of Equity and the Environment

12

Industrial and Resource Location, Trade, and Pollution[1]

Duane Chapman, Jean Agras, and Vivek Suri

The literature on trade and environment is extensive. Taken together, Cropper and Oates (1992) and the World Bank (Low, 1992) reviewed more than 30 papers published prior to 1992. Recently, Agras et al. (1994) reviewed more than 40 papers, of course with coverage of earlier work. Of these, no more than five authors seem to find trade and environment to be adversely linked (Birdsall and Wheeler, 1992; Chapman, 1991; Gray and Shadbegian, 1993; Hoffnar et al., 1993; and Lopez, 1992).

The dominant view is expressed by the World Bank in the 1992 *World Development Report* (p. 67): "Evidence shows that developing countries do not compete for foreign investment in 'dirty' industries by lowering their environmental standards. Rather ... data ... suggest the opposite: because it is cheaper for multinational corporations to use the same technologies as they do in industrialized countries, these firms can be potent sources of environmental improvement."

Grossman and Krueger (1991, p. 35) carry this point further, arguing that trade will cause "the movement of the dirtier economic activities to the more highly regulated production environments."

Metaphorically speaking, the conclusions cited from the World Bank and from Grossman and Krueger could be assumed to be multiplied 40-fold to represent the dominance of this viewpoint in current economic literature. Briefly, there are four main themes in the literature reviewed by Agras et al.:

1 Environmental costs do not erode international competitiveness, nor are they the chief cause in the migration of dirty industries – although the costs themselves may have been underestimated.
2 Open trading regimes may be better for the environment.
3 Internationally uniform environmental standards (harmonization of standards) are not economically efficient.
4 Cooperation between nations in formulating environmental regulations offers a superior alternative to unilateral action.

In this paper, our modest goal is to make these empirical points:

1 Industrial growth in East Asia is based upon imported resources.
2 Trade between regions with different environmental protection policies can increase total emissions.
3 Global levels of major pollutants are increasing.
4 Living standards, measured by gross economic product per capita, are declining in a number of countries.

Resource dependency and industrialization in Asia

Industrial growth in Japan, South Korea, and Taiwan is widely recognized. However, it is less widely known that these countries depend almost wholly upon the importation of processed industrial raw materials for their manufacturing. Tables 12.1–12.3 show the magnitude of resource dependency for six major resources. These six resources are essentially the basis for manufacturing. For example, the three metals constitute 75 percent of the weight of a new car, and petroleum derivatives add another 14 percent (AAMA, 1993).

In addition, the three energy resources in the tables constitute more than five-sixths of energy consumption for each country and for the group (Dumagan and Drennen (1988), Lofty et al. (1992), OECD (1992), UNCTAD (1991), and USEIA (1992, 1993).

Given this magnitude of industrial resource importation, it is clear that Asian manufacturers contribute to pollution emissions in the regions which supply their industrial resources. Typically, metal ores are processed near mines, and it is the

Table 12.1 Korean industrial resource dependency[2] (1990, units of contained metal or fuel)

Mineral or fuel	Mine production[4] or field output	Consumption of refined primary metal or fuel	Measure of resource dependency (%)
Aluminum ('000 tons of Bauxite)	0	0	100
Coal (trillion Btu)	342	949	64
Copper ('000 mt[4])	0	324	100
Iron ore ('000 tons Fe content)	199	22,870	99
Petroleum ('000 barrels per day)	3	1,025	100
Uranium (tons U)	0	–	100

initial processing which releases most of the pollution associated with metal smelting.

Figure 12.1 shows the distribution of copper from Zambia, one of the world's major copper producers (ZCCM, 1992). Zambia utilizes only 3 percent of its

Table 12.2 Taiwanese industrial resource dependency[3] (1990, units of contained metal or fuel)

Mineral or fuel	Mine production[5] or field output	Consumption of refined primary metal or fuel	Measure of resource dependency (%)
Aluminum ('000 tons of Bauxite)	0	48	100
Coal (trillion Btu)	0	493	100
Copper ('000 mt[4])	0	297	100
Iron ore ('000 tons Fe content)	0	7,760	100
Petroleum ('000 barrels per day)	6	542	99
Uranium (tons U)	0	–	100

Table 12.3 Japanese industrial resource dependency (1985, units of contained metal or fuel)

Mineral or fuel	Mine production[5] or field output	Consumption of refined primary metal or fuel	Measure of resource dependency (%)
Aluminum ('000 tons of Bauxite)	0	2,814	100
Coal (trillion Btu)	530	3,540	85
Copper ('000 mt[4])	43	1,172	96
Iron ore ('000 tons Fe content)	212	179,419	100
Petroleum ('000 barrels per day)	3,929	1,517,676	100
Uranium (tons U)	7	650	99

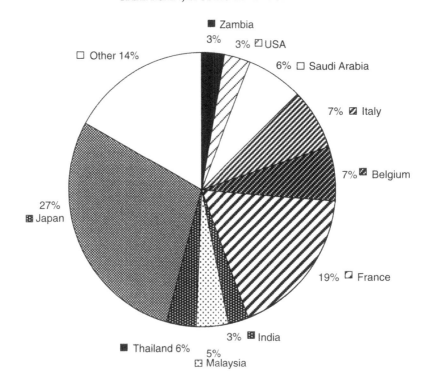

Figure 12.1   Sales distribution of Zambian copper (own production copper-tonnes). *Source:* ZCCM (1992, p. 49)

own production. As raw materials are processed and shipped to manufacturing centers, the pollution remains behind. This is typical. Six developing countries (Chile, Zaire, Philippines, Peru, and South Africa, in addition to Zambia) produce 60 percent of the world's copper identified by country of origin. They utilize only 5 percent of their own mine production locally.

The problem then, is this: developing country raw materials producers supply industrial resources. The pollution-intensive initial processing takes place in their countries. The industrial resources are then exported for manufacturing in Europe, North America, and Asia, whose final products play a significant role in world trade.

Consequently, the economic beneficiaries of the absence of industrial pollution control in developing countries are the manufacturing centers, and the final consumer. In the USA, for example, it was estimated that one third of total copper consumption was embodied in imported goods (Chapman, 1991, p. 457), and this amount exceeds the quantity imported as metal for direct use in manufacturing in the USA.

Increasingly, the world's manufactured goods are fabricated in Asia. Table 12.4 shows an approximate 6 percent annual growth rate in East Asia in industrial production. Now, consider this rapid growth in industry in the context of resource dependency. The three leading East Asia manufacturers in table 12.4

Table 12.4 Industrial production and growth in Asia, 1965–1990 (1990 US dollars)

	Industrial production (US$ million)		Growth factor
	1965	1990	
East Asia			
Taiwan (China)	485	66,774	137.6
Indonesia	2,722	42,743	15.7
Korea, Republic of	6,984	109,819	15.7
Thailand	2,985	31,810	10.7
Malaysia	2,084	16,536	7.9
Japan	320,914	1,234,938	3.9
Philippines	4,567	15,466	3.4
Total	340,256	1,435,537	5.9
South Asia			
Pakistan	1,964	10,010	5.1
India	22,212	85,772	3.9
Bangladesh	1,130	3,359	3.0
Total	26,010	101,769	3.9
China			
Total	20,937	155,331	7.4
Other countries comparison			
Australia	46,893	91,571	2.0
Germany	402,585	583,608	1.5

Source: Adapted from Brandon and Ramankutty, (1993, p. 65).

(Japan, South Korea, Taiwan) are all, essentially, wholly dependent on imported industrial raw materials. Much of their contribution to global pollution is actually released in the countries of origin that process their raw materials.

It bears repeating that the beneficiaries of the lower cost goods produced without pollution control are typically the consumers in North America and Europe. In addition to the pollution released in the countries of origin of raw materials, there is significant growth in pollution in manufacturing centers in Asia. The pollution impact is significant, as may be expected. One analysis projects that Asia will contribute 45 percent of the global growth in CO_2 emissions in this decade. In SO_2 emissions, Asia will exceed the combined total of European and US emissions in ten years (Brandon and Ramankutty, 1993).

Figures 12.2–12.4 show the historic lower growth in GDP relative to the major pollutants for three East Asian countries. The lower shaded line represents the slower growth of GDP, relative to the rapid rise of pollutants, including sewage, sulfur dioxide, and toxic chemicals and metals.

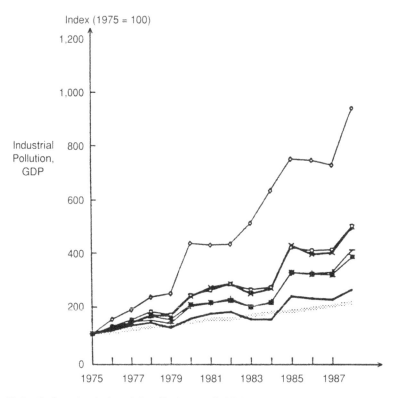

Figure 12.2   Indonesia: industrial pollution and GDP.
Source: Brandon and Ramankutty (1993)
■ Biochemical oxygen demand, + Suspended solids, * Sulfur oxides, ⊟ Particulates,
* Toxicity, ✧ Heavy metals,   Growth in real GDP.

The additional implication of these data is that global pollution is increasing, in part because of the interaction of trade and industrialization. The limited data available on global pollution will be discussed below.

Trade and environmental protection

Part A of figure 12.5 shows two hypothetical regional supply relationships. Each curve indicates the amount of refined copper that would be offered for sale at the price levels on the vertical axis. S_{IB}, for example, represents the supply function for the world's industrialized region producers before new sulfur regulations are implemented. S_D represents the supply response for developing country producers. Note that S_{IB} is to the left of S_D: at any price level, less quantity will be supplied by industrial region producers. In economic theory, the supply price is equivalent to the marginal or incremental cost of production for increasing quantities supplied.

Part B of figure 12.5 shows the world copper market. Q_{TB} is the total industry

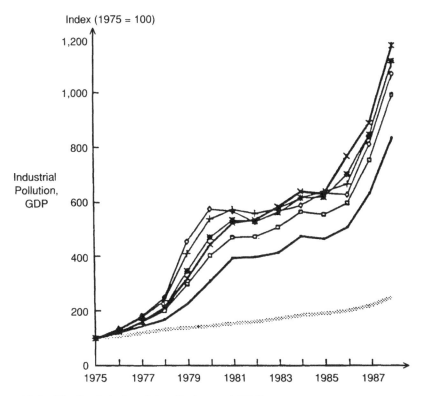

Figure 12.3   Thailand: industrial pollution and GDP
Source: Brandon and Ramankutty (1993)
■ Biochemical oxygen demand, + Suspended solids, * Sulfur oxides, ⊟ Particulates,
* Toxicity, ⟡ Heavy metals,   Growth in real GDP.

supply function for both regions, the sum of the two regional relationships. The downward-sloping customer demand function, Q_C, indicates that customer demand increases as market price declines. Market equilibrium is defined by the intersection of the upward-sloping supply function with the downward-sloping demand function, providing identical prices and quantities to customers and producers. The global equilibrium is at about 7.5 million metric tons (mmt) of world production, at a world price of about 66¢ per pound.

This market equilibrium price in Part B defines the regional production levels in Part A: Q_{IB} is at 3.0 mmt, and Q_D is at 4.5 mmt. The higher marginal production cost for the industrial region reflects a considerable degree of sulfur control. This is about 67 percent, as discussed below. Consequently, global sulfur dioxide emissions are at 11 mmt; 9 mmt from developing country producers, and 2 mmt from industrial country producers. This is assuming a typical ratio of one-to-one for the sulfur–copper ore ratio, and a two-to-one sulfur dioxide–sulfur ratio.

Now suppose industrial regional countries tighten their sulfur control to 95 percent removal. In figure 12.6, supply function S_{IG} reflects the higher cost of the

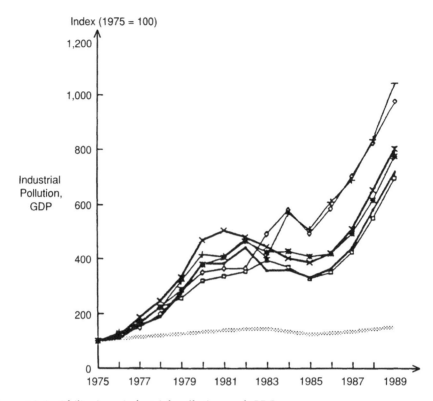

Figure 12.4 Philippines: industrial pollution and GDP
Source: Brandon and Ramankutty (1993)
■ Biochemical oxygen demand, + Suspended solids, ⋆ Sulfur oxides, ⊟ Particulates,
* Toxicity, ◇ Heavy metals,　Growth in real GDP.

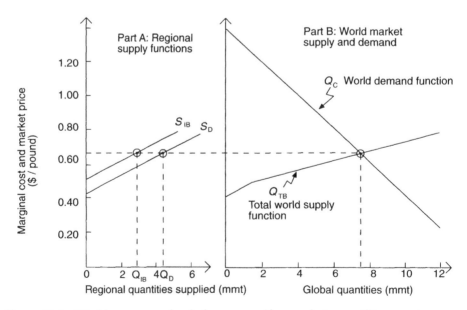

Figure 12.5 World copper market before new sulfur regulations, million metric tons

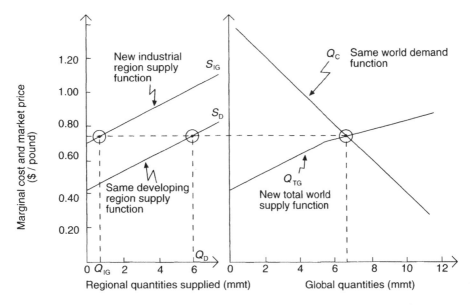

Figure 12.6 New industrial region sulfur regulations and global copper market (million metric tons)

new regulations control level. S_D for developing countries is unchanged. The new total supply function is Q_{TG}. The world demand function is unchanged at Q_C. Supply and demand are now in equilibrium at 76¢ per pound, and a world use level of 6.7 mmt. The dramatic change is the displacement of industrial country producers. Their production level is 0.7 mmt. Q_{IG} market share is now 10 percent, compared to 40 percent before the new regulations.

This theoretical analysis has purposefully been constructed to give this result: global sulfur dioxide emissions are higher. For the industrial region, 95 percent control on 0.7 mmt copper production means 0.07 mmt sulfur dioxide emissions. The developing country sulfur dioxide emissions are 12 mmt for the Q_D production level of 6 mmt copper. Total world sulfur dioxide emissions have grown to 12.1 mmt. Incidentally, Moller (1984) estimates total global anthropogenic sulfur pollution emissions at 70 mmt, and associates 10 mmt with sulfur emissions from metal processing.

In this exercise, a further tightening of industrial region sulfur emission control is associated with

1   a rise in global emissions
2   a rise in world prices
3   falling world output, and
4   a severe contraction in production in the controlled region and displacement to uncontrolled regional producers.

The same argument can be stated more formally. Suppose an international manufacturer can use the same technology in regions A and B, and assume that trade and capital movements are unrestricted. Cost minimization is the goal, with these three assumptions.

$$E_T = E_A + E_B \tag{12.1}$$

$$E_j = \varepsilon_j(1 - S_j)Q_j \quad j = A, B. \tag{12.2}$$

$$MC_j = \beta_0 Q_j^{\beta_1} S_j^{\beta_2} \quad j = A, B. \tag{12.3}$$

E_T represents total global or continental emissions from regions A and B. ε is the uncontrolled ratio of emissions to production. MC is the marginal cost of production of Q in region j and comes from a Cobb–Douglas production function. S is an index of control, ranging from 0 to 1. So β_1 is the economy of scale in production, and β_2 is the "diseconomy" of scale in pollution control.

Assuming there are no pollution controls in region B ($S_B = 0$), the following first order condition results:[6]

$$\frac{dE_T}{dS_A} = \varepsilon Q_A\left(\frac{\beta_2}{\beta_1} - 1\right) \tag{12.4}$$

So, if β_2 (the diseconomy of scale in percentage pollution control) exceeds β_1 (the economy of scale in output parameter), then (12.4) is positive. Higher standards in region A result in higher overall global pollution levels.

In many actual applications, β_2 may be approximated by integers. The first increment of pollution control can be very inexpensive. For example, moving from high to medium sulfur coal when both are readily available at comparable cost can be done at low incremental cost. As scarcer low sulfur coal is purchased, the cost of reducing emissions rises. Sulfur scrubbing is still more costly, and the increment in cost from 90 percent to 95 percent sulfur removal could be comparable to the increment from 50 percent to 90 percent. In (12.4), if β_2 is greater than β_1, the interaction of trade with increasing regulation in region A leads to an increase in total global emissions: the dependent variable is positive.

Obviously, again, the empirical reality is very important. If β_2 is small, then there is no problem. However, if β_2 is much larger than β_1, the interaction of trade with differential environmental standards may be significant.

GATT, NAFTA, and Rio

As the global economy becomes formalized through new world and regional agreements, it is evident that environmental protection has not been considered a significant domain of trade policy, nor has trade been considered relevant to environmental policy.

The General Agreements on Tariffs and Trade (GATT) has no explicit discussion of the problem of reconciliation or harmonization of environmental policies. The GATT Secretariat (GATT, 1992, p. 10) explicitly offered this judgment: "In principle, it is not possible under GATT's rules to make access to one's own market dependent on the domestic environmental policies or practices of the exporting country." Similarly, NAFTA's attempts to address this question have been to no avail (NAFTA, 1992; USTRO, 1992).

In practice, GATT has generally been interpreted as prohibiting import taxes or controls based upon environmental cost or policy differences. In the dolphin/ tuna case, the GATT panel simply overturned the applicability of the US Marine Mammal Protection Act on the apparent basis that the Act regulated dolphin catches, and could not therefore be a basis for regulating tuna imports. Consequently, the status of GATT and the Act seems to be this: tuna boats cannot sell tuna caught with dolphins if they are US boats selling their product in the USA. But, if a US boat moves to Mexico, it can sell tuna caught with dolphins in the US market, and, under GATT, the USA cannot regulate or tax this practice (USITC, 1992). As Strand et al. (1992) have pointed out, US boats moved and dolphin populations continue to decline.

In a similar industrial case, the US tax on imported chemical products was overturned by a GATT panel. The USA had sought partially to equalize environmental protection costs by applying a tax on imports equivalent to the Superfund tax borne by domestic production (USITC, 1991).

If NAFTA and GATT are implemented as structured in 1992, it is apparent that the ability of US policy to influence environmental practice in its trading partners will be strictly limited (Chapman, 1992). While this general prediction seems straightforward, it may be more difficult to define the future practices where significant transboundary pollution occurs.

Consider a hypothetical situation. An Asian auto manufacturer develops a new facility and community in Mexico, near the border, for producing vehicles for sale in the USA. Since municipal sewage control is not common in the new Asian manufacturing centers (WRI, 1992; Chira, 1985), municipal taxes are not collected and no facilities are built. The untreated sewage from the facilities' new workers enters the USA. Can trade or environmental policy be invoked? Apparently not, according to current NAFTA and GATT provisions.

Further, NAFTA institutionalizes a de facto exemption for Mexico to continue its nonreporting of pollution emissions.

In a speech to the GATT Plenary Committee, US Vice President Al Gore (1994) discussed the creation of a Committee on Trade and Environment within GATT's World Trade Organization. As yet, there is no formal program of analysis or policy which will affect trade–environment interactions.

The Rio Environmental Summit in June 1992 focused on a very different facet of trade–environment relations. Its major emphasis was on the global environment, for which the Climate Convention was particularly important. One of the most significant parts of this treaty may be its commitment for signatories to publish greenhouse gas emission data (Schnoor, 1992). However, there is no agreement to limit growth of CO_2 emissions. Is it possible that increased energy efficiency in the sense of reduced energy per dollar of GNP may provide a partial solution?

Howarth et al. (1991) analyzed eight OECD countries and found continuing

Table 12.5 Aggregate world energy and GNP data: 1965, 1990

	World		OECD		Rest of world	
	1965	*1990*	*1965*	*1990*	*1965*	*1990*
Energy intensity (kBtu/$ growth rate/year)	15.997	15.436 −0.1%	13.600	10.461 −1.0%	23.231	28.053 +0.7%
Total GNP (trillion 1990$)	$9.602	$22.299	$7.235	$15.993	$2.367	$6.306
Population (billions)	3.317	5.284	0.649	0.777	2.668	4.507
Per capita values						
Energy (MBtu/capita[a])	46.3	65.1	151.6	215.3	20.7	39.3
GNP ($/capita)	$2,895	$4,200	$11,148	$20,170	$887	$1,399

[a] MBtu means million Btus. Some calculations will differ because of rounding error.
Source: World Bank (1992)

declines in energy-industry GNP ratios. But it must be remembered that many consumer and intermediate goods are manufactured in rapidly industrializing countries, and this displaces energy previously required in developed countries to manufacture the same products.

Table 12.5 shows changes in aggregate energy intensity on a macro basis between 1965 and 1990. Note that energy used per dollar of GNP for the OECD countries declined as expected from 13,600 Btu/$ to 10,000 Btu/$. This supports the Howarth et al. argument. But, in contrast, the rest of the world increased from 23,300 Btu/$ to 28,100 Btu/$. The apparent world average declined very slightly from 16,000 Btu/$ to 15,400 Btu/$ over the 25-year period.

Conclusion

The dominant perspective on trade and environment among US economists is that increasing trade raises living standards, which provides the economic basis for reduced pollution.

Of more than 40 papers on the subject reviewed by the authors, only five held the other position, that trade is likely to increase overall pollution levels, or that the absence of pollution control can be a positive factor in industrial location.

The studies reviewed by Agras, Suri, and Chapman (Agras et al., 1994) usually used Federal survey data, which have excluded a number of potentially significant types of environmental and worker protection costs. The analysis which follows is based upon discussion with personnel in the Bureau of Economic Analysis, the Bureau of the Census, and management personnel at factories, mines, and smelters in the USA, Mexico, Chile, Zaire, Zimbabwe, Russia, and South Africa. It is adapted from Chapman (1991). There are six sources of error in the types of cost factors which have been excluded.

One important factor is that many labor-intensive environmental activities that are part of a production process may not be reported. For example, the labor, fuel, and equipment costs of dust control in a pit mine by use of watering trucks may not be reported. Similarly, collateral protection devices that are a secondary part of production equipment may not be reported. Relevant examples here would be the capital and labor costs of a dust hood on an ore conveyor, or fans and hoods on a grinder.

Second, monitoring and planning activities may be excluded. Four examples of environmental protection expenses that have been excluded would be:

1 professional time spent with visitors inspecting protection systems
2 meteorological monitoring of ambient air quality
3 environmental planning, and
4 time and expense in report preparation and meetings with State and Federal regulatory personnel.

A third omission from survey data is the cost of protecting workers from environmental hazards. Roll bars, respirators, monitoring: all of these types of items are excluded from environmental cost reports.

Also, interest expense or opportunity cost for investment in protection equipment is not included in the survey data. This could be significant for capital-intensive pollution control practices.

A fifth factor in under-reporting environmental costs in surveys may be vintage: current management may not perceive practices which preceded them as protective; current management may focus on environmental practices introduced during their tenure. Examples here are respirators and tall stacks.

Finally, productivity loss has been excluded from the surveys. When production stops or is slowed because of environmental problems, this output loss is not counted as an environmental expense. New work by Gray and Shadbegian (1993) and at the Bureau of the Census finds that the cost of productivity loss may be three or four times higher than the cost implied by capital expenditures data.

Recent analysis by the US Office of Technology Assessment (1994, pp. 196–200 and elsewhere) generally supports the minority view held by us and given here.

Our perspective raises very different points from those held in the current dominant perspective. First, the dramatic growth of manufacturing in East Asia for global markets is based entirely (or nearly so) on the importation of processed pollution-intensive raw materials. For a typical product in this global system, a US consumer benefits from a lower price and a cleaner local environment for an Asian product made from imported resources. However, energy use and pollution

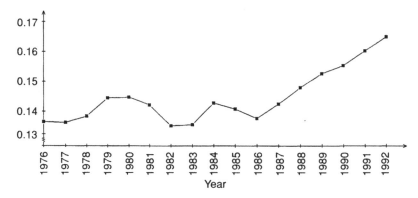

Figure 12.7 World trade as a proportion of gross world product. Brown et al. (1993)

associated with the fabrication of the product occur in the country of origin of the raw materials, and in the country where the final product is manufactured.

A modest logical exercise in economic theory shows the presence of trade between two regions with strongly different pollution control practices can increase total world pollution.

In reality, the implementation of GATT and NAFTA excludes any impact on actual environmental practices. It seems likely that in reality total global pollutant levels are increasing exponentially.

It is widely believed that world living standards have been rising, in part because of the growth of world trade (figure 12.7). However, as figure 12.8 shows, Gross World Product per capita in real dollars has been fluctuating for 15 years. The highest value in the series was actually 1980, with another peak in 1990 not quite reaching that level. The current value is somewhat below the 1980 value.

Turning again to empirical data, the decline in energy per real dollar of GNP in the OECD countries has been exactly offset by an increase in energy intensity elsewhere. As a result, world energy intensity (energy use per real dollar of GNP) has stayed almost constant, and world energy use has been accelerating.

Actual data on global emissions are very limited. One recent report showed accelerating emissions of sewage and air pollutants in association with rising GDP in three countries with major growth in industry and GDP. The question arises as to whether this is a global trend.

Figure 12.9 reports estimates of four major world pollutants, each of which shows accelerating growth. It is likely that actual data, if available, would also show exponential growth now for sewage, toxic metals and chemicals exposure, and other types of pollutants.

The empirical perspective we see is very different from the commonly held viewpoint. In summary, on a global basis, the international economy is characterized by increasing trade and world economic product, stagnation in gross economic product per capita, accelerating energy use, and exponential growth in emissions of major pollutants.

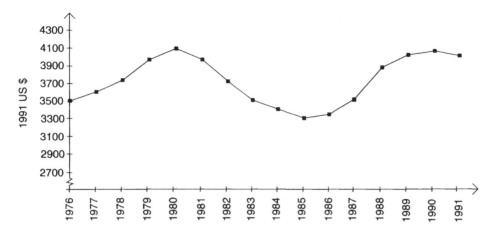

Figure 12.8 Gross world product per capita (real US dollars)
Sources: World GNP data in current prices from World Bank (1993) are deflated by the
US GDP deflator from US Council of Economic Advisors (1993). (V. Suri, November
1994)

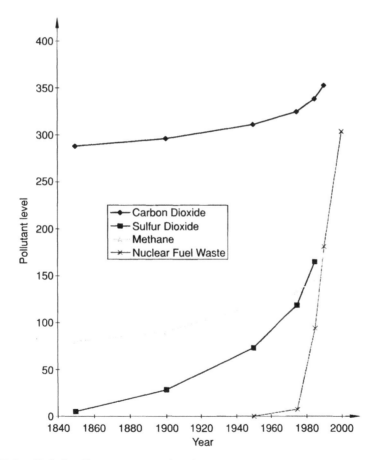

Figure 12.9 Global pollutants are accelerating
Sources: Carbon Dioxide, Boden et al., 1990; Houghton et al., 1990; Sulfur dioxide,
McClive, 1990; Methane, Houghton et al., 1990; Nuclear Fuel Waste, Chapman, 1994
(E. Smith, Nov. 1994)

Notes

1   The authors wish to thank Eleanor Smith for her invaluable assistance in the preparation of this manuscript.
2   Korea does not import any bauxite, but for their aluminum production they import alumina and unwrought aluminum, making their resource dependency measure 100 percent.
    Korea has substantial uranium reserves, but they are currently not economically retrievable. Current nuclear fuel is imported.
3   The consumption of uranium for Taiwan was not reported, but any amount consumed will make them 100 percent dependent on outside resources.
4   "mt" means metric tons.
5   "Mine Production" means the metals content of mined ore.
6   Commencing with (12.3) in the text, the following calculations are used to derive (12.4).

$$Q_i = \left(\frac{1}{\beta_0}S_i^{-\beta_2}MC_i\right)^{\frac{1}{\beta_1}}, \qquad S_i > 0$$

$$E_T = (1-S_A)\varepsilon Q_A + (1-S_B)\varepsilon Q_B$$

$$\frac{dE_T}{dS_A} = (1-S_A)\varepsilon\frac{dQ_A}{dS_A} - \varepsilon Q_A + (1-S_B)\varepsilon\frac{dQ_B}{dS_A}$$

$$\frac{dE_T}{dS_A} = (1-S_A)\varepsilon\frac{dQ_A}{dS_A} + (1-S_B)\varepsilon\frac{dQ_B}{dQ_A}\frac{dQ_A}{dS_A} - \varepsilon Q_A$$

$$\frac{dE_T}{dS_A} = \varepsilon\frac{dQ_A}{dS_A}\left[1-S_A + (1-S_B)\frac{dQ_B}{dQ_A}\right] - \varepsilon Q_A$$

Assuming $S_B = 0$ and $dQ_B/dQ_A \cong -1$

$$\frac{dQ_A}{dS_A} = -\frac{\beta_2}{\beta_1}\frac{Q_A}{S_A}$$

$$\frac{dE_T}{dS_A} = \varepsilon Q_A\left[\frac{\beta_2}{\beta_1} - 1\right]$$

Alternatively, if $dQ_B/dQ_A \neq -1$

$$\frac{dE_T}{dS_A} = \varepsilon\frac{\beta_2 Q_A^\varepsilon}{\beta_1 S_A}\left[S_A\left(1-\frac{\beta_1}{\beta_2}\right) - \left(\frac{dQ_B}{dQ_A}+1\right)\right]$$

If $dQ_B/dQ_A \cong -1$ and $S_B > 0$

$$\frac{dE_T}{dS_A} = \varepsilon Q_A\left[\frac{\beta_2}{\beta_1}\cdot\frac{S_A-S_B}{S_A} - 1\right]$$

References

AAMA (American Automobile Manufacturers Association) (1993) *AAMA Motor Vehicle Facts and Figures '93*. Detroit, MI: Government Affairs Division.

Agras, J., Suri, V. and Chapman, D. (1994) Environment and trade: A review of the literature. Working paper 94–11. Ithaca, NY: Dept. of Agricultural, Resource, and Managerial Economics, Cornell University.

Birdsall, N. and Wheeler, D. (1992) Trade policy and industrial pollution in Latin America: Where are the pollution havens? In P. Low (ed.) *International Trade and the Environment*. World Bank discussion paper, No. 159. Washington, DC: World Bank.

Boden, T. A., Kanciruk, P. and Farrell, M. P. (1990) *Trends '90: A Compendium of Data on Global Change*. ORNL/CDIAC-36. Oak Ridge, TN: Carbon Dioxide Information Analysis Center, Environmental Sciences Division, Oak Ridge National Laboratory.

Brandon, C. and Ramankutty, R. (1993) *Toward an Environmental Strategy for Asia*. World Bank Discussion Paper #224. Washington DC: The World Bank.

Brown, L. R., Kane, H. and Ayres, E. (1993) *Vital Signs, 1993*. New York: Worldwatch Institute, W.W. Norton.

Chapman, D. (1991) Environmental standards and international trade in automobiles and copper: The case for a social tariff. *Natr. Resources J.* 31, 449–61.

Chapman, D. (1992) *Environmental Costs and NAFTA: Potential Impact on the US Economy and Selected Industries of the North American Free Trade Agreement*. Testimony, US International Trade Commission. November 18.

Chapman, D. (1994) *Notes on Nuclear Fuel Waste Accumulation Data*. Ithaca, NY: Cornell University.

Chira, S. (1985) Most Japan houses still lack comfort of those in the U.S. *New York Times*. October 30.

Cropper, M. L. and Oates, W. E. (1992) Environmental economics: A survey. *Journal of Economic Literature*, 30 (2), 675–740.

Dumagan, J. and Drennen, T. (1988) Resource Dependency, Japan. Compiled for the Seminar on the Economics of Resource Use. Ithaca, NY: Cornell University.

GATT (1992) *Trade and the Environment*. Geneva, Switzerland. GATT Secretariat.

Gore, A. (1994) Remarks Prepared for Delivery, Meeting of the GATT Plenary Committee, Marrakesh, Morocco. Washington, DC: White House Press Office, April 14.

Gray, W. B. and Shadbegian, R. J. (1993) Environmental regulation and manufacturing productivity at the plant level. Discussion paper CES 93-6. Washington, DC: Center for Economics Studies, US Department of Commerce.

Grossman, G. M. and Krueger, A. B. (1991) *Environmental Impacts of a North American Free Trade Agreement*. National Bureau of Economic Research Working Paper Series. No. 3914. Cambridge, MA: National Bureau of Economic Research.

Grossman, G. M. and Krueger, A. B. (1992) *Environmental Impacts of a North American Free Trade Agreement*. Discussion Papers in Economics, No. 158. Princeton, NJ: Woodrow Wilson School.

Hoffnar, E., Molina, D. and Parish, N. (1993) Mexico's maquiladora trade and the industrial flight hypothesis. *Journal of Borderland Studies*, 8 (2), 91–104.

Houghton, J. T., Jenkins, G. J. and Ephraums, J. J. (eds) (1990) *Climate Change: The IPCC Scientific Assessment*. Intergovernmental Panel on Climate Change. New York: Cambridge University Press.

Howarth, R. B., Schipper, L., Duerr, P. A. and Strom, S. (1991) Manufacturing energy use in eight OECD countries. *Energy Economics*, 135–142.

Lofty, G. J., Hillier, J. A., Cooke, S. A., Linley, K. A. and Singh, H. R. (eds.) (1992) *World Mineral Statistics, 1986–1990, Volume 1: Metals and Energy Production: Exports: Imports.* London: British Geological Survey.

Lopez, R. (1992) Environmental degradation and economic openness in LDCs: The poverty linkages. *American Journal of Agricultural Economics*, 74 (5), 1138–43.

Low, P. (ed.) (1992) *International Trade and the Environment.* World Bank Discussion Paper No. 159. Washington DC: The World Bank.

McClive, T. (1990) Estimation of global SO_2 emissions: An economist's perspective. Working Paper 90-1. Ithaca, NY: Dept. of Agricultural, Resource, and Managerial Economics, Cornell University.

Moller, D. (1984) Estimation of the global man-made sulphur emission. *Atmospheric Environment*, 18 (1), 19–27.

NAFTA. US International Trade Commission (1992) *North American Free Trade Agreement.* Washington, DC: September 6.

OECD (1992) *Uranium, 1991 Resources, Production, and Demand.* Paris: OECD Nuclear Energy Agency and the International Atomic Energy Agency.

Schnoor, J. L. (1992) *Earth Summit and Environmental Policy.* University of Iowa.

Strand, I. E., Bockstael, N. E. and Siegal, R. A. (1992) Trade, institutions, and preference for living marine resources. *American Journal of Agricultural Economics*, 74 (5), 1150–4.

UNCTAD (UN Conference on Trade and Development) (1991) *UNCTAD Commodity Yearbook.* New York: UNCTAD.

US Bureau of the Census (1993) Measuring the Productivity Impact of Pollution Abatement. *Statistical Brief* SB/93-13, US Bureau of the Census.

US Council of Economic Advisors (1993) Economic Report of the President together with the Annual Report of the Council of Economic Advisors. Washington, DC: US Government Printing Office.

USEIA (Energy Information Administration) (1992) *International Energy Annual 1991.* DOE/EIA-0219(91). Washington, DC: USEIA.

USITC (International Trade Commission) (1991) *International Agreements to Protect the Environment and Wildlife.* Publication No. 2351. Washington, DC: USITC.

USITC (International Trade Commission) (1992) *The Year in Trade: Operation of the Trade Agreements Program 1991, 43d Report.* Publication No. 2554. Washington, DC: USITC.

US Office of Technology Assessment (1994) *Industry, Technology, and the Environment.* Washington, DC: USOTA.

USTRO. (Trade Representative Office) (1992) *Review of US–Mexico Environmental Issues.* Washington, DC: Executive Office of the President. February 25.

World Bank (1992) *World Development Report 1992. Development and the Environment.* New York: Oxford University Press.

World Bank (1993) *World Tables, 1993 Edition.* Baltimore, MD: Johns Hopkins University Press.

WRI (World Resources Institute) (1992) *World Resources 1992–1993.* New York: Oxford University Press.

ZCCM (Zambia Consolidated Copper Mines Limited) (1992) *Annual Report.* Lusaka, Zambia: ZCCM.

13

Sharing Common Property Resources: The North Atlantic Cod Fishery

Daniel V. Gordon and K. K. Klein

The management of ocean fisheries is a troublesome area for governments. The difficulty occurs due to the failure of the market to provide the correct price signals to achieve an efficient outcome. It is complicated because of the many nations, coastal states, and distant water fishing nations who demand the right to harvest a share of the resource, and because the market fails to achieve an efficient solution because of the open access, common property nature of the resource (Gordon, 1954; Christy and Scott, 1965). Thus excess amounts of fishing effort are used in harvesting the stocks, causing an over-exploitation of the resource in both biological and economic terms. Although governments are well aware of these problems, in practice, international management policies generally have failed. The North Atlantic cod fishery is a case in point.

The management of the North Atlantic cod stocks is currently shared by Canada, which has jurisdiction within the 200-mile coastal exclusive economic zone (EEZ), and by the North West Atlantic Fisheries Organization (NAFO), which has jurisdiction within the adjacent high seas. Both parties share similar management objectives in the stated desire to sustain the stocks and achieve economic benefits, but the cooperation and enforcement of regulations have not been uniform. In short, the outcome of many years of Canadian and international management and regulation of the North Atlantic cod fishery has been the almost complete desolation of the stocks. In 1992, Canada initiated a moratorium on the cod fishery within the 200-mile EEZ and, in 1994, under pressure from Canada, NAFO imposed a moratorium on the southwestern cod stocks in the adjacent high seas.

The purpose of this chapter is twofold. First, we seek to review the international management practices that have been used to regulate the North Atlantic cod fishery and to determine why the policies have failed. Second, we discuss the obstacles and opportunities for management of the high seas cod fishery.

Economics of market failure

Before we can discuss and evaluate the problems of managing the North Atlantic cod fishery, it is important to describe the economic factors that give rise

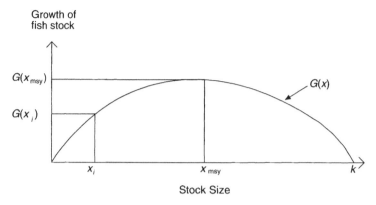

Figure 13.1   Growth function of the stock of fish

to over-exploitation of the resource and thus dictate management intervention. This will set the stage for the analysis as well as identify those factors that governments must address to achieve a better outcome in both biological and economic terms.

Even in a very simple model, the analysis must consider both biological and economic factors that affect the fishery (Conrad, 1994). We define the carrying capacity of the habitat as the size of the stock or biomass of fish that would exist in the absence of harvesting. An important biological parameter is the growth of the fish stock at stock levels less than the carrying capacity of the fishery. A simple assumption is that the growth in the stock of fish depends only on the size of the stock itself. At very low stock levels and plentiful but limited food supply, growth in the stock of fish increases with the size of the stock. As the size of the stock of fish increases, increased competition for the limited food supply will cause the growth of the stock eventually to reach a maximum and then to decline to zero as the stock reaches the carrying capacity of the habitat.

Based on this simple model, growth as a function of the stock can be shown graphically (figure 13.1). Let k be the carrying capacity of the habitat in the absence of harvesting. The growth curve $G(X)$ shows the change in the rate of growth of the stock as the stock size changes. At any given stock size (X), the level $G(X)$ is available for harvesting without depleting the stock of fish. A harvest level less than $G(X)$ will allow both for harvest and for increases in stock size, whereas harvest levels greater than $G(X)$ will cause a decline in the stock of fish. As long as harvest does not exceed growth, harvest levels can be maintained on a sustained yield basis. What is more, in the absence of any economic information on harvesting, the maximum harvest, $G(X_{msy})$, is obtained at stock size X_{msy}, which is defined as the level of maximum sustainable yield.

Prior to the mid 1970s, the principal objective for the fisheries was one of maintaining total harvest levels at the maximum sustainable yield. This appeared to be a simple and effective way to manage the fishery, requiring only biological information about the size of the stock and its net growth rate. However, the economic structure of open access common property fisheries is unlikely to lead

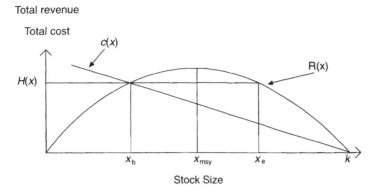

Figure 13.2 Bioeconomic and optimal economic equilibrium

to an equilibrium output level equivalent to maximum sustainable yield. In addition, there is no economic justification for such an objective.

Following Munro (1980), we can assume that the demand for fish is perfectly elastic, implying a constant price for fish. If harvesting is carried out on a sustained yield basis, then total revenue available from the fishery is defined as price times the quantity of fish harvested. For simplicity, we let output price equal one. This allows the net growth function, $G(X)$ in figure 13.1, to be defined also as the total revenue generated on a sustained yield basis. To complete the economic model, we must consider the cost of harvesting. A simple assumption is that the cost per unit of fishing effort (where fishing effort is the amount of labor and capital used in harvesting) is constant, but that the amount of fishing effort required to harvest increases as the stock size decreases. This argument is based on the notion that the more plentiful the supply of fish, the less effort needed to harvest. The total revenue, $R(X)$, and cost of harvest, $C(X)$, are shown in figure 13.2. The downward sloping total cost curve represents the decreased effort needed to harvest fish as stock size increases. It is also important to keep in mind that economists define the cost function to represent the price that the inputs would receive in their best alternative use. In other words, the cost curve represents the true opportunity cost of the labor and capital used in harvesting fish.

In an open access fishery, fishing vessels will harvest the stock if the revenue generated from doing so at least covers the true opportunity cost of the labor and capital used in the fishing effort. As seen in figure 13.2, as harvesting is initiated, stocks decline and total costs increase, but revenue exceeds the true cost of harvesting. This indicates that a profit or a rent is generated by the use of labor and capital in harvesting. In other words, labor and capital are earning a rate of return in excess of what is necessary to keep them fishing. This profit encourages increased fishing effort as fishing vessels try to maximize their profit.

Note that no one fishing vessel has an incentive to conserve the fish resource, which would increase the stock of fish and make it easier (and less costly) for other vessels to capture fish. Consequently, single vessel conservation efforts are useless.

Fishing effort will continue to expand, causing costs to increase, until all economic profit is exhausted (where total revenue is equal to total cost), because the expansion of fishing effort will continue as long as labor and capital inputs receive a greater return through fishing than could be earned in their best alternative use. The point of equilibrium is reached (in figure 13.2) at a stock size of x_b, and is defined as the open access equilibrium that would prevail in the absence of regulatory controls on the fishery. Economists refer to this point as a bioeconomic equilibrium, i.e. the unrestricted equilibrium that would prevail based on the interaction of the biology and economics of the fishery.

An important question to ask is whether the bioeconomic equilibrium is also the optimal economic equilibrium We address this question directly in figure 13.2. The level of harvest, $H(x)$, obtained at the bioeconomic equilibrium (i.e. stock size x_b) could also have been harvested at a larger stock size, x_e. In other words, the same level of harvest could be obtained with a larger stock of fish and much less fishing effort. Consequently, the bioeconomic equilibrium is both economically and biologically inefficient because excess fishing effort is used in harvesting and results in over-exploitation of the fish stock.

If the objective of government intervention is not only to sustain the stocks but also to maximize economic profit, the optimal harvest level is obtained at a stock level of x_e (i.e. the greatest distance between total revenue and total cost), in figure 13.2. The difference between revenue and cost for the harvest up to this point represents the maximum profit possible in the fishery. Since the cost curve represents the true cost of labor and capital, profit generated in the fishery can be considered as the return to the fish stock itself and should be collected by the owners of the resource.

In coastal state territorial waters, the ownership of the fishery is not an issue; however, on the high seas ownership is the main issue (Munro, 1990). It is worth pointing out that, even for coastal states, the ability to capture profit is not a trivial matter and, it is fair to say, that for the North Atlantic cod fishery, profits, in general, have been non-existent.

It is important to note that the optimal economic equilibrium is characterized by a larger stock level than the maximum sustainable yield level. Consequently, economic rationale calls for a more conservative management strategy in terms of stock size than required under the objective of maximizing sustainable yield.

Although it is simple and static in nature, this model helps to identify the most important management issues in fisheries economics. Furthermore, if the fishery is open access and unregulated, the results are predictable: excess fishing effort, over-exploitation of the stock and dissipation of profit earned in the fishery. The biological problem with such an outcome is that there exist no natural checks or restrictions to ensure that the bioeconomic equilibrium occurs at a positive stock level. In other words, the unregulated interaction of biological and economic factors could well lead to complete depletion of the stock. The economic problem is that unregulated fishing leads to all profits being dissipated. In the long run, neither the fishers nor the "owners" of the resource capture the profit.

The second important issue identified by the model is that the main cause of the dilemma of open access is the excess fishing effort used in harvesting the fish stock. In general, government policies to achieve an improvement over the bio-economic equilibrium must restrict fishing effort. Moreover, it is not sufficient for government policy to concentrate only on rebuilding stock levels, say by imposing total allowable catch (TAC) quotas, because if profits are earned in the fishery, fishing effort will increase and competition among fishers for a share of the restricted harvest will drive profits to zero.

Government policy must control both harvest level and fishing effort to achieve the maximum economic benefits from the fishery. To do so, governments must have information on the stock and growth of the species and the economic parameters that characterize both revenue and cost of harvesting (Dupont and Phipps, 1989).

One additional problem governments must face is the distribution of the share of the harvest among the different agents. In coastal state territorial waters, the government must distribute the potential harvest among its own fishers. On the high seas, the distribution of the harvest is made more difficult because many nations demand a share. As management policies increase stock levels, causing profits to increase, the number of nations demanding a share can also be expected to increase.

Management of North Atlantic cod stocks: 1950–1977

The cod stock in the North Atlantic is really a complex formed by a number of distinct cod groups. These different cod groups have been subject to different management strategies in the past. Figure 13.3 provides a map of the North Atlantic region that has been subject to Canadian and NAFO cod management policies. For example, the Northern cod stock, which plays such an important role in both the Canadian inshore fishery and the international offshore fishery, has been designated by biologists as the 2K3JL cod stock. An interesting charac-teristic of ocean groundfish, like the cod, is that they tend to concentrate in waters above the continental shelf. In figure 13.3, the continental shelf off the Canadian coast is designated by the dotted line. The Canadian shelf extends some distance out to sea, and in the case of the Grand Bank, this extension exceeds the currently recognized coastal state 200-mile EEZ. Furthermore, the shelf stretches even further out to sea in an area called the Flemish Cap. The large Canadian continen-tal shelf has attracted fishers from many nations for several centuries.

After World War II, Canada, USA, and several European countries formed the International Commission for the Northwest Atlantic Fisheries (ICNAF). The purpose of the ICNAF was to collect scientific data and to recommend manage-ment policies to member countries that would allow a maximum sustainable yield harvest level (ICNAF, 1965). Up to the 1970s, the only management tool used by the ICNAF to regulate the fishery was a restriction on mesh size to allow younger fish to escape capture. Subject to this restriction, it was an open access fishery (Munro and McCorquodale, 1981).

Prior to 1977, Canada's territorial waters extended no more than 12 miles to sea. Within this region, Canada maintained exclusive management control over

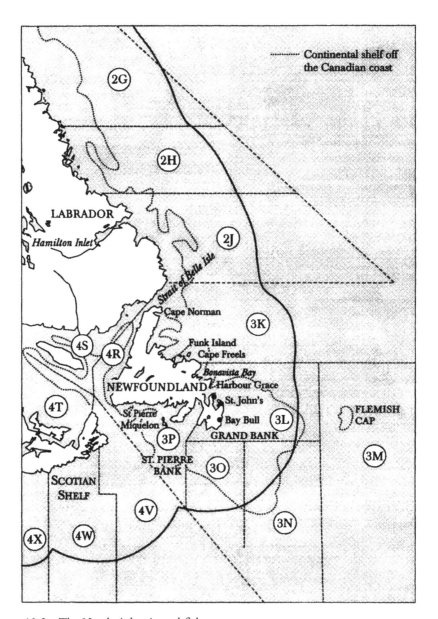

Figure 13.3 The North Atlantic cod fishery

cod stocks; its interests were primarily in the inshore cod fishery. However, the inshore cod fishery was based on the segment of the Northern cod stock that had escaped offshore harvest and had migrated inshore during the late spring and early summer to feed. Consequently, Canada had a very strong interest in the establishment of the ICNAF and, in particular, policies imposed for regulating the Northern (2J3KL) cod stock. At this time, both Canadian and ICNAF management goals were consistent in striving for a maximum sustainable yield harvest level.

The first major problem for ICNAF management of the cod fishery occurred during the late 1960s and early 1970s when there was a substantial increase in fishing effort directed at the offshore Northern cod stocks. With expanding demand for fish products, fish prices had increased, causing increases in revenue and profits to the fishery, and thus encouraging greater fishing effort. The problem for the ICNAF was that policies were not in place to allow for a regulated reduction in fishing effort if fishing pressure on the stocks became excessive. At this time, the ICNAF was little more than an advisory group to member countries and lacked the policies and ability to enforce management decisions.

Munro (1980) reported that, as a measure of this increased fishing effort, the offshore fishing vessels in the ICNAF region increased from a total of 500,000 tons at the end of the 1950s to over 1.5 million tons by the mid-1970s. The expansion in offshore fishing effort resulted in a substantial increase in harvest levels which, in hindsight, were larger than maximum sustainable yield levels and led to a drastic decline in the Northern cod stock. This decline precipitated a crisis in the Canadian inshore fishery.

In table 13.1, the Northern cod harvests for the distant water fleet and for the Canadian inshore fleet are reported for various years from 1956 to 1976. In the late 1950s, Canada held the largest share of the cod fishery, about 60 percent, but this declined to about 15 percent by the mid-1970s. On the other hand, in 1968,

Table 13.1   Harvests of Northern cod: 1956–1976 (000's tonnes)

Year	Total harvest	Canada		Distant water nations	
		Harvest	*Share (%)*	*Harvest*	*Share (%)*
1956	300.5	183.1	60.9	117.4	39.1
1960	393.6	164.7	41.8	228.9	58.2
1964	562.0	141.5	25.2	420.5	74.8
1968	783.2	123.4	15.8	659.8	84.2
1972	454.6	66.5	14.6	388.1	85.4
1974	372.6	36.1	9.7	336.5	90.3
1975	287.5	42.7	14.8	245.0	85.2
1976	214.2	63.0	29.7	151.2	70.6

Source: ICNAF, *Statistical Bulletin*, Economics Branch, Fisheries and Oceans Canada, St John's (various years).

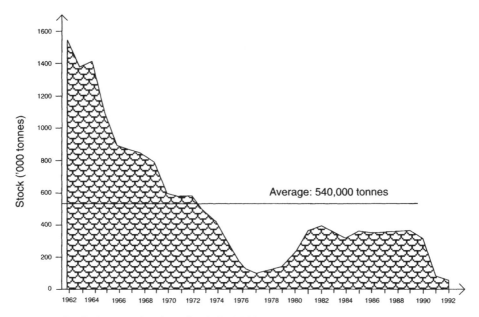

Figure 13.4 Estimates of cod stock 1962–1992

the distant water nations, with increased fishing effort, recorded their largest ever harvest of about 660,000 tonnes of cod. It is clear that the increased fishing effort by the foreign fleets directed at the Northern cod stocks resulted in a substantial increase in harvest levels, thus reducing the stock and causing a serious decline in the Canadian inshore cod harvest.

In an attempt to reduce fishing effort on this stock, in 1973, the ICNAF introduced TAC quotas for cod in the 2J, 3K, 3L, 3N, 3O and 3P areas of its jurisdiction; see figure 13.3. The ICNAF management policy at this time was based on a maximum sustainable yield harvest level. For the years 1973–5, the TAC quota was set in excess of the then accepted maximum sustainable yield of 550,000 tonnes. However, during this period, an average harvest of only 300,000 tonnes was landed. In 1976, the TAC was set at 300,000 tonnes, less than half its 1973 level of 665,500 tonnes, but again harvest fell to just over 200,000 tonnes. In 1977, the TAC was cut again to 160,000 tonnes, roughly equal to that year's harvest of 172,800 tonnes (ICNAF, 1978).

Based on the simple model presented earlier, these data are consistent with setting quotas at levels thought to give maximum sustainable yield (X_{msy} in figure 13.2) but with actual stock levels to the left of that which would provide such a yield. The effect of these actions was to drive stocks to ever lower levels (to x_b or even lower in figure 13.2), which not only dissipated economic profits in the industry but also put the long-term survival of the entire fishery in jeopardy.

It appears that a policy of maximum sustainable yield was not adequate to manage the fishery. One of the problems was that accurate measures of maximum sustainable yield were not available and it turned out that TAC levels were set more in line with harvest levels than with stock levels. It should be noted that accurately estimating stock levels is very difficult, and estimates are not *ex-ante*, which is more useful for policy purposes, but rather, *ex-post*. The inability accurately to forecast stock level was a major handicap to ICNAF regulation of the cod fishery.

In figure 13.4, the estimated stock of Northern cod is graphed for the period 1962–1992. A noticeable trend in the graph is the continuous decline in the stock between 1962 and 1977. For this period, it is clear that the policies and regulations of the ICNAF were not sufficient to halt the decline in the stock of Northern cod.

Management of North Atlantic cod stocks: 1977–1994

Under the Third Law of the Sea conference, sponsored by the UN, Canada and many other coastal states extended economic jurisdiction over the coastal seas to include a 200-mile EEZ off the coast. Unfortunately, this EEZ did not include all the continental shelf; therefore Canada's problems with distant water fishing nations and international management of the cod stock were not over (Mitchell, 1978). However, it was estimated that the EEZ accounted for 95 percent of the total stock of Northern cod fish (Canada, 1981). The Third Law of the Sea conference allowed coastal states complete jurisdiction over fisheries management within the 200-mile EEZ. In other words, the EEZ transferred ownership over fishery resources to the exclusive right of coastal states (McRae and Munro, 1989). The only restriction was that any stocks of fish designated as surplus by the coastal state had to be allocated to distant water fishing nations. Not surprisingly, coastal states, including Canada, worked very hard to exclude distant water fishing nations from the 200-mile EEZ. It is worth noting, however, that some coastal states (e.g. the Pacific Island countries) continued to rely on foreign fleets to harvest offshore tuna stocks (Doulman, 1987).

With the development of the EEZ, the ICNAF was dissolved and a new commission, the Northwest Atlantic Fisheries Organization (NAFO), was formed to manage cod stocks on the continental shelf outside the Canadian 200-mile EEZ and stocks that straddled the boundary of the EEZ. Canada maintained jurisdiction over the Northern cod stock. The Law of the Sea conference encouraged cooperation among coastal states and distant water fishing nations and required that management policy within the EEZ and adjacent high seas be consistent (Munro, 1989).

Two factors relating to the introduction of the 200-mile EEZ are of particular interest. First, with unilateral property rights over fish in the new EEZ, it was concluded that the problems caused by the international management of the cod stocks could be quickly corrected and Canada would reap the economic benefits (Copes, 1978). The optimism was so great at this time that the Canadian Department of Fisheries and Oceans published reports with such titles as "A Fisheries Success Story" (Canada, 1980). However, this euphoria was short lived. Second, nobody knew what would be the fate of the large non-Canadian distant water fishing fleet. Canada made some allowance for foreign nations fishing vessels within the EEZ under the assumption that this would provide leverage over foreign fishing in the adjacent high seas.

The problem of foreign fleets is not exclusive to Northern cod. In the Bering Sea, the extension of the 200-mile EEZ by the USSR and USA forced foreign fishing vessels into a small international sea between the two countries known as the "donut hole." Not surprisingly, pressure on fish stocks in the "donut hole" increased substantially.

It was widely acknowledged that previous international management of the Northern cod fishery had been a failure. The cost was borne most heavily by the Canadian inshore fishery. At about the same time as Canada's exclusive fishing zone was extended to 200 miles, the Canadian government also shifted its management objective for ground fisheries from one of maximum sustainable yield to an attempt to maximize the economic benefit of the resource. This would increase stock size to X_e in figure 13.2. Under heavy pressure from Canada, the ICNAF also changed policy objectives. The new policy included a harvest formula known as the $F_{0.1}$ rule (Munro, 1980). For cod, this rule meant an annual catch of about 20 percent of the stock. Although a very rough measure to approximate the harvest which would give the maximum sustainable economic yield, it none-theless led to a far more conservative approach to preserving stock levels than did the maximum sustainable yield approach. However, even under the alter-native management objective, the "estimated" stock of Northern cod continued to decline.

Following the implementation of the 1977 EEZ, estimated stocks of Northern cod appear to have increased (figure 13.4); Canadian harvests grew substantially to reach a maximum of 245,000 tonnes in 1988. Of course, this was at the expense of the foreign fleets. The problem for Canada was that fishery policy was designed not so much for optimal fishery management, but rather to develop an industry of last resort to encourage employment in the Atlantic provinces (Tobin, 1994). Canada still maintained an objective of maximizing economic profit from the fishery, but a policy of almost unlimited free access to the fishery resulted in little profit earned.

With foreign nations' fleets pushed outside the EEZ, the pressure on straddling cod stocks increased (Miles and Burke, 1989). Munro argued that, at least initially, Canada and NAFO cooperated in setting TAC quotas and in managing the Atlantic cod fishery. However, as a direct result of Canada's policy to eliminate foreign fishing within the EEZ, this cooperation deteriorated.

The level of the Canadian quota for foreign nations' harvest of Northern cod (2K3JL) for the period 1984 to 1994 is shown in table 13.2. This quota was set at 20,000 tonnes in 1984, declined to zero from 1988 to 1990 and increased to about 2,000 tonnes in 1991–92. A moratorium on all cod fishing was imposed in 1993 and 1994. In spite of the quota, foreign harvest substantially exceeded the quota in each year except 1994. Not only was the Canadian quota ignored by NAFO members, but NAFO imposed quota levels also were not maintained. For example, the NAFO quota for 3NO cod (figure 13.3) for the 1986 to 1989 period was set at an average annual harvest of 15,400 tonnes but the harvest averaged

Table 13.2 Foreign quota and harvest of Northern cod
(2J3KL) (000's tonnes): 1984–1994

Year	Quota	Harvest
1984	20.0	28.6
1985	16.3	43.3
1986	16.3	67.6
1987	9.5	36.1
1988	0.0	26.8
1990	0.0	38.8
1991	2.3	25.5
1992	2.1	24.8
1993	moratorium	14.9
1994	moratorium	0

Source: Department of Fisheries and Oceans, Canada.

almost 25,000 tonnes over this period. After 1989, NAFO policies were more successful in maintaining catch levels in line with quota allocations.

One additional problem arose for NAFO management of Atlantic cod, and was caused by non-NAFO flagged vessels fishing off the Southwest bank of the continental shelf. These vessels failed to abide by restrictions on mesh size or NAFO TAC levels. This was a particular irritant to Canada, which suspected that the vessels were supported by some NAFO members attempting to avoid fisheries regulations.

In addition to the over-fishing, it became clear that the scientific estimates of stock size during the 1980s were overly optimistic. By 1992, the estimates of the stock of cod in the North Atlantic were at their historic lowest recorded levels. Canada imposed a moratorium on the Northern cod within the EEZ in 1992. However, stock size continued to decrease and the moratorium was imposed on all cod stocks within the EEZ (Canada, 1994). In addition, NAFO responded in early 1994 by imposing a moratorium on the Southwest cod stock in its jurisdiction. Although the future of Atlantic cod is bleak, one can view the problem as an opportunity to start anew with fisheries policies to allow for an optimal management of the cod fishery (Canada, 1993).

Obstacles for future management of North Atlantic cod

The problems in management of North Atlantic cod can be separated into three general areas:

1 population dynamics of the codfish
2 allocation of fishing rights, and
3 allocation of fishing benefits.

Population dynamics of the codfish

The simple models of economic equilibrium for fish stocks shown in figures 13.1 and 13.2 imply that once the relationship between stock size and growth rate is known, the maximum sustainable biological or economic yields can be selected. It also implies that these relationships are symmetric and constant over time. Although such models are useful for understanding the basic characteristics of the fishery, management policy based on such models can be seriously biased (Munro and Scott, 1993). For example, if the growth curve in figure 13.1 is skewed to the left and becomes more skewed over time, then the growth of the stock relative to the size of the stock becomes a much more important policy parameter at low stock levels and as time progresses. The direct implication is that a depleted stock would take much longer to recover. In addition, if the growth curve was of that nature, a conservative harvest would be required to maintain adequate stock levels.

The implications of a non-symmetric growth curve for the fish stock may be more serious than just a longer recovery period from stock depletion. The consequences of non-symmetric growth may be irreversibilities in the size of the stock itself. In figure 13.1, irreversibilities would be illustrated by the growth curve intersecting the horizontal axis at positive but low stock levels. Some empirical evidence for such a possibility does exist, e.g. the stock of cod off Southern Greenland has never recovered after being depleted by excessive harvesting in the early 1960s.

The point of this discussion is that without reliable estimates of the stock of fish and a complete understanding of the dynamics of the growth of the fish population, including the minimum stock levels needed to avoid irreversibilities, an optimal management strategy is not possible. What makes this problem so intractable is that we will never know with certainty the size of the stock simply because it cannot be observed. Estimates of fish stocks will always be subject to error and uncertainty. The population dynamics of the cod stock is complicated and depends on the effects of changes in water temperature, natural predators, diseases and other important factors. Codfish cannot be considered in isolation from other species when considering management policies. They depend on stocks of Capelin and other fish species for their food. These fish, in turn, are dependent on still other species for their survival. The relationships among these multi-species is poorly understood and provides little basis for effective management of codfish stocks.

Allocation of fishing rights

It is clear that some mechanism is necessary for allocating available codfish in the North Atlantic. The current sorry state of the fishery is ample evidence that high (unsustainable) quotas, open access to the fishery, and the non-enforcement of quota allocations have led to exploitation and possible ruination of the resource. Many countries have a demonstrable interest in the resource. Canada, for example, has endeavoured to protect its economic interest by declaring and en-forcing the 200-mile EEZ, but other countries also have a justifiable stake in the outcome.

What makes this such an obstacle to management is that the three major forms of setting property rights for fishing in the North Atlantic cod fishery – open access, international control of fishing rights, and sole country control of fishing rights – have already been attempted. Unfortunately, in terms of maintaining stock levels or in generating economic profits, all three organizational methods have failed.

Nevertheless, some method needs to be developed which would ensure survival of the fishery for future generations by strictly limiting the number of codfish which can be caught each year. The countries that have a long-term interest in the fishery need to agree on and respect some allocation and enforcement mechanism for the available fish. Then, within each country, some mechanism must be found for allocating that country's share among private or public operators who will fish the stocks.

Allocation of benefits

A question separate from who gets to catch the fish is who gets the benefits. Economic profits generated from fishing activities do not necessarily have to go to those who do the fishing. However, distribution of benefits has historically been based on fishing rights and makes an agreement on alternative procedures for allocating the benefits difficult.

The allocation of benefits is essentially a question of equity: which countries get a share, how much goes to each country, how much goes to various groups within each country, and what proportion goes to this generation as opposed to future generations? These are important issues, not only for efficiency in operat-ing the fishery, but also and especially for equity. Distributive justice demands a consideration of the rights of those who have little opportunity to present their demands or to defend themselves; the economic proceeds from the North Atlantic cod fishery need not (and indeed, should not) go to merely those who are the strongest militarily or economically.

Opportunities for future management

Although many problems beset management of the North Atlantic fishery, par-ticularly those resulting from apparent mismanagement in the past, opportunities do exist for more sustainable management schemes in the future (Munro, 1993). These must be based on solid biological, economic, and ecological research as well as improved international cooperation over this important resource. The better our knowledge concerning the growth and dynamics of codfish stocks and how codfish interact with other species in their environment, the better will be management schemes. Increased scientific effort in ecological modelling and data collection is needed to understand the role of codfish as part of a large system in the ocean.

Although increased research is warranted, an even more important factor is how this information is used. For many years, biologists provided the best possible estimates of stock size and growth of the codfish. However, such information is irrelevant if the fishery management scheme is designed more as a program to maintain employment in coastal areas than as a fisheries program to maintain fish stocks and generate economic profits. Often, predictions of declining stocks have been ignored to maintain short-run employment benefits.

Although improved estimates of stock size can be achieved with increased research, stock uncertainty will remain a characteristic of the industry. Efficient management policy must allow for this uncertainty. Economic models that account for both the uncertainty in stock size and the biological dynamics of the cod fish would certainly aid in developing efficient management strategies.

Previous management efforts in the North Atlantic have involved both international and Canadian administration. However, third party vessels have been allowed to avoid TAC quotas and restrictions on mesh size. Clearly, it is vitally important that someone have authority, not only to set allowable catch levels, but also to be in a position to enforce them. The problem of allowing one country exclusive property rights is that it creates incentives to use the resource for rather short-term economic gains, especially when increasing catch stimulates employment levels in depressed areas. However, an international joint commission would have the authority of the world community and could lead to better enforcement. The most important point is to design an allocation system that protects the long-term sustainability of the fish stock. It is a secondary matter of who gets to fish and who gets the rewards. Given the uncertainty in stock size, an efficient allocation system demands a safety first criterion when setting TAC quotas (UN Food and Agriculture Organization, 1994). Moreover, ecological principles ought to be applied in setting TAC levels to preserve the fish stock for the very long term. This also would permit long-term maximization of economic yield, though not necessarily for a single country or for a single group of fishers.

Once TAC levels have been determined, an allocation scheme must be designed to share the catch among fishers. Economic models can provide a description of the best possible market outcome. The challenge for regulators is to set up rules to achieve this. One possibility is to sell or auction the right to fish. This would lead to improved efficiency and allow the capture of economic profit generated in the fishery, which could then be allocated in any manner deemed desirable.

The rewards from fishing could be distributed in a more fair manner. Social philosophers and economists have discussed the idea of distributive justice whereby the notion of fairness can lead to a higher overall level of utility, i.e. not just making fishers better off (Broome, 1992). Consuming countries, as well as producing countries, legitimately could have a claim to a share of the profits. What may be even more important, future generations also have a claim to the profits (Barry, 1978). The current social calculus is often one of dismissing or ignoring the consequences of current actions on future generations. If we follow a social rule that the current generation should have no right to leave fewer resources than they received, it must be true that the actions of the current generation can not be allowed to disadvantage future generations.

Intergenerational transfers of resources raise additional problems. If current harvest is reduced to increase future stocks, a cost is imposed on the current generation and a benefit accrues to future generations. Because costs and benefits occur at different times, proper decision making requires that these values be discounted to a common period. The choice of an appropriate discount rate is fundamental (Cline, 1992). In the fishery, standard discount rates of 5 percent or 10 percent, which are commonly applied to short-lived private or public capital investments, may not be appropriate where very long-term effects are also important. High rates disadvantage future generations because far away benefits add practically nothing to the present value of the stream of benefits. Cline (1992) and others strongly suggest discount rates of 1 percent to 1.5 percent as more justifiable for projects which effect changes in the environment, such as changes in fish stock. A low discount rate will encourage more investment for the future and, in the fishery, suggest a more conservative harvesting policy.

The collapse of the North Atlantic cod fishery is the result of both international and Canadian mismanagement of this once abundant resource. Notwithstanding the seriousness and perhaps irreversibility of low stock levels, there now exists an opportunity to initiate management schemes to allow for enforcement of new polices and regulations to ensure adequate stock levels, now and for the future, and to provide for an equitable distribution of the benefits generated in the fishery.

References

Barry, B. (1978) Intergenerational justice in energy policy. In D. MacLean and P. G. Brown (eds), *Energy and the Future*. Philadelphia: Temple University Press.

Broome, J. (1992) *Counting the Cost of Global Warming*. Cambridge, UK: The White Horse Press.

Canada, Department of Fisheries and Oceans (1993) *Charting a New Course: Towards the Fishery of the Future*. DFO/4904, November, Ottawa.

Canada, Department of Fisheries and Oceans (1994) *Report on the Status of Ground Fish Stocks in the Canadian Northwest Atlantic*. Stock Status Report 9414.

Christy, F. T. and Scott, A. (1965) *The Common Wealth in Ocean Fisheries*. Baltimore: The Johns Hopkins Press.

Cline, W. R. (1992) *The Economics of Global Warming*. Washington, DC: Institute for International Economics.

Conrad, J. M. (1994) Bioeconomic models of the fishery. In *Handbook of Environmental Economics*, D. W. Bromley (ed.) Oxford: Blackwell Publishers, 405–32.

Copes, P. (1978) Canada's Atlantic coast fisheries: Policy development and the impact of extended jurisdiction. *Canadian Public Policy*, iv (2) Spring, 155–71.

Doulman, D. J. (1987) Licensing distant-water tuna fleets in Papua New Guinea. *Marine Policy*, 11 (2), 16–28.

Dupont, D. P. and Phipps, S. A. (1989) *Efficiency Gains Versus Employment Losses: An Empirical Evaluation of Alternative Fishery Regulation Proposals*, Working Paper No. 89-01. Halifax: Department of Economics, Dalhousie University.

Gordon, H. S. (1954) The economic theory of a common property resource: The fishery. *Journal of Political Economy*, 62, April, 124–42.

ICNAF (International Commission for the NorthWest Atlantic Fisheries) (1965) *Research Bulletin Number Two*. Dartmouth, Canada.

ICNAF (1978) *Redbook*. Dartmouth, Canada, August.

ICNAF (International Commission for the North West Atlantic Fisheries) (various years) *Statistical Bulletin*. Dartmouth, Canada.

McRae, D. and Munro, G. (1989) Coastal state "rights" within the 200-mile exclusive economic zone. In P. A. Neher, R. Arnason and N. Mollett (eds) *Rights Based Fishing*. Dordrecht: Kluwer Academic, 97–112.

Miles, E. L. and Burke, W. T. (1989) Pressures on the United Nations Convention on the Law of the Sea of 1982 arising from new fisheries conflicts: The problem of straddling stocks. *Ocean Development and International Law*, 20 (4), 343–57.

Mitchell, C. H. (1978) The 200-mile limit: New issues, old problems for Canada's East coast fisheries. *Canadian Public Policy*, iv (2) Spring, 172–83.

Munro, G. (1980) *A Promise of Abundance: Extended Fisheries Jurisdiction and the Newfoundland Economy*, Economic Council of Canada, EC 22–86.

Munro, G. (1989) Coastal states and distant-water fishing nation relations: An economist's perspective. *Marine Fisheries Review*, 51 (1), 3–10.

Munro, G. (1990) Extended jurisdiction and the management of Pacific highly migratory species. *Ocean Development and International Law*, 21 (3), 289–307.

Munro, G. (1993) *Issues in Fisheries Management under the New Law of the Sea*, Discussion Paper No. 93–20. Vancouver: Department of Economics, The University of British Columbia.

Tobin, B., Federal Fisheries Minister, Canada (1994) *Canadian Press*, July 25.

UN Food and Agriculture Organization (1994) *The Precautionary Approach to Fisheries with Reference to Straddling Fish Stocks and Highly Migratory Fish Stocks*, New York.

14

Redirecting Energy Policy in the USA to Address Global Warming

Timothy D. Mount

Environmentalists are becoming increasingly skeptical about the validity of recommendations made by economists about environmental issues. Typically, economists believe that unbounded economic growth can continue well into the next century, and that markets (when free from artificial distortions) are efficient mechanisms for governing the use of natural resources such as fossil fuels. Most environmentalists would challenge these assertions. While problems stemming from market failures are recognized by economists, they also believe that solutions to these problems can and will be found. There is no need at the present time to reformulate the established methods of doing economic analysis. Marginal corrections to the existing system are all that is required. The primary objective of this paper is to question this conclusion by considering how energy policy in the USA is dealing with the problem of global warming.

First, four standard limitations of markets are discussed, and the optimism about continued economic growth expressed by economists is based on a belief that governments will be able to correct these deficiencies in the performance of markets. Environmentalists, on the other hand, believe that the effectiveness of governments in modifying markets is decreasing because the influence of competitive markets in the global economy is expanding.

The focus is then put on energy and the history of concerns about running out of supplies of different fuels. High discount rates and omitted environmental costs both contribute to keeping energy prices low in the short run and to reducing the incentives for developing alternative sources of energy. Since there is growing scientific evidence that global warming places a constraint on the rate at which fossil fuels should be used, there is an increase in the social premium for the development of "backstop" technologies and for more restraint in the use of fossil fuels. In spite of this evidence, current forecasts of emissions of greenhouse gases (GHGs), show substantial increases in all regions of the world except the former Soviet Union and Eastern Europe.

Most of the forecasted growth in energy use will be in low- and middle-income countries. Assuming that a policy for stabilizing global emissions of GHGs is desirable, considerations of equity imply that emissions should be reduced in high-income countries to compensate for some growth in low-income countries.

This is the basic predicament for high-income countries that led to the agreement at the UN Earth Summit in 1992 to stabilize emissions at 1990 levels. Since emissions in the USA currently account for over 20 percent of the global emissions of GHGs from fossil fuels, it is argued that the USA must take leadership in the formation of policy for global warming. Without a major redirection of energy policy in the USA, it is highly unlikely that other countries will be willing to make effective changes.

Placing environmental limits on emissions of GHGs will require widespread increases in energy efficiency. For high-income countries, it will also be necessary to have public support for making sacrifices that benefit low-income countries. Current evidence in the USA is that income inequities are growing within the country, and that the public's support of government welfare programs for redistributing income is shrinking. The conclusion (on page 322) is that the government will not be able to build political support in the USA for effective policies to deal with global warming unless public attitudes to energy and equity change.

The objective is then (on pages 322–7) to develop an economic explanation of why the views of economists and environmentalists about energy are so different. It is argued that Hotelling's (1931) rule for managing the extraction of a non-renewable resource underestimates the true value of fossil fuels. Even if the market discount rate equaled the social discount rate, the size of Hotelling's scarcity premium is small until the remaining stock of a resource is low. For most of the economic life of a resource, the price is effectively determined by the direct costs of production. An alternative approach is proposed using Marshall's (1920) concept of nature's stored-up treasures. This approach places the focus on the cost of replacing fossil fuels, and raises the question of whether the rents from fossil fuels are being used wisely under current policies.

Finally we summarize the evidence about current energy policy in the USA. Given public attitudes, it is unlikely that effective policies for addressing global warming will be implemented. For this reason, a series of alternative strategies are presented that address the problem of global warming indirectly. These include improving air quality in urban areas and forming a partnership for improving energy efficiency with a low-income country such as China.

Four chronic problems

In any textbook on resource economics, limits in the ability of markets to reach socially efficient solutions are recognized. The issue is how seriously these limits are taken in actual practice and what measures are being taken to correct them. Attitudes among economists on this issue vary. On the one hand, a leading neoclassical economist, Robert Solow (1992), is relatively optimistic about the current situation. His opening remarks in a paper presented to Resources for the Future on non-renewable resources state "You may be relieved to know that this talk will not be a harangue about the intrinsic incompatibility of economic growth and concern for the natural environment. Nor will it be a plea for the strict conservation of non-renewable resources" (p. 5). In contrast, Herman Daly and John Cobb (1989) consider that the corrective measures proposed by economists "are ad hoc corrections introduced as needed to save appearances, like the epicycles of Ptolemaic astronomy" (p. 37). A major reason for these different attitudes is the amount of faith that they have in the future ability of governments to solve economic and environmental problems. The optimism of economists comes from a belief that appropriate corrections to markets could be made, and the pessimism of skeptics comes from a belief that corrections will not be made. The evidence about global warming, presented in the next two sections, suggests that the skeptics are correct for this particular environmental problem.

In Solow's paper, four limitations of competitive markets are identified. The differences between Solow's optimism over the ability to overcome these limitations and the concerns raised by Daly and Cobb are reviewed in the following discussion to provide a framework for evaluating energy policy. The framework also helps to identify the reasons why environmentalists believe that economists undervalue the importance of energy.

Discounting the future

Many environmentalists and economists recognize the fact that market rates of discount are typically too high to value events in the future correctly from a social perspective. For example, Solow (1992) states "To make conservation an interesting proposition at all, the common discount rate should not be too large" (p. 10). Uncertainty about the future and concerns about receiving returns from investments increase rates of discount, and may also discourage exploration for new reserves of non-renewable resources (Dasgupta and Heal, 1979). Hence the problem for resource economists, in practice, is to determine how the high market rates of discount can be lowered when alternative investments or policies are evaluated. For some projects, governments or NGOs, such as The World Bank, make the decisions and can use social rates of discount in their calculations. Nevertheless, it is unlikely that this type of argument would influence decisions made by an oil company operating an oil-field in a politically unstable region. Getting a financial return on the investment as quickly as possible would be the primary goal. At the present time, it appears that more reliance will be placed on market forces for making economic decisions given widespread public concern about high rates of taxation, the recent collapse of the Soviet system of planned economies, the growing influence of international corporations, and the increasing reliance on competitive markets to make economic choices. Consequently, the problems associated with high rates of discount will not be resolved in a global economy in which international markets are the dominant force behind economic decisions.

It should be noted that many economic decisions are made without government interventions using implicit discount rates that are low. This can happen for any investment that does not require commercial financing. Obvious examples are the investments that parents make in educating their children. These investments may involve the allocation of time by the parents as well as financial expenditures. In spite of the importance of these types of investments, most economists would treat them as items of consumption by the parents.

The concept of family decisions can be extended to include economic production and community activities. One could argue, for example, that one reason for supporting family farms is that these farmers may be more willing to make long-term investments in establishing environmentally sound production techniques and reducing damage such as soil erosion. It seems highly likely that the issue of discounting the future too fast underlies the proposal, made by Daly and Cobb (this volume chapter 11), to rely more on local communities and less on markets for making economic decisions.

Conventional economic models are limited by not considering how people invest their resources outside market activities. Spending time with children, repairing one's home, working on a community project and looking after an elder relative are all real investments of time and money. Since these types of decisions can ignore the high discount rates that exist in the market, the future tends to be taken more seriously when these decisions are made. Hence, it is a sign of serious economic collapse when the options facing people are so limited or their attitudes are so myopic that they destroy their local environment. One can hypothesize that a viable community implicitly uses a low or zero social rate of discount, and therefore, that long-term environmental issues are considered seriously. Given the expanding role of competitive markets in the production of fossil fuels, however, the important implication is that relatively high rates of discount will be used in the energy industry. Governments can offset the effects of high discount rates, to some extent, by taxing the use of fossil fuels, which leads to the next problem of environmental externalities.

Incorporating environmental externalities

The prices paid for commodities in a typical market economy do not include the social costs of many types of environmental damage. These externalities have been discussed in the economic literature for over fifty years. Ignoring these costs leads to market prices that are lower than social prices, and as a result, levels of consumption are too high from a social perspective. Generally, the imposition of Pigouvian taxes is proposed as a solution by economists; see Pearce and Turner, (1990, chapters 4 and 5). These taxes would increase market prices, lower levels of consumption and, if appropriate, encourage polluters to install control equipment to reduce environmental damage.

In the absence of Pigouvian taxes for environmental damage, governments can impose regulations on sources of pollution and levels of safety for the public. Although Coase (1988, chapter 5) has argued that markets can solve environmental problems efficiently without government intervention or Pigouvian taxes, the conditions for this to happen are limited. In many situations, an issue ignored by Coase, transaction costs, is a dominant factor. For the pollution associated with burning fossil fuels that contributes to urban smog or global warming, for example, the number of sources of pollution and the number of people affected are both very large. Transaction costs for solving the problem of urban smog through market forces would be prohibitively high. The ongoing legal battles over the tobacco industry are a good illustration of how difficult it is to assign the blame for adverse health effects to a particular source of pollution. For problems such as urban smog and global warming, the relationships between sources of pollution and the different types of damage are even more complicated. Although the simple bargaining proposed by Coase could solve the problem of sparks from a steam train setting fire to a farmer's field, it would not be effective for global warming.

The prices of natural resources should reflect the correct social discounting of the future as well as incorporate external costs. Solow (1992) states that it is "obvious that every day market prices can make no claim to embody that kind of foreknowledge" (p. 16), but the increasing competition in global markets will not correct these types of deficiencies in pricing. International competition will probably have an adverse effect on existing environmental standards and worker safety because there is no global equivalent to the control that national governments have over national economies. Furthermore, there are no effective market incentives for developing countries like China to avoid repeating the problems experienced in industrialized countries in the use of coal, for example (burning coal at 30 percent efficiency in a conventional power plant with few control devices for emissions is less expensive than using coal gasification with combined-cycle turbines and cogeneration to give 70–80 percent efficiency overall and few emissions). For these and other reasons, Daly and Cobb disagree with the majority of economists, and they are strongly opposed to the expansion of free trade in the global economy, and to the use of market forces to solve environmental problems. Although many economists might support imposing a tax on carbon in fossil fuels to address global warming, the real test posed by Daly and Cobb is whether such a policy will actually be implemented on a large enough scale to solve the problem.

Measuring national production

Conventional measures of a national production such as GNP have been criticized for many years. For example, Baran and Sweezy (1966) argue that certain components such as military expenditures and competitive advertising should be excluded, and Mishan (1972) argues that the expenditures required to offset pollution, such as increased medical expenses, are really costs and not income. More recently, "green" accounting has been advocated to deal with the depletion of forests and fuels and environmental damage; see Serafy (1989). The need to improve the measurement of national income is one area in which economists like Solow agree with critics like Daly and Cobb, and Solow (1992) states "When it comes to measuring the economy's contributions to the well-being of the country's inhabitants, however, the conventional measures are incomplete. The most obvious omission is the depreciation of fixed capital assets" (p. 6). It should be noted that the following discussion is limited to considering the use of GNP as a measure of economic production, and it ignores the serious problems of using GNP as a measure of welfare.

The standard alternative to GNP proposed by Serafy and Solow is net national product (NNP). The basic idea is to measure the attainable level of consumption keeping the stocks of capital, resources and environmental quality intact. Serafy quotes Adam Smith and John Hicks to show that this concept has a long history in economics, and it is a standard part of cost accounting through the calculation of depreciation for expenditures on physical capital. The recent extensions of this concept cover renewable resources (such as forests), non-renewable resources (such as stocks of fuels), and the costs of environmental damage (such as soil erosion and air pollution). In this expanded form, there is a direct relationship between NNP and the concept of sustainability advocated by environmentalists, and these proposed "measurements... play a central role in the only logically sound approach to the issue of sustainability that I know" (Solow, 1992, p. 7).

The importance of measuring national income differently using NNP is illustrated by Daly and Cobb. They develop an "index of sustainable economic welfare" (ISEW) in the USA for the years 1950–86. From 1950 to 1980, the ISEW increased faster than GNP per capita (2.7 percent per year and 2.1 percent per year, respectively). From 1980 to 1986, however, GNP per capita continued to increase at 1.8 percent per year (in spite of a recession in 1982), but ISEW decreased at a rate of −0.3 percent per year (Daly and Cobb, 1989, p. 419). In other words, the implications for the period 1980 to 1986 about economic growth are completely different when the two measures are compared.

One major problem about NNP is the lack of agreement about which items should be included in NNP and how they should be measured. For example, Daly and Cobb include additions to income, such as the value of household services, as well as deductions, such as the depletion of resources. Alternative methods of measurement are being evaluated by the National Research Council in the USA in response to concerns raised in a recent study by the US Department of Commerce. Eventually, conventions for measuring NNP may be established by the UN and adopted by governments in the same way that the current procedures for national accounts were established.

For this paper, the treatment of stocks of fossil fuels is important. In conventional measures of national income like GNP, direct expenditures on exploration, production, processing (e.g. refining oil or generating electricity) and distribution are included. These measures cover only the cost of labor and the labor embodied in physical capital. The additional cost in NNP proposed by Serafy is to assume for accounting purposes that compensating investments in other sources of income must be made to offset the depletion of any non-renewable resource.

If an annual revenue of R_N can be obtained from a stock for N more years into the future, the present value of this revenue is

$$\frac{R_N\left(1 - e^{-rN}\right)}{r}$$

using r as the continuous rate of discounting the future. If the equivalent sustainable revenue is R_∞ per year, it follows that

$$R_\infty = R_N\left(1 - e^{-rN}\right) \quad \text{and} \quad e^{-rN}$$

represents the proportion of the observed revenue from the stock that should be subtracted from GNP. Serafy proposes using the ratio of the stock to the current level of extraction to measure N.

In table 14.1, the percentages of revenue required to offset depletion illustrate two points. First, the percentages are negligible if the ratio of reserves to consumption (N) is larger than 100 and the discount rate is 5 percent per year. Since 50–100 is a reasonable approximation for N in the actual situation for oil (Chapman, 1993) and 5 percent is representative of real market discount rates, the implication is that the practical relevance of the offset of revenue is only just emerging (the values of N for other fuels, such as coal, are larger than the value for oil). Second, the offset percentage is much higher if a lower discount rate is used, providing an excellent example of the point raised earlier about the problem of using a market discount rate that is higher than the social discount rate.

There is some disagreement among authors about the correct measure of revenue (R_N) to use for fossil fuels. Solow (1992, p. 11) assumes that the offset of revenue is identical to the pure profits above production costs – Hotelling's (1931) scarcity premium. Serafy (1989, p. 13) assumes that the appropriate offset corresponds to a proportion of revenue net of extraction costs. In contrast, Daly and Cobb (1989, p. 439) also include the extraction costs in the measure of revenue because extraction costs are "regrettable necessities." In all cases, however, the offsets of revenue would grow exponentially over time at the discount rate (if annual consumption is constant over time and no additions to reserves are discovered). These issues are explored further in pages 322–7.

The widespread interest among economists and environmentalists in improving the measurement of national income will probably lead to actual changes in, or supplements to, national income accounts. These modifications will reflect the depletion of some resources, particularly fuels and minerals, and possibly changes in environmental quality. One reason for being optimistic is that changes in

Table 14.1 Percentage of revenue required to offset the depletion of a stock

Years remaining (N)	Discount rate (100r)		
	1%	2%	5%
500	1	0	0
100	37	14	1
50	61	37	8
10	90	82	61

accounting practices can be implemented by governments and international organizations. For this reason, the accounting procedures can also use social rates of discount in the calculations. However, even if general agreement can be reached among countries on how to measure NNP, there is no guarantee that the availability of new information will modify market behavior or improve actual decisions about, for example, how quickly fossil fuels are consumed or whether investments in alternative sources of energy are made.

Replacing non-renewable resources

The discussion of measuring national production introduced the argument that the depletion of a non-renewable stock should be treated as a cost in national income accounts. The implication is that offsetting investments should be made to cover these costs. However, "the setting aside of part of the proceds for reinvestment is only a metaphor" (Serafy, 1989, p. 16). This is the fourth problem of resource economics. There is no guarantee that investments in new technologies to replace non-renewable resources will be made. Once again, the problem is recognized by Solow (1992) who states "the cardinal sin is not mining; it is consuming the rents from mining" (p. 20). The question is how seriously the problem is taken in the formation of current economic policy. The importance of developing "backstop" technologies is obvious to environmentalists – for example, see Meadows et al. (1992, chapter 6) – but appears to be much less important to economists; Hartwick (1989) is one exception. Economists typically consider the implications of having backstop technologies available rather than the institutional mechanisms and sources of investment needed for their creation.

One possible source of funds for research on new technologies is to tax the use of non-renewable resources through consumption taxes or profit taxes. For example, the rationale for imposing a petroleum revenue tax on oil from the North Sea is discussed by Dasgupta and Heal (1979, p. 371), and they argue that there is "an unavoidable conclusion that there will in general be a strong case for government support for activities designed to promote a technological advance, and this is indeed the typical situation in the most market-oriented economies" (pp. 475–6). Instead of developing a framework to link the revenues from taxation to research expenditures, they focus on the difficulties of predicting technological advances, and cite the case of a Fellow of the Royal Society in England who in 1876 did not recognize the commercial possibilities of electric power (p. 478). One thing does appear to be clear from history: market forces are generally effective in exploiting new commercial technologies, but they do not necessarily develop these technologies in the first place. Although the future is always uncertain, it will be relatively easy to adapt to new unexpected opportunities, such as inexpensive electric power from fusion, but using fossil fuels with no viable backstop technology may lead to serious problems in the future.

OPEC (Organization for Petroleum Exporting Countries) has had some success over the past twenty years in taxing oil production. The reaction of economists has generally been to discuss the inefficiencies associated with monopolistic behavior and the underutilization of resources. For example, Kay and Mirrlees (1975) state "Economists are well aware that the world's store of exhaustible resources is limited. But in light of the arguments presented here, we wish to suggest that there is a real danger that the world's resources are being used too slowly" (p. 171). An alternative test would be to follow Solow's suggestion and evaluate how the monopoly profits have been spent. To what extent, for example, have these profits been used to establish sustainable levels of income? While there is no simple answer to this question, it is just as pertinent as the question of whether resources are being used too slowly. When issues of global equity are considered (on pages 314–22), economists' concerns about using resources too slowly in industrialized countries are seen to be misplaced.

Summarizing the four problems raised about resource economics, only one appears to have generated some agreement among economists and environmentalists that it can be corrected. This is the problem of incorporating the depletion of resources into national income accounts, and a major reason for this is that the decision to supplement the accounts can be made by governments and international organizations. It is not a market decision. Two of the problems – discounting the future too fast and ignoring environmental externalities – are characteristics of market decisions. Governments must introduce modifications to correct these problems. This does not mean that governments should ignore markets completely to solve the problems. Targets for reducing pollution, for example, can be set by governments, but markets can still have an important part to play in determining how to meet the targets efficiently. Economists and their skeptics generally have different levels of optimism about the ability of governments to enforce the needed modifications of markets. For a problem like global warming that requires international cooperation among governments, it is much harder to implement effective policies than it is for regional and national environmental problems. The discussion in the next two sections shows that there is little evidence for optimism about current efforts to deal with global warming.

Both economists and environmentalists have doubts about the fourth problem of replacing fossil fuels and other non-renewable resources. For example, Solow (1986) has criticized the UK government for using the taxes on North Sea oil for general revenue instead of investment. Incentives to make investments in new technologies and the associated research activities can be supported by governments. However, markets alone will not provide sufficient incentives for replacing non-renewable resources in a timely way as long as discount rates are high and many external costs of using these resources are ignored. This is the underlying reality for energy policy relating to global warming.

The conclusion is that the optimists among economists believe implicitly that governments will be effective in the future, and that modifications will be implemented to offset the inherent limitations of markets in solving economic and environmental problems correctly. The skeptics, on the other hand, assume that the increase of competition in international markets will erode the existing capabilities of governments to modify market behavior. Consequently, rather than making gains, environmental standards will be lowered with more competition, and existing gains in improving the safety and health of production workers, for example, will be lost. Furthermore, there is no guarantee that governments will set appropriate policies even if they have the power to do so. David Price (1996) points out that there is no convincing historical evidence that human populations will stabilize economic activities at sustainable levels. For true pessimism about the future, however, one can turn to Kaplan (1994) who predicts that environmental problems and economic inequities will overwhelm many governments, leading to "The Coming Anarchism". Unfortunately, there are already examples of this situation, particularly in Africa. While it is likely that most governments will retain the ability to modify market behavior and implement environmental policies, there is substantial skepticism among environmentalists that this will actually happen. The specific problems of energy are discussed further in the next section.

Crying wolf: Is energy different?

In Aesop's fable, the boy who was bored being on his own while looking after the sheep decided to cause some excitement by sounding the alarm that a wolf was attacking the sheep. Eventually, the people in the village, who had responded to a series of false alarms, grew tired of being tricked, and when a real wolf appeared, they treated the boy's cries for help as another false alarm and did not go to help him. This story can be viewed as a description of the responses of economists to concerns about running out of resources, and, in particular, different sources of energy. Global warming has raised new concerns about the use of fossil fuels, and the question is whether this is another false alarm or a real sign that changes in economic practices should be made.

In 1973, the first major global oil embargo occurred due to the successful efforts of OPEC to control supplies of oil. The resulting increase in the cost of importing oil initiated an alarm about supplies of energy in many countries. This alarm coincided with discussions of the book *Limits to Growth* by Meadows et al. (1972) which had predicted that physical limits to continued economic growth would be binding in the relatively near future. The reactions of many economists to this thesis were very hostile; see for example Kay and Mirrlees (1975). A similar reaction was made by Nordhaus (1992) who criticized a revised version of the Meadows' (1972) model. The main criticism made by economists was that the model in *Limits to Growth* ignored the potential for technical change and for substituting new types of resources for non-renewable resources. Furthermore, Hotelling had shown over fifty years ago that markets would develop scarcity premiums, and higher prices, automatically for a resource when remaining supplies became limited.

Using experiences with the history of fuels in the UK, economists pointed to a series of false alarms over supplies of energy. When charcoal was used to smelt iron, for example, there was concern about running out of wood and the perceived need to secure new supplies of wood from France (Kay and Mirrlees, 1975, p. 150). The solution to this problem was the discovery of how to use coal to smelt iron. Coal became the new source of energy that made the industrial revolution possible. In the mid-nineteenth century, the economist Jevons (1865) raised concerns about increasing the costs of industrial production as coal seams became harder to exploit. These concerns about coal supplies in Britain were alleviated by the discovery of oil in the Middle East. Oil became the basis for continued economic growth in the twentieth century.

Limits on the rate of use of fuels

Looking back at 1973, it appears that the economists who were skeptical about *Limits to Growth* were correct. The high price of oil stimulated exploration for additional sources of oil, and new fields such as Alaska and the North Sea were developed. Improved methods of extraction were also developed that increased the recoverable reserves from existing fields. Efforts on the demand-side were made to increase the efficiency of delivering services from energy. In addition, there was an expansion in the use of alternative sources of energy such as nuclear power. The situation now is that OPEC has been unable to maintain sufficient control over supplies of oil to keep the price as high as it was in the late 1970s and early 1980s. In the USA, the real price of gasoline is about the same as it was before the oil embargo in 1973. All indications are that competitive markets for oil are working effectively at the present time.

Nevertheless, there are some ominous signs about the current situation. Environmental concerns about global warming imply that there should be limits on the rate at which fossil fuels are consumed; see, for example Houghton (1994). Strategies are now being considered in most industrial countries for stabilizing emissions of GHGs (primarily carbon dioxide from burning fossil fuels) to keep levels at, or below, the levels emitted in 1990. This goal was initiated by the UN Conference on the Environment and Development held in Rio de Janeiro, Brazil in 1992, but it is viewed by many environmentalists as a relatively small step in the right direction. For example, Krause et al. (1992, Scenario D, p. 197) consider that global emissions of GHGs should be cut to one fifth of the current level to avoid long-term environmental damage. More recently in 1995, a new UN conference held in Berlin, Germany concluded with the recommendation that national targets for reductions of GHGs should be set.

The implication of global warming is that concerns are no longer limited to running out of inexpensive sources of fuels. There should also be a limit on the rate of use of fuels. If current levels of emissions already exceed the ability of the biosphere to absorb GHGs without causing long-term harm to the environment, there are important implications for energy policy. First, there is one more external environmental cost of using fossil fuels that is not captured by conventional market forces. Second, and more importantly, equity becomes a central issue. For a given total level of use, one should question the highly skewed situation that currently exists with a small proportion of the world's population having high levels of consumption and most people having low levels. These issues are explored further later; see page 314.

Replacements for fossil fuels

Non-economists like Meadows et al. (1992) and Hall et al. (1991) treat energy and other natural resources differently from economists. Economists consider energy as just another input, and put their faith in substitution as the solution to scarcity. However, Hall et al. (1991) state "elasticities of substitution between natural resources and capital and labor calculated at the level of the firm or industry do not necessarily reflect true substitution possibilities over the economy as a whole. Including the direct and indirect energy costs of producing capital and labor reduces the degree to which capital and labor can be substituted for fuel in production" (p. 893). Their conclusion is that economists typically do not recognize "the realities of physical constraints imposed on our economic possibilities" (p. 896). Even if one questions this view, it seems reasonable to expect that substitution for energy is easier at the high levels of consumption per capita that are observed in industrialized countries than it would be if major increases of energy efficiency were achieved. Observed possibilities for substitution between capital and energy, for example, generally imply reducing the amount of energy wasted. Eventually, energy from fossil fuels must be replaced by another source of energy.

The original plan for replacing fossil fuels in the USA, that was implemented after the oil embargo in 1973, was to use electricity from nuclear power plants. Unfortunately, nuclear power in the USA appears to be much less viable as an alternative to fossil fuels than it did in the 1970s. The choice posed by Lovins (1977) between nuclear power and renewable sources of energy is even more pertinent now. With no major new source of energy available at a reasonably low cost, the optimism that many economists expressed after the oil embargo in 1973 must be questioned. Current policy simply assumes that a replacement for fossil fuels, particularly oil, will emerge in time to avoid major disruptions to economic production and lifestyles. At the present time, nuclear power is still the most economically viable alternative if the environmental costs of nuclear waste and the political costs of nuclear terrorism are ignored.

Among economists, Daly shares many of the concerns of the critics of conventional economics, and, in particular, concerns about the sustainability of continued economic growth. Daly proposes three goals for sustainability:

1   to keep the harvest of renewable resources at or below the levels of regeneration
2   to expand production from renewable sources to match the depletion of non-renewable sources such as fossil fuels, and
3   to keep the amount of pollution at or below the levels that can be absorbed by the environment without adverse effects.

The second goal is the most important for this discussion, and it requires some additional explanation. Although it applies to all types of non-renewable resources, the implications for fossil fuels are more serious than for other resources, such as metals, because recycling is not a feasible option. For fossil fuels, improving the efficiency of use is equivalent to replacing them by renewable sources of energy (Rubin et al., 1992), and these two alternatives can be treated as synonymous.

Although deforestation and the plight of many international fisheries are current examples of violations of the first of Daly's goals, this goal is still generally accepted as valid by resource economists. Furthermore, the continuing debate over global warming and GHGs is a good example of the growing recognition of Daly's third goal that limits do exist on the capacity of the environment to absorb pollution. Economists may not be the leaders in these debates, but they are involved; (for example, see Nordhaus (1991), and Pearce (1991)).

Daly's second goal, however, is the one that is being ignored at the present time. Even though fossil fuels are being consumed at ever higher rates, there is relatively little concerted effort by governments or industry to develop alternative sources of energy. Following the discussion in the previous section, the current costs of conventional sources of energy are too low to bring about major investments in alternative sources. (In the USA, expenditures on nuclear power are being directed to determining how to clean up existing nuclear sites and how to store nuclear waste rather than on expansion. Expenditures on renewable sources of energy are relatively low, and energy from renewables is still very limited in comparison to the energy from burning fossil fuels.) Although many economists would accept the need for a backstop technology to replace fossil fuels in the future, e.g. Manne and Richels (1992), Hartwick (1989), Cline (1992), and Chapman (1993), the main problems with current energy policy are

1   the imbalance between the limited expansion of renewable sources of energy and the growing consumption of fossil fuels, and
2   the absence of a coherent plan for investing in the development of new technologies for renewable sources of energy.

The contrast between the recommendations of economists and those of environmentalists can be illustrated by comparing the models of Nordhaus (1994) and Meadows et al. (1992). The optimum tax on carbon to deal with global warming is found by Nordhaus to be relatively small. Imposing this tax has only minor effects on economic growth, and emissions of GHGs continue to increase. Stabilizing emissions at the level in 1990 (i.e. the proposal adopted at the Earth Summit) is considered to be an expensive and unjustified alternative. (In another study, Rose and Stevens (1993) estimate positive net benefits from a 20 percent reduction in carbon emissions.) In contrast, Meadows et al. (1992) conclude that continued economic growth will lead to a collapse of the global economy. Consequently, there is a pressing need to adopt new practices and technologies now, because feedback delays in environmental systems make it important to recognize potential problems in advance.

Given global limits on the rate of use of fossil fuels imposed by the environment, attitudes towards economic equity will affect how fast the transition to

renewable sources of energy should occur. If the current inequitable situation
among countries is accepted, then there is less urgency to develop new technologies for energy. On the other hand, if it is recognized that the use of energy should
increase in developing countries to allow for economic growth (without increasing global emissions of GHGs), there is no viable way to achieve this at the
present time without substantial reductions in the use of fossil fuels and living
standards in industrialized countries. (Ignoring the environmental problems of
global warming may also have adverse effects on income inequality. For example,
Rosensweig and Parry (1993) reach this conclusion because of the vulnerability of
subsistence agriculture to higher temperatures.) The main conclusions are that
energy is different, because

1   fossil fuels must eventually be replaced by another source of energy, and
2   there are environmental limits on the rate at which fossil fuels should be
    used.

The associated issue of economic equity is discussed further in the next section.

Economic growth and energy use

The importance of low income countries

The information in table 14.2 is derived from the 1992 World Development
Report of the World Bank. It shows the size of the world population, the level of
global production (GNP), and the total use of energy in 1965 and 1990, with
three alternative sets of projections for 2025. Countries are grouped into three
categories representing high, middle and low levels of income per capita. In 1965,
over one-fifth of the world's population lived in high-income countries, and they
produced over four-fifths of total GNP and used nearly four-fifths of total energy.
By 1990, however, the share of population in high-income countries was less than
one-fifth, the share of total GNP was still over four-fifths, but the share of energy
had fallen to just over three-fifths. This share of energy is projected to fall to less
than two-fifths by 2025. Although global GNP increased by 50 percent from
1965 to 1990, global energy consumption more than doubled. Table 14.3 shows
that 50 percent of the increase in energy use from 1965 to 1990 occurred in low-
and middle-income countries, compared to only 21 percent of the increase of
GNP and 92 percent of the increase of population. The implication is that the
growth of energy use in low-income and middle-income countries is becoming
increasingly important, and policies to deal with global warming must reflect
this reality.

The projections for 2025 in tables 14.2 and 14.3 are based on the assumptions
summarized in table 14.4. Projections of growth rates for population correspond
to current UN forecasts and imply lower rates of growth in the future (Population
Reference Bureau, 1991). Projected growth rates in GNP per capita are held
constant at the annual rates observed from 1965 to 1990. The high projected
growth rates for energy correspond to the same annual rates as the period 1965

Table 14.2 Population, economic output and energy consumption

		Level[b]	Percentage share[a]		
		All countries	Low-income countries	Middle-income countries	High-income countries
1965					
	1. Population	3 billion	58	20	22
	2. GNP	8 trillion	4	10	86
	3. Energy	3 billion	7	15	78
1990					
	1. Population	5 billion	62	22	16
	2. GNP	19 trillion	6	12	82
	3. Energy	7 billion	15	22	63
2025[c]					
	1. Population	8 billion	65	24	11
	2. GNP	55 trillion	9	16	75
	3. Energy (high)	21 billion	34	29	37
	(medium)	15 billion	34	29	37
	(low)	11 billion	34	29	37

[a] Country groups are defined in the Source.
[b] The units are 1990 $US for GNP, and metric tons of oil equivalent for Energy.
[c] Derived from the assumptions summarized in table 14.4.
Source: Values for 1965 and 1990 are derived from tables 1 and 5 of the *World Development Report 1992* (World Bank, 1992).

Table 14.3 Changes of population, economic output and energy consumption[a]

		Change of levels[b]	Percentage share		
		All countries	Low-income countries	Middle-income countries	High-income countries
1965–1990					
	1. Population	2 billion	68	24	8
	2. GNP	11 trillion	7	14	79
	3. Energy	4 billion	22	28	50
1990–2025					
	1. Population	3 billion	70	27	3
	2. GNP	36 trillion	11	18	71
	3. Energy (high)	14 billion	41	33	26
	(medium)	8 billion	48	35	17
	(low)	4 billion	64	42	−6

[a] Derived from table 14.2.
[b] Same units as table 14.2.

Table 14.4 Average annual growth rates (percent)

	Low-income countries	Middle-income countries	High-income countries
1965–1990			
1. Population[a]	2.2	2.2	0.8
2. GNP/capita[a]	2.9	2.2	2.4
3. Energy/capita[a]	4.1	2.6	1.5
1990–2025			
1. Population[b]	1.5	1.6	0.3
2. GNP/capita[b]	2.9	2.2	2.4
3. Energy/capita (high)[b]	4.1	2.6	1.5
(medium)[b]	3.1	1.6	0.5
(low)[b]	2.1	0.6	−0.5

[a]Derived from Tables 1 and 5 of the *World Development Report 1992* (World Bank, 1992).
[b]Specified values.

to 1990, and the medium and low rates are 1 percent and 2 percent less than the high rates, respectively. Using the low energy rates, energy use declines slightly in high-income countries. In all three cases, however, global energy use increases from 1990 to 2025. Table 14.2 shows the levels in 2025, and table 14.3 shows the changes in levels from 1990 to 2025.

Even though the rate of population growth decreases, the increase of population from 1990 to 2025 in table 14.3 is still larger than the increase from 1965 to 1990, and only 3 percent of this increase occurs in high-income countries. The increase in global GNP from 1990 to 2025 is over three times bigger than the increase from 1965 to 1990. This is also the case for energy use for the high energy rates of growth. Even with the low energy rates of growth, the increase in total energy use from 1990 to 2025 is the same as the increase from 1965 to 1990, and all of the increase is in low- and middle-income countries in this case. The implication is that the prospects for stabilizing emissions of GHGs are daunting even if the level of population eventually stabilizes at 11 billion. The important question is how closely economic growth and energy use are linked together. Most economists would agree with Nordhaus that the cost of reducing emissions of GHGs from fossil fuels would be substantially lower rates of economic growth.

The results presented in tables 14.2–14.4 about the future are simple accounting calculations to illustrate the factors that are contributing to global warming. These results are, however, generally consistent with the current forecasts of energy consumption and the corresponding emissions of carbon made by the Energy Information Administration (EIA, 1997) for different countries for 2000 and 2015. The EIA forecasts of carbon emissions summarized in table 14.6 are derived using three sets of economic forecasts summarized in table 14.5.

Table 14.5 Annual growth rates of real GNP

Region	1970–80	1980–90	1995–2015		
			Low	Reference	High
USA	3.0	2.6	1.9	2.4	2.9
Other N. America	3.0	2.6	1.9	2.4	2.9
Western Europe	3.0	2.6	2.0	2.5	3.0
Industrialized Asia	4.3	4.0	2.3	2.8	3.3
Industrialized	3.2	2.8	2.0	2.5	3.0
Eastern Europe/Former Soviet Union	3.2	2.1	2.1	3.6	6.6
China	5.8	8.9	4.3	7.3	8.8
India	6.4	6.3	3.8	5.3	6.8
Other Asia	6.4	6.3	3.8	5.3	6.8
Middle East	4.8	1.5	1.2	2.7	4.2
Africa	4.2	1.4	1.9	3.4	4.9
Central & S. America	5.8	1.1	2.0	3.5	5.0
Developing	5.4	3.3	na	4.7	na
Total	3.5	2.8	na	3.1	na

Source: EIA (1997)

Table 14.6 Global emissions of carbon (million metric tons)

Region	1990	1995	2000			2015		
			Low	Reference	High	Low	Reference	High
United States	1,337	1,424	1,515	1,543	1,575	1,688	1,798	1,939
Other N. America	224	240	278	283	289	351	372	396
Western Europe	1,016	1,014	1,059	1,081	1,098	1,209	1,279	1,346
Industrialized Asia	408	473	499	514	523	584	625	661
Industrialized	2,985	3,151	3,352	3,421	3,485	3,831	4,074	4,341
Eastern Europe/ Former Soviet Union	1,339	893	967	1,012	1,087	1,087	1,251	1,625
China	625	821	930	1,031	1,076	1,294	1,838	2,167
India	159	221	252	276	296	384	490	612
Other Asia	307	432	511	557	597	716	904	1,122
Middle East	203	254	244	265	282	276	344	418
Africa	205	248	251	267	281	290	352	422
Central & S. America	189	220	243	263	282	343	452	585
Developing	1,687	2,197	2,431	2,660	2,815	3,303	4,379	5,325
Total	6,012	6,241	6,750	7,093	7,387	8,222	9,704	11,292

Source: EIA (1997)

Countries are grouped into industrialized, Eastern Europe and the former Soviet Union (EE/FSU) and developing. The high-income group in tables 14.2–14.4 corresponds roughly to industrialized plus EE/FSU, and the middle- and low-income groups correspond to developing.

Comparing the assumptions about future economic growth in table 14.2 and the reference case in table 14.5 shows that the global growth rates are both close to 3.1 percent per year; note that the time periods are 1990–2025 in table 14.2 and 1995–2015 in table 14.5. The growth rates for the EIA reference forecasts in table 14.5 are lower for industrialized countries (2.5 percent) compared to high-income countries (2.7 percent implied in table 14.2), but combining industrialized and EE/FSU would increase the EIA growth rate. The EIA growth rates for developing countries are slightly higher (4.7 percent) compared to low-income countries (4.3 percent implied in table 14.2). The range of EIA growth rates from low to high is relatively small for industrialized countries (1 percent) compared to most developing countries (3 percent), China (4.5 percent) and EE/FSU (4.5 percent).

An important implication of the EIA forecasts of carbon emissions in table 14.6 is that the underlying growth of energy use will be lower than economic growth in all countries (2.2 percent per year for aggregate energy compared to 3.1 percent for global GNP in table 14.5). It should be noted that this implies a major change from the historical experience for low-income countries in table 14.4 (4.1 percent for energy per capita compared to 2.9 percent for GNP per capita over the period 1965–1990). The reason given by EIA (p. 16) is "energy efficient technologies used in industrialized nations will increasingly be adopted in the developing nations." To this extent, the EIA forecasts of energy use are optimistic, and greater dependence on electricity as a source of energy in developing countries, for example, could result in higher growth rates for energy use.

The growth rates in future carbon emissions corresponding to the forecasted levels in table 14.6 are very similar to the corresponding growth rates for energy, and the growth rates for total emissions and total energy are identical (2.2 percent per year for 1995–2015). This is the same growth rate for energy as the medium energy scenario in table 14.2, and consequently, the simple accounting procedures used in tables 14.2–14.4 for the medium energy scenario are in general agreement with the EIA reference case. The main difference is that it is assumed in tables 14.2–14.4 that the ratio of growth of energy and GNP are lower (higher) in high (low)-income countries than the EIA forecast, implying that greater restraint over energy use is exhibited in the high-income countries. An alternative way to match this restraint would be to subsidize the transfer of energy-efficient technology to low-income countries, and this is a valid way to interpret the assumptions made by the EIA about technology transfer. Either way, substantial economic sacrifices will be required in high-income countries beyond business-as-usual assumptions. The willingness of the public in high-income countries to make such sacrifices for people in low-income countries is discussed later in this section.

The most important implication from the forecasts of carbon emissions in table 14.6 is that all of the low economic forecasts for 2000 and 2015, with one exception, are substantially higher than the levels in 1990. The exception is EE/FSU due to the recent collapse of these economies. There is no indication that emissions of carbon from fossil fuels, the major source of GHGs, will stabilize at 1990 levels in any of the industrialized regions even with pessimistic assumptions about economic growth. Under the low economic scenario, emissions from industrialized countries in 2015 increase by almost 30 percent from 1990, and in developing countries, the equivalent increase is almost 100 percent. These forecasts are much higher than the levels required to meet the commitments agreed to at the Earth Summit in 1992. In the reference and high economic scenarios, forecasted emissions from developing countries are higher than emissions from industrialized countries in 2015, reinforcing the point made earlier about the importance of the growth of energy use in low-income countries (table 14.3).

Another important implication from table 14.6 is the current position of the USA which contributed over one-fifth of total emissions of carbon in 1990 and 1995. On a per capita basis, emissions of carbon and energy use are much higher in North America than they are in Western Europe or Japan, for example. This is the primary reason why any global policies to stabilize carbon emissions will require leadership and action from the USA. If there is a reluctance to reduce emissions in the USA, it is highly unlikely that other countries will do so. There are responsibilities associated with being a super energy consumer as well as being a super power.

Attitudes towards economic equity

Many non-economists are probably quite skeptical about the central argument of market economists that the world will be a better place leaving economic decisions to the self-interests of individuals and firms. Few would doubt that self-interest is a powerful motivating force, but it is not immediately obvious why indulging one's own desires is going to help other people. Nevertheless, profits for firms and consumption for individuals are treated as the dominant factors influencing decisions in market transactions. Sen (1977) discusses this problem in his paper *Rational Fools*, and he states that "the exclusion of any consideration other than self-interest seems to impose a wholly arbitrary limitation on the notion of rationality."

There are economic problems which must be solved in practice and are related directly to equity. For example, Sen (1992) discusses the plight of people who are incapacitated and are unable to earn a living. He discusses their "entitlements" to receive support, and shows the limitations of conventional utilitarian models which focus on consumption rather than the capabilities that can be attained. In welfare economics, the problem of equity is implicitly left to governments through the scheme used to weight the utilities of individuals. This provides the rationale for progressive taxation of incomes and the existence of welfare programs, see, for example, Atkinson (1983). However, established procedures used by governments to redistribute income from the rich to the poor are being

challenged in many countries. In particular, there has been a substantial redistribution of income after taxes in favor of the rich; see Phillips (1990) and
Bronfenbrenner et al. (1996). Frank and Cook (1996) characterize these changes
as a central feature in a "winner-take-all" society.

Frank (1988) also addresses a different question. He notes that some people
are altruistic and others simply follow their own interests. The latter group
represents the typical individuals modeled by economists. Frank asks the question
of how can altruists survive in a competitive economy. He argues that certain
problems, such as the prisoner's dilemma, can be solved better by altruists who
are willing to cooperate with others; Frank calls this the "commitment model".
Reassuringly, people with self-interested motives find it difficult to cheat when
solving these problems by pretending to be trustworthy. In experiments, people
tend to behave in a fair way more frequently than the predictions from the self-
interest model would imply. These findings are also supported by Andreoni and
Miller (1993), and such behavior influences "warm glow giving" to charities and
payments for public goods such as Public Radio. It is interesting to note that
taking graduate courses in economics appears to reduce the likelihood of behav-
ing cooperatively and to increase self-interest (Frank, 1988, pp. 226–9).

To summarize the current situation in the USA relative to other countries,
ranges of wages have been reported by Gottschalk and Smeeding (1966) using
data from 1991 from the Luxembourg Income Study. Comparing real income per
household (based on purchasing power parity and corrected for household size)
shows that the income level for the tenth decile in the USA is lower than the
equivalent levels in 13 other industrialized countries, primarily in Europe. On the
other hand, the median income in the USA is the highest among the 14 countries,
and the income for the ninetieth percentile is substantially higher than it is in the
other countries. In other words, the range of incomes from the tenth to the
ninetieth decile in the USA is the largest by a long way. In fact, current economic
conditions in the USA do not stand up very well to Samuel Johnson's standard
that "a decent provision for the poor is the true test of civilization" (quoted by
Atkinson, 1983, p. 224).

In a recent study, *The State of Americans* by Bronfenbrenner et al. (1996), a
number of "disturbing facts and figures" about the population are discussed that
present a different perspective on the aggregate picture of real economic growth
over the past two decades. The issues considered include crime, education, health
and income. To focus on the single characteristic of household income in the
USA, McClelland (1996, figure 3–5) compares the changing distributions of
incomes for different time periods. From 1947 to 1973, real incomes in all
quintiles increased at over 2 percent per year, and the rate of growth in the lowest
quintile (2.9 percent) was the biggest and the rate in the highest quintile (2.42
percent) was the smallest. Increasing affluence led to greater equity, following a
traditional Kuznets curve for a high-income country. The situation from 1973 to
1992 was exactly the opposite. Real incomes in the lowest two quintiles actually
decreased, and the highest annual rate of growth (0.93 percent) occurred in the
highest quintile. Overall, there was a small decline in the real median income, and
the inequality of the distribution of income increased substantially.

To some extent, the decline in real incomes for poor families over the past twenty-five years in the USA can be associated with a loss of manufacturing jobs for unskilled workers due to increasing competition in international markets. The result is that a significant number of families in the USA are under economic stress and feel threatened by competition for jobs with low-income countries like China and Mexico. This segment of the public is unlikely to be sympathetic to increasing taxes on fuels or subsidizing the transfer of energy-efficient technology to competing countries. These, however, are exactly the policies that are needed to address global warming.

Attitudes towards the environment

Demonstrating that public attitudes towards economic inequality can change in a competitive world is an important step. It raises a similar question of how public attitudes affect the solutions chosen for environmental problems like global warming. Identifying the origin of attitudes about the environment in a society is difficult, but education, religion and political leadership can and do modify the attitudes of individuals. Roderick Nash (1989) describes how attitudes towards nature have evolved from survival and self-interest to "ecological egalitarianism" with legal rights for nature as well as for people. In spite of the current success of market capitalism relative to planned economies, many people see the need for changes in public attitudes. For example, Aleksandr Solzhenitsyn (1993) argues for more self-restraint by individuals to protect the environment, and he states "The time is urgently upon us to limit our wants. It is difficult to bring ourselves to sacrifice and self-denial because in political, public and private life we have long since dropped the golden key of self-restraint to the ocean floor." Bill McKibben (1995) has argued that people in the USA must learn to live "lightly on the Earth," and the current Vice-President, Al Gore (1992), has described a moral basis for his approach to solving environmental problems. However, these efforts to change public attitudes have yet to achieve tangible effects on current energy policy relating to global warming.

The need for a broader vision for economic analysis is recognized by some economists. For example, Heilbronner (1992), in reviewing a biography of John Maynard Keynes by Robert Skidelsky, quotes "Keynes addressed the world as a priest, not as a technician. And though he rearranged its theology, economics spoke, through him, as a church, not as a branch of differential calculus." Heilbronner concludes "I suspect that we will not discover the way out of the present impasse until we find an economics that projects a moral vision along with a technical diagnosis comparable to that of the General Theory [of Employment, Interest and Money] . . ." (p. 9). A corollary to this statement is the question of whether economists should remain passive and treat current public attitudes as given and fixed, because it is unlikely that satisfactory solutions to global warming will be implemented unless changes in public attitudes occur.

Stabilizing global emissions of GHGs will require reductions of emissions in

industrialized countries, lower rates of growth of emissions in developing countries and the development of new sources of energy and energy-efficient technologies for use in all countries. There is little hope that these policies will be adopted
unless there is widespread support in high-income countries for reducing income
inequities among countries, and public attitudes throughout the world accept the
need to stabilize emissions of GHGs. It was argued above that the USA must take
leadership in addressing global warming because the levels of energy use and
emissions of GHGs in the USA are so large in total and on a per capita basis. It
is also true that unilateral action by the USA will not be sufficient to solve the
problem unless it leads to equivalent actions in other countries. The predicament
is that public attitudes in the USA are not compatible with taking leadership at
this time. Attitudes towards energy are reflected by the low taxes paid on gasoline
relative to most other countries. The vulnerability of imported supplies of oil has
always been an influential factor in most industrialized countries, but the tradition in the USA is based on abundant domestic supplies. At the present time,
the evidence in the USA about the use of fossil fuels supports the pessimism
of environmentalists about the inability of competitive markets to deal with
global warming.

A Marshallian perspective on fossil fuels

Many environmentalists find it hard to understand the economic logic that makes
the price of a gallon of gasoline lower than the price of a gallon of beer. Beer is
a renewable product that is easy to make at home and has been in production
from the time of the ancient Egyptians. Petroleum, on the other hand, is a
complex chemical product that is expensive to synthesize, is a valuable feedstock
for producing plastics and a compact source of energy for transportation. Beer is
relatively inexpensive to produce, but there are other costs and beer is generally
subject to special taxes on alcohol (the tradition in UK income accounts is to treat
alcohol as a "vice"). The price of gasoline includes the costs of extraction, refining
and distribution as well as some taxes. In European countries and Japan, the taxes
on gasoline are high (over 70 percent of the total price in Europe, for example).
In the USA, only 27 percent of the average price of gasoline is for taxes, and most
of this revenue is directed to highway improvements; this is based on data for
1992 (EIA, 1994). The actual costs of production are less than a dollar per gallon
in all of the European countries, Canada and the USA. The low cost of producing
oil reflects many improved techniques for the extraction and refining of oil that
have been introduced by the oil industry. In the USA, for example, substantial
increases in oil reserves have been made since the discovery of oil in Alaska, but
these increases came from improved methods of recovery and not from finding
new oil fields. Globally, current projections are that the real price of crude oil will
not increase over the next twenty years, in spite of continued growth of consumption at a projected rate of increase of 2.1 percent per year in the reference case
(EIA, 1997). Given the prospect of increasing growth of oil consumption with
low prices, most economists would argue that this is an example of competitive

markets working well. For example, the efforts by OPEC to capture monopoly profits in the mid-1970s were undermined by the mid-1980s through increases in production capacity in other regions of the world.

Hotelling's scarcity premium

The theoretical explanation of how owners of a non-renewable resource like oil behave under competition was developed by Hotelling over sixty years ago. The basic structure is that the present value of true profits (the scarcity premium) above the total cost of production, including a fair return on investment, must be the same for every point of time in the future. If this was not the case and an owner believed that discounted profits would be higher at some time in the future, it would be economically rational to cut current production and wait until profits increased. Since these decisions would be based on market rates of interest, which are generally higher than social rates of discount (see pages 303–4), there is still a tendency to produce too much in the current period. To varying degrees, this overproduction is offset by governments through consumption taxes on fuels such as gasoline. These taxes could also reflect internalizing environmental externalities such as urban smog.

The implication of Hotelling's rule is that the true profit or scarcity premium measuring the future exhaustibility of a non-renewable resource will grow at the market rate of interest. This is exactly the same feature exhibited by the adjustment factors in national income accounts for the depletion of a stock (table 14.1). Consequently, the scarcity premium has similar characteristics to the adjustment factor, and it is trivially small if interest rates are high and the time horizon to exhaustion is long. For actual levels of reserves, Kay and Mirrlees have shown that the scarcity premium would be essentially zero, and the economically efficient price of crude oil, for example, should be very close to the long-run marginal cost of extraction. (In another study, Flaim and Mount (1978) have argued that actual oil prices have traditionally been based on average cost pricing rather than marginal cost pricing, and as a result, market prices are lower than the efficient prices.)

With this background, how would economists address the problem of global warming? The two main arguments for modifying market behavior would come from the discussion on pages 302–10. First, one could argue that there are environmental externalities, associated with future damage from global warming, that are not reflected in the prices paid for fuels. A tax on carbon emissions should be imposed to internalize the externality. Second, one could argue that high market discount rates make investment in research on renewable sources of energy commercially unattractive. Some government expenditure on this research should be made to develop economically viable alternatives for fossil fuels.

The standard economic arguments for taking action to address global warming depend on balancing the costs of reducing emissions of GHGs with the future benefits of moderating the changes of climate. Measuring these costs and benefits is extremely difficult to do. Many conflicting recommendations would be developed by different special interests, illustrated by the contrast between the minor adjustments proposed by Nordhaus and the more drastic changes proposed by Meadows et al. (see pages 310–14). Given the difficulties in reaching agreement over these economic magnitudes, it seems probable that greater dependence would be placed on the natural sciences by recommending a physical limit on annual emissions of GHGs. This is the strategy that is emerging from the series of UN conferences on climate change following the Earth Summit in 1992. Given a target level of emissions, economists could develop economically efficient ways to meet the target by, for example, establishing markets for carbon emissions. To be effective, all policies would require cooperation among governments over monitoring and enforcement on a global scale, and this could not be accomplished without widespread support from the public throughout the world.

Taking stores from Nature's storehouse

A constructive step towards winning public support for policies to address global warming would be to develop an economic evaluation of fossil fuels that is more compatible with the concerns of environmentalists (see pages 310–14). More specifically, it would be desirable to understand why environmentalists place more value on fuels than the economic rules of efficiency established by Hotelling. Many environmentalists would support Daly and Cobb in wanting to see more than the "*ad hoc* adjustments" that measure external costs, for example. The basis for developing a reconciliation between economists and environmentalists is to use the concept of "Nature's storehouse" proposed by Alfred Marshall (1920), and I am indebted to Mohammed Dore for encouraging me to read Marshall's *Principles of Economics*.

Modern neoclassical economics follows the tradition of Walrasian general equilibrium theory. The decision to follow this path can be traced back to the beginning of this century. "Alfred Marshall, the founder of neoclassical economics, was highly sensitive to the historical character of the actual economy. Nevertheless, economists on the whole wanted economics to become increasingly scientific, and their idea of science was based on physics rather than evolutionary biology . . . Milton Friedman notes of economists that we 'curtsy to Marshall, but we walk with Walras'" (Daly and Cobb, 1989, p. 20). The theory proposed by Hotelling for determining the scarcity premium on the extraction of fossil fuels is an extension of the static Walrasian general equilibrium model to include forward markets. Hence, it is appropriate to consider what differences would exist if a Marshallian approach had been followed.

Marshall (1920) made a clear distinction between the economic return to land and the economic return to a mine. "This difference is illustrated by the fact that the rent of a mine is calculated on a different principle from that of a farm. The farmer contracts to give back the land as rich as he found it: a mining company cannot do this; and while the farmer's rent is reckoned by the year, mining rents consist chiefly of 'royalties' which are levied in proportion to the stores that are taken from Nature's storehouse" (p. 167).

Marshall goes to considerable lengths to understand how the determinants of market prices differ in the short run and the long run, and the corresponding dynamic effects of imposing taxes. As part of the discussion in Chapter IX, Marshall (1920) considers the implications of placing taxes on a windfall if a "meteoric shower of a few thousand large stones harder than diamonds fall in one place" (p. 415). These stones are ideal for use in machine tools. Three different situations are considered. The first assumes that there are no production costs to the owner of the stones if they are sold to manufacturers. The second assumes that some effort must be expended by the owner to find the stones, but the total supply is still fixed, and the third assumes that an unlimited number of stones can be produced at some uniform cost. In the first case, the price is determined by the demand for the services of the stones or by the cost of producing alternative cutting tools, and "the value of a stone could not much exceed the cost of producing tools" (i.e. the backstop technology) (p. 416). At the other extreme, the third case is an example of a conventional supply situation with an infinite supply elasticity. Consequently, the price is determined by the cost of production. The second case is an intermediate situation, which is a reasonable approximation to the characteristics of mining, and the price is determined by the intersection of the demand for the services and the supply of the effort to find the stones.

Placing a tax on the stones in the first case, which would have to be bounded at less than the cost of the backstop technology, would reduce the rental income of the owner of the stones. In the third case, a tax would increase costs for all production processes using the stones. The tax would be paid indirectly by anyone purchasing the products and not by the original owners (producers) of the stones. For the second case, the tax affects both the owners of the stones and the production costs of the users of the stones. The relative effects of the tax on the owners and the users change over time and are determined by the rates of adjustment.

Marshall raises three concepts that are relevant to understanding the use of fossil fuels. First, fossil fuels are examples of Nature's "stored up treasures." Second, the cost of a backstop technology places a limit on the level of taxes that can be imposed, and third, dynamic adjustment processes matter when evaluating the effects of different policies. The implications of these concepts can be illustrated by considering the cost of extracting oil, C, the market price for crude oil, $P_m \geq C$, and the price of a replacement source of renewable energy (the backstop technology), $P_b \geq P_m$. The Marshallian value of nature's treasure is $(P_b - C)$, and this difference also measures the maximum tax that could be imposed (this was the issue identified by Mohammed Dore in his unpublished paper, Dore 1994). In contrast, the primary concern of most economists is to compare the "profits" from extraction, $(P_m - C)$, to Hotelling's scarcity premium.

The important difference between the conventional Hotelling approach and the Marshallian approach is in the measure of value used. Using Hotelling's rule, the market price P_m and profits $(P_m - C)$ are the focus of attention. Concern is expressed if profits are too high due, for example, to monopoly behavior. This leads to statements about using resources too slowly because prices are too high. When market rates of discounting are used, Hotelling's scarcity premiums are very small until stocks of the resource are nearly exhausted, and they then increase rapidly in magnitude. Solow and Serafy use profits $(P_m - C)$ as the measure of income from the resource (see pages 302–10). Daly and Cobb use market price (P_m) as their measure. For a Marshallian, however, the correct measure is the rent $(P_b - C)$.

Consider a simple example for oil. Chapman uses an ethanol fuel to represent the backstop technology in his analysis of depleting reserves of oil. He shows that the transition to this renewable source of energy occurs about sixty years from now using $50 per barrel as the price of the backstop technology. Assuming that the average cost of production is currently $10 per barrel and the market price is $15 per barrel, the standard measure of profit (e.g. due to the monopoly behavior of OPEC) is $5 per barrel. For a Marshallian, however, the rent is $40 per barrel.

In reality, the cost of a backstop technology in the future is uncertain, and furthermore, the cost can be reduced through expenditures on research. Consequently, a Marshallian should judge current practices governing the depletion of oil in terms of how effectively the $40 profit is being used. Currently, most of the profit is being dispersed to people using oil in the form of low prices for oil. In the example, only $5 of the $40 rent is being collected by monopoly power or through taxes on fuels. The justification for these taxes is generally to account for external environmental costs (e.g. urban smog) or to pay for complementary products (e.g. roads). In other words, they are examples of the conventional corrections to markets discussed earlier; see pages 302–10.

To a Marshallian, the availability of inexpensive sources of non-renewable energy is treated as a temporary phenomenon. It is unwise under these circumstances to develop social systems that are heavily dependent on the continued availability of inexpensive energy. One reason is that the rate of adjustment to higher prices would be relatively slow, e.g. changing the dispersed lifestyle of suburbia in the USA. It would be better to look at stocks of fossil fuels as a gift from Nature that can be used to develop better social systems in the future. The only way to reconcile this Marshallian view with standard economic theory, and current energy policy, is to assume that an inexpensive backstop technology can be developed to replace fossil fuels.

If one accepts the view that nuclear power (both fusion and fission) is not a viable alternative to fossil fuels, then the importance of renewable sources of energy is clear. Since renewable sources of energy are relatively expensive, the Marshallian and environmentalists' critique of current energy policy stands. Furthermore, the total amount of energy obtained from renewable sources is likely to be relatively small compared to typical projections of global energy needs made by economists. A major reason for this is that many renewable sources, such as biomass, compete for land with agriculture. With growing populations throughout the world, the demand for agricultural land will increase to expand the production of food. Brazil provides an example of the problems of high food prices associated with allocating prime agricultural land to the production of sugar for ethanol. Keeping this land out of food production provided a major incentive for the deforestation of the Amazon to support the expanding population in Northern Brazil.

The overall conclusion is that current energy policy is incompatible with a Marshallian perspective. The gift of fossil fuels should be used by society to develop new technologies that improve energy efficiency and lower the costs of energy from renewable sources. Daly's concept of sustainability for energy is more than an accounting scheme. At the present time, only a small proportion of the Marshallian profit is being used to develop appropriate technologies to replace fossil fuels. The biggest share of the profit is going to support the current consumers of oil and to encourage high levels of consumption. By focusing on the importance of the cost of alternative sources of energy, the Marshallian approach provides a rationale for greater restraint in the use of fossil fuels, and it is more consistent with the view of environmentalists that the value placed on fossil fuels in competitive markets is much too low.

Conclusions

The primary objective of this paper is to explain why many environmentalists are critical of current economic theory about fossil fuels, and to provide an alternative economic framework for analyzing energy issues. The transition from using non-renewable to renewable sources of energy and the environmental problem of global warming are used to illustrate these issues. There are five main conclusions:

1 Markets discount the future, and the importance of developing alternatives for fossil fuels, too much.
2 The contribution of energy to the economy is under-valued by economists.
3 The environmental costs of energy use are also under-valued.
4 Most growth in the use of fuels will be in countries with low incomes per capita.
5 Limiting the rate of use of fossil fuels for environmental reasons has implications for economic equity.

Problems with market solutions to resource problems have been recognized by economists. These include

1 discounting the future too fast
2 ignoring environmental costs
3 ignoring the depletion of stocks of resources in measuring national production, and
4 the low level of investment in developing alternatives for non-renewable resources.

Economists who are optimistic about the future for energy must believe that governments can and will correct these deficiencies in markets (or that the deficiencies are of minor importance). Pessimists about the future, on the other hand, consider that increasing competition in the global economy will undermine the role of governments, and may erode gains that have already been made in addressing environmental problems.

Criticisms by economists of the gloomy predictions made by environmentalists about energy implicitly assume that inexpensive substitutes for fossil fuels will be found, but there are two important changes that have occurred over the past twenty years in scientific knowledge about the use of fossil fuels. First, concerns about global warming have put a limit on the global rate at which fossil fuels should be used. Second, current prospects for the nuclear industry are poor, and it appears unwise to assume that large amounts of inexpensive energy will come from this source in the future. Consequently, the lack of economically viable sources of renewable energy should be of great concern. In addition, placing limits on the rate of use of fossil fuels puts economic equity among countries as a central issue for energy policy. It is interesting to note that this is consistent with the conclusions reached by Eric Hobsbawm (1996) in his economic history of the twentieth century. He recognizes that demographics and ecological problems will be decisive in the long run, and concludes "If these decades proved anything it was that the major political problem of the world . . . was not how to multiply the wealth of nations, but how to distribute it for the benefit of their inhabitants."

Turning to the specific issue of energy policy and the problem of global warming, it was argued on page 319 that the high levels of energy use in the USA make it essential for the USA to take leadership in implementing solutions. This can be done by showing more restraint in the use of fossil fuels and developing new technologies for increasing energy efficiency and for renewable sources of energy. Many existing technologies for improving energy efficiency are already cost effective – see Rubin et al. (1992) – but they have not been adopted due to various market distortions (e.g. different incentives for renters compared to owners of buildings). Nevertheless, an underlying problem is the public's belief that energy should continue to be inexpensive. Even though the USA has shown leadership in reducing many sources of air pollution (e.g. acid rain, urban smog and cigarettes), little restraint has been shown in the use of fossil fuels, particularly for automobiles and road transportation. In this respect, the USA lags behind other countries in leading the way to finding solutions for global warming.

Although leadership from the USA is required, most of the growth in the global use of energy will occur in low-income countries. Increased energy efficiency and a greater reliance on renewable sources of energy will also be needed in these countries. In fact, it may be easier to build the foundations for efficient energy systems in low-income countries now than it would be to change established and inefficient systems sometime in the future. To the extent that knowledge about improved energy technologies exists in high-income countries, it will be necessary to find ways to encourage (e.g. through subsidies) their adoption in low-income countries. On the fiftieth anniversary of the Marshall plan, it is appropriate to remember how this act of generosity by the USA helped to rebuild Western Europe after World War II. A similar plan to deal with global warming is needed at this time. Unfortunately, the increased inequities of income that have developed in the USA, and the economic pressures faced by many people from global competition, make it unlikely that the public will be willing to support steps to stabilize emissions of GHGs before other countries take action.

Existing policies for reducing emissions of GHGs in the USA are ineffective. The lack of interest in "no regrets" options for improving energy efficiency and the dependence on "voluntary restraints" in the President's Climate Change Action Plan are examples. The results of the policies are illustrated by the forecasts of substantial increases of carbon emissions in the USA shown in table 14.6. The public's indifference over restraint in the use of energy and tolerance of growing economic inequities are not conducive for developing effective policies to address global warming. Consequently, it is appropriate to consider whether there are alternative approaches to the problem.

One approach is to change the public's attitudes towards energy in the USA. The Marshallian perspective (developed on pages 324–7) provides an economic explanation of why environmentalists believe that economists undervalue energy. The distinguishing feature is that Marshallian rent measures the difference between the cost of a backstop technology and the cost of production. In contrast, the conventional concern of economists is the difference between the market price and the cost of production. Historically, most of the Marshallian rent has been used to encourage consumption by charging low prices, and this, in turn, has led to the growth of a dispersed suburban lifestyle in the USA. Although changing public attitudes about energy is desirable, it will be a slow process even if the efforts to change attitudes are successful. More immediate action is needed.

A second approach is to use another type of environmental problem to encourage the same actions needed to address global warming. The obvious choice is to reduce urban smog. Since automobiles are a major source of air pollution in urban areas, improving transportation and reducing emissions would be desirable. A reason for expecting policies for reducing smog to be more acceptable to the public than policies for global warming is that the adverse health effects of smog are more obvious than the uncertain future effects of global warming. Improvements in fuel efficiency and public transportation would both contribute to reducing emissions of GHGs.

A secondary benefit from developing new technologies for reducing urban smog in the USA, such as hybrid electric buses, is that the same technologies could be used in other countries to improve urban air quality. Urban smog is a global problem, and smog in many developing countries is worse than it is in the USA. Hence, there is a potential for developing new global markets for environmental technologies if governments in other countries make a commitment to internalize the external health costs of air pollution. Establishing production facilities in developing countries may be a practical way to introduce new technologies into these countries.

An effective global policy to stabilize emissions of GHGs will require cooperation from a large majority of countries. A few major dissenters could jeopardize
the viability of any policy. In particular, the governments of low-income countries
like China and India must participate because these are the countries where most
of growth in emissions will occur in the future. As a practical step towards
achieving this goal, it would be desirable for the USA to form a partnership with
a low-income country like China. (In the reference scenario in table 14.6 the
forecasts of emissions in China are larger than the forecasts for the USA by the
year 2015.) The objective of this partnership would be to evaluate the feasibility
of different policies for stabilizing emissions. In this way, leadership would be
shared between a high-income and a low-income country, and the knowledge
about new technologies would be of value to countries at different stages of
development. Other countries might form similar partnerships at the same time or
choose to adopt polices on their own. Discussions among governments organized
by the UN will continue, and they may lead to countries meeting targets for
emissions in the future, unlike the current situation. Eventually, sanctions on
trade for non-participating countries could be used as an incentive for limiting
emissions. However, a joint commitment made by China and the USA to adopt
specific actions for limiting emissions of GHGs would go a long way toward
encouraging other countries to deal with the problem of global warming
seriously.

References

Andreoni, J. and Miller, J. H. (1993) Rational cooperation in the finitely repeated
   prisoner's dilemma: Experimental evidence. *The Economic Journal*, 103 (418), 570–84.
Atkinson, A. B. (1983) *The Economics of Inequality*, 2nd edn. Oxford: Clarendon Press.
Baran, P. A. and Sweezy, P. M. (1966) *Monopoly Capital: An Essay on the American
   Economic and Social Order*. NY: Monthly Review Press.
Bronfenbrenner, U., McClelland, P., Wethington, E., Moen, P. and Ceci, S. J. (1996) *The
   State of Americans*. Free Press.
Chapman, L. D. (1993) World oil: Hotelling depletion or accelerating use? *Nonrenewable
   Resources*, Oxford University Press, 2 (4), 331–9.
Cline, W. R. (1992) *The Economics of Global Warming*. Washington, DC: Institute for
   International Economics.
Coase, R. H. (1988) *The Firm, the Market, and the Law*. University of Chicago Press.
Daly, H. E. and Cobb, J. B. Jr (1989) *For The Common Good*. Boston: Beacon Press.
Dasgupta, P. S. and Heal, G. M. (1979) *Economic Theory and Exhaustible Resources*.
   England: Cambridge Economic Handbooks.
Dore, M. H. I. (1994) *The Theory of Exhaustible Resources and Intergenerational Equity:
   A Marshallian Approach*. Unpublished manuscipt: Brock University.
EIA (1996) *International Energy Outlook 1997: With Projections to 2015*. US Depart-
   ment of Energy.
Flaim, S. J. and Mount, T. D. (1978) Federal income taxation of the United States
   petroleum industry and the depletion of domestic reserves, SERI/TR-52-041. *Solar
   Energy Research Institute*. Golden, Co.
Frank, R. H. (1988) *Passions Within Reason: The Strategic Role of the Emotions*. NY:
   W. W. Norton & Company.

Frank, R. H. and Cook, P. J. (1995) *The Winner-Take-All Society*. NY: Free Press.

Gore, A. (1992) *Earth in the Balance: Ecology and the Human Spirit*. New York, NY: Plume.

Gottschalk, P. and Smeeding, T. M. (1996) Cross national comparisons of earnings and income inequality, unpublished paper. Boston College and Syracuse University.

Hall, D. O., Mynick, H. E. and Williams, R. H. (1991) Cooling the greenhouse with bioenergy. *Nature*, 353 (6339), 11–12.

Hartwick, J. (1989) *Non-Renewable Resources*. Hardwood Academic Press.

Heilbronner, R. (1992) John Maynard Keynes Vol. II: The economist as saviour 1920–37, by Robert Skidelsky. In *The New York Review*, 6 (4), 6–9.

Hobsbawm, E. (1996) *The Age of Extremes: A History of the World, 1914–91*. NY: Vintage.

Hotelling, H. (1931) The economics of exhaustible resources. *Journal of Political Economy*, 39, 137–75.

Houghton, J. T. (1994) *Global Warming, The Complete Briefing*. Oxford, England: Lion Publishing.

Jevons, W. S. (1865) *The Coal Question*. London: Macmillan.

Kaplan, R. D. (1994) The Coming Anarchy. *The Atlantic Monthly*, 273 (2). See also online at: www.theatlantic.com/election/connection/foreign/anarchy.html.

Kay, J. A. and Mirrlees, J. A. (1975) The desirability of natural resource depletion. In D. W. Pearce and (assisted by) J. Rose (eds) *The Economics of Natural Resource Depletion*. London: Macmillan Press, pp. 140–76.

Krause, F., Bach, W. and Koomey, J. (1992) *Energy Policy In The Greenhouse*. John Wiley and Sons, Inc.

Lovins, A. B. (1977) *Soft Energy Paths: Toward a Durable Peace*. Cambridge, MA: Ballinger Publishing Company.

Manne, A. S. and Richels, R. G. (1992) Buying greenhouse insurance: The economic costs of carbon dioxide limits. Cambridge, MA: MIT Press.

Marshall, A. (1920) *Principles of Economics*, 8th edn. New York, NY: Macmillan Company.

McClelland, P. (1996) *The State of Amerians*. Free Press.

McKibben, B. (1995) *Hope, Human and Wild*. NY: Little, Brown & Company.

Meadows, D. (1972) *The Limits to Growth: A Report for the Club of Rome's Projection on the Predicament of Mankind*. New York: Universe.

Meadows, D. H., Meadows, D. L. and Randers, J. (1992) *Beyond the Limits*. Post Mills, VT: Chelsea Green Publishing Company.

Mishan, E. J. (1972) *Elements of Cost-Benefit Analysis*. London: UNWIN University Books.

Nash, R. F. (1989) *The Rights of Nature: A History of Environmental Ethics*. The University of Wisconsin Press.

Nordhaus, W. D. (1991) To slow or not to slow: The economics of the greenhouse effect. *The Economic Journal*, 101 (407), 920–37.

Nordhaus, W. D. (1992) Lethal model 2: The limits to growth revisited. *Brookings Papers on Economic Activity*, 2. CN: Yale University, pp. 1–59.

Nordhaus, W. D. (1994) *Managing the Global Commons: The Economics of Climate Change*. Cambridge, MA: MIT Press.

Pearce, D. W. (1991) The role of carbon taxes in adjusting to global warming. *The Economic Journal*, 101 (407), 938–48.

Pearce, D. W. and Turner, R. K. (1990) *Economics of Natural Resources and the Environment*. Baltimore: Johns Hopkins University Press.

Phillips, K. (1990) *The Politics of Rich and Poor*. Random House.

Population Reference Bureau, Inc. (1991) *World Population Data Sheet*. Washington, DC: Population Reference Bureau, Inc.

Price, D. (1996) Unthinking carrying capacity. Unpublished paper. Ithaca, NY: Department of Anthropology, Cornell University.

Rose, A. and Stevens, B. (1993) The efficiency and equity of marketable permits for CO_2 emissions. *Resource and Energy Economics*, 15 (1), 117–46.

Rosensweig, C. and Parry, M. (1993) Potential impacts of climate change on world food supply: A summary of a recent international study. In H. M. Kaiser and T. E. Drennen (eds) *Agricultural Dimensions of Global Climate Change*. Delray Beach, FL: St Lucie Press.

Rubin, E. S., Cooper, R. N., and Frosch, R. A. (1992) Realistic mitigation options for global warming. *Science*, 257, 148–9, 265–6.

Sen, A. K. (1977) Rational fools: A critique of the behavioral foundations of economic theory. *Philosophy & Public Affairs*, 6 (4), 317–44.

Sen, A. K. (1992) *Inequality Reexamined*. MA: Harvard Press.

Serafy, S. E. (1989) The proper calculation of income from depletable natural resources. In U. J. Ahmad, S. E. Serafy and E. Lutz (eds) *Environmental Accounting for Sustainable Development*. Washington, DC: The World Bank, pp. 10–18.

Solow, R. M. (1986) On the integenerational allocation of natural resources. *Scandinavian Journal of Economics*, 88 (1), 141–9.

Solow, R. M. (1992) *An Almost Practical Step Toward Sustainability*. Washington, DC: Resources For The Future.

Solzhenitsyn, A. I. (1993) To tame savage capitalism. *The New York Times*, November 23, p. 11.

World Bank (1992) *World Development Report*. Washington, DC: World Bank.

Epilogue

According to Walrasian general equilibrium theory, the market mechanism allocates private goods in an incentive-compatible manner, but the theory assumes that there are no public goods and no common property resources, that there is a complete set of futures markets and that there exists a set of market-clearing prices for all goods. The assumptions clearly recognize the limits to markets; there are some things that the markets just cannot do. The Walrasian theory can only reflect an "equilibrium" which is a function of "initial endowments," and, as Binmore has said, it is disingenuous to claim the theoretical equilibrium a "social optimum." As the Introductory chapter argued, the first theorem of welfare economics (that every competitive equilibrium is a Pareto optimum) is vacuous and the second (that any particular Pareto optimum can be reached by policy makers by a suitable redistribution of the initial endowments) is incentive-incompatible as no one would want to reveal their initial endowments if it was known that the "state" would confiscate their wealth. Furthermore, as the market-driven equilibrium is not a social optimum, it has nothing to recommend it from the point of view of fairness or equity.

A logical extension of general equilibrium is welfare economics, but fairness and equity are not well served by welfare economics either. We are therefore inevitably led to the Rawlsian view that the market mechanism must be used but its limitations require political intervention. According to Rawls, fairness is a procedural norm that must be played out through political institutions. Achieving sustainable development will require norms and rules for resolving conflicts between social groups and between generations. In the end, we hope that there will emerge new processes and new institutions that are based on the concept of justice as fairness, as Rawls has argued. In the meantime, we must work with what we *have*. There is a theorem, due to Richard Bellman, which says that if we do not do the best with what we happen to have, we will never do any better with what we should have had! Therefore, let us turn to what we have.

The papers in this book show the limits to markets, as demonstrated by the evidence of global environmental degradation. We have been concerned about climate change and its skewed adverse impacts which will fall mainly on those least able to defend themselves, such as small island nations facing rising sea levels, or very poor nations that may lose a lot of land, such as Bangladesh.

We have also been concerned with energy policy or the lack of it, as in the case of the USA which could provide world leadership by planning to reduce urban smog or by a phased transition to renewable energy use. If the developing countries all proceed to increase their per capita incomes by following the same intensive use of fossil-fuel energy as was the case in the USA and other industrialized nations, we may bring in irreversible changes to the biosphere. What seems clearly essential is that the developed North should agree to extend the principles of the Montreal Protocol to all action on global climate change and offer to developing countries the necessary resources and technology so that they also may plan a transition to the use of renewable energy sources.

We have been concerned with industrial location policy and the migration of dirty, energy-intensive industry to newly industrializing countries of South Asia and Latin America, and the distributional impacts of such changes: the North enjoying cleaner environments while their consumers are able to import the products of such industries. We do not believe that we can simply rely on the so-called environmental Kuznets curve, which says that as the incomes of developing countries rise, they will be able to clean up their environments, and so the faster the growth there the better. This argument has been adequately refuted in Arrow et al. (1995) and we do not propose to go into it here. Arrow et al. also show why equity matters and why markets may not be up to the task of caring for the environment.

We have also been concerned with common property resources and a lack of international will to agree on formulating and enforcing a sustainable ocean harvesting policy, in spite of several international accords. Market-driven methods of harvesting take more from the oceans than can be replaced by the ability of the fish species to reproduce themselves. A number of fish species are threatened, and future generations may inherit oceans that do not support the biodiversity the present generation itself inherited. In fact, equity to future generations has ramifications in all the areas mentioned above, as future generations do not have a vote in the marketplace, and the markets fail them more than anyone else.

When markets fail, it is clear that collective action is necessary, and there are indications that the international community is aware of this, as witnessed by important international agreements in the late 1980s and also in the 1990s. The limits to markets are recognized in these accords. There are also signs that equity too is beginning to play the role that it should in these agreements. We comment briefly on the Montreal and the Kyoto Protocols and contrast how weak and inadequate the Kyoto Protocol is compared to the Montreal Protocol.

In the Montreal Protocol, it was agreed that a 14-member Executive Council would administer the Protocol; seven of the Council members were to be from the developing countries. This parity in decision-making between developed and developing countries was unprecedented. All parties were aware of the path-breaking nature of this protocol, and all parties were positioning themselves for the *next* set of global negotiations which would be on global warming and a program of reduction of the GHGs (which was to follow in December 1997). The USA strongly argued that the Montreal Protocol be *not* treated as a precedent for the future negotiations. This proved to be a stumbling block, but in the end the USA succeeded in having the words "without prejudice to any future arrangements" included in the preamble, but not the words "without precedent." This was an acceptable compromise to all, considering that the power-sharing agreement was a major breakthrough and was unlike the administrative structures of other world bodies, including the UN and the Bretton Woods institutions.

Most of the developing countries, led by India, finally agreed to sign the Montreal Protocol after significant bargaining in which they made coping with global change a matter of international justice, and forced the *de facto* recognition of the principle of equity. This could be done only by making ozone protection a matter of North–South conflict. What India achieved through the protracted negotiations was to demonstrate that coping with global change would impose unequal costs and hardships, with the worst hardships falling on the poorest of the world. This brought the equity dimension to the center of the negotiations.

If the projections of future chlorine loading that will occur due to the Montreal Protocol (as amended several times) are to be believed, the Protocol is indeed a tremendous success. The ozone hole will be wiped out by 2075. Periodic reviews (every four years) will bring in revised and accelerated phase-out schedules: first the CFCs, then the (less damaging) HCFCs, and then a move to even less damaging HFCs. The agreement is a clear recognition of the rights of future generations. It is also clear that the Montreal Protocol also recognized the rights of developing countries and the need for compensation for them to make the transition to ozone-friendly technology. The creation of the 14-member executive committee for the Protocol has also given the developing countries a veto. As stated earlier, this is a significant departure from the Bretton Woods formula of decision making which leaves power concentrated in the hands of the rich nations.

In comparison to the Montreal Protocol, the Kyoto Protocol on GHGs, signed in December 1997, is a weak and pale imitation. In the Kyoto Protocol, there are legally binding targets for CO_2 reductions, with differential targets, but no 14 member decision-making council and no financial compensation for developing countries for adapting their capital stock to the use of renewable energy. For this reason alone, India and China are not even party to the Protocol, when these two countries are poised to accelerate industrialization, and, given their huge populations, to increase their CO_2 emissions to unprecedented levels. Why was Kyoto so unlike Montreal?

Unlike ozone-depletion, global warming is not a *direct* threat to the main industrialized countries – indeed the USA and Canada may even benefit from it. The USA may benefit the most as it will have the technology to sell to others who have to cope with the consequences of global warming, such as rising sea levels, and also the instruments and tools required to cope with extreme climate events. The adverse consequences of global warming are badly skewed against the poorest. For example, Bangladesh will face increasing flooding due to rising sea levels; tropical Africa and Latin America will face declining food production due to droughts and desertification resulting from increased variability of climate.

Moreover, unlike the CFC producing industry, oil corporations such as Exxon, Mobil or Shell-BP do not face class action suits. Automobile and airline companies face no threat from consumers. Industry faces no serious pressure to reduce GHGs, and consequently the ratification of the Kyoto Protocol is itself in jeopardy, let alone its implementation. In fact, the precedent of the equity provisions of the Montreal Protocol may be a deterrent to implementing the Kyoto Protocol, as all nations wait to see whether any possible revisions to the Kyoto Protocol might in some way go in the direction of Montreal.

The Montreal Protocol was indeed a path-breaking departure in which the industrialized countries not only agreed to an accelerated phasing out of ozone depleting substances, but also gave the developing countries more or less equal say on the executive committee. They also agreed to a fund for developing countries to aid their transition to newer technologies. The most important factors that led to such a revolutionary agreement were:

- the new scientific evidence of ozone depletion posing a threat to the *Northern* hemisphere
- the fear of class action suits in the USA
- globalization of international trade and its importance to the larger developing countries
- the relatively small segment of the chemical and manufacturing sector that would be affected by the Protocol, and
- the existence on the horizon of new technologies, which are essentially fairly continuous process innovations rather than radical departures.

It was thus the factor of self-interest, led by public pressure particularly in the USA, which enabled the developing countries to insist on the "polluter-pays" principle and on equitable compensation for China and India. In the case of GHGs, the threat to the health of people is considered remote and, in any case, the adverse effects of global warming are distributionally skewed against the poorer nations. Richer countries have now lived with third-world poverty for decades, and will view more disasters there, aggravated by extremes of climate, as nothing new. The consequences of global warming are more likely to be treated as calling for voluntary acts of charity rather than as a matter of equity, requiring compensation for the actions of the industrialized countries. This is indeed a gloomy conclusion. One can only hope that such a pessimistic conclusion may mobilize collective action on global warming.

The Kyoto Protocol as it stands may be regarded as no more than a beginning and as a gesture: much more needs to be done. The Protocol must be strengthened along the equity principles agreed upon in the Montreal Protocol, bringing both India and China into the accord. Indeed, it is the distributional consequences of global warming that will have to be the central focus of any future revisions to the Kyoto Protocol on GHGs.

References

Arrow, K., Bolin, B. and Costanza, R. (1995) "Economic Growth, Carrying Capacity and the Environment," Science, 268, 520–21.

Dore, M. H. (1997) "The Montreal Protocol: Lessons for a Protocol on Global Warming." Paper presented at the Trade Convergence Climate Complex Workshop "Impacto de la variabilidad climática en salud pública," *CATHALAC*, Panamá, June 16–18, 1997.

Name Index

Abrams, R. A. 97
Agarwal, A. 221, 222, 236(5), 237(26)
Agras, J. 267, 279
Altieri, M. 151
Alvarez-Buylla, E. 159(1)
Anderson, M. 151
Andreoni, J. 320
Ansari, Z. R. 222, 233, 236(6)
Arizpe, L. 141, 151, 159(2), 162(19)
Arrow, K. J. 6–7, 10, 12, 13–14, 22, 62, 86, 88, 93, 94–5, 96, 97, 101–2, 334
Atkinson, A. B. 10, 211, 319, 320

Balestrino, A. 36(3)
Ballard, G. M. 133(3)
Baran, P. A. 305
Barbier, E. B. 83, 111(2)
Bardhan, P. K. 161(17)
Baron, J. 97
Barrett, S. 203, 212
Barro, R. J. 82
Barry, B. 10, 43, 51(6), 298
Bartra, A. 161(17)
Basili, M. 111(1)
Basterrechea, M. 144
Becker, G. 72(6)
Beitz, C. R. 52(19)
Bell, D. 63
Bellman, R. 333
Benedick, R. E. 223, 232, 235(3), 236(10, 11, 13)
Bentham, J. 80, 86
Berlin, I. 134(16)
Bhaduri, A. 161(17)
Bharucha, E. 218, 234, 236(4)
Bidwai, P. 231
Binmore, K. 10, 12, 13–14, 36(1), 333
Binswanger, H. 161(17)

Biraben, J-N. 188(5)
Birdsall, N. 189(13), 267
Bishop, R. 59
Blackwell, D. 103
Blaikie, P. 156, 157
Blake, J. 189(9)
Boadway, R. W. 21
Bohm, P. 96
Bohnenblust, H. F. 103
Bondestam, L. 162(19)
Bongaarts, J. 140
Boserup, E. 145–6, 150
Bradford, G. 157
Brandon, C. 271–4
Brandt, W. 162(25)
Bromley, D. W. 47–8
Bronfenbrenner, U. 320
Brookshire, D. 59
Broome, J. 21, 298
Brown, J. W. 222, 232, 235(1), 236(5)
Brown, L. R. 280
Brun, W. 97
Burke, W. T. 294
Burniaux, J. M. 201

Cabellero, R. 97
Camerer, C. 97
Carlsson, G. 189(9)
Carson, R. T. 31, 68, 94
Cassen, R. 189(13)
Chapman, C. B. 133(3)
Chapman, D. 36(1), 267, 270, 277, 279
Chapman, L. D. 307, 313, 326
Chesnais, J-C. 178
Chipman, J. 21
Chira, S. 277
Christy, F. T. 285
Clark, W. 162(25)

Subject Index

adaptive rationality 80, 81–2
advantage (capability set) 32–4
Africa 171, 310
ageing population 178, 179
Agenda 21 255
aggregate world energy 278
agriculture: effect of global warming 199;
  food supply 242–3, 326–7; *jhum*
  system 242, 245, 259(1, 2); population
  growth and 241–2, 244; poverty
  and 242–3, 245–6; rehabilitation of rural
  landscape 250–3, 261(5), 262(6), 263(7);
  sustainable 246–7, 250
agroecosystems 243, 246–7, 260(3)
air conditioning 224, 227–8
air pollution (urban smog) 18, 305, 323,
  326, 329
allocative efficiency 133(2), 210–11
allocative justice 11, 12
altruism 68, 71, 320
American Automobile Manufacturers
  Association (AAMA) 268
"anchoring and adjustment" 64
anthropogenic greenhouse warming 194–5
Arrow-Debreu model 30
ASEAN Agreement on the Conservation of
  Nature and National Resources 257
Asia: industrial location 17–18, 267–82;
  state policy and population growth 171,
  172, 181–2, 187–8; tropics 241–3, 245–8,
  250–4, 257, 259(1, 2), 261(5)
asset liquidity 105–6, 109, 112(7)
assets, environmental (non-use values) 15,
  54–72, 94–7
attitudes: to environment 321–2; to risk
  126
auction market 60–1
autoroute (development) 247, 260(3)

backstop technology 301, 308, 313, 325,
  326, 329
bargaining: contingent compliance 229–31;
  ozone regime and 219–21
basic contraction consistency 58
basic expansion consistency 58
Bayesian approach 118, 122
Beijing Ministerial Declaration of
  Environment and Development 205, 206
belief systems 104–5, 133
benefits, allocation of (fisheries) 297
bequest value 67–8, 94
Bergson-Samuelson social welfare
  function 7, 8, 12
bias in estimating probabilities/valuing
  outcomes 126–7
binariness (of choice function) 58
biodiversity 85, 89; protection in
  Tropics 17, 240–63; use (policy
  framework) 255–6
Biodiversity Convention 17
biomass 241–2, 326
biophysical limits 142–3, 147, 149, 151
biotechnology 255
birth control 156–8, 175–7, 183–4, 186–
  8
birth rates 172, 176–80, 187
Black-Scholes conditions 107
black market 51(11, 13), 67
body/bodily injury (rights) 15, 38–43
Boolean based comparative method 161(14)
Brazil 16, 150, 219, 221, 223, 240, 245,
  326–7
Bretton Woods institutions 233, 335
Brundtland Report 83, 117
Bureau of the Census (US) 279
Bureau of Economic Analysis (US) 279
Bureau of National Affairs 44

Printed and bound by CPI Group (UK) Ltd, Croydon, CR0 4YY

23/04/2025

14660951-0005